MW00333967

FRANKENSTEIN WAS A VEGETARIAN

FRANKENSTEIN WAS A VEGETARIAN

Essays on Food Choice, Identity, and Symbolism

Michael Owen Jones

University Press of Mississippi / Jackson

The University Press of Mississippi is the scholarly publishing agency of
the Mississippi Institutions of Higher Learning: Alcorn State University,
Delta State University, Jackson State University, Mississippi State University,
Mississippi University for Women, Mississippi Valley State University,
University of Mississippi, and University of Southern Mississippi.

www.upress.state.ms.us

The University Press of Mississippi is a member
of the Association of University Presses.

Copyright © 2022 by University Press of Mississippi
All rights reserved

First printing 2022
∞

Library of Congress Cataloging-in-Publication Data

Names: Jones, Michael Owen, author.
Title: Frankenstein was a vegetarian : essays on food choice, identity,
and symbolism / Michael Owen Jones.
Description: Jackson : University Press of Mississippi, 2022. |
Includes bibliographical references and index.
Identifiers: LCCN 2022007614 (print) | LCCN 2022007615 (ebook) |
ISBN 9781496839930 (hardback) | ISBN 9781496839947 (trade paperback) |
ISBN 9781496839954 (epub) | ISBN 9781496839961 (epub) |
ISBN 9781496839978 (pdf) | ISBN 9781496839985 (pdf)
Subjects: LCSH: Food habits—Political aspects. | Food habits—
Health aspects. | Food habits—Moral and ethical aspects. | Food habits—
Social aspects. | Food habits—Religious aspects. | Food preferences. |
Food consumption. | Vegetarianism.
Classification: LCC GT2850 .J663 2022 (print) | LCC GT2850 (ebook) |
DDC 394.1/2—dc23/eng/20220222
LC record available at https://lccn.loc.gov/2022007614
LC ebook record available at https://lccn.loc.gov/2022007615

British Library Cataloging-in-Publication Data available

supported with grant
Figure Foundation

CONTENTS

PREFACE

To clarify, it was actually the eight-foot-tall wretch made of parts from the graveyard and slaughterhouse, not Frankenstein who created it, that was a vegetarian in Mary Wollstonecraft Shelley's novel *Frankenstein; or, The Modern Prometheus* (1818). But since the mid-nineteenth century, much of the public has bestowed the name Frankenstein on the demon.

The creature in *Frankenstein* says, "My food is not that of man; I do not destroy the lamb and the kid, to glut my appetite; acorns and berries afford me sufficient nourishment." The being also extolls the pleasure of consuming vegetables from a farmer's garden, much like Mary's husband, the poet Percy Bysshe Shelley. A fervent vegetarian, Percy edited and added wording to Mary's manuscript. Percy also penned an influential pamphlet on the radical reformation of society through a vegetable diet, which is one of the matters I explore in this book regarding fundamental concepts in food studies along with several topics that have received too little attention.

Eating is a necessity for us. Matters of food choice, symbolism, and the communicative role of food in everyday life, however, were largely ignored by scholars except for occasional works in ethnography, history, and nutrition. As a field, the multidisciplinary study of food finally came into its own by the late twentieth and early twenty-first centuries. International conferences were organized. Universities began offering courses, concentrations, and eventually degrees in food studies. Journals are devoted to the subject, such as *Digest: An Interdisciplinary Study of Food and Foodways, Gastronomica, Anthropology of Food, Canadian Food Studies,* and *Food, Culture & Society,* among others.

In the bibliography of this book I provide citations to several publications that chronicle and describe numerous works in the development of food studies, especially in the disciplines of food history, folkloristics, anthropology, cultural studies, and sociology. They are Ken Albala (2009), "History on the Plate: The Current State of Food History"; Lucy M. Long (2009), "Introduction" (to the special issue "Food and Identity in the Americas" in

Journal of American Folklore); Lucy M. Long, editor (2015), *The Food and Folklore Reader*; Cornelia Gerhardt (2013), "Language and Food—Food and Language"; Sidney W. Mintz and Christine M. Du Bois (2002), "The Anthropology of Food and Eating"; and Nicklas Neuman (2019), "On the Engagement with Social Theory in Food Studies."

Here, as a folklorist, I note only a few points in Long's two surveys of research concerning foodways, that is, the customs and traditions, knowledge, and competencies related to food that are typically learned and manifested in everyday interactions among people. The term "foodways" embraces a wide range of activities, from producing, procuring, preserving, and transforming foodstuffs to presenting, sharing, consuming, and disposing of what is not eaten. The topic of foodways also involves people's conceptions (food-linked meanings and meaningfulness, values, beliefs, and aesthetics), routine occasions and special events for preparing and partaking of the fare, and communication through food regarding self and others. Because foodways are associated with hearth and home, however, their importance is often overlooked or underestimated in understanding human behavior and social dynamics as well as addressing issues of health, politics, and identity, which concern me in much of this book.

As Long observes, folklorists' analyses of foodways owe a great deal to the work and influence of Don Yoder (1921–2015), Professor of Folklore and Folklife at the University of Pennsylvania. Yoder is noted for his research on the customs, beliefs, and practices of Pennsylvania Germans, including religion, art, and, in the early 1960s, food (schnitz, sauerkraut, and mush).

Rather than restrict the study of traditions to oral lore, he conceived of the consistencies and continuities in behavior, or people's traditions, as "folklife" (which encompasses objects and their making and use). He modeled his orientation on the European ethnological approaches characteristic of the German *Volksleben* and Swedish *folkliv*. Yoder set forth the method in his essay "Folk Cookery" in 1972 (cited in the bibliography), emphasizing the need to investigate the totality of practices, processes, and beliefs surrounding food and eating. His foodways classes inspired the publication of research by at least nine of his students, Lucy Long among them, and the founding of the journal *Digest*, mentioned above.

Several people have asked me how I became interested in food studies (and, as well, folkloristics, which I explained in *Exploring Folk Art*, 1987, pp. 1–2). From 1973 through 1975, I taught several classes at UCLA on foodways but then ceased owing in part to the limited number of folklore studies available and also in order to focus more on folk art, folklore in organizational settings, and research methods, in addition to having greater administrative responsibilities. I did, however, edit a special issue of *Western Folklore* in 1981 about foodways. In the mid-1990s I resumed offering a course regularly on food customs and symbolism in the United States. By then an array of works had been published by folklorists.

When I was growing up, the preparation and presentation of food in our home was not a priority or a display of artistic skills and aesthetic subtleties. My father limited his cooking to frying a small range of fare. My mother was scarcely more adept. In her youth on a small farm in southeastern Kansas, the children were given a choice of chores; my mother and her brother opted for those outdoors, while their two sisters picked cooking and other indoor activities. Additionally, my parents suffered financial constraints their first years of marriage, so we ate to live rather than lived to eat. My mother was teaching for small recompense at a rural elementary school; my father worked first on a painting crew, then on the shop floor in an aircraft factory, while also struggling to farm the acreage where we lived. Further, when I was eleven, my mother suffered injuries in an automobile crash caused by another driver; she lost her sense of smell like some coronavirus patients in 2020 and 2021. Her anosmia led to food aversions and other changes in her food habits, which I discuss in "The Proof Is in the Pudding," listed in the bibliography. Then, too, I had my own health issues. Our home was surrounded by wheat fields, and I was fed a steady diet of freshly baked bread and macaroni-based casseroles in high school. The food, prepared by two local women, was delicious, but for years I suffered severe bouts of hay fever and abdominal cramping; I was unaware until diagnosed in my late teens that I was allergic to wheat and products made from it (fortunately, the sensitivity lessened over time).

As a freshman at the University of Kansas, I was intrigued upon learning from another student about his documentation of recipes from households in the southeastern part of the state. My interest grew further when a guest lecturer in a Latin American political science course I was taking spent the first minutes asking students to identity each country whose cuisine he described. I also worked for a while as a waiter in a college café and tavern noted for its extensive use of food handlers' argot; that led to my first analytical article as a second-year graduate student in folklore at Indiana University. Titled "Creating and Using Argot at the Jayhawk Café: Communication, Ambience, and Identity," the essay appeared in *American Speech* (1967) and later in a collection of some of my writings (*Exploring Folk Art*, referenced in the bibliography). By fall 1968, I had moved to Los Angeles, where I relished dishes at ethnic restaurants.

In the 1960s and 1970s I was affected, as were many others, by environmental and health food movements opposing the reliance on chemical fertilizers and pesticides, antibiotics injected into farm animals, and additives to our food. Rachel Carson's *Silent Spring* (1962) indicted the chemical industry, agribusiness, and the federal government for the indiscriminate use of pesticides, such as DDT, which was widely sprayed on crops in my youth and finally banned in the United States in 1972, that harmed people, wildlife, and the environment; indeed, over the years the media published stories about poisonings and warned consumers to scrub or peel fruits and vegetables before eating them. In her influential *Diet for a Small Planet* (1971), Frances Moore Lappé argued for the health and ecological benefits of a plant-based diet, contending that we were squandering most of our food by feeding grains to animals, depleting our soil and water, and adversely affecting our health with heavy reliance on meat. The back-to-the-land movement appealed to me, particularly the writings by poet, activist, and farmer Wendell Berry at whose home in north central Kentucky in 1966 we dined one night on fresh produce from his garden. His books *A Continuous Harmony* (1972), *Meeting the Expectations of the Land* (1986), and others and his essay "The Pleasures of Eating" in *What Are People For?* (2009) engage the reader to participate in food production even in small ways, such as a planter box in the window.

In the mid-1980s I joined the Southern California Culinary Guild, where I became acquainted with several food writers. As director of our research center in folklore at UCLA, I organized a two-day conference with the Guild in 1989 on the folklore and mythology of food (and gave Charles Perry the name of his column in the *Los Angeles Times*: "Forklore"). I had also joined the Co-opportunity Market in Santa Monica, California, a food-buying club founded in 1974 by a UCLA graduate in science along with a community organizer, a musician, and an activist; the Co-op is a member-owned store promoting organic food and responsible, typically local, sourcing. After I became the principal cook in our household in the early 1990s, I met and learned a number of techniques from Cajun chef Paul Prudhomme and Emeril Lagasse, who has his own interpretation of Creole cuisine. On the academic front, I began presenting papers and publishing about foodways again, initially with my 2005 presidential address to the American Folklore Society on food choice, symbolism, and identity, which are topics in this book, and continuing with aesthetics, morality, politics, and applying insights in food studies to address two significant health issues also figure among the themes in my analysis.

I begin the book with a chapter on the language of food. People communicate through what they eat, how they prepare and consume food, and with whom they partake of it. Our speech is sprinkled with food metaphors:

carrot top, a hunk, a peach, a nut. Proverbs give us counsel, whether "too many cooks spoil the broth" or "cast your bread upon the waters and it will return to you a thousand fold." Often food defines events, such as hotdogs at ball games, popcorn at the movies, and picnics on the beach. Particular fare may be invested with feelings, and it can console, reward, or be used to punish. The symbolic discourse involving foodstuffs is complex; there are multiple meanings, ambiguities, and conflicting messages and interpretations, along with the influence of circumstances and the impact of habits, customs, and identities.

"Food is everything we are," insisted the celebrated chef and world traveler Anthony Bourdain. "It's an extension of nationalist feeling, ethnic feeling, your personal history, your province, your region, your tribe, your grandma." In the second chapter, I examine the interrelationship of food choice and who a person is, was, or wants to be. Identities consist of ethnicity, religion, class, occupation, peer group, family, gender, and more; there is also an individual's self-concept, body image, values, and temperament. The type of food preferred as well as its quantity, status, and manner of consumption reflect or influence who or what one is. Sometimes you eat what others think you are, conveyed by what they serve you; or your hosts prepare food for you based on who they think you think they are. You might also at times eat what you wish you were. Regardless of the situation and messages, alimentation and identity are solidly linked.

In efforts to understand what people eat, it is also important to discover what they do *not* ingest, and especially why some things elicit revulsion, a matter taken up in the third chapter. Charles Darwin, in his book on the expression of emotions (1872), defines "disgust" as meaning "something offensive to the taste." He attributes this reaction to a strong association "between the sight of food, however circumstanced, and the idea of eating it." This chapter explores the role of nurture, culture, and cognitive development in accounting for feelings of disgust. It also considers why some individuals sometimes eat things that repulse others. Finally, it addresses what the moral correlates and social consequences of the emotion are, for disgust is about ideas of civility and propriety, distinction and class, and differentiating and segregating people.

When feeling out of sorts, nostalgic, or in need of a hug, most of us turn to comfort food. One frequently mentioned item tied to memorable occasions, emotional eating, thoughts of others, sensory experiences, and perhaps physiological processes is chocolate, which is the most commonly craved food in North America. In the fourth chapter, I focus on various reasons we yearn for particular fare, along with the allure of the "food of the gods," why indulgence sometimes causes discomfort, and the impact of popular culture and folklore on eating patterns that provide feelings of comfort.

More than two million individuals in the United States are forcibly separated from society behind bars, as I indicate in the fifth chapter. Many contend that, whether by design, neglect, or indifference, their food contributes greatly to "the pains of imprisonment." Sometimes disgusting, it often is monochromatic, bland, and monotonous. Long deprived of food's sensory appeal, commensal eating, and personal autonomy, what do those in isolation on death row choose as their final repast? How does race, class, ethnicity, gender, or other identity affect their requests? What are the origins of the last meal ritual, and why is it perpetuated? Ultimately, what does the offer of a last meal before dying symbolize about public attitudes, the power of the state, and our humanity?

In the sixth chapter I investigate efforts by the Federal Bureau of Prisons, as well as several institutions abroad, to ban pork products from the menu. Although swine are the most widely eaten animals in the world, several religions proscribe their consumption. The Bureau's prohibition of pork, which was based on faulty data and methods, was met with incredulity and sarcasm on one hand, and on the other, it was lauded as a means of adding to the punishment of prisoners. Moreover, pork sanctions in the United States and Western Europe engendered bigotry, Islamophobia, and a rise in culinary nationalism exploited by politicians claiming that various pork items define national character and symbolize their country's uniqueness. For many individuals, institutional restrictions represent an attack on their personal food habits, freedom to choose what to eat when they wish, and who they are.

Like Dr. Frankenstein's creature, which ate wild berries and garden produce, some people reject the partaking of any kind of flesh. Among them was one of England's greatest lyricists, Percy Shelley, who advocated a vegetable diet, atheism, free love, and the reformation of society that could begin with changing an individual's eating habits. In the seventh chapter, I first present background on his wife, Mary Shelley, who experienced a nightmare that she described in a chapter in her novel *Frankenstein*. Then I focus on Percy's denunciation of meat consumption in poetry and in a pamphlet in 1813 promoting the salubrious effects of a "natural diet." Employing arguments resonating today, Shelley adamantly opposed killing and eating animals on grounds of health and morality, but also in criticism of wealth, power, and commercial interests. He marshaled evidence defending his vision of a world of benevolence, equality, and the cure of various diseases; he included as

testimony his own switch to vegetarianism, from which, however, he sometimes lapsed.

As it did in Shelley's time and place, the interrelationship of eating and
politics obtains in the United States, which I discuss in chapter 8. Of special
concern is how candidates' culinary choices relate to their personality and
values. Principal among the politicians are two finalists in contention for the
2016 presidential election, Hillary Rodham Clinton and Donald J. Trump.
Both used food in efforts to express character and to manipulate food symbolism for political gain, albeit in significantly different ways.

In the ninth chapter, I pursue other aspects of food habits on the campaign
trail. These encompass insults, gaffes, gender issues, body image, pandering
to the public, and purveyors naming foods to honor or ridicule contenders
for office. I also consider why "retail politics" remains popular, as well as why
the Iowa State Fair is an important arena for politicking.

The last two chapters provide ways to apply an understanding of symbolism and identity to two sets of problems involving food. The first issue, in
chapter 10, involves how to alter penal policy and practice. Prisoners and jail
inmates in 2017 numbered 2,245,000. Unfair fare has been a frequent complaint of the incarcerated. "The food shouldn't be part of the punishment,"
said one prisoner. "We're still human beings, and we care about what we eat."
Too often those behind bars must sue, riot, or subvert the system to obtain
better provisions. A few changes not only in the quality and variety of meals
but also in recognition of how food embodies a sense of self and commu-
nicates attitudes, feelings, and values might help solve or avert a number of
problems now and in the future.

The final chapter concerns type 2 diabetes, which afflicts 27 million Americans. The second application of insights in this book is how to enhance
nutrition education and counseling, especially among Latinx, nearly half of
whom born in the year 2000 are likely to develop diabetes during their lives.
Emphasis has long been on instructions in taking medications and reading
glucose levels. Guidance also should help individuals understand how they
utilize foods symbolically and as markers of who they are.

ACKNOWLEDGMENTS

I am indebted to Lucy M. Long, Daniel Wojcik, Elliott Oring, and my wife, Jenny, for their pointed discussions with me regarding what I have written. Any errors of fact or interpretation, however, are mine.

The essays in this book first appeared as articles or chapters in other books, albeit in different form and often bearing another title. I am grateful to the readers of the manuscripts, and to the editors and their assistants, for corrections and helpful suggestions. I thank the publishers for permission to reprint these essays in revised form in this book.

Chapters 1 and 2 are from the first two-thirds of "Food Choice, Symbolism, and Identity: Bread-and-Butter Issues for Folkloristics and Nutrition Studies (American Folklore Society Presidential Address, October 2005)," *Journal of American Folklore*, vol. 120 (2007), pp. 129–77. Chapter 3 is a revised version of "What's Disgusting, Why, and What Does It Matter?" *Journal of Folklore Research*, vol. 37 (2000), pp. 53–71. Chapter 4 derives from "'Stressed' Spelled Backwards Is 'Desserts': Self-Medicating Moods with Foods," *Comfort Food Meanings and Memories*, edited by Michael Owen Jones and Lucy M. Long (UP of Mississippi, 2017), pp. 17–41. Chapter 5 appeared in longer form as "Dining on Death Row: Last Meals and the Crutch of Ritual," *Journal of American Folklore*, vol. 127 (2014), pp. 3–26. Chapter 6 is from "Pig Tales: Assumptions, Beliefs, and Perceptions Regarding Pork Bans Real and Rumored," *Western Folklore*, vol. 76 (2017), pp. 379–414. Chapter 7 appeared without the introduction regarding Mary Shelley as "In Pursuit of Percy Shelley, 'The First Celebrity Vegan': An Essay on Meat, Sex, and Broccoli," *Journal of Folklore Research*, vol. 53 (2016), pp. 1–30. Chapters 8 and 9 are from "Politics on a Plate: Uses and Abuses of Foodways on the Campaign Trail," *Journal of Folklore Research*, vol. 57 (2020), pp. 47–79. Chapter 10 is excerpted from the longer article "Eating behind Bars: On Punishment, Resistance, Policy, and Applied Folkloristics," *Journal of American Folklore*, vol. 130 (2017), pp. 72–108. Chapter 11 is a shortened version of "Latina/o

Local Knowledge about Diabetes: Emotional Triggers, Plant Treatments, and Food Symbolism," *Diagnosing Folklore: Perspectives on Disability, Health, and Trauma*, edited by Trevor J. Blank and Andrea Kitta (UP of Mississippi, 2015), pp. 87–114.

FRANKENSTEIN WAS A VEGETARIAN

Chapter 1

THE LANGUAGE OF FOOD

The early months of the coronavirus pandemic in 2020 brought food to the consciousness of Americans, both as sustenance and its nonnutritional meanings. Panic buying emptied market shelves of canned goods, pasta, and bags of rice and beans. Fears of meatpacking plant closures caused stores to severely limit customer purchases.[1] A period of mandated isolation or self-imposed quarantine witnessed a dramatic increase in home cooking, especially baked goods and recipes using pantry items; during a five-month period, mentions of "sourdough" on Twitter rose 460 percent and "baking bread" shot up 354 percent.[2] Having to while away the hours, striving for a sense of control, and seeking comfort loomed large as did recalling past events of socializing around food. Those who were housebound likely would have agreed with David Mas Masumoto,[3] an organic farmer in Central California, that "Like an additional flavor, meanings are carried with food."

Indeed, reminiscing in March 2021 about the large Southern meals he experienced growing up, Ben Mims notes in regard to meanings that "Serving a surplus of food was the way we showed love to one another, especially when vocalizing it was not our strong suit."[4] Unable to talk about their feelings, the family conveyed them through a Sunday lunch of plates piled high with mouthwatering morsels. Food, then, "is a potent mode of communication," contends Annie Hauck-Lawson,[5] a registered dietician, who coined the term "the food voice" in the course of her ethnographic study of a Polish-American family. "Listening to the *food voice*," she writes, revealed how individuals "used food to express their views about themselves and their culture," making it possible for her to interpret "each participant's perspective about community, economics, gender, nutrition, ethnic identity, and traditions." Among other researchers who have adopted the concept, folklorist Lucy M. Long utilizes "food voice" in teaching nutrition majors and other students to become aware of how food often serves as "expressions of identity and carriers of memory."[6] Further, in regard to food as communication, the linguist Dan Jurafsky postulates a "grammar of cuisine" with "an implicit structure, a set of rules" concerning the dishes, meals, and entire cuisines.[7] As food historian Ken Albala remarks,[8] a cuisine's grammar can be discerned from which ingredients are (or are not) paired, the order in which dishes are served, or the utensils appropriate for their consumption.

An observation by folklorist Richard Raspa of two neighboring populations in Utah illustrates the rules governing dishes and meals.[9] "In Mormon cooking, casseroles and roasts are presented simultaneously on a platter with, say, creamed vegetables and buttered potatoes, followed by ice cream or pie or other confection for dessert." The Italian immigrants, however, "are accustomed to individual and sequential servings of *pasta* or *minestra* followed by a sauteed veal or beef, an oil-and-vinegar green salad, then fruit to complement the meal."

Symbolic discourse involving cuisine is pervasive and complex, manifesting itself in a wide variety of contexts.[10] The language of food exhibits multiple connotations that may be ambiguous, conflicting, or even pernicious. Understanding how messages are conveyed through culinary behavior requires an examination of not only victuals but also the preparation, service, and consumption of food, for all are grist to the mill of symbolization. As Margaret Visser writes,[11] "Food is never just something to eat."

Human beings feed on metaphors in order to talk about something else. We hunger for, spice it up, sugarcoat, hash things out, sink our teeth into, and find something difficult to swallow.[12] Terms of endearment partake of the gastronomic: sugar, honey, pumpkin, cupcake, sweetie pie. Foodstuffs inform descriptions of people: a ham, a nut, or someone with a peaches-and-cream complexion, cauliflower ears, or potato masher nose. There is a bountiful array of proverbs and proverbial expressions, such as you can catch more flies with honey than with vinegar, you reap what you sow, you can't have your cake and eat it too, half a loaf is better than none, variety is the spice of life, a watched pot never boils, out of the frying pan and into the fire, and an apple a day keeps the doctor away. In other words, as Lévi-Strauss said, "Food is not only good to eat, but also good to think."[13] "I wanted to live deep and suck out all the marrow of life," wrote Henry David Thoreau in *Walden*, explaining his quest for nutriment beyond the physical.[14] More pointedly, Rosalind Russell proclaimed in *Auntie Mame*, "Life is a banquet and most poor suckers are starving to death. So live, live, live!"

The omnipresent role of food in communication and interaction as metaphor or other symbolic form should come as no surprise, given the fact that we experience food from birth to death. We often eat in social settings, which generates associations between food and people; restrictions on social gatherings during coronavirus upsurges galled many individuals deprived of spending time with loved ones and maintaining traditions among family and friends.[15]

In addition, few activities as food-related ones involve so many senses.[16] We hear stomach rumblings and suffer hunger pangs, see the food, smell it, salivate in anticipation of eating it, sense its weight and density as we lift it, and feel its heat or coldness as it enters the mouth. We detect an item's sweet, sour, salty, bitter, spicy, bland, and umami qualities on the tongue. We enjoy the feeling of satiety after consuming food while also perceiving renewed physical and mental energy. As Oscar Wilde remarked: "After a good dinner, one can forgive anybody, even one's relatives."

Jean Anthelme Brillat-Savarin wrote in *The Physiology of Taste, or Meditations on Transcendental Gastronomy* (1825), "The pleasures of the table are for every man, of every land, and no matter of what place in history or society; they can be a part of all his other pleasures, and they last the longest, to console him when he has outlived the rest." Or as Garrison Keillor of *A Prairie Home Companion* fame put it, "Sex is good, but not as good as fresh sweet corn."

Dictionaries define symbol as a visible sign of something invisible, as an idea, a quality: one thing stands for, represents, or re-presents another. In 1944 philosopher Ernst Cassirer wrote that "instead of defining man as an animal *rationale*, we should define him as an animal *symbolicum*."[17] Three decades later, the anthropologist Raymond Firth noted that human beings do not live by symbols alone, but they certainly order and interpret their reality, and even reconstruct it, through symbols.[18]

We create symbols when we assign meaning to elements of lives and the world that extend beyond their intrinsic content. Any activity, object, concept, or utterance may be rendered symbolic anytime and anywhere by anyone.[19] This is particularly so in regard to food and eating. Items of food are often imbued with special significance, be it Maine lobster or Native American frybread, along with cuisines such as soul food and Cajun cooking.

Even the physical characteristics of a foodstuff can be emblematic, conveying values and ideas.[20] For example, the American Food for Peace Program once sent yellow corn from the United States to Botswana for distribution in schools as drought relief. Shamed and humiliated by the tons of yellow grain given them as food, secondary school students in Serowe rioted, burning the headmaster's car and destroying stockpiles of it. Only white maize is fit for human consumption; yellow is fed to animals.[21]

In another instance, the absence rather than presence of a dish on the menu caused consternation.[22] The food manager-dietitian at a Maryland correctional facility with a large African American population planned a

Thanksgiving meal consisting of turkey, yams, macaroni and cheese, collard greens, and corn bread. Inmates angrily confronted the servers behind bulletproof glass demanding, "Where's the sauerkraut?" Years earlier, institution workers who commuted from Pennsylvania had introduced the pickled cabbage as a side dish. A regional food was incorporated into an ethnic cuisine and became associated with a national holiday. Its absence at mealtime left people feeling deprived and bereft.

Utensils may be iconic for some eaters. In the newsletter *American Food & Wine*,[23] John Thorne interprets the fork as a "claw" with "long sharp nails" and hence

> an unconscious emblem of the hunt. . . . As coda, consider the fork in relation to the chopstick. . . . Of the two, the fork is the arrogant one, for it imperiously seizes where the other only plucks. But chopsticks are by far the more sensual instrument, delicately sexual in the gentle but urgent tugging of morsel after morsel out of the savory mess. . . . Where the skewering fork ensures yet again each morsel's death, chopsticks tenderly grasp and deposit it, still pulsating with metaphoric life, into the waiting mouth.

People define events through food. "Some habits never change: a hot dog on a stick at the beach, hot chocolate at the ice skating rink, and popcorn at the movies," one of my students said. Although fraught with meaningfulness, such food choices may have unpleasant consequences. A friend of mine always eats Dodger Dogs at baseball games in Los Angeles. He does not like them, he eats too many, he feels sick later, but he insists that it's not a Dodger game without the hotdogs.

On the other hand, events can define consumption, such as the ribald bachelorette parties celebrating a friend's upcoming wedding analyzed by folklorist Diane Tye.[24] "Juxtaposed to how they usually see and conduct themselves, participants . . . demonstrate their sexual agency through a playful display of hypersexualized femininity."[25] This includes mixed drinks with names like Blow Job shooters and food in the shape of male genitalia, such as meatballs and cookie balls, appetizers created from cucumbers and bananas, and phallic cakes, cookies, or cupcakes.

Special occasions marked by food, such as family reunions, Sunday dinners, or holiday meals pose problems for people whose dietary needs make them feel excluded. In my interviews with Latinx suffering type 2 diabetes, one woman said, "I feel bad when I refuse to eat food that friends offer me. I don't like to explain my health to everybody so I say no thank you, and they say, 'Why don't you like this?'"

For some, food identifies place. The locale could be a region, city, neighborhood, or home.[26] Examples include pasties in Michigan's Upper Peninsula,[27] Cincinnati chili in Ohio,[28] green bean casserole in the Midwest,[29] and a giant hamburger in the little berg of Harrison, Nebraska (population 360), where Delores Wasserburger of Sioux Sundries serves up twenty-eight-ounce cheeseburgers with a bag of potato chips. Years earlier a rancher, Bill Coffee, brought in a few ranch hands and asked for a large hamburger. That was when she whipped up her first Coffee Burger. Since then the diner has been featured on the Food Network and visited by tourists from around the world.[30]

Fairs and festivals abound throughout the United States in summertime. Sponsoring chambers of commerce acknowledge their intention of promoting the place, the people, and the products, benefits, and achievements as emblematic of the town and surrounding area. Shining the spotlight on agriculture, they emphasize bounty by giving away great quantities of popped corn or ears of roasted corn. They foster agrarian lifestyles, values, and a sense of self-reliance. Nostalgia for bygone days prevails: heating corn on the cob in iconic steam engines, throwing horseshoes, pitting men and their machines against one another in tractor pulls, hosting a midway with carnival booths and barkers, and encouraging visitors to attend an old-time blacksmith demonstration.[31]

Other themes reign as well. Festivals extol a sense of community in the locale, as suggested by the buttons in figure 1.1. Hundreds of volunteers work together to produce the events, which includes shucking and cooking thousands of ears of corn. Parades draw their participants from town folks. The Sweet Corn Queen is chosen from girls in the local high school. There are street dances, contests featuring local talent, and musical performances by the high school vocal ensemble, a church choir, or bands in the area, such as Doc Ashton and the Root Canals. Proceeds from the fair support local charities and next year's event. A festival is geared to the whole family with its games, carnival rides, "kiddie" parade, face painting, crafts, petting zoo, and, at the National Sweet Corn Festival in Hoopeston, Illinois, a Little Corn Eaters Run as well as the Cream of the Crop Pretty Baby Contest. Not only the symbolic but also the sensual element looms large, for a festival is filled with a cacophony of sounds and panoply of sights. The aroma of cooking food wafts through the air day and night. BBQ chicken and pork, buffalo burgers and vegetarian patties sizzling on a grill, and fry bread and cornbread beckon the hungry and make mouths water.

Figure 1.1 Souvenir badges celebrating Corn Chaff Days
in Hector, Minnesota. Author's collection. Photo by
Laura Layera.

In addition to defining existing places, food can also "make" place. This occurred for Japanese Americans in internment camps during World War II. They reterritorialized their surroundings by using mess halls, gardens, hot plates in living quarters, tofu-producing facilities, and memories of food as "spaces" in which to expand political activity and create collective identities.[32]

Frequently food is invested with emotion resulting from or contributing to its symbolic import. "I have a sense of well-being when I eat any kind of meal on a special occasion," one person told me. "The well-being is generated by enjoyment of the people I am with. I have a sense of well-being when I eat oatmeal. I am sure this feeling is associated with TV commercials about Quaker oats in which oatmeal is synonymous with motherhood."

As one of its "voices,"[33] food consoles. "'Stressed' spelled backward is 'desserts'" reads a sign in a bakery near me. Sweets provide solace for all those actors on television shows who dig into a container of ice cream when they are depressed; their actions tell the viewer what their emotional state is.

Comfort food is a primary source of consolation, signifying a particular time and place in the past that evokes feelings of peace and happiness as well as association with others. "No food can ever mean as much to you as that food [which you grew up with]," writes John Lancaster in the *New Yorker*.[34] It is comfort food, "designed to remind us of familiar things, to connect us with our personal histories and our communities and our families. That has always been true and it always will be true."

Many people give food as a way to convey sympathy and support when a friend falls ill or suffers a death in the family. In *Up a Country Lane Cookbook*, Evelyn Birkby includes a recipe for Mabel Lewis's Jell-O dish (pineapple and grapes in red gelatin with whipped topping). "This was truly a comfort salad, for Mabel always took this to a family at the time of serious problems." Birkby comments further, "We learned, during those long, painful days that the quiet offer of food provided sustenance for our bodies and comfort for our aching hearts, as our family weathered the terrible storm of our daughter's death."[35]

The meanings of edible items may conflict or evoke ambivalent emotions. Chocolate is a case in point. It may be eaten either as a reward for an achievement or as therapy for a difficult, trying day. Viewed as sinful because it provides sensual pleasure, chocolate occasionally evokes a sexual analogy. Excessive consumption of chocolate by an individual, however, might signal to that person and others a lack of self-control and a sign of moral failing. An individual might use eating as retribution. For example, one person told me, "Many times, when I eat little other than 'junk' food during the day, I will maliciously punish myself by eating more junk food, perhaps feeling that I will compound the crime and so remind myself of my terrible eating habits."

Sometimes food-derived assessments of other people, not just oneself, are negative. An example is French president Jacques Chirac's remark about Britain to leaders of Russia and Germany on the eve of the G8 summit in the summer of 2005: "You cannot trust people who have such bad cuisine. It is the country with the worst food after Finland." In reaction, *The Sun* declared that Chirac should not "talk crepe."[36] Chirac also said unkind things about the Scots' haggis (composed of cows' lungs, intestine, pancreas, liver, and heart mixed with onions, suet, and oatmeal stuffed into a sheep's stomach) as well as the American hamburger. Two years earlier, in this international food fight, cafeterias in the US House of Representatives changed "french fries" to "freedom fries" and "French toast" to "freedom toast" as part of a Republican protest at Chirac's opposition to the war on Iraq. Renaming items on the menu was "a small but symbolic effort to show the strong displeasure of many on Capitol Hill with the actions of our so-called ally, France," said Representative Bob Ney (R, Ohio) whose committee was in charge of the eateries.

Food-based slurs, stereotypes, and nicknames not only denigrate others but also dehumanize the Other, as in such ethnophaulisms or *blasons populaires* for Germans, French, English, and Indochinese as kraut, frog, limey, and fish head,[37] or, along the Texas border, greaser, chili, pepper belly, taco choker, and beaner aimed at those of Mexican descent.[38] Visceral metaphors that marginalize populations have been employed to promote adverse social policies such as the Immigration Acts of 1921 and 1924, which severely restricted the number of people from Southern and Eastern Europe. Foreigners in the United States were described as "indigestible food," as in the remark that "the stomach of the body politic" is "filled to bursting with peoples swallowed whole whom our digestive juices do not digest." Voicing a common attitude at the time, President General Sarah Mitchell Guernsey of the Daughters of the American Revolution contended that "You can never grow an American soul so long as you use a hyphen. . . . What kind of American consciousness can grow in the atmosphere of sauerkraut and Limburger cheese? Or, what can you expect of the Americanism of the man whose breath always reeks of garlic?"[39]

A more recent food-related instance of assailing others is the action of a woman from Upstate New York. In January 2020, in a display of anti-Semitism, she threw a package of pork chops on the front steps of a synagogue. Returning a few hours later, she photographed her symbolic statement. Police charged her with first-degree harassment as a hate crime.[40]

Reprehensible though these verbal and physical metaphors are, they indicate an important point for research and application: symbols evoke emotions, act upon opinions, and influence actions. For example, Larry Hirschhorn, a consultant trained in psychodynamics, was asked to facilitate a retreat for senior scientists in a research organization. In a brief conversation a delegate told him that the controller and president were "nickel and diming" the labs to death. Hirschhorn asked about provisions for food. Everyone was to bring a brown bag lunch. He urged the delegate to tell the president that it would be better to provide lunch for the retreat as a symbol of support, but the delegate hesitated. "Puzzled and irritated," remarks Hirschhorn, "I realized that I was experiencing the same feelings that bothered the scientists of the company." Retreat participants would be less able to work well if the president did not meet such simple dependency needs as food, and Hirschhorn as consultant would feel less effective. "So the president, even before I met him and before I even had a contract, was nickel and diming me to death as well!"[41]

As noted above, not only a food's physical traits but also an item's absence at table, the utensils employed to eat it, the locale in which it is consumed, and its association with comfort are the ingredients for meaning making. In addition, the preparation and service of foodstuffs can send signals, for instance burning dinner as the coding of seeming incompetence in the kitchen in order to escape a social role.[42] Ostensibly occasions to celebrate family unity, holiday meals can become arenas where diners pass hostility rather than bread around the table as exemplified fictionally in Guriner Chadha's movie *What's Cooking?* It is described as "Thanksgiving. A celebration of food, tradition, and relative insanity."[43]

Moreover, the very act of eating conveys meanings through one's deportment at table. Like parents today who teach manners to their young children, a rash of etiquette books in the late nineteenth century advised a growing middle class in the city on how to dress, walk, and talk properly to impress others, as well as how to meet, greet, and eat. Rules of decorum comprise a catalog of symbolic behaviors to communicate messages about oneself; hence, you are how you eat.[44]

Food also projects anxieties through symbolic form.[45] The sexual dysfunction of men in military boot camp or in other institutional settings is blamed on adulteration of the food with saltpeter.[46] The Kentucky Fried Rat legend about a couple taking home chicken only to discover that they had been munching on a rodent expresses alarm over the loss of community control by large impersonal corporations displacing local vendors.[47] The rumor that Church's Fried Chicken is owned by the Ku Klux Klan, which contaminates the food with a chemical to sterilize Black males, projects racial fears.[48]

Consider, too, the reactions in some quarters to bioengineering. In the mid-1990s, the sweet visage of Dolly the cloned sheep, named after country singer Dolly Parton, was quickly replaced by the face of Victor Frankenstein's monster. Corn and other genetically modified foodstuffs have been dubbed "Frankenfood." In addition, a rumor spread that the federal government required Kentucky Fried Chicken to change its name to KFC because a study at the University of New Hampshire had discovered that genetically manipulated organisms rather than real chickens are being used. These creatures lack beaks, feathers, and feet, and in some accounts they possess two breasts and three legs. Tubes to pump blood and nutrients inserted into their bodies keep them alive. In another version, the gigantic breasts of chickens are so pumped up by chemicals the birds tip over while trying to walk.[49]

Be they objects, acts, or linguistic formations, symbols stand ambiguously for a multiplicity of meanings. Context, therefore, often determines content, that is, circumstances affect whether or not meaning emerges as well as what messages are conveyed or inferred. Eating everything on one's plate may appear to be gluttony or it might mean that one follows the dictum "Waste not, want not" or that there is an actual scarcity of food or money. Hirschhorn interpreted having a brown bag lunch at the retreat he was to lead as a sign of organizational stinginess, but in other situations it might speak to a desirable informality among participants.

Because of the ambiguity or multiple meanings of symbols, an act may be misunderstood. For instance, a youth from Taiwan moved in with an American family to learn English. On Sunday, the hostess prepared a special family meal, setting a beautifully roasted chicken on the table, the neck cavity facing him. He picked at his food and finally said, "It was delicious, and I will leave here just as soon as I find another place to live." The tradition familiar to him was that when a person is not welcome, the host places a chicken with its head facing the unwanted party.[50]

Ignorance or transgression of cherished traditions and their meanings can cause large-scale disruption and dissention, as it did after the Marriott Corporation took over food service at Dodger Stadium in Los Angeles distressing many of the fans by no longer grilling Dodger Dogs, downsizing the double bag of peanuts to a single, barring Roger the Peanut Man from hurling peanut bags to customers because of company policy against throwing food, and trying to force employees to continue working during the singing of the "Star-Spangled Banner."

Food has a political dimension exercised not only by corporations that own land, operate processing plants, or secure space for products crowding market shelves, but also by departments of government devoted to the environment, land use, and health and human services.[51] The political is also manifest in everyday activities. A household member who shops for groceries, decides on the night's menu, prepares the food, or designates where in the home a meal will be consumed exerts power over others. The person who dines with another at a restaurant and insists on paying for the meal might be motivated for several reasons but ultimately asserts dominance.

To conclude, people assign meanings to what, where, how, when, and with whom they eat. While food, including its preparation, service, and consumption, is a vehicle of communication, the message may be intended or unintentional and what is inferred might correspond to or conflict with it; both encoding and decoding depend greatly on the context involving the individuals, their relationship, and the event. Food can be used to mark place, express individuality as well as community, and erect boundaries between or among people. It can create or project anxieties. Ignorance or transgression of rules and expectations can result in social disruption. Whether family members, corporations, or government agencies, those who control the production, procurement, distribution, preparation, or serving of foodstuffs exert power over others as expressed through words and actions.[52] If food-related symbolism is complicated, then the relationship between food and identity is no less problematic, which I take up in the next chapter.

Chapter 2

EATING WHAT YOU ARE, WERE, OR WANT TO BE

Through what we eat as well as when, where, and how, we convey values, attitudes, and who we are to other people as well as ourselves. Often the process is unconscious; sometimes it is intentional, a result of self-making and also the consequence of identifying with or being categorized by others as a member of a nationality, region, ethnicity, race, religion, occupation, age group, and so on.[1] I begin this chapter with an analysis of eating behavior in relation to one's personal food system, then discuss gendered eating and provisioning mythology followed by food choice in social contexts, and end with a section on the dynamics of identity.

SELF-MAKING AND PERSONAL EXPRESSION THROUGH FOOD

To take up the first matter of self in relation to food consumption (i.e., a personal food system), some self-images derive from the *range of fare* consisting of foods viewed as acceptable to the individual. One person admits to being, or is characterized by others as, a picky or fussy eater unwilling to try new foods,[2] another is a food snob, and someone else boasts a willingness to eat anything and, even being an invasivore, is willing to consume offensive species such as feral hogs in Texas and nutria ("swamp rats") in Louisiana.[3] Yet others identify themselves as omnivores or as one of the six kinds of vegetarians from occasional meat eater to ovo-lacto vegetarian to vegan.[4] Some people refer to dietary restrictions as hallmarks of their identity, such as fare that is free of eggs, gluten, nuts, or soy. A few individuals, succumbing to orthorexia nervosa, obsess over eating healthfully; they fixate on the inclusion or exclusion of particular foods as preventing or curing disease or critically affecting their daily well-being.[5]

Regarding the actual *types of food* preferred and consumed as distinct from what is within acceptable limits, there is the self-proclaimed junk food junkie (immortalized in Jim Croce's song by this title), fast-food freak, meat-and-potatoes man, salad lover, sushi addict, chocoholic, adventurous eater or culinary tourist, or pasta person (Sophia Loren once said about her voluptuous figure, "All you see, I owe to spaghetti").

The relationship between identity and types of food eaten is illustrated in the cult classic *The Breakfast Club* (1985), directed by John Hughes, in which the lunches of the five main characters correlate with their personalities. Claire (the princess), who wears diamond earrings from her mother and drives her father's BMW, opens up a neat, gray bag from which she withdraws a Japanese wood plate, napkin, chopsticks, and black lacquered box of sushi, along with a decanter of soy sauce. Andrew (the jock) plops a large shopping bag on his desk containing a big bag of chips, three thick sandwiches, cookies, a banana, an apple, and a quart carton of milk; he is carbo-loading for a wrestling match. Brian (the geek), a straight-A student and member of both the chess and physics clubs, has brought a peanut butter and jelly sandwich with the crusts removed, a Thermos of soup, and a container of apple juice. Allison (the outcast), hides her face in the hood of her jacket, opens a sandwich, peels off a thin slice of meat, tosses it over her shoulder where it sticks to a sculpture, grabs two straws, pours sugar out of them onto each slice of bread and into her mouth, and slurps soda. John (the outlaw) has no food for lunch, only a can of Coke; he comes from a home of domestic violence and is abusive toward others, remarking sarcastically about their food choices and personalities.

"The way you cut your meat reflects the way you live," observed Confucius. Indeed, *how an individual eats* speaks to identity, whether one be fastidious, messy, a formal diner, or someone who does not stand on formality. Tolstoy's joy in expressing intensely felt physical sensations in some of his writings bears a direct relationship to his eating with his hands, absorbing sensory qualities as directly as possible.[6] The method of eating includes ritualistic behavior, such as a person's consuming all of one food on the plate before moving on to the next; the manner in which the character portrayed by Barbra Streisand in the movie *The Mirror Has Two Faces* always cuts her salad into small bits, which endears her to Jeff Bridges's character; the way a young man invariably tears open and flattens a fast-food bag to use as a place mat for the items inside that drove his (now ex-)girlfriend to distraction; and the systematic techniques that people employ to eat wedges of cake, fried eggs on toast, corn on the cob, and Oreos.[7]

Sometimes *meal patterns* correlate with identity, as in the three-meals-a-day person, the individual who professes to not being a breakfast eater ("I don't do mornings"), the frequent snacker, or the person who often eats on the run because of a hectic schedule. The *quantity consumed* relates to self when one admits to being a hearty eater, light eater, nibbler, a person who eats like a bird, or, conversely, like a horse. Finally, *consistency of alimentary practices* bears a relationship to identity, as in the regular eater, a stable eater, or someone who "grabs lunch when I can."

In addition to the numerous identities related to consumption practices, there are those corresponding to personal characteristics, which in turn manifest themselves in eating behavior. One of these traits is *orientation toward health*. A diet of organically grown, free-range, and brown, coarse, or raw foodstuffs as opposed to conventionally grown (often with a helping of pesticides), factory-raised, and white, refined, and processed items testifies to health consciousness.[8] For instance, Jacob Chansley, also known as Jake Angeli and the self-professed QAnon Shaman wearing a horned hat and fur pelts and covered in tattoos of Norse symbols, was among those storming the Capitol in Washington, DC, 6 January 2021. He refused to eat in jail for several days. His mother told reporters, "He gets very sick if he doesn't eat organic food. Literally, he'll get physically sick."

As a corollary, there is the patent disregard of fitness. In 1981 the punk rock band Jody Foster's Army belted out a song at a couple of hundred beats per minute consisting of "Coke and Snickers is all I eat," repeated eight times in rapid succession followed by "Health Sucks!" sung eight times in a row. Food writer Calvin Trillin who often reviewed "rib joints" remarked, "Health food makes me sick." A man who was an undergraduate student when the counterculture health movement was strong said, "Because it is so fatty and a hazard to one's health, eating Spam," which he did, "was sort of like an anti-statement, the antithesis of perfection and health."[9]

"The body is not the same from day to day. Not even from minute to minute," acknowledges Emily Jenkins.[10] "Sometimes it seems like home, sometimes more like a cheap motel near Pittsburgh." A second trait as part of personal characteristics is *body image*. Often fat is implicated, particularly among females. For many college-age women, growing fat betokens *loss of control*, which is another personal characteristic related to identity and hence food intake (and an issue for countless anorexics). In contrast, the bodies of thin people symbolize restraint in eating that gives these individuals power over others through self-righteousness and moral rectitude.[11]

In addition to orientation toward health and concerns over body image as well as control, another trait by means of which people may identify themselves related to food choice is *salience of food*, as in "I love to eat; I love to cook" or "I eat to live, not live to eat." Yet another is *degree of satisfaction and gratification* apparent in the person who gushes about being an enthusiastic eater or the remark by George Bernard Shaw that "I am no gourmet, eating is not a pleasure to me, only a troublesome necessity, like dressing or undressing."[12] An additional characteristic consists of *physiological conditions and attributes*, as in "I have a nervous stomach" or one's being ill with a cold or the flu, suffering from a disease (e.g., diabetes, celiac disease, acid reflux, colitis), having an allergic reaction to shellfish, potato skins, citrus, tomatoes, wheat products, or monosodium glutamate (MSG), experiencing disgust and cravings while pregnant, and so on. *Lifestyle*,[13] such as the self-proclaimed cosmopolitan, beach bum, fitness buff, or outdoors-oriented individual, comprises yet another personal trait giving rise to an identity that in turn expresses and determines food choice.

One final component of identity to be mentioned, reproduced in, or constructed by eating behavior is that of *values, philosophy, or ideology*. At a county fair, for instance, the food booths of fraternal, religious, and civic organizations sell virtually the same fare; customers may purchase their food from one rather than another vendor because of their identification with and allegiance to that organization.[14] For some individuals who identify with a racial or ethnic group, preparing and consuming foods associated with that identity helps keep memories and traditions alive.

GENDERED DIETS IN PROVISIONING MYTHOLOGY

According to widespread provisioning mythology both past and present, many foodstuffs bear the mark of gender. This in turn can influence individuals' behavior.[15] For many people in Western society, milk and eggs have associations with women, as do vegetables that contain seeds (the ovaries of plants) and that are round, smooth, small, soft, sweet, and juicy. In contrast, tubers are linked to men; traits consist of the long, thin, rough, tough, heavy, filling, and strongly flavored. Vivid, bright, warm colors in produce represent the feminine (emotional, expressive), while cool greens and blues betoken the masculine (calm, controlled, e.g., "cool as a cucumber").

In explaining how such links develop, Marshall Sahlins[16] suggests that societies seize natural facts, apply them socially, and then reapply them naturally. The metaphor of sweetness, for instance, is employed in socializing women to be supportive and kind; sweet objects subsequently are viewed as feminine. Although "real men don't eat quiche," many in fact do consume milk and eggs as nutrient-rich, strength-building foods and perhaps, it has been hypothesized, as symbolic domination over women and their reproductive capacity.[17] Finally, red meat is masculine—as in "he-man food," "hero" sandwiches, and bowls of Campbell's hearty beef stew referred to as "the manhandlers"—while the more delicate chicken and fish tend toward the feminine.

Most of the literature on gendered eating centers on binary models.[18] In concentrating on cisgender individuals—those who have the same gender identity as their birth-assigned sex—these studies ignore people who identify as gender nonbinary. In addition, the bulk of research on food consumption among gays and lesbians concerns disordered eating. Little has been published about the diets of transgender individuals other than food insecurity and alterations in food preparation in the course of aging when many have outlived their companions and, during the coronavirus epidemic, lost their systems of social and mental health support.[19]

Regarding the attributes of masculinity and femininity assigned to foods, for centuries red meat has been associated with strength, power, aggression, and hence male identity.[20] Not surprisingly then, Lawry's Restaurant in Los Angeles has long sponsored an annual Beef Bowl coinciding with the Rose Bowl. Since 1956 the competing football teams have been treated on alternate nights to prime rib. A competition once pitted players against one another to consume the most meat. Ed Muransky of the University of Michigan Wolverines set the all-time record in 1979, when he ate eight pounds of beef. The 11 January 1965 issue of *Sports Illustrated* notes that (whether coincidentally or not) in each of the eight preceding games the team that ate the most went on to win the Rose Bowl.

Blood carries aspects of violence, arousal of the passions, and bestiality itself. Ballad publisher Joseph Ritson writes in his *Moral Essay upon Abstinence* (1802),[21] "use of animal food disposes man to cruel and ferocious actions" evident in the fact that the ancient Scythians, "from drinking the blood of their cattle, proceeded to drink that of their enemies," while Hindus, abstaining from meat, are of "gentle disposition." Blood appears metaphorically in everyday language: there is noble blood, tainted blood, and a union in blood as well as the thin-bloodedness of the elderly. "Spilled blood" refers to a deed of violence, "cold blooded" connotes a merciless act, and "hot blooded" signifies anger and impulsiveness.[22]

Omnivores are often thought of as aggressive in contrast to the more passive herbivores.[23] Voltaire was horrified at the cruel inhumanity of consuming flesh, Emanuel Swedenborg saw meat eating as a symbol of our fall from grace, and Percy Shelley viewed it as the root of evil and source of disease.

In regard to falling ill from flesh eating, Sylvester Graham, who bequeathed us whole wheat bread and Graham crackers, railed in the mid-nineteenth century against meat eating as weakening health and promoting lust. Ellen G. White, who established the Seventh-day Adventist Church with her husband and a friend, endured weakness and fainting spells from consuming flesh although she loved the taste. In June 1863, she experienced a vision; revealed to her was God's plan for a reform diet without animal products that would greatly lessen disease and agony, including her own, which became a tenet of the religion. Three years after her vision, she opened the Western Health Reform Institute in Battle Creek, Michigan. A decade later John Harvey Kellogg, an Adventist medical doctor, who is shown in figure 2.1, became director and eventually changed the name to the Battle Creek Sanitarium, where he and his dietitian wife, Ella, invented eighty meatless dishes including corn flakes. He lectured in the 1870s on the theory of "autointoxication": meat literally rots in the stomach causing the body to be "flooded with the most horrible and loathsome poisons."[24]

Figure 2.1 John Harvey Kellogg portrait. Library of Congress.

The notion of contagion informs some of these pronouncements: one literally *becomes* what one eats. George Bernard Shaw, for example, worried that "If I were to eat meat, my evacuations would stink" because an animal's stench of terror at being slaughtered is conveyed to its flesh and hence to the eater. On the other hand, one likely eats what one *already is*. A few studies suggest that flesh eating figures prominently in the diets of those who emphasize social power, hierarchical domination, and conservatism, while people who place greater value on equality, peace, and social justice gravitate toward vegetarianism.[25]

Many nineteenth-century vegetarians promoted what were considered radical causes at the time, including temperance, anti-vivisection, and women's suffrage,[26] their identity and that of contemporary vegetarians symbolizing a lifestyle and set of values rather than being simply a matter of taste regarding what to ingest. Although grains and vegetables were recommended in place of flesh, the word "vegetarian" did not come into use until the 1840s. Rather, eschewing meat and meat products while eating only fruit and vegetables was referred to as a "natural diet." The word "vegetarian" was not taken as cognate with "vegetable" but with the Latin *vegetus*, meaning "lively" or "vigorous."[27] A Vegetarian Society was founded in England in 1847, an American Vegetarian Convention was formed in 1850, and a Vegetarian Society was established in Germany in 1867. By the early 1800s, the principal objections to consuming flesh expressed by vegetarians today had been articulated. They include such contentions as creophagy, or flesh eating, is unhealthful, animal slaughter brutalizes human character, raising animals for food inflicts suffering on our fellow creatures, and stock breeding is a waste of environmental resources.

I devote a section of this chapter to the symbolism of meat and nonflesh food because of how fundamental they are to diet and identity: we eat one or the other or both and in the process generate or convey a sense of self. Moreover, sex and gender are basic identities biologically and through social construction. The symbolism of meat and vegetables in relation to identity has greatly impacted, and continues to determine, people's behavior in a multitude of ways, which has implications for contemporary nutritional programs. Sometimes men who assume the role of cooking, for instance firefighters, masculinize their assumption of "women's" work by using profanity profusely during food preparation.[28] Although masculine identities may be multiple, such as "strong," "healthy," "wealthy," "sensitive," "traditional," "smart," or "pure" men, the fact remains that there has long been a "hegemonic masculinity" serving as a prototype or ideal that associates men with meat rather than with "sissy" or "wimpy" foods.[29] A study of gay men in Brazil who refer to themselves as "bears" found them consuming bovine meat and drinking beer to build an ideal "macho," unfeminine body.[30]

Probably as a result of long-standing notions about meat, produce, and "stimulants," health manuals in the nineteenth and early twentieth centuries recommended a diet low in meat for adolescent boys as a means of combating masturbation, along with reduced consumption of hot spicy foods, which inflame the passions. They also advocated a lower intake of red meat in pregnant and lactating women, promoting instead the ingestion of "delicate," "light" female foods like fruit, soups, milk, vegetables, chicken, and fish that reflect a woman's own delicate feminine condition as well as avoid stimulating red-bloodedness inappropriate to those fulfilling a nurturing role. By contrast a man required a diet heavy in flesh because of his expenditure of energy in hard work and creative thinking, which also used up his blood that must be replenished.[31]

Toward the end of the nineteenth century, many Victorian young women rejected meat, associating a carnivorous diet with sexual precocity, abundant menstrual flow, and even nymphomania and insanity.[32] Spices and condiments also excited the sensual nature rather than moral character of a young woman. "Indulgence in foods that were considered stimulating or inflammatory served not only as an emblem of unchecked sensuality but sometimes as a sign of social aggression," writes Joan Jacobs Brumberg in *Fasting Girls*,[33] "Women who ate meat could be regarded as acting out of place; they were assuming a male prerogative." In addition, eating could quickly lead to gluttony and physical ugliness; slimness signified spirituality, beauty, and gentility. "In this milieu food was obviously more than a source of nutrition or a means of curbing hunger; it was an integral part of individual identity. For women in particular, how one ate spoke to issues of basic character." Then and now, denial of appetitive "expressed an ideal of female perfection and moral superiority." Limited research suggests that those identifying as sexual minorities, including some cisgender women as well as individuals identifying themselves as members of the LGBTQ community, report higher levels of addictive-like eating to cope with negative emotions caused by stress from heterosexist rejection, harassment, and discrimination.

In the past and to some extent now, provisioning mythology has affected which foods men and women of different classes select in their diet. Several studies indicate that working-class and professional women in the United States and United Kingdom appear to prefer a more feminine array of foodstuffs than do working-class men.[34] Although many professional males give lip service to a penchant for the same items as their female counterparts, they are inclined to consume a more masculine set of items, particularly when away from home and in the company of their fellows. Countless working-class women in households prepare and eat a more masculine diet than they would like because they accommodate themselves to their spouses' preferences, write Marion Kerr and Nicola Charles in "Servers and Providers: The Distribution of Food within the Family." This often was the case in the American Midwest in my youth and perhaps continues. "Well I *know* my husband's taste in food so I stick to just plain things," said a woman whom Kerr and Charles interviewed. "We live on beef, pork or lamb . . . so I tend to stick to the same thing most weeks—I rarely buy anything for myself." Men typically eat more meat than do women, observed the authors, because they expect it as males and owing to the fact that many females think they need it. As one woman remarked, "A man that's been at work all day doesn't want to come home to fish fingers. He wants something a bit more substantial."[35]

Having examined the identities of male and female in relation to food symbolism, it is time to consider other ways in which people indicate who they are through alimentary activities. This entails a consideration of social contexts and such matters as class, ethnicity, family, and peers.[36]

FOOD CHOICE IN SOCIAL CONTEXTS

Not only gender but also class, ethnicity, race, family, and affinity groups, including occupations, dominate the list of social categories and contexts affecting eating behavior. In the best-seller *The Status Seekers*, for example, Vance Packard describes the downs and ups of food associated with class. A man grew up in a poor family of Italian origin that subsisted on blood sausages, pizza, spaghetti, and red wine. After high school, he worked in logging camps, where he learned to prefer beef, beans, and beer. Later, in an industrial plant in Detroit, he worked his way up the ladder and cultivated the favorite foods and beverages of other executives: steak, seafood, and whiskey. Ultimately gaining acceptance in the city's upper class, he won culinary admiration by serving guests, with the aid of his servant, authentic Italian treats such as blood sausage, spaghetti, and red wine.

As suggested by Packard's example, high-status foods are those that are expensive because of rarity, cost of ingredients, labor-intensive preparation, the prominence of animal protein, and their nonnutritional meanings and associations. A staple item, if prepared in elaborate ways and served infrequently, can attain or preserve prestige value ("prestige," from Latin *praestigium*, illusion or delusion).

For centuries, white bread, white rice, and meat have commanded admiration.[37] In the seventeenth century, for example, Elizabethan England had five kinds of wheat bread, each of which had its class associations. Manchet, the bread of higher aristocratic tables, consisted of six-ounce loaves, "white and sweet." An inferior brown for the poor was composed almost entirely of bran; other breads were made of rye, barley, oats, beans, peas, corn, or mixtures, but not wheat. Ground acorn bread was for the very lowliest.

In regard to meat, visitors to America were amazed at the amount of flesh ingested. In *Domestic Manners of the Americans*,[38] Frances Trollope wrote, "They consume an extraordinary quantity of bacon. Ham and beef-steaks appear morning, noon and night." Letter after letter to relatives in the Old World proclaimed, "We eat meat three times a day"; in one instance an immigrant wrote "twice a day," fearing that readers would not believe the actual frequency.[39] The nineteenth century was an age of dyspepsia owing to the staggering amounts of fatty meat, fried foods, and rich gravies that people wolfed down. Gout, dysentery, and digestive disorders were pervasive, which vegetable-based regimens were designed to correct. Today, heart disease, diabetes, and colon cancer are implicated in a meat-heavy diet.

The specific foods considered high status and "luxury" items have varied through time and among groups and subcultures. A general rule seems to be that delicacies provide refinement in texture, taste, and fat content. They also are distinguished by quantity or such qualities as complexity, exotic origin, style, or expense compared to standard staple foods.

As symbols, status foods may have a significant impact on people's behavior. Being served an inexpensive dish might upset one guest, while a luxury item could impress others. Three nights before the Super Bowl game in 1991, as an example of the second point, Coach Fred Hoaglin treated the eight-man New York Giants offensive line to eleven pounds of lobster, fifteen pounds of steak, twenty-five pounds of side dishes, and $400 bottles of wine: "I wanted them to experience real quality food so they would play real quality ball," he said.[40] The Giants edged out the Buffalo Bills 20–19. (On the other hand, UCLA football coach Chip Kelly came under fire in 2020 for the expensive, high-quality food he ordered for players, and for the team's frequent game losses.[41])

What one individual esteems, another may reject. To many, a table centerpiece of Jell-O with tiny marshmallows, bits of pineapple, julienne carrots, and other fruit or vegetables exemplifies a woman's creativity and sophistication.[42] To others it is déclassé. "Cold or hot, Spam hits the spot" might be true for a number of people; cooking contests highlight it with award-winning entries like Savory Spam Cheesecake. Hawaiian identity seems to revolve around this canned meat, which is known to many as "Hawaiian steak." But Spam is not prestigious to all, for some view it as unhealthful and others as beneath their status.

The tradition of using convenience foods and prepared mixes, whether Tater Tots, Shake 'n Bake, or Hamburger Helper, is appreciated by some, ridiculed by others. *The National Lampoon* satirized "the Cooking of Provincial New Jersey" in an article by Gerald Sussman mimicking the beautifully photographed images of haute cuisine and class-based rhetoric in *Gourmet Magazine*.[43] Subtitled "Twenty-one Cuisines, One Great Taste," it features frozen, canned, and processed items. Ernest Mickler's *White Trash Cooking* inverts food and status correlations, however, privileging lower-class food.[44] It is a language of cheap ingredients: swamp cabbage, hog lights (lungs), lard, 'gater (alligator) tail, cooter (turtle), and such commercial products as mayonnaise, Reddi-Wip, and Ritz crackers. His recipes are for dishes like Aunt Donnah's Roast Possum, Mock Cooter Soup prepared with oleo, Potato Chip Sandwich, and Paper-Thin Grilled Cheese made with white bread ("no other will do") and two slices of Velveeta cheese ("no other will do").

As Lucy M. Long writes regarding her research on green bean casserole in the Midwest,[45] "Such foods [made with commercial products] can become surprisingly meaningful carriers of identity and memory"[46] and therefore integrated into family foodways. A baked dish of green beans and cream of mushroom soup topped with a sprinkling of canned fried onions, the green bean casserole was invented by the Campbell Soup Company. Through the process of traditionalization or folklorization, this processed food became a common feature of everyday meals, potlucks, and holiday fare regionally and even nationally. Cheap, dependable, easily transportable, and requiring little culinary skill to make ("Open cans, mix, and bake"), the casserole appeals to many people for its salty, crunchy taste and familiarity. The dish is subject to multiple variations: "The beans can be fresh or frozen; they can be french-cut (i.e., in thin strips) or regular," writes Long. "The soup can be replaced with a homemade white sauce (very daring!) and sautéed fresh mushrooms; the canned onions can be substituted with potato sticks, crumbled potato chips, or toasted slivered almonds."[47] Such alterations along with additions such as capers, pimentos, and green pepper demonstrate individuals' artistry and personal aesthetics as well as suggesting a degree of wealth and refined taste.

Individuals, then, may define themselves symbolically through not only the food they consume but also what they prepare and serve. "I use the word 'rich' to describe the effect I strive for in company meals," one person told me.

Rich to me means abundant, varied, interesting, and aesthetically pleasing. I describe the people whom I want to have as my guests as rich
in personality. When I have company, I try to make the meal, the surroundings, and the conversation rich in order to give my guests the
impression that I too am a richly interesting person. When I am a
guest in another person's house I evaluate the experience on the basis
of its richness: good company, good conversation and abundant food,
and aesthetically pleasing surroundings.

Evident in the speaker's concluding remark is the fact that people may
evaluate others on the basis of food.

In social interactions involving food, individuals often make decisions
about who they want to appear to be, who they do not want to appear to be,
and what the best way to behave is in order to be perceived as they wish.
Several studies indicate that people who eat with friends consume more
food (especially dessert) than when dining with strangers, and that men
ingest more than women.[48] Research on female college students demonstrates that being thin and eating lightly function as social indicators of
femininity because of their importance in achieving status, popularity, and
sexual partners.[49]

While food or its consumption may be intended to signify identity, status,
or social relationship, at times people take pains to convey that the meals
they serve should not be taken as an expression of feelings toward others.
For instance, one individual told me that after having had a trying day she
prepared a simple, light repast for guests rather than something elaborate.
But then she worried that "they would think that I did not care about them
and that they would translate the meal to mean 'annoyance' or 'obligation.'
I apologized frequently for not providing a more interesting dinner, for I
feared being judged negatively."

The relationship of food to ethnic identity has long been a staple of foodways documentation, analysis, and presentation.[50] Such a linking of food
to ethnicity or nationality may appear at farmers' markets, as shown in figure 2.2. Traditional fare is often a significant element of festivals, as well,
whether homegrown or organized by ethnographers.[51] For ethnic displays
at festive events, disagreements can arise as to which food should be served:
an Americanized one or a more "authentic" dish (often the researcher's preference but whose unfamiliar flavors might offend the palate of many festi-
valgoers).[52] Participants in regional events highlighting ethnic identity usually consume esoteric dishes behind closed doors while publicly displaying
those that have been accepted by the dominant society, even rechristening

Figure 2.2 Vendor booth at Farmers' Market, Mar Vista, CA. Beneath "Good Morning Vietnam," the banner reads: "Preserving culture through culinary traditions." Photo by the author.

concession fare to suggest ethnic relevance; for instance, vendors at an Italian American festival in Indiana calling soda pop *gassoso*, lemonade *lemonatto*, and a ham and cheese sandwich *pasticcetto di prosciutto*.[53]

As often noted, many members of the first generation of immigrants attempt to retain their cuisine to the extent that similar ingredients are available, economics and social context do not pose hurdles, and the food items continue to symbolically tie them to their place of origin. But alas, "Old Confucius ways don't work anymore, you know," says Uncle Tam in Wayne Wang's movie *Dim Sum: A Little Bit of Heart*. "Things can't stay the same. Something happens here. Whoosh! It changes. You only keep what you can use." Typically the children of immigrants opt for the foods of the dominant culture; in England and the United States, it is often fast, junk, frozen, or convenience items pervading the wider society that the youth feel, or wish to appear to be, a part of rather than apart from.[54] Members of the third generation, however, may hunger for emblems of ethnicity, selecting certain foods as representations of their heritage.[55] Fears of losing ethnic or racial traditions and other symbols of identity associated with food can surface when individuals with diabetes or heart disease face the prospects of having to change their diet to conform to clinicians' recommendations.[56]

Researchers often dwell on ethnic identities that they suppose people assume for themselves, but my colleague Robert A. Georges at UCLA

contends that you often eat what others think you are, and those who prepare the food for you choose it on the basis of who they think you think
they are. He draws on personal experiences, including one occasion when
he visited Greek immigrant relatives for the first time who vied with one
another to prepare him a Greek meal although they rarely cook Greek dishes
and he did not ask for such cuisine. After examining a number of situations
in which he was host or guest, he set forth a theorem regarding food choice
and social identity:

> We and others select and reject certain foods, prepare the selected
> foods in particular ways, and serve them to specific individuals be-
> cause we identify them or ourselves as Southerners, natural food ad-
> dicts, men or women, old or young; and our decisions may be based
> on assumptions, inferences, or hypotheses rather than on "facts" and
> may be made unilaterally rather than cooperatively, regardless of the
> nature or the source of the identities we ascribe to others and con-
> ceive them to ascribe to us.[57]

A final point about ethnicity is that sometimes it serves up chagrin, not
pride or pleasure. During a televised interview, film director Luis Valdez
asked to tell his taco story.[58] "Mother's tacos, I mean, they're wonderful things,
especially if the tortillas are warm, they're hot off the stove, the beans are hot,"
he said. "And it is everything that symbolizes the warmth of home, mother.
It's a symbol of the solidarity of Mexican family life." The child carries the
taco to school wrapped in newspaper or waxed paper inside a paper bag."
At lunchtime the other children bring out their food. "They're eating these
things called sandwiches," said Valdez, "which are these scientific, you know,
square things that are kind of even, and inside they've got, you know, very
neatly fine cut slices of ham, lettuce, or tomato, or what have you." They differ
so much from the taco.

> And you look at it and suddenly that taco, which symbolized that
> warmth, is no longer the same thing. . . . For one thing, it's no longer
> warm, it's cold. So the tortilla has undergone, you know, . . . a wrin-
> kling process that makes it look like this long, ugly, dried up thing
> with spots on it, and the beans are cold, and all of a sudden, it rep-
> resents everything that you're ashamed of, and you don't want to
> pull that sucker out and eat it in public. It's disgraceful. The taco has
> become . . . this obscenity. And you want that . . . nice, white scientific
> sandwich. . . . And rather than eat your taco and proclaim yourself

Chicano in front of all these young gringo kids eating their sandwiches, you go without lunch sometimes. Or you go in the bathroom to eat it, but certainly not in public.

In addition to gender, class, and ethnicity, the categories of family and peers relate to identity and food choice.[59] According to one study,[60] in socializing the tastes of children, American families tend to give priority to food in three major ways. One is food as nutrition, for example, "Eat your vegetables; they're good for you." A second is food as a material good manifested by frequent reference to cost of ingredients and labor in preparation; hence, accepting food entails a moral obligation to consume it. And third, food as a reward, particularly dessert. Several studies of anorexia implicate childhood experiences with food in the home, particularly struggles with issues of power and the lack of autonomy and control.[61] Finally, an investigation of teenage girls' foodways found that the teens distinguish between "healthful food," served at home, and "junk food" (potato chips, candy, sodas, burgers, fries) that they purchase at the mall.[62] The former symbolizes ties to family, the latter loyalty to peers and independence from home. The tensions that arise over whether to eat junk food or healthful food signal the conflicts teens feel between maintaining familial relations and gaining autonomy as adults. A paradox results: nutritionists insist that junk food is unhealthful and inappropriate, yet for teens such "fun" food is a symbolic way to act out the independence necessary for psychosocial maturation and well-being.

People develop self-images through multiple experiences and sources of information, be it in the home, at work, in school, or from the media. In regard to the last, advertising plays a vital part in shaping eating behavior, social roles, and bodies.[63] "To the extent that we are what we eat, and what we eat has been influenced by advertising," writes Arthur A. Berger,[64] "advertising has helped determine what we are, physically as well as emotionally." Sidney W. Mintz goes further, contending that "in the modern Western world, we are *made* more and more into what we eat, whenever forces we have no control over persuade us that our consumption and our identity are linked."[65]

THE DYNAMICS OF IDENTITY

Whatever the sources and their initial impact, identities are not static, but dynamic. Once enacted, the multiple ways one identifies oneself are affected by self-reflection, challenges from various quarters, clarification, alteration, and reinforcement.[66]

Illness can call into question one's consumption practices, along with identities to which they are linked, thus precipitating changes. George Bernard Shaw was already an herbivore when he contracted smallpox. Friends who thought his resistance had been lowered because of "those wretched vegetables" convinced him to take up meat eating; feeling worse after doing so, he reasserted his former identity and eating practices, vowing never to abandon his diet again because of illness.[67] In contrast, Sylvester Graham, a staunch crusader against "overstimulating" foods, including flesh, alcohol, spices, condiments, and refined flour, resorted to meat and whiskey toward the end of his short life in a desperate effort to stimulate a failing body.[68]

Self-making, as symbolically expressed in or constructed through food choice, engages the processes of monitoring, evaluation, and revision,[69] as the behavior of the nameless African American migrant in *Invisible Man* by Ralph Ellison illustrates so well. In chapter 9, he enters a diner for breakfast. The counterman assumes that he is from the South and offers him stereotypical Southern food: pork chops, grits, eggs, biscuits, and coffee. "He leaned over the counter with a look that seemed to say, There, that ought to excite you, boy." Ashamed, and rejecting this badge of regional and racial heritage, the Invisible Man orders orange juice, toast, and coffee. "A seed floated in the thick layer of pulp that formed at the top of the glass. I fished it out with a spoon and then downed the acid drink, proud to have resisted the pork chop and grits. It was an act of discipline, a sign of the change that was coming over me."

In chapter 13, as the Invisible Man wanders through the Black section of the city, he grows angry upon seeing one window display after another advertising products to alter or hide an African American identity. Then he comes upon an elderly man warming his hands against a cart from which wafts the enticing aroma of baking yams, "bringing a stab of swift nostalgia. I stopped as though struck by a shot, deeply inhaling, remembering, my mind surging back, back. . . . we'd loved them candied, or baked in a cobbler, deep-fat fried in a pocket of dough, or roasted with pork and glazed with the well-browned fat; had chewed them raw—yams and years ago." The vendor offers him a yam, butter spooned over it. "I took a bite, finding it as sweet and hot as any I'd ever had, and was overcome with such a surge of homesickness that I turned away to keep my control." Munching on the yam as he walks along, the Invisible Man is "suddenly overcome by an intense feeling of freedom. . . . It was exhilarating. I no longer had to worry about who saw me or about what was proper." He ceased attempting to deny who he is or to be ashamed of such signs of identity as yams: "'They're my birth mark,' I said, I yam what I am!'"

Developing, assessing, and altering or reasserting one's sense of self, and expressing it symbolically, occur over the life course.[70] Self-image is influenced by personal experiences, including illness, along with social and environmental factors, and it aggregates elements from a multiplicity of identities. A case in point is Gary Robertson (1939–2016), who lived alone on his farm in Manitoba, Canada.[71]

Born of a Scottish immigrant mother, Gary was reared by her as an assimilated Anglo-Canadian Roman Catholic in the city of Winnipeg. He later cultivated an image composed of several identities directly opposite the earlier ones: rural, Ukrainian, and Orthodox lay monk. He was the only child of abusive parents; in his teenage years he sought refuge with his Polish-Ukrainian grandparents from whom he learned a smattering of household dialect, religion, and ethnic traditions. He despaired of city life, bought a farm, spent twenty years building a house from two abandoned log cabins, within which he constructed an Orthodox chapel replete with icons that he painted, seen in figure 2.3, and attempted to live a monastic life of prayer, chanting, and iconography.

Gary long suffered from colitis, rheumatoid arthritis, headaches, hernias, sinusitis, hemorrhoids, depression, and an enlarged prostate, he told me. He suffered hives and diarrhea for three weeks; soon his weight dropped from 190 to 145 pounds. "My poverty was chronic and I did without

Figure 2.3 Gary Robertson in log home, Manitoba, Canada, with triptych he painted. Photo by the author.

proper food. . . . The arthritis had been getting worse and every other ailment with age setting in. . . . Here I was about to turn 56 and my whole
system collapsed."

He began reading books on health and diet, querying a local dietitian and
a doctor, reviewing what he knew about folk remedies, purchasing commercial herbal preparations, and growing herbs. He started keeping a daily log
of what he ate, at what time of day, the supplements he took, and any illness
that he suffered. Over time he developed a diet containing little dairy and
eliminating sugar, most meat, and alcohol. He developed a regimen of eating six to eight times a day, avoiding food or drink that is either hot or cold,
which he attributed to the tradition of his Eastern European grandparents,
and consuming only a single item at a sitting but varied from one day to
the next.

The last time I interviewed him, he had been free of colds and flu for three
years and his bouts of colitis had diminished. In addition, as he settled into
a new diet reflecting different values, greater control, and a new orientation toward health, he built a grotto next to the river near his house, where
he prayed and meditated, let his hair and beard grow long, and donned
the black cassock of an Orthodox monk, thereby completing his ethnic-
religious transformation.

In conclusion, the proverb that "you are what you eat" may be true in a
broad sense, but on closer examination the situation is more complex. We
have seen that you become what you eat literally and figuratively because
consumption practices construct identity; you eat what you already are owing
to the fact that alimentation reflects self-concept (as in the expression "If
you are what you eat, then I'm fast, cheap, and easy"); you are how you eat
in regard to comportment and class; you often eat what others think you
are, which is conveyed by what they serve you; those who prepare food for
you to eat may do so on the basis of who they think you think they are; and
you sometimes eat what you wish you were or want others to think you are
but might not be. Whoever we are, we express or symbolically construct
an identity linked to eating practices related to the range and type of food
consumed, personal characteristics including values and lifestyle, and social
categories and reference groups with which we are associated.

But what if we think a food that others eat is repulsive? Why do we react
this way? What are some of the social consequences and moral correlates of
disgust? These and other questions are addressed in the next chapter.

Chapter 3

WHAT'S DISGUSTING, WHY, AND WHAT DOES IT MATTER?

In *The Expression of Emotions in Man and Animals* (1872), Charles Darwin writes, "The term 'disgust,' in its simplest sense, means something offensive to the taste. It is curious how readily this feeling is excited by anything unusual in the appearance, odour, or nature of our food." For example, "In Tierra del Fuego a native touched with his finger some cold preserved meat which I was eating at our bivouac, and plainly showed utter disgust at its softness; whilst I felt utter disgust at my food being touched by a naked savage, though his hands did not appear dirty." Continues Darwin, "A smear of soup on a man's beard looks disgusting, though there is of course nothing disgusting in the soup itself. I presume that this follows from the strong association in our minds between the sight of food, however circumstanced, and the idea of eating it."[1]

While the indigenous person took offense at the softness of tinned meat and Darwin was disgusted by a naked man poking his food, other people are repulsed by the thought of eating beef, pork, fish, carrion birds, hyenas, reptiles, amphibians, eggs, milk, and butter, to name a few items. Whether or not disgust is universal in the human species, which seems likely, the objects of revulsion appear not to be. They vary so widely as to challenge attempts to find a common denominator.

In the search to understand why people eat what they do, it is equally important to discover what they do *not* eat and why they don't eat these things. Disgust has moral implications, too, evident in people's reactions to someone else's appearance, odors, and table manners as repugnant or loathsome—reactions that, in turn, have justified class distinctions, social stratification, and segregation. This chapter considers what people find disgusting and why they do, reasons that some individuals sometimes eat disgusting things, and the moral correlates and social consequences of the emotion.

Feelings of revulsion constitute a distinct emotion, like love, hate, and fear. These feelings are marked by physiological characteristics. The reaction is emotional recoil combined with wrinkled nose and narrowing of nostrils to defend against penetration, downturned mouth, and constriction of the throat to prevent swallowing, nausea, and even vomiting.

Disgust differs from distaste or dislike. According to one report, researchers for the US Army who track food preferences found that the most widely disliked item is liver, followed by lima beans, squash, creamed onions, eggplant, and beets.[2] To "not like" a food means that one does not enjoy its sensory qualities: appearance, texture, odor, temperature, touch, mouth feel, or taste. Or a person prefers not to serve or consume the item because it carries negative associations and symbolism, such as poverty, low social status, or unpleasant experiences. Distaste can result from surfeit, such as overeating a sweet, fatty, or rich food. This reaction is usually not permanent, nor is queasiness at the prospect of taking one more bite accompanied by strong emotional recoil and other characteristics of revulsion typical of the disgust response.

Disgust leads to aversion: avoiding the noxious object. But disgust is not the same as aversion learning or "bait shyness." Aversion learning involves associating illness with a particular food, especially a substance novel (or "strange") both in aroma and taste. Food aversions develop even when the interval between the stimulus and the illness is so long that the food could not have caused us to be sick or when nobody else who consumed the same food at the same time fell ill.[3] On the other hand, when recovery from illness follows ingestion of a particular food we enjoyed and linked to recovery, we tend to like that food in the future; hence the positive associations that some people have with Jell-O or chicken soup served by a caring parent or grandparent.

Probably common in the human species, disgust appears largely to be the product of nurture, culture, and cognitive development. In experiments, psychologist Paul Rozin and associates discovered that 62 percent of subjects aged two or less were willing to eat imitation dog feces crafted from peanut butter and smelly cheese; 58 percent had no aversion to a whole, small, dried fish; and 31 percent would ingest a whole grasshopper (which the experimenters had sterilized). Rarely did children under age seven or eight reject a beverage after a contaminating substance (e.g., a grasshopper) was removed with a spoon. Children younger than eight who rejected such objects as feces or grasshoppers did so on the grounds of distaste (dislike of sensory qualities) or some vague sense of danger rather than the disgust response. Few had a notion of trace contamination—invisible residues from one object on another—or the principle of contagion. In other words, these studies suggest that one must develop certain cognitive structures to conceptualize contamination as tiny, invisible particles that corrupt an object even if contact is brief and does not leave a detectable trace.[4]

Typically, objects of animal origin arouse disgust, and further, waste (or bodily excretions thought of as waste) is universally disgusting. This list includes animals, parts of animals, or animal products (especially feces, urine, mucus) or objects such as foods that have come into contact with these or that resemble them.[5] "Yuck!" said one of my students in regard to eating tongue. "Just think of everything the animal has used it for!" The implication is that, should the food be consumed, the history of what the organ had touched and done would become a contaminating part of the eater's own history.

Certainly some people abhor particular creatures or their parts as potential food. Consider any flesh among vegetarians, beef for Hindus, pork among many Jews and Muslim, and viscera as well as dogs, grasshoppers, and grubs for many if not most Euro-Americans.[6] For those who eat what might easily disgust others or themselves, two common behavioral responses occur. One is disguise; the other, transformation. Chopping up parts of an animal and cooking them in a stew hides their origin. Calling the creatures or their parts by other names diverts attention from their nature,[7] for example, referring to a calf's thymus gland as "sweetbreads" or a bovine's diaphragm muscle as "hanging tenderloin" or naming a dish "escargot" rather than "snails" or "menudo" instead of "cow stomach soup." Purchasing a piece of meat attractively displayed on a "sanitary" white foam tray wrapped with plastic helps alter the meaning from "part of a dead animal" to "food." Cooking, smoking, or using spices helps mask the original properties of the flesh.[8]

Even fecal matter, the quintessential disgust object for many, can be rendered acceptable for human contact in the form of, say, dried cow or ox dung used for cooking fires. It could even be transformed into food. A few years ago the Environmental Assessment Center in Okayama, Japan, announced that it had managed to make a sausage out of recycled Tokyo sewage by adding soybean protein and beef flavoring. However, it did not intend to market the product commercially owing to the main ingredient's "image" problem.[9]

While bodily waste is generally disgusting, we especially tend to recoil from *other* individuals' secretions and wastes, particularly those of strangers. Unflushed public toilets, another's spittle on the ground, or someone else's sweat on the gym's workout equipment may seem disgusting, though we are not so repulsed by the wastes and secretions of ourselves or loved ones.[10] Plant life also may be loathsome, especially when it smells foul, feels slimy, or looks rotten, or when it resembles something else disgusting; for instance, one of my students commented that watery, overcooked spinach "looks like hair in the shower drain."

Several examples from my research illuminate what some Americans consider vile, which senses dominate in triggering revulsion, and possible origins of disgust. When I asked a group of students to write down something disgusting (not necessarily food-related items), one mentioned spit, another "creepy, crawly things"; three wrote "slimy things"; four indicated moldy or dirty food; five said feces or flatulence; six referred to people who were obese, coarse and vulgar, gluttonous, or filthy (one suggested "a fat man snoring"); twelve mentioned cruelty, violent death, and child abuse or molestation; thirteen said vomit. Asked which animal parts they found disgusting, the students dwelled on eyes, brains, tongue, stomach, intestines, liver, heart, kidneys, spleen, genitals, feet, fat, veins, and tails. When I asked them which vegetables were repulsive and why, I received such responses as brussels sprouts ("slimy"), okra ("slimy, squishy seeds, gluey"), asparagus ("smells bad"), spinach ("feels awful in my mouth: stringy, mushy, slimy"), eggplant ("creepy, soft skin"), marinated vegetables ("Yuck," wrote the respondent, probably because they are oily), and yellow squash ("looks like ABC baby food," i.e., "already been chewed").

Some things threaten us because they are uncanny, possessing an unnatural power. For instance, corpses, mutilated parts of the body, or amphibia—cold, clammy, often pale and possessing an unusual mode of locomotion—all may provoke revulsion.[11] Carnivorous animals may disgust because they feed on material that is itself repulsive; scavenger birds and hyenas, along with rats, snails, and insects, possess uncanny qualities that threaten through the prospects of contact or ingestion. For example, when asked which of three categories of animals are edible, twenty-seven of my students indicated herbivores (cows, sheep), five said omnivores (pigs, chickens), and only two mentioned carnivores, a category that comprises such creatures as cats, vultures, coyotes, hyenas, snakes, and rodents. So abhorrent are rats to many Americans that they are used as the principal symbol of urban decay.

In *The Anatomy of Disgust*, legal scholar William Ian Miller stresses that both animals and vegetative matter repulse: he mentions gooey mud, a scummy pond, a murky quagmire smelling of rotting plant life. The generator of disgust is generation itself, posits Miller: surfeit, excess of ripeness, the fecundity of the slippery, wiggling, teeming "life soup" that arises from putrefying vegetation. "It is not that animal bodies decay, excrete, suppurate, and die that makes these processes sources of disgust to us: it is that ours do," he contends. The stuff inside us is a polluting mess of oozy, slimy, gooey, smelly things, and "the animals that disgust us do not disgust us as animals but because they have characteristics that are disgusting: sliminess, slitheri-ness, teemingness." They remind us—these insects, slugs, worms, rats, bats, centipedes—of "life, oozy, slimy, viscous, teeming, messy, uncanny life."[12]

Developmentally, human beings probably become particularly aware of offensive substances at the time of toilet training.[13] During a second impor-tant period in our lives, that of adolescence, writes Miller, we acquire "excep-tional sensitivity to disgust, primarily provoked by the vertigo of sexual awakening and bodily changes: menstruation, pimples, voice changes, emis-sions, unpleasant body odors, and hair in all the wrong places."[14]

People sometimes purposefully participate in disgusting behavior or con-sume revolting objects. J. G. Bourke, in his ethnological *Scatological Rites of All Nations*, describes a Zuni ceremony he witnessed in 1888 in which a handful of male participants, amid rapid-fire comments and exclamations, passed excrement and urine to one another and consumed them heartily. One of the men vomited after the ceremony was over. According to Bourke, "Some of the sallies of the actors were received with laughter, and others with signs of disgust and repugnance, but not of disapprobation."[15] Swallow-ing live goldfish was a craze among college students in the late 1930s. In the early 1980s, folklorist Ken Thigpen filmed young men and women downing live salamanders at the Phi Delta Theta fraternity house on a Pennsylvania State University campus.[16]

All three examples suggest that participants are boasting of what they are able to do, overcoming their own feelings of revulsion in order to do something repellent to others. The participants in salamander swallowing engage in one-upmanship. As a tradition unique to this fraternity, gorging on salamanders became a symbolic marker of identity that differentiated this house from its nearest rivals, the straight-laced Beta Theta Pi fraternity. Additionally, in the film some of the women tongue their salamanders las-civiously, the phallic significance obvious, intimating an association of desire with disgust and insinuating that disgust can have the power to allure. To indulge in the disgusting is to be tempted by the forbidden. As Miller writes, "A person's tongue in your mouth could be experienced as a pleasure or as a most repulsive and nauseating intrusion depending on the state of relations that exist or are being negotiated between you and the person."[17]

Bravado and the allure of the forbidden are not the only reasons to partici-pate in the disgusting. No sooner do children develop a concept of contagion and learn the disgust response than many of them flaunt it, challenging rules of decorum. A food section of the *Los Angeles Times* carried an article about, and recipes for, party food resembling ants, snakes, snails, and swamp juice that a girl requested for a sleepover on her sixth birthday.[18]

Something that initially seemed attractive might on closer inspection repulse but then inspire acceptance and participation. Figure 3.1 depicts a detail of the fifty-foot wide, eight-foot tall multicolored collage on the side of a theater. This Gum Wall is in an alley next to Pike Place Market, the heart of Seattle's vibrant scene of food stalls and restaurants. The wall is coated with an estimated one million pieces of spit-covered, germ-ridden, used chewing gum exuding a peculiar odor on hot summer days. "I remember being grossed out when I looked at my photos later," said one person. A local landmark, it was started by audience members waiting in line for improv shows at the Market Theater. People continue to contribute to it, even many who find the wall repugnant.[19]

Part of the appeal of courting the disgusting might be sensationalism, as in some news reports about eating insects. One such report dwells on a book by Ronald Taylor called *Entertaining with Insects*, which includes recipes for cricket pot pie, mealworm chow mein, fudge hoppers, and beetle sausage.[20] Another announcement concerns an annual Mosquito Cook-Off at Ridge State Park in Walcott, Arkansas. The first prize was awarded for

Figure 3.1 Detail of a local landmark in downtown Seattle, WA. The Gum Wall is covered in a million pieces of used chewing gum, which exude a strong odor on hot summer days. Photo by the author.

mosquito cookies that consisted of crushed mosquitoes stirred into boiling syrup mixed with brown sugar; the heat sterilizes the mosquitoes, notes the article, which "carry up to 16 disease bacteria."[21] In April 2020, *The Guardian* reported that in a "breakthrough moment" the EU's European Food Safety Authority is expected within weeks to endorse whole or ground insects as safe for human consumption: "Food safety agency's decision could put mealworms, locusts and baby crickets on menus," reads the article's subhead.[22] A photo depicts a decorative plate containing mealworms on a tortilla.

Desperation is often given as a reason for engaging in such disgusting behavior as eating insects, dogs, or humans. The soccer players who survived an airplane crash on a mountain top in the Andes in 1972 ate the corpses of their colleagues, albeit, as one said, "With respect. In little bits."[23] In the first scene of Howard Hawks's film *Rio Bravo*, Claude Akins portrays a mean-spirited cowboy at the bar who tosses a coin into a spittoon for a destitute and desperate Dean Martin to retrieve, an act that conveys just how depraved the alcoholic Martin character has become.

Yet another reason for engaging in disgusting behavior is tied to religion: numerous women during the Middle Ages humiliated themselves in order to gain sanctity.[24] A noted example is Catherine of Siena (*ca.* 1370), who nearly vomited when caring for a sick nun with a foul-smelling cancer on her breast. To overcome her squeamishness, she bent down, holding her mouth and nose over the sore. On another occasion, while she dressed the nun's wound, the stench again overpowered her, causing her to vomit. Appalled at her reaction, Catherine took the washing from the sore together with the scabs, put them in a cup, and drank the mixture heartily. That night Christ came to her in a dream, she claimed, and in reward for drinking cancerous pus he drew her mouth to the wound in his side and allowed her to drink her fill.[25]

Up to this point I have considered the nature of the disgust response and how it differs from related phenomena, examined some of the things that people find disgusting as well as possible reasons for this response, and suggested why some people choose to embrace disgusting behavior. I conclude with attention to two other issues.

The first matter is the "cause" or perhaps "function" or consequence of disgust. One contention is that the disgust reaction helps prevent people from eating something that will sicken or kill them; it has "survival value," like the aversion learning or "bait shyness" in human beings and some other animals. A problem with adaptive explanations is that they tend to be applied selectively. A "hygienic" account often has been given for the Jewish prohibition against eating pork, which spoils more rapidly than other meats in a hot climate and may harbor trichinosis. Proponents of this explanation ignore the many diseases transmitted by other animals and neglect to apply the same kind of argument to other dietary restrictions or "taboos."[26]

A second problem regarding a functionalist explanation of food disgust as having survival value is that it seems dysfunctional to starve rather than eat insects, worms, reptiles, or algae. Such items are high in protein and potentially delicious foods; many people around the world in fact eat such things. Entomologist C. V. Riley pleaded with Americans in 1876 to eat grasshoppers, and a century later C. W. Schwabe published tasty recipes in *Unmentionable Cuisine* for grilled snake and fried caterpillars as well as interesting ways of preparing reptiles, fish sperm, and offal.[27] In the context of scarce resources and concerns about food insecurity and sustainable nutrition, insects provide cheap, high-quality proteins; five hundred tons of insect-based food is already produced annually, much of which can be found in Dutch, Belgian, Finnish, and British supermarkets.[28]

Finally, many people relish the odor, taste, or mouth feel of bacteria-ridden Stilton cheese, "high" pheasant, slimy raw oysters, clabbered milk, and so on; items whose sensory qualities or semi-"spoiled" state should trigger a disgust response. For instance, the great French gastronome Brillat-Savarin, author of *Physiologie du goût* (The Physiology of Taste) was said to carry dead game birds in his pocket to "savor" their aroma.[29]

In the final analysis, I suspect that disgust simply *is*; perhaps it cannot be reduced to a particular cause but to a set of conditions. Among the factors involved in developing the disgust response, at least among Euro-Americans, may be the customs, concerns, and experiences that surround toilet training, as well as the period of bodily changes in adolescence. Others likely include the generation in childhood of cognitive structures such as the idea of "contagion," along with accompanying fears of contamination. Disgust has important correlates and consequences, including moral judgment.

"The lower classes smell," wrote George Orwell in *The Road to Wigan Pier*, which documented working life in northern England. This, he contended, is "the real secret of class distinctions in the West."[30] Disgust is about class, wealth, education, and distinction.[31] It also involves notions of civility, propriety, and deportment; of differentiating, ranking, and segregating people; of prejudice and discrimination; and of expressing social and moral sentiments. Hence, those behind bars are often referred to as "scum" or "slime" while homeless people camped on sidewalks or begging at street corners provoke antipathy in some because of their appearance, smell, or rudeness.

A typical moral sentiment is that the people or behaviors we find disgusting have a will to offend. Obese people are unwilling to not be fat. In one study, for example, participants viewed photos of both slender and excessively

overweight individuals performing everyday activities. Respondents exhib-
ited more stereotypes, negative attitudes, and expressions of disgust toward
the obese as well as a desire to distance themselves from these people.[32]

Many anorexics feel disgust at the sight of obese persons or even those
who are normally fleshed out and curvaceous, contempt for those in this
condition, and revulsion at the thought of resembling them. This fat phobia
involves feelings of disgust at the sight of overweight individuals, fat itself, or
older people with sagging flesh and skin folds.[33] One woman told a researcher,
"I always feared being compared to a female body like that. I want to avoid
curves—I always avoided looking like a woman. . . . I always felt, 'I do not
want to look like that, bulged, drooping breasts, flabby behind'—it's just not
pretty, and that's what I'm trying to avoid."[34]

Thus, being overweight can be interpreted as intentional behavior, for
it demonstrates lack of self-control; it is the sin of gluttony, a moral judgment against surfeit, intemperance, and nondenial of fleshly pleasure.[35] In
her biography *Solitaire*, fashion model Aimee Liu concludes a description
of gorging with the sentiment that "I loathed myself for such weakness and
raged at my failure of willpower." Further, she states, "When, at the end of a
three- or four-day fast, my pelvis sank to a hollow shell once again, I gloried
in this proof of strength and determination. Loss of weight had become my
personal path to honor; starvation was the goal of my adolescence"—both
a means and a symbol of control in her life.[36]

Etiquette has developed as a symbol of social refinement as well as personal control; gluttony, exposing masticated food while talking, and all other
"bad manners" offend precious sensibilities and good taste. The consumption
of etiquette books burgeoned in America in the late nineteenth century. In
a young, mobile society, social status was based on dress, conversation, and
manners at table rather than on inherited title or estate. "By structuring content, the manner books clarified social divisions," writes historian Arthur M.
Schlesinger, Sr.[37]

Putting people in their place appears to be one motive for telling stories
about the disgusting things individuals eat and the ill-mannered ways they
behave. Tales of degrading acts mark individuals and specific groups as
socially inferior, requiring segregation from the rest of society. Similarly, as
discussed in the first chapter, which was on symbolism, food-based slurs or
ethnophaulisms denigrate and dehumanize others, providing a rationale for
adverse social policies, including governmental anti-immigration acts that
restrict or exclude entire populations from asylum in a country. Expressing repugnance at women he dislikes (and their bodily functions), particular sociocultural groups from "shithole countries," and the ill manners of a

political rival, as Donald J. Trump has done (which I deal with in the eighth chapter), generates disgust and the rejection of others.

In this chapter I have characterized the disgust response and surveyed what some people find disgusting, but I have also considered why individuals may sometimes consume disgusting things, discussed hypotheses about why disgust exists, and examined some moral correlatives and social consequences of disgust. I suspect that the disgust response is general in the human species, and perhaps peculiar to it, because it seems to involve the consciously held concept of "contamination" that has yet to be demonstrated in other animals.

To return to Darwin, who first identified disgust as a distinct emotion, he was repulsed at the sight of, as he said, a "savage" coming in contact with his food. He mentions the incident not only in *The Expression of Emotions* (1872) but also in *Journal of Researches* (1845) and cites Fuegians in yet a third work, *The Descent of Man* (1871) to make a crucial point. All of this suggests that the native's behavior indelibly impressed him, and did so in the most visceral and negative way.

In his *Journal of Researches*, Darwin noted several aspects of foodways in Tierra del Fuego, a frozen landscape off the southern tip of South America. "They liked our biscuit," observed Darwin, "but one of the savages touched with his finger some of the meat preserved in tin cases which I was eating, and feeling it soft and cold, showed as much disgust at it, as I should have done at putrid blubber." Further, he wrote, "If a seal is killed, or the floating carcass of a putrid whale is discovered, it is a feast; and such miserable food is assisted by a few tasteless berries and fungi." Regarding other food customs, Darwin noted that "Mr. Low believes that whenever a whale is cast on shore, the natives bury large pieces of it in the sand, as a resource in time of famine; and a native boy, whom he had on board, once found a stock thus buried. The different tribes when at war are cannibals."

In setting forth the principles of evolution in the second edition (1874) of *The Descent of Man*, Darwin comments, "The main conclusion arrived at in this work, namely that man is descended from some lowly organized form, will, I regret to think, be highly distasteful to many. But there can hardly be a doubt that we are descended from barbarians." He continues, "The astonishment which I felt on first seeing a party of Fuegians on a wild and broken shore will never be forgotten by me, for the reflection at once rushed into my mind—such were our ancestors. Those men were absolutely naked and bedaubed with paint, their long hair was tangled, their mouths frothed with excitement, and their expression was wild, startled, and distrustful. They possessed hardly any arts and like wild animals lived on what they could catch." Darwin concludes, "For my own part I would as soon be descended from . . . [a monkey or baboon] as from a savage."[38]

Darwin's remarks imply that much more than biological development was involved in human evolution; in his mind, the existence of a population like the Fuegians attested to ongoing intellectual and cultural evolution within the species itself. This later led to the concept of unilineal cultural evolution, the notion that culture evolves like biological species do, from the simple to the complex, from savagery to barbarism to civilization. This idea is grounded in an immediate and personal experience of Darwin's. A long-haired, paint-smeared, naked, distrustful native who eats rotted whale blubber during times of famine—this socially inferior, ill-mannered, degraded human being actually *touched* Darwin's food and left a memorable impression upon him. Not only did Darwin find the Fuegian's action disgusting, but he also felt that his theory about humankind's descent from similar creatures would be "highly distasteful to many." Better if we could claim a monkey or baboon as our direct progenitor.

The subject of disgust thus involves more than simply food avoidance. It encompasses aesthetics and moral judgments and, sometimes, rejection of our fellow human beings as well.

A topic that embraces rather than spurns others, however, is the subject of the next chapter. "Comfort food" provides solace, brings to mind memorable occasions, and may serve as a social surrogate when feeling lonely. Many of us self-medicate our moods with the gratifying sensations and memories afforded by food, even if the things we eat are not always the most healthful.

Chapter 4

"STRESSED" SPELLED BACKWARD IS "DESSERTS"

Self-Medicating Moods with Foods

During the early months of the COVID-19 pandemic in the United States, when many state governors insisted we isolate ourselves from others, a study by three psychologists appeared in the journal *Self and Identity*. The authors found that "nontraditional strategies" of fulfilling the need to belong include "symbolic social bonds . . . such as comfort foods" that buffer "against loneliness, isolation, and rejection," help "individuals to feel supported and connected,"[1] and contribute "a unique spice to everyday social interactions, which more traditional social connections do not."[2] Moreover, home baking had spiked by April 2020, with banana bread at an all-time high and pizza, French toast, and chocolate cake not far behind, as people sought comfort during a period of anxiety.[3]

A survey of grocery store food sales across the country following the 11 September 2001 terrorist attack in New York City showed an upturn of more than 12 percent over the previous year in the purchase of snack food items and an almost 13 percent rise in the sale of instant mashed potatoes.[4] Restaurateurs reported increased sales of soup, macaroni and cheese, puddings, and similar fare.[5] Conventional wisdom has it that we crave and often eat comfort foods—typically high in fat, starch, and sugar—because we feel "depressed" or "stressed out" about events. Numerous greeting cards, bumper stickers, rubber stamps, beverage mugs, and T-shirts refer to chocolate in particular: "Next to you, the best thing in life is chocolate!"; "Chocolate is proof that God loves us"; "Chocolate: It's not just for breakfast anymore." A popular saying claims, "Chocolate is cheaper than therapy and you don't need an appointment."[6]

I begin this chapter with surveys reporting the association of comfort food choice with gender, age, and locale. Then I consider definitions of comfort food, some of the biological, hedonic, emotional, and social bases for cravings and consumption, as well as instances of discomfort and illness resulting from indulgence. Following that is a section on chocolate—the "food of the gods" with a history spanning thirty centuries—which has its self-proclaimed chocoholics, sayings, rituals, celebrations, jokes, folk knowledge, and stories about hoarding and clandestine consumption. The final topic is the impact of folklore and popular culture on establishing eating patterns, which turns an item into comfort food that provides symbolic social bonds and relief from stress.

SELF-MEDICATING MOODS WITH FOODS

Although comfort food choice is idiosyncratic, patterns are evident, for example, the preference among many in the United States for such side dishes as mashed potatoes and macaroni and cheese. Responses to questionnaires indicate that men are more likely to choose hot foods and main meal items such as steak, casseroles, and soup, while women have a propensity for sweets or snack foods including chocolate, ice cream, and potato chips. Generally speaking, the male choices possess a nostalgic quality associated with meals prepared by others in their youth. Female selections more often exhibit convenience, indulgence, and perhaps in some instances an implicit rejection of the traditional role of homemaker.[7]

Younger people gravitate toward flavor-saturated options of saltiness and intense sweetness.[8] In one survey of 3,700 respondents, 46 percent said they preferred sweets. Fifty-one percent of women versus 36 percent of men opted for ice cream, chocolate, and brownies. In terms of age categories, a larger percentage of baby boomer respondents favored braised meats, casseroles, and ice cream; Gen Xers tended to desire fast food such as burgers and burritos, as well as particular brands of packaged cookies, candies, and snacks; and Generation Y respondents fancied burritos, ramen noodles, and global comfort food in the form of Indian and Thai curries and Vietnamese noodle soup.[9]

Mashed potatoes headed the list of favorites in one survey; 27 percent of respondents said they were reminiscent of mom, 18 percent found them soothing when stressed, and others remarked on associations with childhood, security, and warmth. Thirty-six percent of women versus 19 percent of men ate comfort food under stress, while 36 percent of men versus 27 percent of women chose feel-good food to put them in a positive mood. With respect to seasons, 51 percent of people in the survey consumed more comfort foods during the winter; 29 percent mentioned holidays. Those self-medicating with food when stressed differed regionally: 57 percent in the Northeast and 48 percent in the West, in contrast to 24 percent in the South and 23 percent in North Central United States. In regard to the rate of craving mood foods, 51 percent desired them one to three times per week and 58 percent ate comfort foods as often as thrice weekly. Thirteen percent longed for them daily, while 11 percent enjoyed a dose of this kitchen therapy every day of the week.

As implied by the plaque in figure 4.1, the *Oxford English Dictionary* defines "comfort food" as "food that comforts or affords solace; hence, any food (freq. with a high sugar or carbohydrate content) that is associated with childhood or with home cooking. orig. N. Amer." Merriam-Webster's eleventh edition *Collegiate Dictionary* defines comfort food as fare "prepared in a traditional style having a usually nostalgic or sentimental appeal."

The term's first appearance in print may have been on Sunday, 6 November 1966 in a column by psychologist Dr. Joyce Brothers titled "Psychological Problems Play a Part in Obesity." Published in the *Des Moines Register* and many other newspapers, the essay states, "Studies indicate that most adults, when under severe emotional stress, turn to what could be called 'comfort food'—food associated with the security of childhood, like mother's poached egg or famous chicken soup." The *OED*, however, dates the expression's earliest use to an article in the *Washington Post* on 25 December 1977 in which restaurant critic Phyllis Richman describes a Southern dish: "Along with grits, one of the comfort foods of the South is black-eyed peas." Whatever its origins, the term has become widely adopted into everyday speech, restaurant menus, cooking shows, recipe books, magazines, and advertising.

The co-owner of a restaurant specializing in Japanese comfort food, learned from his mother and grandmother and popular along the streets of Tokyo, summed it up: Comfort food is "familiar, flavorful, and filling." A reviewer of the eatery adds, "No matter the ethnic origin, it invariably involves a degree of nostalgia; a familiar component that resonates with your past."[10]

Definitions and conventional wisdom frequently relate comfort food consumption to stress. Several experiments and observations offer a degree of confirmation. Male rats and mice subjected to extreme levels of stress, including frequent exposure to social subordination by an older aggressor, engaged in frantic wheel running and compulsive eating of high-energy foods such as pure lard and a 30 percent sucrose solution. Female rhesus monkeys harassed by higher ranking females showed an increased intake of a high-sugar diet of banana-flavored pellets.[11]

Figure 4.1 Wooden wall plaque: "Keep calm and eat a cupcake." Author's collection. Photo by Laura Layera.

Stress produces a state of hypervigilance, the fight-or-flight response. Normally, fat deposits in the body generate a signal that reduces the amount of a stress-related chemical. In chronic stress, however—when there is a torrent of anxieties, threats, and burdens over days or weeks—the hormone cortisol in the adrenal gland remains elevated, which often appears to be correlated with compulsive, pleasure-seeking behavior and a marked preference for high-energy foods.[12]

Experimental research also suggests that some people might be more sensitive to the presence of fat in foods owing to their bodies' production of a greater amount of a protein referred to as CD36.[13] In addition, there appears to be a fat receptor in the tongue along with the sweet, salty, sour, and bitter tastes and that of umami (savory).[14] Rats and mice in controlled taste tests show a decided preference for foods with fat. Eating fat might reduce vulnerability to sadness. After experimentally inducing feelings of unhappiness in human subjects, clinical investigators found that a gastric infusion of a fatty acid solution apparently lowered the intensity of this emotion by nearly half, which is comparable to the pharmacological effects of antidepressants.[15]

In addition to biological explanations, several of which are at present speculative, experiential evidence points to a number of reasons for craving or consuming comfort food. One is the hedonic response: the sensory pleasures derived from the taste, texture, aroma, and mouthfeel of certain foods. As an example, each month in Florida, prison inmates purchase 270,000 honey buns, the dense, glazed snacks that weigh in at six ounces and boast 680 calories, 30 grams of fat, and 51 grams of sugar. Craved and consumed avidly, they sometimes are fashioned into cakes for cellmates' birthdays or to celebrate release from prison, bet on sports events, and barter in the underground economy. According to one inmate, a honey bun "sticks to the gut and fills the gap left from the state food that's badly prepped . . . and at times spoiled to a point that it's uneatable."[16]

Comfort foods vary across societies, from the warm, soft-textured, soupy rice congee in China to the stir-fried rice noodle dish Pad Thai served as street food and in casual eateries in Thailand to vegemite, the dark brown, salty paste rich in umami favored by Australians. Dining on death row, many prisoners about to be executed request a calorie-loaded last meal of savory fried chicken, juicy burgers, and sugar-laden pastries and sodas that they have been deprived of for years and that often encode emotional meanings. The reviewer of a book about what top chefs would choose as their last meal writes that "when it comes to our deepest desires, it turns out that food isn't just about taste. It's tied right into memory and the longing for the sensations of when we felt happiest or most loved." The reviewer quotes a restaurant owner: "If someone can hand us those memories . . . it's the culinary equivalent of a big hug."[17]

The desire for comfort food is often social, emotional, or associational. One account about food brought to a prison conveys the sense of reassuring memories that food may conjure up. At Christmas, a woman took her husband some homemade biscuits, "not because I can bake good biscuits but because he asked me to try. They turned out . . . different." He shared his Christmas food with others who had received none, including an elderly man with no teeth who consumed nothing but the biscuits. No one else liked them. Asked if he thought they were good, the man replied, "Every morning when I was a little boy, my mama baked biscuits for breakfast. When I came to prison, she still baked biscuits for me every Christmas. My mama died a few years ago, and I ain't had any homemade biscuits since then. Your wife's biscuits taste just like my mama's—God rest her soul, that woman never could bake a decent biscuit! They taste awful, but they remind me of my mama."[18]

Some prisoners and many in the free world endeavor to combat feelings of boredom, unhappiness, frustration, anxiety, loneliness, resentment, enmity, and grief by seeking comfort in food. A woman in a British prison said, "You've got to get solace somehow . . . so I eat. I eat the sweets because the dinner's disgusting, but also because it makes me feel better, cheers me up."[19] As a female college student put it: "Food is a friend, a consolation, a hobby, a companion."[20]

In a survey of comfort food by Julie L. Locher and associates, the researchers who queried 264 undergraduate students determined that the choices and reasons for them fell into four categories.[21] One is *nostalgia*: the identification with a particular time and place in one's past evoking feelings of peace and happiness. A male student said that SpaghettiOs symbolized being taken care of by his mother when ill. *Indulgence* food, a second category, was exemplified by a desire for something expensive and calorically rich, often chocolate but also in one instance a student recalled her impoverished childhood in which her mother sometimes had enough money to prepare breaded pork chops. A third is *convenience* food. One woman explained: "When I am feeling depressed . . . I want something that is convenient. It is more convenient for me to go to the store and buy some cheese curls than it is for me to go in the kitchen and cook."[22] The fourth category consists of *physical comfort* food: the sensory aspects of a food that is warm, soft, smooth, easily eaten and digested, and provides a sense of fullness.

An article by a team of three nutrition scholars and a folklorist that concerns emotional eating during the COVID-19 pandemic found that motivations included mood (especially feelings of stress), convenience, sensory appeal, price, and familiarity.[23] The investigators invoke the concept of liminality, a state of in-betweenness, to further interpret food choice motives related to the increased intake of comfort food; that is, "the uncertainty of the future, not only in terms of food but of everyday life in general, is suspending the usual rules" about healthful eating.[24]

A theme running through many accounts is that individuals turn to comfort food when alone—and perhaps when feeling lonely.[25] In an essay concerning the consumption of chicken soup, Jordan Troisi and Shira Gabriel find that comfort food serves as a social surrogate, fulfilling a need to belong.[26] As numerous definitions indicate, comfort food tends to be identified with family tradition, holidays, and special events in which an individual participated. The physiological experience of ingesting a palatable food activates emotional associations with other people that become encoded with the food. After losing her olfactory sense owing to head injuries suffered in an auto accident, my mother sometimes prepared chicken and dumplings like the dish made by her grandmother who had reared her and about whom she reminisced fondly. Mother could not smell the food, which is much of its sensory satisfaction, but she recalled her grandmother, whose dish was "soooooo good!"[27] Comfort food, then, may serve as a social surrogate.[28] For my mother, chicken and dumplings held "autobiographical meanings."[29]

Comfort foods are often considered to be junk food or harmful to health. Mashed potatoes, macaroni and cheese, pasta dishes, ice cream, and even chocolate are not inherently unhealthful, however. Nevertheless, fifty-two out of ninety-four teenage respondents to a student opinion poll on the *New York Times* learning blog indicated that their choices, and comfort foods generally, are bad for one's health.[30] But several added comments such as: "I don't care if it's healthy or not"; "I don't think it matters"; and "People just want to feel good, and if their comfort food makes them feel that way for a moment then that's all that matters."

Nearly a dozen of the ninety-four teens referred to emotional motivations for and consequences of consuming comfort foods. Among the remarks were "it does make me feel better when I'm eating them"; "they [mashed potatoes and french fries] just hit the spot and make my life feel like I have been lifted up"; and "When I am upset or if I had a stressful day I go to the store and buy a Reese's candy or something. Another comfort food that I have is ice cream. It's not very healthy for you, but I swear it takes your problems away the second you put a spoonful in your mouth."

Emotional reasons for partaking of comfort foods differ with age. Older individuals tend to consume them when feeling positive while younger people are somewhat more inclined to turn to them when in a dysphoric state.[31] Gender is also a factor. In one survey, more than one-third of the women, compared to one-fifth of the men, found solace in comfort foods when feeling "stressed"; and more than one-third of the men ate them to maintain or enhance positive emotions in contrast to one-fourth of the women who did so.[32] Hunger triggers food cravings in many men regardless of the substance; postconsumption feelings are apt to be positive. Women often attribute their cravings to television commercials, boredom, and stress[33]; after succumbing to their craving, many feel anxious and guilty, particularly if they have been on a restricted diet.[34]

In the late 1990s, two practitioners utilized their understanding of comfort food to help elderly anorexic clients in a nursing home who frequently refused to eat and whose quality of life had diminished greatly. Dieticians design and serve meals representing a "balanced diet" to all patients even though the food remains uneaten meal after meal. "Comfort foods may be a viable alternative," suggest the creators of an alternative approach that proved successful. Comfort foods, they write, are "associated with bygone years, intended to trigger recollections of pleasant childhood experiences and feelings of caring and healing."[35] The authors surveyed 115 individuals in an Iowa care facility, asking them "to identify special foods fed to them by their mothers when they were sick or having an especially difficult time."[36] At 44 percent, chicken soup ranked highest on a list of forty-eight items, followed by toast (33 percent), milk toast (29 percent), ice cream (19 percent), and other items. Offers of comfort food to the patients were accompanied by solicitous comments from the staff to help them recall early experiences in which caring individuals gave them the food. The goal was "to use family traditions, ethnicity, and religious or traditional beliefs to stimulate digestion and trigger hunger," write the authors. "Many residents are comforted by nostalgia. They enjoy thinking of times past and people they loved."[37]

Thoughts of loved ones, earlier days, and attachments to family, community, and birthplace abound as a result of transnationalism—the migration of people from one country to another—and are manifested in culinary longings. Every few weeks and at holidays, couriers transport coveted comestibles to the *oaxaqueña/os* in California from their relatives in Mexico. Items consist of peppers, cheese, seeds, and particularly homemade foods such as *mole* (a cooking sauce consisting of twenty or more ingredients, including chili peppers, seeds, nuts, and often chocolate), *tlayudas* (a tortilla unique to Oaxaca), and *chapulines* (fried grasshoppers, which are considered a delicacy). "If my mom sends me things, it's such a treasure," said one person. "When I receive these things, I'm receiving something from my family. It makes us feel connected to our people."[38]

The *envios* (shipments) are prepared by the senders, paid for by the recipients, and carried by representatives of community-based businesses. Beneficiaries "commonly talk about the 'authenticity' of the food, both in regards to the taste and the fact that it came from their homes and was made by their mother." Although the "'home' may be the anchor, the food, be it tlayudas or grasshoppers, is the chain connected to the anchor."[39] A cultural nutrient thus provides emotional comfort, for "food represents 'home,' the family, the household, and the local community.... It signifies a person's identity."[40]

One or another food might be or might once have been comforting, but ingesting it can also produce negative feelings, discomfort, and even anxiety.[41] Those who are dieting to lose weight sometimes feel remorse after having succumbed to their gustatory and emotional cravings for calorie-laden comfort foods, especially sweets. Some Latinas with diabetes bemoan having to adhere to a restricted diet or chastise themselves for not abiding by it. One woman told me: "Desserts: those are my comfort foods." Another admitted, "The day of Thanksgiving . . . that one pie made of pumpkin: I know that I shouldn't eat it, but I get tempted and I take nibbles . . . nibbles."[42]

While Spam is a highly desirable food for many Hawaiians and Southerners, partaking of it can evoke issues of class. "Being an African American, looking good was always important, showing some kind of status," said one man who quit eating it after eight years. "Being associated with Spam would take that away from that good image."

Consuming foods rich in positive associations with home, family, and identity can also trigger alarm. The American-born children of Oaxacan immigrants in Monterey County, California, exhibit exceptionally high levels of lead poisoning caused by ingesting lead through fried grasshoppers and other homemade foods sent to them as *envios*.[43] "My first thought was, 'What's going to happen to us, to our unique way of getting what makes us who we are, our traditional foods,'" said a community worker.[44]

THE FOOD OF THE GODS

An oft-mentioned comfort food tied to memorable occasions in childhood, emotional eating, thoughts of others, sensory experiences, and perhaps physiological processes is chocolate, which is the most commonly craved food in North America.[45] Several questions arise: Which gender is more susceptible to chocolate's allure? Is chocolate craving culture-specific or is it cross-national? Are some people addicted to chocolate as they claim?

American folklore and popular culture have a field day with this food item. T-shirts read: "If the answer is chocolate, who cares what the question is." "Save Planet Earth. It's the only one with chocolate." "A balanced diet is chocolate in both hands." The Complete Chocoholic First Aid Kit, advertised on the internet several years ago, consisted of bite-sized chocolate bandages, "quick fix" chocolate tablets, chocolate "aspirins," and a chocolate "diet pill." Sayings on shirts, mugs, and rubber stamps refer to chocolate as therapy: "When no one understands you, chocolate is there." "Here, have some chocolate. Feel better now?" There are also jokes on the internet concerning why chocolate is better than sex: "You can get chocolate," "You can have chocolate in public," "No need to fake your enjoyment of chocolate," "Size doesn't matter—though more is still better."

Consumption of cacao or chocolate—the "food of the gods"—originated in the New World with the Olmec, Maya, and Aztec at least three thousand years ago and diffused to Europe in the mid-1500s. From the sixteenth century to the present, more than one hundred medicinal uses have been proposed.[46] Frequently mentioned today is chocolate as a stimulant, relaxant, antidepressant, and aphrodisiac.[47] People describe chocolate as heavenly, irresistible, decadent, naughty, dangerous, erotic, immoral, sinful, unhealthful, and addictive—but also therapeutic.[48]

Surveys indicate that substantially more American women than men crave chocolate; for example, in one study the ratio was 40 percent female to 15 percent male.[49] According to a T-shirt: "Chocolate is a girl's best friend." Remarked actor Sandra Bullock: "Chocolate is the greatest gift to women ever created, next to the likes of Paul Newman and Gene Kelly. It's something that should be had on a daily basis." Then there's the joke about the man who finds a bottle on the beach containing a genie that grants him three wishes. The first is for one million dollars. The second is for a convertible. For his third wish, the man asks to become irresistible to women. The genie turns him into a box of chocolates.

For years, researchers and the public have puzzled over chocolate's appeal and effects. One rationale is that the craved food serves homeostatic needs; that is, ingesting the substance will redress a nutritional deficiency. Sometimes women cite this belief in "the wisdom of the body" to account for chocolate craving in relation to their menstrual cycle, contending that chocolate restores depleted magnesium or aids in the release of serotonin to improve mood.

Arguing against magnesium deficiency, however, is that other foods—including rice bran, flax seeds, cornmeal, and seaweed—are high in magnesium but not craved.[50] Moreover, individuals could simply take a magnesium pill but don't.[51] Dark chocolate contains cacao mass, coco butter, and some sugar. Milk chocolate, which most people prefer with its added milk solids and sugar, contains lower amounts of cacao and hence less magnesium. White chocolate does not include cocoa solids at all. Many women contend that they crave chocolate perimenstrually, but few eat more chocolate during the two to three days before and after the onset of menses, and non-PMS sufferers do not show signs of cyclic changes in eating.[52]

In one of the rare cross-national studies, a survey indicates that while 40 percent of American female respondents associated chocolate craving with their menstrual cycle, only 4 percent of Spanish females did.[53] Among people craving sweets, the difference between men and women in Spain who desired chocolate was relatively small—22.2 percent and 28.6 percent, respectively—compared to 17.4 percent men and 44.6 percent women in the United States.[54] The white chocolate preferred by Spanish women has no cacao base. In a questionnaire study undertaken in Egypt, researchers found that the craved foods first mentioned by both men and women were savories, not sweets. Only 6 percent of women and 1 percent of men named chocolate.[55] These responses raise further doubts about a homeostatic cause, suggesting instead a cultural origin for chocolate cravings.

A second popular claim is that chocolate improves mood and counters depression. Among the 380 chemical elements in chocolate are tyramine and phenylethylamine, which are arousing and might stimulate the release of dopamine. But these compounds are higher in some sausages, cheddar cheese, and pickled herring.[56] Chocolate contains caffeine although the amount is insignificant compared to coffee and tea.

A common belief is that chocolate or carbohydrate craving addresses serotonin deficiency, especially in depressed individuals who then self-medicate. Carbohydrates stimulate insulin production, which increases the proportion of tryptophan, which is converted into serotonin. The fat content in chocolate slows the absorption of carbohydrate, however, and 5 percent of chocolate's calorie content is protein, negating the serotonin effect.[57] Therefore, a "depressed mood cannot be the sole trigger of chocolate cravings," writes a set of researchers. "Many women report ingesting chocolate to improve mood, but these individuals exhibit no more depression-like symptomatology than women who do not use chocolate for these purposes."[58] Alleviating a negative mood more likely occurs through the hedonic effects of eating, not a nutritional or physiological mechanism. Concludes a pair of investigators: "This proposed link between serotonin, mood and 'craving' for carbohydrates . . . has become part of the folklore of the psychology of eating."[59]

Self-identified chocoholics often insist that psychoactive constituents in chocolate cause addiction to it, which explains their intense desire for and overconsumption of it as suggested by the message on the refrigerator magnet in figure 4.2. "I'm sure it's addictive; I do think that," remarked one individual. It has a "druglike effect," said another. "Some of the ingredients in chocolate, it works on your brain and then you feel happy."[60] But theobromine is a weak stimulant, caffeine concentrations are low, and other compounds exist in greater amounts in foods that are not craved or said to be addictive.[61]

A T-shirt proclaims, "When it comes to chocolate, resistance is futile." Indulgence, however, is stigmatized in our current climate of "healthism,"

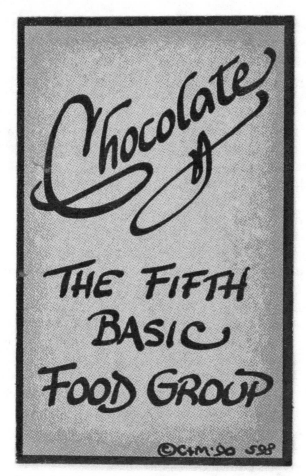

Figure 4.2 Refrigerator magnet: "Chocolate. The Fifth Basic Food Group." Author's collection. Photo by Laura Layera.

in which chocolate is considered "bad" and the 2.8 billion pounds consumed annually in the United States (11.7 pounds per capita) is said to contribute to an obesity epidemic. Notably, the Swiss eat twice as much chocolate, and the Austrians are not far behind them. Employing a medical model to justify overindulgence in eating chocolate, to explain why one succumbs to its "moreish" quality (wanting to consume more), and to account for failing to exercise restraint relieves individuals of personal responsibility; they are victims of forces beyond their control.[62] A T-shirt advises that there are "3 steps for chocoholics. Admit you have a problem. Admit there is no cure. Don't worry about it anymore."

Not a staple but rather a highly palatable treat, chocolate possesses oro-sensory properties providing immense gratification. It dissolves at a slightly lower temperature than a person's body warmth; one observation is that "if you've got melted chocolate all over your hands, you're eating it too slowly." Because it is calorically dense and exhibits a unique combination of sweetness, creamy texture, characteristic taste, and tantalizing aroma, chocolate "seduces the palate."[63] As the cartoon character Dennis the Menace remarks to his friend while eating a chocolate ice cream cone, "Joey, the only thing better than chocolate is . . . well . . . nothing!"[64]

Chocolate, which is "a real pleasure thing," commented one person,[65] may be eaten either as a reward for an achievement or as therapy for a difficult, trying day. In other words, to celebrate or to medicate.[66] Its excessive consumption is viewed as evidence of lack of self-control; hence, one lay construction views it as unhealthful, harmful, or simply "bad." Little wonder that there are stories about people hoarding, hiding, and clandestinely consuming chocolate. "The taste of chocolate is a sensual pleasure in itself, existing in the same world as sex," observed the therapist and media personality Dr. Ruth Westheimer. "For myself, I can enjoy the wicked pleasure of chocolate . . . entirely by myself. Furtiveness makes it better." Viewed as sinful because it provides sensual pleasure, chocolate often evokes a sexual analogy: "Eating chocolate is a bit like having sex. . . . It just feels so good," said one woman in a study of alleged chocoholics.[67] Remarked the actor Alicia Silverstone: "My favorite thing in the world is a box of fine European chocolates which is, for sure, better than sex."

Encounters with chocolate are unavoidable. Thoughtful hotel staff leave a piece on your pillow at night; chocolate bars and bags of Hershey's Kisses sit temptingly near the cash register in pharmacies and grocery stores; greeting cards incorporate references to it; and it appears in various forms at major holidays, including chocolate eggs and bunnies at Easter, chocolate coins on Hanukkah, chocolate snowmen and Santa Claus at Christmas, chocolate skulls, cats, bats, witches, and jack-o'-lanterns at Halloween, and red, heart-shaped boxes of gold or silver foil-wrapped chocolate cherries, caramels, truffles, nougats, fudge, and bonbons on Valentine's Day. Gift boxes of chocolates in advertisements and shops often emphasize femininity, luxury, and allure.[68] They are glossy white, gold, silver, or chocolate brown; a colorful ribbon adorns one corner; and images on the cover depict some of the delicious confectionaries inside. A symbol of romance and sexuality, chocolate figures in the ritual of seduction. Often one individual gives the sweets to another person as a symbol of adoration or as a step in breaking down resistance.

A topic rarely investigated is unusual food mixtures involving chocolate and other ingredients, which are eaten clandestinely.[69] The single survey of "secretive food concocting" describes the incorporation of not only chocolate but also sugar and peanut butter. Examples include topping scrambled eggs, peanut butter, and chocolate chip sandwiches with sugar; partaking of oatmeal with Oreo cookies; eating bananas with peanut butter wrapped in cheddar cheese; and consuming tortilla chips and peanut butter, french fries in ice cream, and ham and cheese with syrup. The researchers report that a majority of respondents simply had a craving rather than being hungry or bored. Judging from my own occasional queries to others, it seems that sometimes the consumption of unusual combinations provides or is motivated by a desire for not only gustatory but also emotional satisfaction, and hence what is prepared might well be considered "comfort food."

THINKING ABOUT A FOOD AS COMFORT GIVING

Several articles implicate yet another set of influential factors in accounting for the consumption of comfort food. The researchers who mentioned that carbohydrate "addiction" has "become part of the folklore of the psychology of eating"[70] also note that a "widely believed motive to eat chocolate is to improve mood" and they refer to "belief," "a popular idea," and "everyday discourse." Others comment on "popular claims" and "a popular hypothesis,"[71] a "lay definition" and a "conventional explanation,"[72] and "the popular media and personal anecdotes."[73] There are references as well to "socially constructed" notions, "folk wisdom," and the "vernacular of everyday life," along with "family traditions," "cultural traditions," and "traditional beliefs." In other words, folklore and popular culture play a significant role in establishing patterns of comfort food choice, perpetuating ideas about certain food items, influencing expectations, and affecting cognitive processes.

The process of conceptualizing an item as comfort food seems to follow a particular set of occurrences. It entails having a pleasurable gustatory experience, repeated exposure to the item, emotional meanings attributed to the food, learned expectations of the alleviation of an aversive mood or maintenance of a positive frame of mind, and social reinforcement.

To elaborate: Certain foods are highly palatable owing to their sweet, salty, savory, aromatic, or other properties. Combined with the hedonic satisfaction they offer as well as the simple pleasure of eating and feelings of satiety, carbohydrate-rich fare and the fatty acids in some of the items may have physiological consequences affecting moods.[74] Foods providing such desirable outcomes will be sought again as a conditioned response; some items are given in childhood as treats and rewards, the indulgence leading to learned behavior patterns and anticipation.[75]

Often an item is associated with one or more individuals, and these emotionally charged connections become part and parcel of the food. For example, one of the teens who mentioned a comfort food on the *New York Times* blog noted, "It is a special recipe that only my aunt knows." Another commented, "My comfort food is my mom's fried chicken, mashed potatoes and gravy, hot biscuits and gravy (or Honey) and corn or green beans. Nobody can cook it like my mom. . . . It's just a wonderful meal and makes for a great family time together." A dish, then, becomes cognitively linked to family or other relational partners.[76] A repast might also carry markers of ethnicity because of the "flavor principle," a distinctive taste owing to herbs, spices, and manner of preparation.[77] As either family fare or cultural cuisine, the food becomes conceived of as "traditional," that is, exhibiting continuities through time and consistencies in space,[78] and therefore it is imbued with value and perpetuated.[79]

One example of taken-for-granted understandings, or "folk knowledge,"[80] is the oft-heard remark at a Thanksgiving feast that tryptophan in the turkey has caused a person's fatigue. Amino acids are natural sedatives metabolized into the neurotransmitters serotonin and melatonin. But the food needs to be eaten on an empty stomach, and turkey contains no more tryptophan than does pork, beef, chicken, or beans, the devouring of which is not alleged to put people to sleep. The drowsiness owes much to the carbohydrate-rich side dishes and sugar-laden desserts that lead to increased serotonin levels, not to mention the depressant effect of the accompanying alcohol or the fact that the body redirects blood from elsewhere to the digestive system, a process that is pronounced after overeating.[81]

Another popular notion on the internet is that bananas improve mood because of their serotonin content. Although it is true that bananas contain serotonin, it does not cross the blood–brain barrier.[82] Lay constructions like this one are not necessarily misguided and without some basis. Rather, members of the public may have incomplete information in their efforts to understand their behavior and that of others.

Surveys, conducted largely among college students, have identified some comfort foods, but ethnographic studies can contribute additional insights. Direct observation and interviews, or having people keep diaries for a period of time, usually produces more accurate records of behavior and cognitive processes than does soliciting recall on a questionnaire. Daily journals that document what was eaten, when, and in what circumstances can be discussed with the diary keepers in regard to items they identify as comfort food, thus providing understanding about eating patterns during normal and stressful circumstances, the variety of foods that were consumed and their manner of preparation, items claimed to alleviate or maintain particular moods, and other data revealing what is conceived of as comfort fare and why it was consumed, when, where, and by whom.

The eleven studies in *Comfort Food Meanings and Memories*, edited by Lucy M. Long and me, illustrate the use of information-rich sources beyond surveys. Researchers draw upon diverse documentation ranging from personal interviews and observations to autoethnography, cookbooks, films, internet blogs, advertisements, and works of fiction. The foods they focus on vary widely from bologna to chocolate, sweet and savory puddings, dairy products, fried rice, cafeteria fare, "one-eyed Jacks," Rhode Island "doughboys," soul food, and others. Authors explore numerous concepts and issues associated with comfort food such as identity, nationality, ethnicity, sense of place, family, stress, discomfort, guilt, betrayal, and loss, thereby contributing to a deeper understanding of people's relationship to what they eat.

To conclude, in recent years the term "comfort food" has become a household word. Many restaurants, blogs, and cookbooks now promote comfort food or propose ways of preparing less fattening versions of it, cutting one-third to one-half or more of the calories in chicken pot pie, Philly cheesesteaks, and tuna melts. A large percentage of the American population partakes of comfort food, often wittingly and willingly, as either celebration or medication. Laboratory studies of stress among animals and their increased intake of fat and sucrose suggest that there are implications for human beings, principally in regard to eating disorders, depression, corpulence, and cardiovascular disease. Some note the rising incidence of stress in our lives, along with a growing obesity epidemic, wondering if there is a correlation.[83]

Further research on comfort food can reveal more fully the process by which individuals attach meanings to food, how and why they self-diagnose and self-medicate with food, and the ways in which they draw upon multiple sources of authority, including tradition, personal experience, and the media.[84] In sum, additional studies can contribute to a greater understanding of comfort food consumption and to how and why food is as much a symbolic object as it is a substance to nourish the body.

An extension of research on comfort food concerns what people facing the existential precipice of life's ending choose as their final repast. Why do they select these foods? How did the custom of a last meal before execution begin, and why is it perpetuated? Such matters are addressed in the next chapter.

Chapter 5

LAST MEALS AND THE CRUTCH OF RITUAL

Questions, misconceptions, and controversies surround the offer of a final meal before execution. When did the tradition of a last meal begin? What do prisoners choose to eat, including the most popular items, and why? Are limits imposed on requests? Do inmates eat all the food? What meanings have been attributed to providing a final repast, and why is the custom perpetuated? Answering these questions requires more specifics than presented in the small number of studies to date.[1] Possessing varied meanings for different participants in the drama of execution, the ceremonial last meal is one of the most powerful symbolic elements within a larger phenomenon laden with rituals and symbols.

LAST MEALS THROUGH TIME

The origins of a final repast are elusive. Sacrificial and scapegoating rituals in ancient Greece during calamities or in efforts to avert a future catastrophe sometimes involved selecting a criminal, poor man, or other marginal individual to be chased out of the city or even killed. The victim was treated to special food or an excellent repast in order to make this stand-in for the community appear to be a more valuable and representative member.[2] In Rome on the eve of entering the arena, gladiators and *bestiarii* (those who fought against wild beasts) received an elegant dinner, the *cena libera*, provided by the host of the show as symbolic compensation to those about to die. The Romans considered gladiatorial contests to have developed from human sacrifice to propitiate the souls of the dead. Rather than kill free and noble members of society, prisoners or slaves were chosen, but they had to be made to appear higher in status, such as by extending a special meal to them.[3]

In Nuremberg in the late 1500s, the condemned "was allowed a liberal table, provided by charitable people" (not by the state) three days before execution.[4] In England, some prisoners with funds, such as John Rann and

Renwick Williams, who were executed in the late eighteenth century, hosted their own dinner party in prison on the eve of hanging.[5] Other condemned inmates had only bread, water, and gruel, or were even starved. Following an execution, the prison warden might schedule an official repast as a closing ceremony: "We hang at eight, breakfast at nine" read one invitation.[6]

By the late nineteenth century in America, the provision of a distinctive end-of-life meal for the condemned was a firmly established tradition. The custom was well enough known that on 9 December 1891, the *Roanoke Times* could print the following joke[7]:

"The Design Frustrated"
WARDEN: Now you can select anything you like for your last meal before execution.
CONVICTED MURDERER: All right. Send in a New England boiled dinner.
WARDEN: No you don't. I can't let you cheat the law by committing suicide.

Newspaper reportage of execution rituals was so pervasive that on 13 September 1891, the *Fort Worth Gazette* published the following editorial:

Some day some newspaper will forget to report the articles of food comprising the last meal eaten by a murderer under sentence of death and then the whole bottom will fall out of newspaper enterprise. It is terrible to contemplate the fearful results that might ensue were the public allowed to remain in ignorance whether a murderer, just before going to the scaffold, ate beef-steak or chicken, or whether he drank tea or coffee. There is too much attention paid to sickly details in setting forth the fact of the execution of a man too dangerous to live.

In the *Washington [DC] Times* on 13 February 1903, an anonymous author reports on the sale of relics from the infamous Newgate Prison in England, then segues to the remark, "You are familiar with the nature of the breakfast often prepared in this country [the United States] by the sheriff's wife as the last meal of the condemned: coffee, rolls, chops, eggs." The writer concludes, "There is a strange fascination in the accounts of executions."

Many people have been attracted to executions as well as inquisitive about the crimes and final actions of condemned prisoners. England banned public executions in 1868, and they ceased in America by the 1930s. But from the Middle Ages onward, executions were popular amusements attended by hundreds, sometimes thousands, in all ranks of society. Reasons varied, including the satisfaction of witnessing the restoration of law and order through ritu-alized retribution, catharsis in escaping from resentful or deprived lives, feelings of pleasure in the excitement of being in a crowd, morbid curiosity, sympathy with the condemned, or the need for strategies of defense against the fear of death.

THE EXECUTED AND THEIR LAST MEALS IN POPULAR CULTURE

The lives and deaths of criminals continue to intrigue, as evident in popular culture. Known as the "pickax murderer" whose conversion to Christianity gained worldwide publicity, Karla Faye Tucker is celebrated in song by four bands in addition to being the subject of two plays, several documentaries, and an interview on *Larry King Live*; her story also inspired the movies *Last Dance* (1996) and *Crossed Over* (2002). Aileen Wuornos, a Daytona Beach sex worker who became a serial killer, has had two documentary films, one comic book, a song, an opera, and a movie about her.[8] Charlize Theron won a Golden Globe and an Academy Award Oscar for her portrayal in *Monster* (2003), said to be based on the life of Wuornos. Eating Krispy Kreme dough-nuts helped the actor gain thirty pounds for her role.[9]

Convicted of robbing and murdering a gas station attendant one night and a motel manager the next evening, thirty-two-year-old Gary Gilmore was executed by firing squad in Utah, a method that he chose. His last meal consisted of steak, potatoes, milk, and coffee although he consumed only the beverages along with contraband whiskey. His last request was for his eyes to be used for transplants (two people received corneas). His last words were "Let's do it!"[10] Norman Mailer won a Pulitzer Prize for *The Executioner's Song* (1979) based on Gilmore's story, and Tommy Lee Jones garnered an Emmy for his portrayal of Gilmore in a 1982 television movie. Five weeks before his execution, the cast of *Saturday Night Live* sang a medley of Christmas songs with altered lyrics titled "Let's Kill Gary Gilmore for Christmas."[11] *Playboy* published a lengthy interview with him that appeared shortly after his death. He is celebrated in song by two musical groups, the Adverts and the Police. In a *Seinfeld* episode, Jerry finally decides to buy a particular jacket and says to Elaine: "Well, in the immortal words of Gary Gilmore, 'Let's do it.'" Dan Wieden, one of the founders of the ad agency for Nike, credits the inspiration for his "Just Do it" to "Let's do it."[12]

A last supper industry emerged, replete with official and unofficial web-sites reporting final meal requests and last words, displaying a last meals trivia game, and offering Dead Man Eating T-shirts, underwear, and coffee mugs. News articles concerning those just executed often mention final repasts. Several books have appeared, such as *Last Suppers, Last Meal, Meals to Die For,* and *Their Last Suppers.* Although no longer accessible online, a Canadian company called Last Meals Delivery Service provided clients in Toronto "a replica of the 'last meal' consumed by someone executed in the United States." Begun in 2003, but eventually discontinued, the highly popular blog *Dead Man Eating* posted end-of-life meals in prisons throughout the United States. Other websites have listed the more extravagant orders. Some bloggers ask readers to ponder: what would you request as *your* last meal?

A FEAST BEFORE DYING: FOOD CHOICES AND THEIR IMPLICATIONS

Texas has carried out the death sentence with the greatest zeal, accounting for about one-third of the executions since the death penalty resumed in 1976.[13] Between 7 December 1982 and 10 September 2003, 245 of 310 Texas inmates on the eve of execution ordered special last meals. French fries headed the inventory of items at 48 percent of requests. At 35 percent, burgers were second in popularity, often cheeseburgers and frequently with double meat patties. Chicken, almost always deep fried, was included in 19 percent. Steak occurred in 18 percent of orders. Ice cream, including shakes, appeared in 29 percent. Pie (usually pecan), cake (most often chocolate or white with white icing), cheesecake, peach cobbler, banana pudding ("with real bananas"), and cookies, cinnamon rolls, and doughnuts figured in 29 percent of orders. Seven inmates asked for multiple desserts. Sodas (typically Coke or Dr Pepper) were included in 30 percent of the requests.[14] Although the last meal in Texas is served at 4 p.m., two hours before execution, 21 percent of the inmates ordered breakfast, mostly eggs, sausage (occasionally bacon, steak, or pork chops) and hash browns, sometimes with biscuits and gravy; the exception was one man who asked for two boxes of frosted flakes and a pint of milk.

Certain items turned up infrequently. Only 16 percent of meals contained salad, and 12 percent included milk. Other than deep-fried potatoes and onion rings, vegetables were evident mainly by their absence, found in only 4 percent of meal requests; they included carrots, peas, green beans, cauliflower, broccoli with cheese topping, corn on the cob, and fried okra.

Many last meal orders sought beverages, food, and preparations that rarely appear on prison menus. Hot coffee and tea have been eliminated as nonnutritional and as possible assault weapons. Milk tends to be available only at breakfast but not every day in some facilities. Water, an artificial fruit drink, or a beverage resembling Kool-Aid is provided at other meals. Casseroles, goulash, and soy-stretched chicken dishes are common on daily menus, with pudding or Jell-O for dessert.[15] In order to boost calories while cutting costs, meat is often extended through grinding and adding textured vegetable protein. Increasingly, cold cuts are served at lunch. Some prisons have banished fried foods, thus eliminating the cost of cooking fat, decreasing equipment maintenance, lessening sewage and drain problems, and for reasons of health.[16] Meals have been trimmed in some prison systems from three to two on weekends and holidays, or to days when inmates are not working, a cutback that led to a dramatic increase in prisoner assaults in some facilities.

In circumstances of deprivation, therefore, an emphasis on sensory experiences looms large in food choice among condemned prisoners who miss the taste and texture of savory fried chicken, juicy burgers, and sugar-laden pies, cakes, and sodas. Brian Price, an inmate at the Walls Unit in Huntsville, Texas, who prepared about two hundred last meals over a ten-year period, said he seasoned burgers with Worcestershire sauce, garlic powder, salt, and pepper. "Then I'd grill the onions right there beside it and toast the buns with butter. I did the best I could with what I had and I'd always use fresh lettuce and tomato to garnish it with."[17] The first last meal that Price cooked was Lawrence Buxton's request for steak, pineapple upside-down cake, tea, punch, and coffee. He was touched when the inmate sent word back about how much he enjoyed the meal: "I gave this guy a little bit of pleasure—just something to distract him for a brief moment before his execution. It's a very humbling and emotional experience and I always prayed over each meal."[18]

A number of prisoners combined two, three, or even four types of meat in a meal request and also asked for multiple sodas and pastries. If a single helping of meat, starch, and sweet represents the "normal" meal, then 73 of 245 requests (30 percent) of Texas prisoners involved excessive amounts of food. Hilton Crawford, for example, ordered "twelve beef ribs, three enchiladas, chicken fried steak with cream gravy, crisp bacon sandwich, ketchup, a loaf of bread, cobbler, three cokes, three root beers, French fries, and onion rings." Kia Johnson specified "flour fried chicken breasts, onion rings, fried shrimp, French fries, fried catfish, double-meat cheeseburger with grilled onions, strawberry fruit juice, and pecan pie."

Final meal requests, however, are subject to restrictions of expense and availability, which vary. According to Brian Price, the inmate cook, it was $20 in Texas and limited to what is maintained in the kitchen or butcher shop (never lobster, and not steak since 1993). The cost in Florida was $40 using ingredients that are present locally, $40 in Indiana and the meal may be ordered from one of a half-dozen restaurants in town, and $50 in California. Legend has it that a prisoner on death row in San Quentin scheduled for execution in late fall asked for fresh strawberries. When told that "we can't get fresh strawberries in November," the inmate replied "I'll wait."[19] Sometimes the prison chaplain or other officials have bent the rules to provide inmates with items "from the free world,"[20] including fruit[21] and Häagen-Dazs instead of ice cream from the commissary.[22] On several occasions, officials brought Price food items to prepare that they had purchased: "Venison, liver, shrimp, bacon, fresh tomatoes, lettuce, and even a 'blooming onion' appeared suddenly on the day of execution."[23]

Because of restrictions, orders for large quantities of food may be pared down. Texas inmate David Allen Castillo stipulated twenty-four soft shell tacos; he received four. He also wanted six tostados, but was given two; two cheeseburgers, which were refused him; and two whole onions, five jalapeños, one chocolate shake, and a quart of milk, which were granted.[24] Substitutions occur. When Pedro Muniz in Texas asked for salad and shrimp, which were not available, he received a cheeseburger, fries, and cola. If nothing particular is requested, then a Texas prisoner is given whatever is scheduled that day for the general prison population.[25] The "Final meal requests" link on the website of the Texas Department of Criminal Justice issues the caveat, "The final meal requested may not reflect the actual meal served," something overlooked or ignored by many who utilize food choice as a basis for pro-death penalty sentiments. Even inmate Brian Price, who prepared last meals for a decade, said he initially assumed that a death row prisoner received what he ordered.[26]

Clearly, a desire for particular sensory experiences, long denied, accounts for some meal requests. Other factors also influenced what prisoners sought as a final repast. One is social class based on education and income. An examination of 196 biographies of prisoners executed in Texas reveals that 11 percent had seven years or less of schooling, 26 percent made it only through middle school, and 15 percent graduated from high school. The largest number at 35 percent dropped out of school in the tenth or eleventh grade, that is, by age sixteen, when they were no longer legally compelled to attend.

Two-thirds of executed prisoners committed murder for financial gain, or in some fashion benefited materially.[27] Often amounts were paltry: $250 from a feed and farm supply; $140 from a laundry; a pistol, purse, and $8 from a home; a $2.70 six-pack of beer from a store clerk.[28] Given their underprivileged backgrounds and underclass status, they likely chose the kind of food as a last meal—burgers, french fries, fried chicken—that had been readily obtainable and familiar before incarceration. Moreover, steak, lobster, and shrimp have long been considered prestige or luxury items owing to price, and they are certainly not part of ordinary prison fare, which probably accounts for their presence in many last meal requests.

In addition to certain sensory qualities and the possible impact of social class, food choice sometimes is influenced by ethnicity but more often by regional upbringing. Of 245 meal requests in Texas, 16 were for tacos, burritos, quesadillas, enchiladas, or simply "Mexican platter" or "Mexican lunch," five inmates asked for tortillas with their meal, and twenty-eight specified the addition of jalapeños, picante sauce, salsa, red pepper, or chili powder to their food. Not all of these prisoners bore a Latinx identity, but many grew up in Texas, and hence were familiar with these foods and condiments. The five requests for chicken fried steak, usually with "country gravy" or "white gravy," two for fried okra, two for a "big bowl of grits," nine for barbecued beef, ribs, or chicken, one for mustard greens and spiced beets, and one for a half-pound of chitterlings suggest regional influence from different areas of the South, not necessarily ethnic identity.

Among the fifty-seven African Americans requesting a final repast out of the 187 last meals prepared by Brian Price, only four asked for something that can be construed as "soul" food, of which barely one fits the stereotype: "1/2 pound of chitterlings, fried chicken (dark meat), 10 slices of bacon, 1 raw onion, fried shrimp, peach cobbler, 1 pitcher of whole milk."[29] Like their White counterparts, twenty-nine Blacks asked for burgers, steak, or chicken. Nine requested other foods, two wanted fajitas or enchiladas, and three specified hot sauce, a bowl of chili, or jalapeño peppers as part of their meal.

Of the twenty-three Latinos, only three stipulated Mexican cuisine exclusively. Seven Latinos specified a combination of Mexican and American foods, two preferred only ice cream, one wanted venison steak, and one indicated shrimp but was given a cheeseburger instead. The lone Asian, born in South Vietnam and raised in Texas, ordered steak, french fries, beans, and water. Again, rather than ethnicity, the data indicate that regional association or upbringing in a particular geographical area affects food choice.

Dietary restrictions owing to religious beliefs and practices seem to have played no part in last meal requests, at least not in Texas. Is gender a factor? As discussed in the second chapter, provisioning mythology declares that red meat is masculine while the more delicate chicken and fish, along with fruit, vegetables, and salad, tend toward the feminine.[30] While they account for 10 percent of murder arrests, only 1 percent of women have been executed since capital punishment resumed.[31]

Of the dozen women executed in seven states since 1976, seven declined a final meal (Wanda Jean Allen, Velma Barfield, Betty Lou Beets, Linda Lyon Block, Francis Elaine Newton, Marilyn Plantz, Wuornos), but one of these women (Barfield) did have a bag of Cheez Doodles and a soft drink, and another (Wuornos) was given a cup of coffee and ate some snack food.[32] One moderate meal was for salad, pickled okra, pizza, strawberry shortcake, and cherry limeade (Christina Riggs), and another consisted of sweet peas, fried chicken, Dr Pepper, and apple pie (Teresa Lewis). Two other selections epitomized feminine food preference: Judias Buenoano requested steamed broccoli and asparagus salad, strawberries, and a cup of tea, and Tucker asked for a banana, a peach, and garden salad with ranch dressing, which she did not eat.[33] In contrast, Lois Nadean Smith—who earned the sobriquet in high school of "Mean Nadean"[34]—stipulated barbecued ribs, onion rings, strawberry banana cake, and cherry lemonade.

In sum, 58 percent of the twelve women in the United States, including three in Texas, declined a meal, in contrast to 21 percent of men in Texas, one woman demanded a masculine plate of barbecued ribs and fried onion rings, and four women (33 percent) preferred restrained servings of mainly feminine cuisine. More than 90 percent of these twelve women, then, chose nothing or female foods in moderate amounts, in contrast to men in Texas, who ordered substantial portions of meat and fried food but little fruit, salad, or fresh vegetables. (A mere 12 of 243 men requested meals without red meat; seven orders were for fruit, salad, and/or vegetables, while five others involved fish, eggs, and/or cheese.)

Several inmates, both male and female, asked for only a beverage such as Coke, freshly squeezed orange juice, or coffee. Perhaps because of anxiety, others nibbled on snack food, ate sparingly, or requested little: an apple, a plain cheese sandwich, a flour tortilla, and water. John Ramos, on death row until the Florida Supreme Court reversed the conviction, said, "I thought about my last meal. . . . I was gonna tell them, 'Just feed me the same s—. It's disgusting of you to offer me the best food when I'm gonna puke it back in your face.'"[35]

Since 1995, a condemned prisoner in Indiana is served a "special meal,"[36] as it is called, at least two days before the execution because many inmates told officials they were not hungry in the twenty-four hours before their death; on the last day, they are given regular prison fare.[37] Hence, when Joseph Trueblood in Indiana refused a special last meal as a means of "protesting what the state is getting ready to do," he was given the same dinner as other inmates: a bologna sandwich, a cheese sandwich, fruit, and cookies, which he did not eat.[38]

Do most of the condemned consume their last meal? A few prison spokes-persons contend that inmates eat a good part of their final meal—including the steak they have to saw through with plastic knives or that is precut and eaten with a plastic spoon or "spork."[39] Other accounts indicate that while some eat heartily, most do not. One reporter writes: "On Thursday evening, however, [Claude H.] Ryan was so nervous he couldn't eat his last meal and, as his final hour approached, he suffered a near breakdown."[40] Another informs readers, "Prison officials described [David Kevin] Hocker as antsy but upbeat the day of his death. He asked a lot of questions about the execution procedure and talked about his religious beliefs. Hocker had no breakfast or lunch Thursday. He requested a last meal of frankfurters, French fries, American cheese and chocolate cake, but he did not eat it."[41]

"I wouldn't be able to eat," said former warden Donald Cabana, "and I've never seen very many who do except to push the food around."[42] Robert Johnson in *Death Work* maintains that most prisoners "eat little or nothing at all."[43] He quotes an officer who said that "food is the last thing they got on their minds." The last meal, noted Johnson, is usually ordered the day before execution, when the condemned still harbor the hope of reprieve; by the time the meal arrives, however, "Your appetite goes with your hope."

In sum, it appears that a number of prisoners consume part of the meal while others order nothing or eat nothing they ordered. Yet other inmates request hearty meals, even inordinate amounts of food. There seems to be no general trend, however, no direct correlation between size of meal and kinds of food ordered on the one hand, and on the other, expressions of remorse, insistence on innocence, unbridled contentiousness, or manifestations of bravado.

A few prisoners have utilized the occasion to make political or moral statements. In North Carolina, Ricky Lee Sanderson explained: "I didn't take [the last meal] because I have very strong convictions about abortion and the 33 million babies that have been aborted in this country. Those babies never got a first meal and that's why I didn't take the last in their memory."[44] On the card for setting forth the final meal request, one inmate in Texas wrote, "Justice, temperance, with mercy." Another penciled, "God's saving grace, love, truth, peace and freedom." A third indicated "Justice, Equality, World Peace."

Lawrence Russell Brewer, a white supremacist gang member executed on 21 September 2011 for chaining an African American man to the back of a pickup truck and dragging him to his death, asked for an enormous meal of steaks, triple bacon cheeseburger, barbecued meat, omelet, pizza, fried okra, ice cream, fudge, and root beer. He did not eat any of whatever food he actually received.[45] An outraged state legislator said that the Texas inmate had ordered the meal in an attempt to "make a mockery out of the process,"[46] that is, he exploited the meal request as a subversive act.

In Tennessee, Philip Workman asked that his final meal be a vegetarian pizza donated to any homeless person near the prison. The state refused. A local woman called friends; together they bought 150 pizzas for $1,200, which were delivered to a rescue mission. "I just felt like I had to do something positive," she said. The president of the People for the Ethical Treatment of Animals (PETA) added another fifteen veggie pies, and a Minneapolis radio station sent seventeen pizzas to a center that helps teens in crisis.[47]

"Some of the condemned prefer to fast," observes the inmate cook Brian Price.[48] "Others order favorite foods from their childhood, recalling happier times to somewhat comfort themselves." In *My Last Supper*, photographer Melanie Dunea asked fifty of the world's top chefs what they would have for their final meal. The majority described simple foods like fried chicken, a hot dog, or a big bowl of spaghetti. One picked a roast, reminiscing to the book's reviewer[49] about his family's Sunday lunch in Scotland when he was growing up. The reviewer writes, "When it comes to our deepest desires, it turns out that food isn't just about taste. It's tied right into memory and the longing for the sensations of when we felt happiest or most loved." He quotes a restaurant owner: "If someone can hand us those memories . . . it's the culinary equivalent of a big hug." Another chef remarked about answers to the question of last meal: "There's always a return to childhood. . . . The word mom comes up at least a third of the time."

Only the notion of physical and emotional comfort as well as pleasant memories triggered by the taste, texture, aroma, and mouth feel of food can account for the overwhelming presence of cakes and pie and ice cream and milk shakes in so many final repasts, or breakfast served late afternoon a couple of hours before execution. Indiana granted a death row inmate's last request for his mother to be allowed to prepare his two favorite meals, which she cooked on-site with ingredients provided by the prison and then shared with her inmate son and several other relatives as well as his spiritual adviser.[50]

The comforting physical sensations of warm, easily eaten, filling foods and the emotional association of food with particular individuals and pleasurable events provide relief of distress for some inmates facing their execution.[51] As we have seen, food selection is also influenced by social class, ethnicity or regional upbringing, provisioning mythology regarding gender, and the desire to make a political or philosophical statement. Often anxiety accounts for prisoners turning down a last meal, opting for what is being served to the general population or eating little or no food at all.

FOOD, CRIMES, AND SYMBOLS

A question sometimes asked is whether or not the last meal sheds light on the psyche of the condemned prisoner. In a word, no. Little can be inferred about character, guilt, or innocence from the final repast owing to the circumstances, that is, years of deprivation of certain foods and their preparations, anxiety, and the desire for solace offered by "comfort food" and the memories evoked.

Based on records combining last words and last meals of 237 inmates executed in Texas over eleven years,[52] it appears that nearly half of the prisoners requested a meal of normal size, while one-fourth asked for disproportionate amounts of food, and the other fourth wanted little or nothing. Thirty-three percent expressed remorse, of whom the largest number (44 percent) specified a normal meal. The remarks of 39 percent of the inmates indicated resignation to their fate; slightly more than half (53 percent) asked for meals of normal size. Of the 13 percent insisting in their final statements on their innocence, the largest number requested either little or nothing to eat (41 percent) or a normal meal (35 percent). Of the three contemptuous prisoners issuing barbed statements ("Kiss my proud Irish ass"; "The prosecutor and Bill Scott are sorry sons of bitches"), two wanted normal measures of food, and one sought a meal of disproportionate size.

Last meals and the items in them serve as symbols in the discourse on crime and punishment. Jacquelyn C. Black created photographs of inmates' final repasts juxtaposed with each individual's photo, last statement, and other information. She writes that in 1984, she read a news article about Velma Barfield, whose final meal before execution consisted of Cheez Doodles and a Pepsi. "That image stayed with me and years later became the impetus for educating myself about capital punishment,"[53] which she now opposes. Those contesting retributive justice, particularly in regard to the mentally handicapped, sometimes start or end an essay with reference to a meal request.

A frequently mentioned instance is that of Johnny Paul Penry, with an IQ less than sixty, who, on hearing of his second last-minute stay of execution, asked if he could still eat his "last" meal—cheeseburgers and french fries.[54] Rickey Ray Rector has been cited by both advocates and opponents of the death penalty, albeit at cross-purposes. After shooting a police officer, he attempted to commit suicide but succeeded only in inflicting severe brain damage, thereby becoming so mentally disabled he did not know what an execution was. For his final meal he requested steak, fried chicken, cherry Kool-Aid, and pecan pie. He left the pecan pie on the side of the tray, however, telling the guards who came to take him to the execution chamber that he was saving it "for later."[55] One blogger writes about seemingly aberrant last meals and eating behavior: "The obvious joke here is that you can't look at some of these requests and not know these guys are retarded."[56] In contrast, an attorney representing a mentally disabled man on death row titles her op-ed piece "What Do We Gain by Taking These Child-Like Lives?"[57] And an editorial in the *Dallas Morning News*[58] concerning Penry and Rector is called "Executing Mentally Impaired Prisoners Is Unjust and Cruel." (In June 2002, the US Supreme court ruled that the execution of mentally disabled people is unconstitutional, violating the Eighth Amendment.)

A trope found in remarks by proponents of the death penalty is the construction of the offender as a "monster." Extravagant food requests or enormous amounts of food—monstrous portions—represent the unfettered appetites of condemned inmates, a lack of restraint also manifested in their crimes and inherent in their character. As the coup de grâce, several justify their position by noting that prisoners on death row for killing people "didn't give their victims a last meal of their choice." One even titles his article "They Didn't Get to Choose Their Last Meals."[59] White supremacist Lawrence Russell Brewer requested a last meal of great quantities of meat, sweets, and soft drinks but ate nothing of what was served him in ridicule of the custom. A Texas state legislator who chaired the Senate Criminal Justice Committee demanded an immediate end to the tradition of providing a special end-of-life meal.[60] "He never gave his victim an opportunity for a last meal," said Senator John Whitmire. "Why in the world are you going to treat him like a celebrity two hours before you execute him? It's wrong to treat a vicious murderer in this fashion. Let him eat the same meal on the chow line as the others."[61]

The custom nevertheless continues in most states, perhaps not surprisingly given food's significance as daily sustenance and its symbolic import. Ancient Egyptians included it for entombed royalty along with other necessities and comforts in the afterlife, adherents of a host of religions from Buddhism to Catholicism to Lucumí offer food and beverage to spirits and saints as a sign of respect and supplication or to seek favors, and some families host a picnic in the cemetery once a year with gifts of food for the deceased. Widely spread, the postburial practice of providing a funerary meal at a reception, usually in the home of the deceased's survivors, focuses on the needs of the living: "Take time to stuff, o mourner. Full stomachs cannot cry."[62]

THE CRUTCH OF RITUAL

Byron Eshelman, former death row chaplain at San Quentin Prison, writes, "Only the ritual of an execution makes it possible to endure. Without it the condemned could not give the expected measure of cooperation to the etiquette of dying. Without it, we who must preside at their deaths could not face the morning of each new execution day. Nor could you."[63]

At the beginning of their film *Last Supper*, Mats Bigert and Lars Bergström call attention to a "paradoxical ritual" in modern executions, that "human mercy and cruelty . . . share the same dinner table."[64] Like the filmmakers, several commentators have puzzled over this, taking divergent, even contradictory, stances. Tony Karon suggests that providing a special last meal might be "to sugarcoat what remains a grim act of violence by the state [executing the criminal] to redress a previous wrong."[65] Focusing on the bureaucratization and routinization of the "new penology" that dehumanizes prisoners turning them into docile automatons, Daniel LaChance contends that the state allows the condemned to choose whatever they wish for a final meal and to speak freely before dying in order to demonstrate that they possess autonomy and agency; as volitional beings who committed heinous crimes of their own free will, they deserve the punishment meted out to them. To sustain the emotional satisfaction required to uphold the death penalty, "The state turns its offenders into self-made monsters."[66] In contrast to this interpretation, Terri J. Gordon proposes that the ritual of the last meal constitutes "both an implicit *call* for forgiveness on the part of the citizens of the state" and "a *demonstration* of forgiveness as well, in that it shows kindness to the condemned and a recognition of their humanity and our shared humanity."[67]

"I always thought of the last meals I prepared as a version of the Last Supper, when Christ knew that he would die the next day," said prison cook Brian Price.[68] Some abolitionists of the death penalty draw upon the crucifixion in pleading for "mercy, forgiveness, and respect for the dignity of life,"[69] while retentionists, calling for retribution, often invoke the "eye for an eye, life for life" passage in Mosaic Law in Exodus 21:22–25. The situation is complicated by the diversity of roles, actors, and scripts in the performance of executions, beginning with the prisoners and the kitchen staff.

A number of inmates have found the offer of a special meal offensive, such as a prisoner described by Johnson[70] who "was horrified by the last-meal ritual, which struck him as barbaric and cruel." On the other hand, before dying, Lawrence Buxton sent word to Texas prison cook Brian Price thanking him for his meal. Patrick Sonnier in Louisiana remarked: "Warden, tell that chef, tell him for me that he did a really great job. . . . And you tell him, warden . . . that I am truly, truly appreciative." Warden Maggio, who earlier had said that the cook was giving "real special attention" to the meal, told Patrick: "He put himself out for you, Sonnier, he really did."[71] Brian Price, who associated the prisoner's last meal with the Lord's Supper, commented,

"I took my job seriously, and it made me feel good that I was able to give the condemned at least a piece of a free world as they remembered it." He continued: "The meal requests were rarely complicated; many prisoners ordered food that they had eaten as children. I think that through their meals, they were seeking a small bit of comfort and courtesy. Food can take you back to a better time in your life, and it gave me comfort to give these dying men and women some comfort in their last hours."[72]

Other participants in the drama of execution include the warden and the execution team, while members of the public, for whom capital punishment is an abstract symbol,[73] make inferences from the little information reported by the media. Former warden Donald Cabana maintains that the last meal is a welcome distraction in having to cope with putting someone to death: "I think you'd feel somewhat naked walking out and there was no last meal issue to talk about. Even if he doesn't want a last meal, you still have to talk to him about that. . . . That takes time away from thinking."[74] During the final five or six hours, two officers are required to distract and comfort the prisoner as part of the task of "getting the man dead."[75] This includes a steady stream of conversation and even eating with him. "Shoot, one of 'em actually asked what to order and we didn't know what to order so we ordered McDonald's food for 'im. He ate Big Macs and I ate Big Macs, you know."[76] Given the ambivalence over the death penalty in the United States,[77] members of the public either develop a sympathetic identification with prisoners by recognizing their common humanity through eating and coming to terms with death, or they infer that "monstrous" meal portions represent an uncontrollable, monstrous character justifying death for the safety of all.[78]

In commenting on the etiquette of dying and the ritual of execution, former death row chaplain Byron Eshelman remarked, "No matter how you think you feel about capital punishment, no matter how you imagine you would face the legal giving or taking of life, you would meet the reality of it by holding tightly to the crutch of ritual."[79] One scholar asks, "What purpose does all this routinization and ceremony serve?" The answer, he says, lies in the "loss of tolerance for suffering," and hence the need for a "carefully groomed image of humaneness": "The modern orchestration of death lends assurance that everything is in order, everything is humane and civilized and that we aren't, after all, barbarians."[80]

When executions in America were carried out in small towns and rural areas before the advent of a centralized state prison, the condemned and the local sheriff were in close contact. Not surprisingly the prisoner's last meal became transformed into a special one before dying. To extend food to another is a profoundly human act, a kindness that symbolically acknowledges a shared humanity. Whether the offer of food was intended as hospitality, a method of calming the prisoner, or a coping mechanism helping relieve the officer of stress or guilt, the fact remains that by the late nineteenth century, the tradition of a custom meal was firmly entrenched in America and often reported in newspapers. As former warden Cabana noted, this and other customs and rituals became incorporated into official procedures, which "helps the warden and the prison staff get on through the damn execution process because you've got things you have to tend to. . . . It is not something that any individual designed. It's kind of come together over centuries."[81]

After executions were conducted in private with few witnesses, prisons disseminated scant information to the newspapers beyond the name of the condemned, the instrument of death, and the person's dying words and last food requests, which define the event for readers. Aware of little about the ritual of execution beyond the final comments and food choice, the public nevertheless makes inferences or projects feelings and constructs opinions in opposition to or in support of the death penalty. Generally overlooked and sometimes misinterpreted, the ceremonial last meal confirms Margaret Visser's observation in *Much Depends on Dinner*[82]: "Food is never just something to eat"—whether for the living or, in this instance, for the dying.

On death row or in the general population, incarcerated individuals rarely have much choice regarding what they eat. A case in point is the Bureau of Prison's effort to ban pork products, foods that administrators wrongly insisted prisoners disliked. I take up the subject in the next chapter, which also examines public reactions, prejudices, and nationalism.

Chapter 6

PORK BANS REAL AND RUMORED

Fear, Bigotry, and Lost Identity

"Finally, the Government Has Decided to Eliminate Pork—from the Menu in Federal Prisons" proclaims a headline in the *Washington Post*.[1] Lisa Rein, the reporter, begins her account, "The nation's pork producers are in an uproar after the federal government abruptly removed bacon, pork chops, pork links, ham and all other pig products from the national menu for 206,000 federal inmates."

Many of the 572 readers' remarks appended to Rein's article expressed incredulity over the ban, while some criticized the move, others approved the decision, and yet others attributed the interdiction to Muslim machinations. More articles followed as the controversy heated up. Another 1,840 comments appeared at the end of six more reports.[2]

Dubiously claimed by the Bureau of Prisons (BOP) to be based on a survey of inmates' food preferences, the prohibition of pork lasted a little over a week before the agency reversed itself. The bureau voiced blatant exaggerations, errors, and misconceptions during that brief period. At the same time, rumors of other bans circulating in the United States and several European countries promoted culinary nationalism and strident opposition to globalism, migration, and the influx of religious traditions that prohibit the consumption of pork.[3] Politicians railed against restrictions on pork-based foods, claiming that the very essence of national identity was under attack. Public comments warned of threats to individual freedom, personal food habits, and sense of self.

PULLED PORK: THE BUREAU OF PRISON'S BAN
AND ITS REVERSAL

The BOP not only feeds more than 200,000 individuals but also serves as the principal model for many of the 1,719 state prisons that house approximately

1,300,000 inmates.[4] Not surprisingly, then, the agency's intention to pull pork from its menus garnered attention in the news. Lisa Rein published three articles on the subject in 2015. The first (9 October) announces the prohibition, the second (16 October) deals with its reversal, and the third (26 October) focuses on the BOP's admission that the ban was "an error."

Rein's lead-in remark in the first article, that the government had abruptly removed "all pig products," is overstated, given what the prison bureau's assistant director, Newton E. Kendig, said that Rein later quotes (26 October 2015), namely, that it was pork roast that was removed. On the other hand, a spokesperson for the agency, Edmond Ross, is quoted in Rein's first article as referring broadly to "pork." Ross mentioned, without specifics, that the federal prison bill of fare had dropped to only two pork products during the past two years, which was not true.

Speaking on behalf of the National Pork Producers Council, a trade association, Dave Warner quipped, "I find it hard to believe that a survey would have found a majority of any population saying, 'No thanks, I don't want any bacon,'" although bacon had not been served for many years (but was available at the commissary for inmates to purchase).[5] He promised to find out how the decision was made and to resolve the issue. He added that pork is both healthful and economical.

Ross, representing the bureau, had initially contended that the annual surveys of inmates' food preferences indicated pork had lost its luster. He then added that "we were paying more than what we'd like to pay" for it. Last, Ross said, "People are more health conscious these days," that is, "Some people choose to be vegetarian or vegan. That's their preference."[6]

Speaking in the interests of the Council on American-Islamic Relations, Ibrahim Hooper said, "In general we welcome the change because it's facilitating the accommodation of Muslim inmates." He predicted, however, "It will stoke the fires of Islamophobia based on the usual conspiracy theories."[7] This indeed occurred, as evident in readers' responses to news articles about the federal ban and the outrage of politicians in Europe reacting to rumors of institutional pork restrictions in their countries.

Within nine days the BOP reversed its policy to eliminate pork products from prisons. It put pork roast back on the menu a few hours after Charles E. Grassley, a Republican senator from Iowa and then the chair of the Senate's Committee on the Judiciary, sent a letter dated 15 October to the bureau's director. He wrote, "The pork industry is responsible for 547,800 jobs, which creates $22.3 billion in personal incomes and contributes $39 billion to the gross domestic product." He contended that removing pork from federal prisons would "have consequences on the livelihoods of American citizens who work in the pork industry." Grassley's warning was overly dramatic in that the bureau spent only $2,975,685 for pork out of a total of nearly $240,000,000 in food expenses, or only one and one-quarter percent.[8]

Ross, the bureau's spokesman who had announced the ban, did not explain the reversal of it: "I'm not cleared to say anything, and I don't have answers for you."[9] Either Ross or the article's author erred, for Rein remarks that according to Ross, "In the past two years, the menu had dropped from bacon, pork chops and sausages to just one dish with the ingredient: pork roast, the entree now back on federal prison dining halls." In fact, more items than chops and sausages had been available and several pork dishes, including roast, were on the list of offerings.

Senator Grassley was so irked on learning that pork had been banned by the bureau that he demanded copies of the surveys and responses dating back as far as prisoners had indicated losing a taste for pork, the sum incurred to conduct each survey, and the bureau's cost of pork compared to beef, chicken, and soy products. Newton E. Kendig, Assistant Director, Health Services Division, responded to Grassley in a letter dated 23 October 2015.

Kendig replied to the senator that the menu was based on such variables as "inmate eating preferences, operational impact, product pricing, and nutritional content." Kendig also wrote, "We re-evaluated the inmate food preference surveys and costs that were considered when the Bureau made the decision to remove pork roast. This re-evaluation led us to the conclusion that the decision to remove pork roast was an error, which has since been corrected." In an email to the reporter, the bureau's spokesman, Ross, said that in addition to the inmate food preferences, the ban was based on such other factors as "safety and security, the health and welfare of the inmate population, and the cost of our overall operations." Ross did not explain how safety and security were connected to pork. Rein titled her last article "The (Half-Baked) Story behind the Pork Ban in Federal Prisons."

In regard to economy and cost reduction, Assistant Director Kendig wrote to Senator Grassley that "product pricing" was a factor. The pork council's spokesman Warner rebutted, "We cost a lot less than beef," a claim supported by the Bureau of Labor Statistics.[10] Furthermore, the United States had recently enjoyed record pork production, causing wholesale prices to drop 40 percent.[11] Warner also challenged Ross and Kendig's claim that pork is unhealthful. "We're nutritious," he countered. The US Department of Agriculture's calorie count and percentage of nutrients in various meats lends support to Warner's statement in that pork loin is nearly as lean as skinless, boneless chicken breasts and contains almost as many grams of protein in contrast to a boneless rib eye filet.[12] An underlying assumption held by prison administrators seems to be that pork cuts are necessarily fatty and of low nutritional quality, a belief that still circulates in public comments despite the breeding of lean hogs since the mid-twentieth century.[13]

In defending the pork ban, Ross added that some of the inmates are vegetarians or vegans, but he did not indicate how many prisoners restrict their diet in this way. According to a CBS news survey concerning "how and where America eats," however, "only 2 percent of Americans consider themselves vegetarians,"[14] a figure unlikely to warrant the exclusion of pork or other meat from prison menus. In addition, the federal prison system offers a "common fare" program for inmates requesting a religious diet that contains no pork and provides a choice of meat and nonflesh entrées at each meal.[15]

Ross also noted that "safety and security" are of great importance in prisons, which is certainly true. Inmates might challenge institutional dominance with defiant behavior. Potential weapons with which to attack staff and other prisoners include meal trays, plates, corndog sticks, chicken drumsticks, plastic wrap, hot sauce, and scalding liquids. Ross did not explain how this factor relates to banning pork, however. Neither did anyone elaborate on "welfare" as a justification for the pork ban. Nor did bureau officials discuss why "operational impact" warranted banning pork from the menu.

A major reason cited by the BOP for its ban on pork was alleged to be inmate ratings on food surveys. Prisoners' responses were erroneously interpreted, however. "Why keep pushing food that people don't want to eat?" asked Edmond Ross on behalf of the bureau. "Pork has been the lowest-rated food by inmates for several years," he said. This statement, in particular, prompted an incredulous Senator Grassley to demand copies of the surveys. It is not uncommon for the federal BOP and some state prisons to distribute a questionnaire to learn what foods inmates desire, which items in the current diet plan appeal most, and what selections prisoners despise; the goal is to reduce waste, complaints, and unrest. The bureau's survey instruments sent to Senator Grassley are dated 21 November 2012, 16 January 2014, and 26 January–4 February 2015. The 2015 survey states in part, "Your input will help us determine your food preferences and determine if changes need to be made to the National Menu for FY 2016."

The three surveys listing inmate responses contain the notation "*Denotes pork." The only item so designated for 2014 and 2015 was "*Pork Roast." For 2012, "*Pork Roast," "*Pork Barbecue," and "*Pork Chop" appear. Not acknowledged is that "Chili Dogs" and "Kielbasa" are also on the survey for 2012; these items and "Breakfast Sausage" show up on the list for 2014, and "Hot Dogs" and "Kielbasa" are mentioned in 2015. Hot dogs, bologna, and kielbasa are processed meat typically composed of pork to which seasonings, corn syrup, monosodium glutamate, starch, sodium nitrite, and other ingredients are added.

Contrary to the assertion by the bureau's representative, Ross, therefore, pork had not been reduced to one or even two items in the previous three years.

Rather than lacking a desire for pork, two-thirds or more of the approximately thirty-seven thousand respondents in 2012 and 2014 marked a strong preference for chili dogs, pork chops, pork roast, pork BBQ, and kielbasa. On the other hand, the majority greatly disliked fifteen items listed on the 2015 survey, all but two of which featured soy or tofu, such as soy beef stew (72.2 percent), soy sloppy joe (71.6 percent), soy chili (70.8 percent), and soy enchilada (70.8 percent).[16] The use of soy is celebrated in some quarters for being cheap, ecologically responsible, and more healthful than a flesh diet. A number of prisoners insist they cannot tolerate a soy-based diet, however, such as one introduced in Illinois in January 2003, which resulted in complaints by more than two hundred inmates of digestive turmoil, including severe constipation, diarrhea, vomiting, and abdominal pain as well as skin ailments, endocrine disruption (enlarged breasts), and thyroid disorders.[17] The increased reliance on soy in many state prisons grows out of efforts at cost cutting and the contention that it is more healthful than meat, although not in the large quantities in which it sometimes is served.[18]

In sum, none of the claims justified the ban on pork. Over the years there were more pork items on the federal prison bill of fare than acknowledged.[19] The most healthful pork dish was the one the bureau sought to eliminate, for pork roast does not contain the sodium, nitrites, sugar, and other ingredients added to processed meat. Because of a surge in production in 2015, pork prices had dropped 40 percent while beef costs rose owing to shortages. Rather than disparaged for several years, surveys indicate that pork was greatly enjoyed; the preparations most loathed were in fact the numerous soy-based ones. The upshot is that, given the brouhaha, the bureau "re-evaluated" the survey results, canceled the ban, and retained pork roast on the menu along with processed pork items that might be tasty but are less healthful.

The public's responses to news of the ban ranged from incredulity to approval to denunciation. People voiced bigotry, conspiracy theories, traditional beliefs and assumptions, and rumors. Some implied culinary nationalism, which also is manifested in European attitudes toward allegations of pork disappearing from public institutions.

IN A PIG'S EYE: SKEPTICISM, SARCASM, AND ISLAMOPHOBIA

Close reading and analysis indicate that the posts doubting the bureau's explanations for withdrawing pork from the menu fall into six main categories. First, several comments are sarcastic. One response to news about the reinstatement of pig meat reads, "Finally a plan to get rid of the pork in government and now its [sic] ruined!" Another: "Life without parole yes, but life without bacon . . . well THAT is cruel and unusual punishment." A third resembles a blues song: "Ain't no pork up on the table, ain't no pork up in the pan, but you better not complain boy, you'll get in trouble with the man." A high school cafeteria "lunch lady" writes that the students love carnitas sprinkled on nachos, "pepperoni pizza, and pulled pork BBQ. I guess that's what keeps them out of Federal prisons." Another states, "Why bother with any food that might taste good, provide a small measure of enjoyment, or remind a prisoner of something from the recent, or far distant past . . . when they were FREE citizens. This is just insanity by this administration."

Incredulity typifies a large number of the 2,412 responses regarding the ban. "This makes no sense. None," writes one poster. "Cons don't want bacon? Ribs? Pork chops? They're becoming vegetarians? Come on," writes another. Contends a third: "It appears to me they were going to cut down on the food value fed to prisoners and hope the public did not find out."

The posters' skepticism originates in four principal experiences or assumptions. One is that the responder enjoys consuming pork him/herself, for example, "I love it," and "I love pork and I would not like it taken off the menu for good." A second basis is the commentators' inference founded on alleged observation or general knowledge, such as, "The fact they make deep fried, bacon wrapped bacon at county fairs tells you something," and "The collective opinion on food for all prisoners in federal lockup is going to look a lot like the collective opinion of the general population, and bacon is always a winner." Third, some posters cite (erroneously) the presumed race or ethnicity of the prisoners: "1/3 of the prison population is black, 1/3 . . . is Hispanic and 1/3 is White. All of those groups are known for their love of pork and pork products."[20] Finally, a few posters invoke the notion of gendered eating preferences, such as, "I don't believe that many prisoners object to these foods [bacon, hot dogs, pork loin, etc.]. Few men don't love at least some of these foods."[21]

In addition to employing sarcasm or finding the ban and its rationale far-fetched, some who criticized the bureau's claims challenged the allegation of cost on the basis of their shopping background. One individual writes, "Pork is still relatively cheap compared to beef. If any meat were to be removed from the menu because of its high cost, it should have been beef." Another insists, "Cost prohibitive? Last time I looked, pork was but a fraction of the cost of beef at the market!" A third disbeliever writes, "Clearly, this is a completely transparent lie: pork is HALF the cost of beef. The claim that this is being done for cost reasons is 100% baloney."

A fourth set of comments questions the new policy from a gustatory perspective. "I have to agree with the pork industry spokesman [Dave Warner]—the idea that people in prison don't like bacon or barbecue is difficult to believe." Remarks another person, "Why did they drop bacon? Are they seriously suggesting that prisoners don't like bacon? Who doesn't like bacon?" A third writes, "Stupid policy by the BOP to begin with. Prisoners don't like bacon? Give me a break."

The reference to bacon, often thought of as the quintessential pork product, originates in the mistaken impression left by Rein's lead-in sentence in her first essay and her quote from the trade association's spokesman, Warner, that this is one of the pork items that had been dropped. As posters note, bacon is especially popular outside prison walls. According to the North American Meat Institute, in 2013 meat companies in the United States processed 112 million hogs yielding 23.2 billion pounds of pork of which approximately 60 percent was turned into such products as bacon and sausage.[22] Even many ex-vegetarians joke that bacon is "the gateway meat," claiming its aroma, texture, and flavor caused their recidivism.[23]

Many of the skeptical remarks, however, involved a fifth and more insidious charge, one voicing anti-Muslim sentiments and political intrigue. "To ban what probably is one of most prisoners' favorite foods such as bacon—for what is obviously based on catering to a preferred religion is WRONG. These prisoners have so little to enjoy or look forward to in prison they should at least be allowed some tasty food. I'm not only appalled by this obvious catering to radical Islam, but also the LIES that this agency is promoting." Others write, "This is solely a ploy to appease Muslims, nothing else"; "Could it be they're just rolling over for the Muslims?" and "They are doing this to cater solely to Muslims. They aren't even doing it for the Jewish inmate's [sic] benefit, just Muslims. Why are we catering to Muslims?"

Much of the animosity engendered by news of the pork ban was directed toward President Barack Obama. "I think Obama once again reveals himself as a cultural Muslim," reads one post. Another contends, "What this is about is letting a few Muslims decide what everyone else in Federal prisons will eat. I'm surprised Obama hasn't banned pork for all Americans." A third states, "Muslims are the favored group in the Obama administration, and that is because Barack Obama is a cultural Muslim himself, and is personally in sympathy with Muslim goals and beliefs. We see this proven over and over and over again, we need to start telling some hard truths here."

Following several anti-Muslim rants, Rein added her own post to her final article. "I'm told over and over [by bureau spokespersons] that Muslims did not ask for the ban," she writes. "They don't need to; the prisons provide them with a nonpork diet and there are many alternatives." Moreover, a Pew survey of religious affiliations of prisoners in the United States indicates that 71 percent are Protestant, 19 percent are Catholic, 7 percent are Muslim, and 3 percent are Jewish.[24] In other words, the number of those who might require a kosher or halal diet is too low to significantly affect the bureau's food preference survey.

In opposition to charges that Obama is Muslim or supports Sharia law, a comment appended to Rein's first article is larded with sarcasm. The post reads: "He [Obama] eats pork. He drinks beer. He supports same-sex marriage and abortion rights. Sounds just like a Muslim to me!" A Google search on "Obama eating pork" results in dozens of images of the president devouring a variety of products, including bacon, hot dogs, ribs, and chops. In addition, Valois Cafeteria on Chicago's South Side, a frequent haunt of Obama's when he was an Illinois senator, posted a sign in its window concerning "President Obama's Favorites"; two of the six breakfasts feature a choice of bacon or sausage.[25]

Fears of terrorism lay behind a few of the charges that the BOP was appeasing Muslims through diet. "This is yet another sign the government is catering to the terrorists rather than fighting them," writes one poster. Another contends, " 'Islamophobia'? Muslims brutally mass murdered 100 peace activists yesterday. But we should not be afraid?" By early December of 2015 when the bureau announced its pork ban, Americans had already suffered several terrorist attacks, such as the destruction of the World Trade Center on 11 September 2001 by the extremist group al-Qaeda, which killed or injured nearly nine thousand people; the mass shooting at Fort Hood on 5 November 2009 by an Army major who had militant Islamic convictions; and the targeting of a social gathering at the San Bernardino County Department of Public Health on 2 December 2015. The last event linked terrorism and food in a fabricated news report claiming that Syed Farook and his wife, Tashfeen Malik, who killed fourteen and wounded twenty-two persons, were incensed that bacon and pork sausage were served at the staff Christmas Party.[26]

A BONE TO PICK: CRITICIZING THE FOOD OR THE PRISONERS

Comments regarding the bureau's pork interdiction also manifested three long-standing examples of belief and folk knowledge about pork and prisons.

By "folk knowledge," I mean "the everyday, taken-for-granted understandings that shape people's perceptions, thinking, actions, and reactions to events and situations."[27]

One traditional notion is that ingesting meat, in this instance pork, defiles the temple of the body. "Pork is disgusting. Prisons don't need it," contends a poster. Another insists, "Pork is really bad for you. Pigs aren't really clean animals. They eat garbage and other disgusting things. So why eat that nasty stuff? Feed the good inmates whatever they want and feed the bad inmates bad stuff." The underlying principle appears to be that of symbolic osmosis or magical transference,[28] that is, the belief that the characteristics of a food source are transferred to the eater. The notion that the pig is a filthy animal and its flesh therefore abhorrent has persisted for an unusually long time, dating from at least the first millennium BCE.[29] Swine have gained this reputation in part because they are scavengers, root in the dirt in search of food, and wallow in mud in order to cool off.

A second belief invokes the principle of less eligibility, which dates from England in the nineteenth century. Prison dietary theory and practice stipulated that a criminal should not be fed better than a pauper in the workhouse, just as a pauper ought not eat better than the poorest honest laborer. "The logic was simple: the poor labourer might be tempted by the better living standards of the work-house, to give up his job and throw himself and family on the rates [taxes levied on local residents to aid the 'deserving' poor]; and the honest pauper might in turn be tempted to try his hand at criminal ways."[30] The omnipresent less eligibility concept, then, demanded a reduction in prison diet because the public was displeased with the kind and amount of food served to convicts. Many still are.

As one commentator writes, "No prisoner should ever eat better than a single student in the US." Another contends, "The prisoners eat better than I do." Remarking on the image of a pork roast accompanying an article about the ban,[31] one individual writes, "That plate of food looked wonderful to me. . . . prisoners should be thankful they're in a USA Jail. . . . many American Homeless people would love a plate of that food." (ellipses in the original). A fourth person exclaims, "WHERE IN THE WORLD does the government get off worrying about what convicted felons want to eat? How about this, for real economy and health: beans and rice, the same food many of our poor are destined to eat every night . . . and they didn't harm anyone or thing." The writer concludes, "I am sick of this concern for the well-being of our illegals, criminals, and others and ignoring of our children, and working poor."

Among traditional attitudes, the third and the dominant one is that of demanding harsh punishment for those behind bars. As Cyrus Naim

contends, in the United States, "prisoners are, as a whole, hated by the public."[32] Long stigmatized and viewed as among the worst of humankind, the
incarcerated should suffer. "Prison is completely pointless if prisoners are
even asked their preferences for food, religious or otherwise," contends one
poster. "They should have only one choice . . . take it or leave it. That's the
whole point of prison surely." Insists another: "If you're in prison, why do you
get a say in what you get fed? You're a criminal and a prisoner." A third opines,
"Pork lost its appeal???? who cares—feed them whatever and quit worrying
about their so called rights—THEY ARE IN PRISON FOR A REASON."

Several posters urge a sparse, unappetizing, unhealthful diet as retribution
for violating society's laws. Exhorts one person: "They are in PRISON. Feed
them bread & water and put their asses out on street road-gangs." A second
proposes: "How 'bout we cut out the meat all together? Rice, water and some
raisins to stave off the scurvy." A third recommends "Water to drink. Oatmeal
for breakfast. Bread for lunch. Gruel for dinner."

In elaborating on the use of food as added punishment for those who are
incarcerated, another writer challenges the presence of meat in any prison
meal and asks why the government would "pander to food preferences for
any convicted prisoner? Hopefully, one day soon the USA is going to wake
up to how soft it has become." The last remark resonates with the findings
of an NBC television poll in the 1990s "that 82 percent of Americans say
life in prison is too easy."[33] According to this mindset, food should be part
and parcel of the "pains of imprisonment"[34]: the deprivations, frustrations,
and degradations of incarceration. In contrast, however, the pork council's
spokesman Dave Warner contended, "For people who are incarcerated, we
understand that they're denied certain rights and freedoms, but we don't
think bacon should be one of them."[35]

WURST CASES: RUMORS OF OTHER PORK BANS

In the years 2013 to 2016, rumors swirled around pork in other contexts.[36]
They fall into two broad categories. One group asserts that several food
vendors in the United States and Canada have banished pork. A second
set involves the disappearance of pork products from school cafeterias in
Western Europe.

In early January 2015, Chipotle removed from its menu carnitas, the
braised, shredded pork, as a filling or topping for burritos or tacos at about
a third of its outlets. A spokesperson for Chipotle later reassured tweeters
that pork was withdrawn only temporarily (and indeed was soon back on the

menu) owing to a lack of the meat because a major supplier had violated the restaurant's policy of treating the animals ethically. Internet rumors quickly spread after the initial announcement of curtailment, however. Commentators on Twitter attributed Chipotle's action to Muslim pressure. Some tweets threatened to boycott the chain restaurant: "Hope U close down 4 appeasing Muslims[.] I will NEVER eat at your restaurant Again! Neither will friends." Several also imply culinary nationalism, such as "They have banned pork for Muslims. Doesn't matter if Americans like pork. Spend your $ where they care."

Rumors in March 2015 claimed that Target had become "Islamic Sharia-Compliant" by designating specific cash registers as free of pork and alcohol purchases. Allegedly, signs at checkout read, "Attention customs: If your order contains pork or alcohol products, we respectfully ask that you choose another lane." Three years earlier a similar notice was supposedly posted at a single location of Wegmans Food Markets. Reactions to the newer target of the repurposed rumor were similar to those tweeted in regard to Chipotle, but with several additions. One focused on the anticipated frustration of having to wait in a long line of customers whose purchases included pork or alcohol. Another, antagonistic toward "bowing to Muslims," emphasized that America was "founded on Christianity" and, in apparently unintended irony, the country is "the land of freedom."[37]

In May 2016 a fabricated news item declared that the 4,600 outlets of Tim Hortons in the United States and Canada would stop selling pork because of Muslim demand. Two years previously, factual albeit sensationalist reports appeared stating that Subway, the world's largest fast-food restaurant with nearly thirty-four thousand outlets,[38] had removed bacon and ham from stores in Great Britain, offering halal meat instead owing to "'strong demand' from Muslims."[39] Beginning in 2007 the Subway chain has permitted new franchises to cater their menu to local tastes (which McDonald's also does), such as areas with large immigrant populations; this affects about 10 percent of the 1,500 stores in England and Ireland. The motivation is pecuniary, catering to prospective consumers in order to maximize profits. Reactions to removing pork products resemble those mentioned above regarding other vendors: "How stupid"; "I will never buy a Subway again"; and "What the hell is happening to Britain??? You are slowly but surely relinquishing control of your country to nonnatives, but are so bound by the lunatic P.C. [political correctness] brigade that no one is doing anything to stop it!"

Reclaiming and perpetuating culinary hegemony appears to be the goal of some politicians in several European nations and cities that have seen a large influx of migrants on the one hand, and on the other, a seeming decline in pork offerings in the cafeterias of daycare centers and schools. In early March 2016, a British tabloid's headline announced, "Germany Bans Sausages," implying that the country had banished wurst and possibly other pork entirely. Daniel Günther, a politician, had noted that pork appeared to be gradually diminishing in public institutions; he extrapolated that it was being barred because of Muslims taking offense at its presence. Apparently Günther did not consider the growing trend toward a less meat-centric diet in some quarters or, through a policy similar to the "common fare" option of American BOP, the provisioning of children with lunches that their beliefs permit them to consume.

Members of Chancellor Angela Merkel's Christian Democratic Union party began fighting to keep pork on the menu, insisting that it is a crucial element in German culture. "The protection of minorities—including for religious reasons—must not mean that the majority is overruled in their free decision by ill-conceived consideration," said the politician Günther, aware that Germany had offered sanctuary to more than one million refugees fleeing Syria. He argued, "The consumption of pork belongs to our culture." He contended, "We . . . don't want the majority having to refrain from pork."[40] A plan to introduce mandatory pork in state-run canteens, schools, and prisons[41] was later rejected, however.[42]

The fight over food and national identity also occurred in France, as reported in September and October 2015. Right-wing politicians and pro-testors warred against real or rumored menu changes in the nation's schools, insisting that if they are to be truly French, then Muslim or Jewish children must eat roast pork. The mayors of several towns announced that a thirty-year history of providing nonpork alternatives on lunch plates would cease; children whose families do not eat pork for religious reasons would be offered nothing but the side dishes accompanying ham pasta bake, roast pork, and Strasbourg sausage.[43] On 21 September a primary school in Auxerre, Burgundy, required children who did not eat pork to wear a red disk, while those abstaining from all meat displayed a yellow one. A local council member denounced the practice, which lasted only one day.[44]

In Denmark where a traditional Christmas dinner often features pork, potatoes, cabbage, and rice pudding, a long-standing "meatball war" (*fri-kadellekrigen*) peaked in the summer of 2013 with a debate over whether or not public institutions should eliminate pork in deference to religious proscriptions. One side claimed that cherished Danish values were under assault from multiculturalism. Opponents argued that the situation did not pose a serious threat (it was estimated that only about 30 out of 1,719 institutions excluded pork from the menu). On 18 January 2016, the City Council of Randers approved a proposal by the Danish People's Party, voting sixteen to fifteen to require that all municipal institutions serve pork products. This included *frikadeller*, a meatball traditionally made of pork and beef, considered by some to be a cherished symbol of national identity. Regarding the vote on behalf of cultural protectionism through alimentation, a councilman said, "We will ensure that Danish children and youth can have pork in the future."[45]

In another instance of food fights, accounts spread in emails and on social media sites such as Facebook and Twitter in 2013 and 2014 that the mayor of Ath, Belgium, had adamantly refused the demand of Muslim parents to abolish pork, the most popular meat on the country's tables, from school cafeterias. "That no more than other nations, the Belgians are not willing to give up their identity, their culture," he reportedly stated. When informed of the rumor, however, the mayor denounced the alleged statements as "a lie," insisting that the presence of pork in school canteens had never been an issue. According to Snopes,[46] the noted source for fact-checking urban legends, variants of the rumor appeared in Quebec, Canada, and in Maryborough, Victoria, Australia.

THE MEAT OF THE MATTER: PORK IN CUISINE AND CONSCIOUSNESS

Pork is the most widely eaten meat around the globe; it accounts for more than 40 percent of world meat consumption, considerably greater than poultry at 34 percent, beef at 21 percent, and goat and mutton at less than 5 percent.[47] Pork is consequential in American culture and consciousness, as apparent in figure 6.1., and it symbolizes ethnic, regional, or national identity to many.[48] National Pig Day, started by two sisters in 1972, occurs annually on 1 March as homage to hogs, celebrating pigs' importance to Americans. Recall also the highly favorable survey responses of federal inmates, the incredulous remarks by readers of articles about federal prisons banishing pork from the menu, and comments by Dave Warner representing the National Pork Producers Council, who could not believe that most survey respondents would reject bacon.

Historically, pork was "the most important meat on American tables"[49] and up to three times more commonly consumed than in Europe. In many parts of the country, and particularly the Deep South, bacon "invariably appeared at every meal."[50] "The United States of America might properly be called the great Hog-eating Confederacy, or the Republic of Porkdom,"

Figure 6.1 Rachel the Piggy Bank, mascot of Pike Place Market, Seattle, Washington, in place since 1986 for donations to support social services; legend has it that rubbing her snout while making a donation will bring you good luck. Photo by the author.

contended the physician John S. Wilson in *Godey's Lady's Book*.[51] In many areas, continued Wilson, "so far as meat is concerned, it is fat bacon and pork, fat bacon and pork only, and that continually morning, noon, and night, for all classes, sexes, ages, and conditions," not to mention the widespread use of lard to fry breads and vegetables. Whether originating in the United States or elsewhere, American folk speech offers more than two dozen swine expressions, for instance, "clumsy as a hog on ice," "I'd as soon kiss a pig," "to make a silk purse out of a sow's ear," "that'll happen when pigs can fly," "casting pearls before swine," "happy as a pig in clover," "as useless as teats on a boar hog," "bringing home the bacon," "know as much about something as a hog knows about Sunday," "you can put lipstick on a pig, but it's still a pig," "slippery as a greased pig," and "don't try to teach a pig to sing; it doesn't work and only annoys the pig."

My queries to people about what food is quintessentially American typically meet with the response "burgers," either hamburgers or cheeseburgers. In 2015, however, per capita consumption of meat in the United States consisted of fifty pounds of pork, only four pounds less than beef in its many forms, including ground.[52] Usually associated with breakfast, bacon appears as a main ingredient or flavoring in scores of recipes on foodnetwork.com and similar sites—from soups, stews, and chowders to breads and muffins, salads, sandwiches, and even butter, nuts, oatmeal, hot sauce, chocolate, and ice cream sundaes. Testifying to the meat's popularity, a restaurant's bacon bar in Southern California offers eleven types to go (including garlic Parmesan, maple, apple pie, and habanero), and a food truck boasts that it is "where everything is made with bacon." The Wendy's burger chain began selling the Baconator burger in 2007, with six slices of bacon, and in 2015 added bacon fries and a pulled pork sandwich. Applebee's in 2014 touted the Triple Hog Dare Ya sandwich, consisting of a ciabatta bun loaded with bacon, ham, and pulled pork, which proved an instant hit. In 2019, a California woman won a "bacon internship" sponsored by Farmer Boys, devoting a full day to tasting and rating the restaurant chain's bacon dishes.[53]

"The manufactured controversy" of the federal pork ban "is symptomatic of rising Islamophobia," said Ibrahim Hooper, a spokesman for the Council on American-Islamic Relations.[54] Two important consequences relevant to anti-Muslim feelings emerge from the reactions and rumors about pork bans. One is anxiety over the possible disruption of personal alimentation. The other repercussion is the political exploitation of specific foods as symbols of national identity.

Many comments about the proscription of pork in prisons express anti-Muslim sentiment, and some voice fears of attacks on fundamental American values as well as the prospects of terrorism. They criticize the preferential treatment accorded a different diet based on a religion that risks "our freedom" by "letting a few Muslims decide what everyone else . . . will eat." Similar arguments and attitudes regarding Muslims appear also in comments about the alleged removal or diminishment of pork in fast-food restaurants. Distressed to think they might be denied a preferred food and eating routine that construct and convey their personhood, people threaten to boycott these establishments and go elsewhere. "I want ham and bacon, not turkey products. No-one is going to dictate what I eat. I'm voting with my feet and suggest everyone does the same." Implying an attack on his or her personal food habits, another individual writes, "I'm not against people coming to live . . . [here] but when it affects our values and beliefs it really frustrates me[;] why should we not be allowed to eat pork and bacon in Subway like we always have done. I will only eat where I can find food I like."

The second ramification is that for some politicians in Europe who oppose immigration and multiculturalism, any hint of pork's removal from public institutions, for whatever reason, is an attack on the character and distinctiveness of their nation-states (or "imagined communities," in the words of Benedict Anderson).[55] "The consumption of pork belongs to our culture,"

Germans are told. To be truly French, one must eat pork roast even if one's religion proscribes it. Being Danish means consuming pork meatballs. Realizing that a way to peoples' hearts and minds is through their stomachs, politicians have appealed to national identity by referring to what has great immediacy to individuals, namely, food as a fundamental source of pleasure, comfort, sustenance, and selfhood. They have appropriated it, using it to symbolize a collective or contested national identity in an era of growing neoconservatism, antiglobalism, nativist movements, and political and cultural isolationism.

In conclusion, rumors like "legends are richly evocative of society's fears, hopes, anxieties, and prejudices, and folklorists decode these narratives to reveal and analyze the cultural attitudes expressed within," writes Trevor Blank.[56] The main ingredients for concocting rumors are credulity, general uncertainty, importance, and personal anxiety, particularly during periods of major societal change, observes Gary Alan Fine.[57] From teenagers to President Donald J. Trump, increasingly more Americans eschew legitimate news sources and obtain their information à la carte from a menu of opinion blogs, tabloid headlines, hyperpartisan sites, emails, cell phone texts, Facebook, tweets, and retweets.[58] Fabricated news, unsupported claims, and "alternative facts" have proliferated. In addition, while in office, the forty-fifth US president stated many times, "I want to be unpredictable, because, you know, we need unpredictability."[59] Trump promulgated erratic policies that created fear, uncertainty, and doubt.[60] "Holy shitfuck. I can't even believe I'm actually still living in the United States," writes one commentator regarding an article about anti-Sharia bills proposed by several states.[61] Recent rumormongering blames the influx of refugees from Muslim-majority countries for threatening to alter the culinary profile of Western nations in prisons, schools, and restaurants and to interfere with individuals' personal food systems important to defining their identity. The growing presence of social unrest and political debates is a recipe for more rumormongering, some of which likely will be food-centric.

Opposition to consuming meat, not just pork, has a centuries-old history in Western countries. Adversaries have opted for a "natural diet" for reasons of health, the environment, and morality. Vegetarianism is an element in Mary Wollstonecraft Shelley's iconic novel about Frankenstein. It also figured largely in the life and diet of her spouse, Percy Shelley, as I explain in the next chapter.

Chapter 7

MARY SHELLEY'S NIGHTMARE AND PERCY SHELLEY'S DREAM

"It was on a dreary night of November. . . ." Thus begins a chapter of *Frankenstein; or, The Modern Prometheus* by Mary Wollstonecraft Godwin Shelley (1797–1851). She describes Victor Frankenstein's act of creating a being and of his reacting immediately with "breathless horror and disgust" when he saw it move. A nightmare that Mary suffered in June 1816 inspired the chapter.

In her "waking dream," recalled Mary (figure 7.1), "I saw the pale student of unhallowed arts kneeling beside the thing he had put together." This "hideous phantasm of a man stretched out" and, beginning to show "signs of life," continued to "haunt her," she writes in the introduction to the third edition of her novel (1831),[1] long after she had transcribed notes of her nightmare, penned a short story, and then drafted a book-length narrative (1816–1817) that appeared in print on 1 January 1818. By the mid-nineteenth century, many literary adaptations and the public erroneously identified the creature as "Frankenstein."[2]

The "wretch" in Mary's novel, portrayed in figure 7.2, is composed of parts of human and animal corpses. It has yellow skin scarcely covering its muscles and blood vessels, flowing black hair, "teeth of a pearly whiteness," watery eyes, "shriveled complexion, and straight black lips." It stands eight feet tall. Despite its frightening appearance, it is intelligent, articulate, and initially "benevolent and good" but later fiendish because of Victor Frankenstein and society's rejection. The creature (not Frankenstein, its creator) is also a vegetarian, feasting first on nuts, roots, and berries and then on garden vegetables similar to the diet of poet Percy Shelley, whom Mary met in 1812 and wed in 1816 and who edited and added words to the novel as well as contributed a preface.

Critics have explored various themes in Mary's horror story, such as a male giving birth, parental abandonment, guilt, an indictment of a class system, human disgust at malformed individuals, challenges to scientific aims pursued in disregard of consequences, and more. It was Carol J. Adams

Figure 7.1 Portrait of Mary Wollstonecraft Godwin Shelley by Richard Rothwell (1840). © National Portrait Gallery.

in her feminist-vegetarian treatise, however, who called attention to the creature's nonflesh diet.[3]

Throughout her novel Mary seems less idealistic about the overhaul of society, including by means of dietary change, than does her husband, Percy (1792–1822), who converted to vegetarianism in early March 1812; a year later he published his vision or dream of societal reformation. Shelley based his ideas on a vegetable diet that could begin simply, he contended, by altering an individual's eating habits as he had done.

In this chapter, I focus on the utopian goal of Percy Shelley, who is seen in figure 7.3, that challenged wealth, power, commercial interests, and unhealthful food. I also explore his alimentation for what it suggests about his personality and identity utilizing some of the concepts set forth in chapter 2 of this book, why he was able to turn to a vegetable regimen with relative ease, and what accounts for his reverting to animal food at times. For comparative purposes, I add the behaviors of several of Shelley's predecessors and his friends. I also refer to later vegetarians who were influenced by his ideas, including one of the world's best known, who helped overthrow foreign domination of his country by means of a philosophy of nonviolence. Through this inquiry, we can trace continuities in gastronomical beliefs over

Figure 7.2 Depiction by Theodor von Holst of Victor Frankenstein becoming disgusted at his creation. Frontispiece of *Frankenstein; or, The Modern Prometheus* (1831).

Figure 7.3 Portrait of Percy Bysshe Shelley by Amelia Curran (1819). © National Portrait Gallery.

time and gain insight into the challenges confronting those attempting to maintain a nonflesh regimen in opposition to the culinary choices of the dominant culture. This in turn has implications for vegetarians today.

THE SALUBRIOUS EFFECTS OF A SIMPLE DIET

Shelley died in a boating accident at age twenty-nine. For the latter third of his life, he adamantly opposed an animal diet on grounds of health and morality, but also in criticism of wealth and the class system. His works and food choice inspired the founding of the Vegetarian Society in England (1847), the Keats-Shelley House in Rome, the *Keats-Shelley Review* (1909–present), and the Shelley Memorial Award for poetry (1929–present). He is considered one of England's greatest lyricists. An atheist and a political radical, Percy Shelley was denigrated by many during his life and afterward, but also worshipped by generations of writers and vegetarians as well as working-class activists.

The poet Robert Browning was so taken by a book of Shelley's verse, given to him by a cousin on his thirteenth birthday, that he declared himself a vegetarian and an atheist like Shelley (although two years later he reverted to eating meat[4]). In his inaugural address before the Shelley Society in 1886, the Reverend Stopford A. Brooke asked, "Why have a Shelley Society?" Because "it is our humour. We are fond of Shelley." The dramatist George Bernard Shaw, who changed his diet in 1881, paid tribute to the Romantic poet: "I was a cannibal for twenty-five years. For the rest I have been a Vegetarian. It was Shelley who first opened my eyes to the savagery of my diet."[5] Shaw proposed renaming vegetarianism "Shelleyism."[6]

Although classical antiquity had its share of those recommending a vegetable diet (e.g., Hesiod, Pythagoras, Socrates, Plato, Ovid, Plutarch), and vegetarianism is practiced to varying degrees around the world currently, much of the modern Western European and American interest can be traced to seventeenth- and eighteenth-century Britain.[7] Principal motivations consisted of health, spiritual, and ethical concerns, much like today.[8]

Among the early promoters of a fleshless diet were physician George Cheyne (1671–1743), the hatter and radical Thomas Tryon (1634–1703), and ballad publisher Joseph Ritson (1752–1803). Dr. William Lambe (1765–1847) was one of the most distinguished champions of the reformed regimen. A student of his, John Frank Newton (1770–1827), a proponent of "nakedism," temperance, and fleshless diets and author of *The Return to Nature, or, A Defence of the Vegetable Regimen* (1811), occasionally dined at the table of William Godwin, Mary's father. A visitor to the Godwin home, which often served vegetarian fare, and then a "constant guest" of the Newton household,[9] Percy Shelley fed on dinners of vegetables and distilled water as well as arguments against ingesting flesh and drinking spirituous liquors.

Shelley's fervent renunciation of meat eating is most evident in an essay titled *A Vindication of Natural Diet*, which appeared in 1813 under the imprint of the medical bookseller J. Callow. He begins his publication,[10] "I hold that the depravity of the physical and moral nature of man originated in his unnatural habits of life," which he boils down to consuming flesh and fermented drink. Several poems include verses denouncing the killing and ingesting of animals,[11] such as the oft-quoted lines from *Queen Mab: A Philo-sophical Poem* (1813): "No longer now / He slays the lamb that looks him in the face, / And horribly devours his mangled flesh."[12]

A Vindication of Natural Diet, a version of which was incorporated in note 17 of *Queen Mab*, is sprinkled with references to Hesiod, Horace, Pliny, Lambe, Cheyne, and Milton, among others. Newton provided the important idea, referring to a myth, which Shelley fleshed out in the second paragraph of *A Vindication*, namely, "Prometheus (who represents the human race) effected some great change in the condition of his nature, and applied fire to culinary purposes; thus inventing an expedient for screening from his disgust the horrors of the shambles. From this moment his vitals were devoured by the vulture of disease. . . . All vice arose from the ruin of healthful inno-cence."[13] Later Shelley writes, "It is only by softening and disguising dead flesh by culinary preparation, that it is rendered susceptible of mastication or digestion; and that the sight of its bloody juices and raw horror, does not excite intolerable loathing and disgust."[14]

Because "animal flesh and fermented liquors" are "slow but certain poison," insists Shelley, those switching to vegetables and distilled water would "have to dread no disease but old age."[15] He also contends, "There is no disease, bodily or mental, which adoption of vegetable diet and pure water has not infallibly mitigated, wherever the experiment has been fairly tried."[16] As evidence, he cites the families of Lambe and Newton, numbering seventeen individuals, who "have lived for seven years on this diet without a death, and almost without the slightest illness."[17]

Similar to the arguments of vegetarians today,[18] Shelley includes moral, political, social, economic, and ecological justifications in *A Vindication of Natural Diet*, which he sandwiches between claims of health benefits at the beginning and the end of his pamphlet. "The quantity of nutritious vegetable matter consumed in fattening the carcase [*sic*] of an ox, would afford ten times the sustenance" now available.[19] Hence, by not "devouring an acre at a meal," the former "eater of animal flesh" would be "appeasing the long-protracted famine of the hard-working peasant's hungry babes."

Expanding on the notions of agricultural inefficiency and social injustice, Shelley writes: "The most fertile districts of the habitable globe are now actu-ally cultivated by men for animals, at a delay and waste of aliment absolutely incapable of calculation." Only the wealthy, he continues, can "indulge the unnatural craving for dead flesh." He then condemns the "vice, selfishness, and corruption" of commerce and challenges England's dependence on other countries for "the luxuries of life" in the form of spices, wines, and other items.[20] It is the "avarice of commercial monopoly" that has made the gap between the rich and poor "wider and more unconquerable." Shelley attributes to the "unnatural diet" the roots of misery and evil, denounces the "brutal pleasures" in the tradition of blood sports, deplores the horror "in the death-pangs and last convulsions of dying animals," and warns that violence to animals breeds human callousness toward one another.[21]

In sum, Shelley's "simple diet" helps prevent or cure various "bodily and mental derangements," a number of societal ills and injustices, and the abuse of natural resources. By increasing the food supply, a vegetable diet decreases the demand for land and with it class conflict.[22] The change to "a natural diet" that can convert "disease into healthfulness" and usher in "the moral reformation of society" begins not on a large scale with nations but "by small societies, families, and even individuals." Shelley's goal, in a nutshell, was to create a world of benevolence, health, and equality—one in which human beings are in closer harmony with nature (and one another) rather than assuming dominion over other species and the "right" to kill and eat them,[23] or what Peter Singer labels "speciesism,"[24] and an age in which we do not feed upon a diet of violence that whets our appetite for more.[25]

A Vindication is heavily laden with discussions of health and illness. Shelley's vegetarianism, however, was less purely medical than ideological. Yet Shelley alluded to fitness and disease often and at length. Why?

One reason is that his predecessors had emphasized the salubrious effects of a vegetable diet. John Frank Newton, whom Shelley met in November 1812 and with whom he dined, said he had been "for many years an habitual invalid" but recovered by following the new, natural regimen.[26] Furthermore, "The children of our family can each of them eat a dozen or eighteen walnuts for supper without the most trifling indigestion."[27] Such a matter was not insignificant. In *The English Malady* (1724), Cheyne writes,[28] "One of the most terrible objections, some weak persons make against this regimen and method, is . . . they have always found milk, fruit, and vegetables to inflate, blow them up, and raise such tumults and tempests in their stomach and bowels, that they have been terrified and affrighted from going on."

Newton's physician, friend, and mentor, Dr. William Lambe, had turned to a nonflesh diet owing to ill health, and he published works on the value of a vegetable regimen in treating such diseases as cancer, tuberculosis, and asthma.[29] Lambe also found through chemical analysis that the Thames River and other resources were "filthy" and "loaded with animal and vegetable putridity,"[30] hence, his insistence on drinking distilled water.

The condition of waterways was so odious that Tobias Smollett satirized it in his picaresque novel *The Expedition of Humphry Clinker* (1772)[31]:

If I would drink water, I must quaff the mawkish contents of an open aqueduct, exposed to all manner of defilement, or swallow that which comes from the River Thames, impregnated with all the filth of London and Westminster—Human excrement is the least offensive part of the concrete, which is composed of all the drugs, minerals, and poisons, used in mechanics and manufacture, enriched with the putrefying carcases [sic] of beasts and men; and mixed with the scourings of all the wash-tubs, kennels and common sewers, within the bills of mortality.

Drinking wine, beer, and fermented liquors was a common alternative to slaking one's thirst from polluted sources. The "gin craze" in the eighteenth century, when grain was cheap, led to such an insatiable demand for "Madame Geneva" that London saw an annual average consumption of seven gallons per adult.[32]

A second reason for Shelley's emphasis on health is that life expectancy in Britain was short—an average of thirty-five years in the 1700s and forty-one years by 1820—in part because of the high rate of maternal and infant mortality.[33] Early demise resulted from smallpox, typhus, diphtheria, measles, scarlet fever, influenza, and tuberculosis. People suffered rickets, whooping cough, skin and eye diseases, parasitic infections, kidney and bladder stones, rheumatism, ulcers, and bad teeth as well as common functional complaints like colds, gastrointestinal problems, burns, bruises, and broken bones.[34] Infectious diseases accounted for 60 percent of deaths in 1848. An overriding concern was to guard against becoming ill in the first place and to avoid "the risk of poisonous medicines."[35]

Animals themselves were a source of disease in people, as George Cheyne warned his readers in An Essay of Health and Long Life (1724) and as John Oswald reiterated in The Cry of Nature (1791)[36] in which Oswald wrote, "Animals, like men, are subject to diseases. Animal food must therefore always be dangerous." The authors were justified in their concerns. Zoonotic diseases abound from contact with animals and even inhaling barnyard dust, as well as from consuming undercooked meat and because of fecal contamination, parasites, and bacteria in flesh, urine, milk, and birth fluids.

Another reason Shelley steeped A Vindication in medical matters was as a strategy to make his radical views more palatable to readers. His ecotopian vision involving a harmonious relationship with nature, nourished by individuals changing from a meat-based diet to a vegetable one, invokes the essence of our spiritual and physical being. Shelley urges readers to "give the vegetable system a fair trial" by breaking through the "pernicious habit" of flesh eating.[37] The carrot on the stick, as it were, is his promise that the "proselyte to a simple and natural diet" will "acquire an easiness of breathing," "no longer pine under the lethargy of ennui," and enjoy freedom from "a variety of painful maladies."

Vegetarianism was reasonable and readily accessible; it could be achieved easily by any individual through a change in diet. Hence, Shelley addressed *A Vindication* "not only to the young enthusiast" who will "embrace a pure system, from its abstract truth, its beauty, its simplicity, and its promise of wide-extended benefit" but also to "the elderly man, whose youth has been poisoned by intemperance . . . and is inflected with a variety of painful maladies" and to "the mother, to whom the perpetual restlessness of disease, and unaccountable deaths incident to her children, are the causes of incurable unhappiness."[38]

As further inducement to take up his "system of perfect epicurism," Shelley refers to the gustatory delights of a "bloodless banquet": "The pleasures of taste to be derived from a dinner of potatoes, beans, peas, turnips, lettuces, with a dessert of apples, gooseberries, strawberries, currants, raspberries, and in winter, oranges, apples, and pears, is far greater than is supposed."[39] Near the end of *A Vindication* he admonishes those desiring health to attend to two rules that he sets forth in capital letters, the typographical equivalent of shouting: One is to "NEVER TAKE ANY SUBSTANCE INTO THE STOMACH THAT ONCE HAD LIFE." The other is to "DRINK NO LIQUID BUT WATER RESTORED TO ITS ORIGINAL PURITY BY DISTILLATION."[40]

In the final two sentences of an appendix, after listing several individuals who lived 100 years or longer, Shelley provides a testimonial to the beneficial effects of a vegetable regimen.[41] He writes, "It may be here remarked, that the author and his wife [Harriet] have lived on vegetables for eight months. The improvements of health and temper here stated, is the result of his own experience."

Another motive for dwelling on illness is that Shelley had his own health problems, including an early tendency toward tuberculosis. On 7 March 1817, he wrote to his father-in-law, William Godwin, "My health has been materially worse," for yet again he had "experienced a decisive pulmonary attack."[42] He was also subject to sleepwalking, trances, and violent nightmares in youth, which later escalated to hallucinations, bouts of depression, and nervous attacks after periods of emotional distress.[43] In addition, he suffered from hypochondria, chronic nephritis, and infectious diseases, including ophthalmia and boils.[44]

As an example of Shelley's psychosomatic disorders, his friend Thomas Love Peacock writes, "About the end of 1813, Shelley was troubled by one of

his extraordinary delusions. He fancied that a fat old woman who sat opposite
to him in a mail coach was afflicted with elephantiasis, that the disease was
infectious and incurable, and that he had caught it from her. He was continually on the watch for its symptoms."[45] Shelley's friend and biographer, Thomas
Jefferson Hogg (1792–1862) adds, perhaps in exaggeration:

> He was perpetually examining his own skin, and feeling and look-
> ing at that of others. One evening . . . when many young ladies were
> standing up for a country dance, he caused a wonderful consterna-
> tion amongst these charming creatures by walking slowly along the
> row of girls and curiously surveying them, placing his eyes close to
> their necks and bosoms, and feeling their breasts and bare arms, in
> order to ascertain whether any of the fair ones had taken the horrible
> disease. . . . This strange fancy continued to afflict him for several
> weeks, and to divert, or distress, his friends, and then it was forgotten
> as suddenly as it had been taken up, and gave place to more cheerful
> reminiscences, or forebodings.[46]

For instances of melancholy, coughs, and physical pain, Shelley treated
himself with laudanum, a popular nostrum and potent narcotic; however, it
caused spasms serious and frequent enough that colleagues and biographers
remarked upon them. He also took the drug in times "of extreme dejection or
in paroxysms of passion,"[47] for instance, when he suffered a "nervous attack"
in January 1812 after a falling-out with Hogg, who had attempted to seduce
his wife, Harriet. Shelley had included free love and nonexclusiveness of
marriage in his radical views, but Harriet was repulsed by Hogg's advances.
Moreover, the event caused, for a while, "the loss of Hogg as a friend, and
almost—one must insist—as a lover."[48]

Another incident when he turned to laudanum occurred in July 1814 after
sixteen-year-old Mary Godwin professed her love for him and he subsequently abandoned Harriet to elope with Mary. As Peacock describes Shelley at the time, "His eyes were bloodshot, his hair and dress disordered. He
caught up a bottle of laudanum, and said: 'I never part from this.'" Shelley
then added in a calmer tone, "Everyone who knows me must know that the
partner of my life should be one who can feel poetry and understand philosophy. Harriet is a noble animal, but she can do neither."[49]

A third period of despondency and dependency on the drug was late 1816
to 1817, when his estranged wife, Harriet, pregnant with Shelley's or some
other man's child, drowned herself. Adding to his despair, the Chancery
denied Percy's lawsuit to keep his two eldest children to rear as vegetarian

atheists, he suffered financial problems, and doctors informed him that a recent pulmonary attack indicated dangerous tuberculosis.[50]

Many of the ideas in *A Vindication* had precedent in the writings of others, including vegetarians with whom Shelley supped. The pamphlet acknowledged and likely was inspired by the serious health threats of the early nineteenth century, not only disease and illness but also dubious and dangerous medical practices. Dwelling on medical matters, Shelley could appeal to issues of concern to readers, some of whom, especially among the aristocracy, would sour on his radical views. Finally, his work reflects a growing worry about his own health. This brings up the question of his personal food system and its relationship to his identity, ideals, and ideology.

OF BREAD, BUNS, AND DISTILLED WATER

Two years before writing *A Vindication of Natural Diet* and a year prior to commencing a vegetable regimen, Shelley shocked family and administrators at Oxford with *The Necessity of Atheism* (1811), which appeared during his first year in college and for which he was expelled in March 1811 when he refused to recant his views. Five months later, nineteen-year-old Percy eloped to Scotland with sixteen-year-old Harriet Wesbrook. In early March 1812, Harriet wrote to a friend, Elizabeth Hitchener: "You do not know that we have forsworn meat and adopted the Pythagorean system. About a fortnight has elapsed since the change, and we do not find our-selves any the worse for it. . . . We are delighted with it, and think it the best thing in the world."[51]

Although Harriet accepted his unusual choice of diet, it was Shelley's professing atheism and other radical notions that "truly petrified" her. She wrote to her Irish friend Mrs. Nugent that *Queen Mab*, with its note 17 concerning the justification of a natural diet, was not to be published "under pain of death" but privately printed for friends, "because it is too much against every existing establishment."[52] In his *Life of Shelley* (1858), Hogg describes the poem and note as subversive and revolutionary, for it targets religion (Christianity in particular), political tyranny, the destructiveness of commerce and war, and the corruption of love by marriage and prostitution. Having known Shelley during the last year of his short life, Edward Trelawny wondered, "Was it possible this mild-looking beardless boy could be the veritable monster at war with all the world?"[53]

Shelley was as unconventional in his dress and coiffure as he was in ideology. "There was something of singularity in his appearance, it must be admitted," remarks Hogg,[54] Shelley's friend from university. He refused to wear shoelaces.[55] "His throat was often bare, the collar of his shirt open, in days when a huge neckcloth was the mode; other men's heads, like those of private soldiers, were then clipped quite close, the poet's locks were long . . . , streaming like a meteor."[56] Hogg notes that Shelley's "features, his whole face, and particularly his head, were, in fact, unusually small" but appeared bulky because his hair was long and bushy, which he often rubbed "fiercely with his hands, or passed his fingers quickly through his locks unconsciously, so that it was singularly wild and rough."[57]

Shelley's diet, too, was quirky. He licked "with relish" the resinous turpentine (mastic) oozing from the bark of fir and larch trees.[58] When feeling hungry as a student at Oxford, "He would dash into the first baker's shop, buy a loaf and rush out again, bearing it under his arm; and he strode onward in his rapid course, breaking off pieces of bread and greedily swallowing them. But however frugal the fare, the waste was considerable, and his path might be tracked . . . by a long line of crumbs."[59] Shelley complained to his first cousin and neighbor Thomas Medwin that a friend had refused his offer of bread. "I explained to him that the individual in question probably had no objection to bread in a moderate quantity . . . and was only unwilling to devour two or three pounds of dry bread in the street, and at an early hour."[60]

Shelley often carried raisins loosely in his waistcoat pocket, writes Hogg. "He occasionally rolled up little pellets of bread [around the raisins], and, in a sly, mysterious manner, shot them with his thumb, hitting the persons—whom he met in his walks—on the face, commonly on the nose, at which he grew to be very dexterous." At home, "he would shoot his pellets about the room, taking aim at a picture, at an image, or at any other object which attracted his notice."[61]

Shelley's aliment consisted largely of bread in one form or another, and sometimes fruit and sweets. A French woman had taught him to make panada. "When the bread had been steeped awhile, and had swelled sufficiently, he poured off the water, squeezing it out of the bread, which he chopped up with a spoon; he then sprinkled pounded loaf sugar over it, and grated nutmeg upon it, and devoured the mass with a prodigious relish."[62] "Like all persons of simple tastes, he retained his sweet tooth," writes Hogg. "He would greedily eat cakes, gingerbread and sugar; honey, preserved or stewed fruit with bread, were his favourite delicacies."[63] Shelley and Harriet's fondness for penny buns and indifference toward the refinements of entertaining sometimes resulted in this being the only fare on the table when guests arrived.[64]

Shelley's friends and biographers refer to his "abstemious" diet. He was "utterly indifferent to the luxuries of the table, and, although he had been obliged for his health to discontinue his Pythagorean system, he still almost lived on bread, fruit, and vegetables."[65] The artist Benjamin Robert Haydon recalled meeting Shelley at dinner: "I did not then know what hectic, spare, weakly yet intellectual-looking creature it was, carving a bit of brocoli [*sic*] or cabbage on his plate, as if it had been the substantial wing of a chicken."[66]

In 1816 Shelley began keeping an account of his intake, writing in Mary's journal that on 26 October he ate twenty-two ounces and the next day twenty-four ounces at lunch, dinner, and tea.[67] One and a half pounds of food is but a fraction of the current American's daily average of nearly five and a half pounds, much of it animal products.[68] Shelley's fare was even less than the meager rations served to prisoners in New York state at the time, which consisted of bread and a cup of burned rye beverage for breakfast, ox head soup at midday, and mush, soup, and potatoes for the evening meal.[69]

Generally disinterested in food as such and also in mealtime rituals, Shelley ate only when hungry, if even then. Trelawny[70] reports his attempt to entice Shelley from his books to join him in a meal: "Putting his long fingers through his masses of wild tangled hair, he answered faintly, 'You go, I have dined—late eating don't do for me.' 'What is this?'" asked Trelawny, pointing to a plate of food on a bookshelf. "'That,'—colouring,—why that must be my dinner. It's very foolish; I thought I had eaten it.'"

Shelley's habits continued with his second wife, Mary, partaking of food:

> when he felt like it, perhaps standing with a book in one hand. "Mary, have I dined?" he would sometimes ask.... She laid in a store of vegetarian foods, occasionally made him a passable pudding, without sugar, which they boycotted because it came from slave plantations. She liked her tea sandwiches cut neatly, but dinner with proper courses was a rarity unless they had company, and throughout their union friends complained about the quality of her table.[71]

Moreover, "The restraint and protracted duration of a convivial meal were intolerable" to Shelley; "he was seldom able to keep his seat during the brief period assigned to an ordinary family dinner."[72]

Incessantly reading or writing, his "tea and toast . . . often neglected,"[73] Shelley was "a man who lived . . . totally out of the ordinary world and in a world of ideas," remarked Peacock.[74] He had about as much interest in food as a later admirer of his principles, George Bernard Shaw, who admitted, "I am no gourmet, eating is not a pleasure to me, only a troublesome necessity, like dressing or undressing."[75]

Sustaining himself, often indifferently, on a bit of bread and a bite of broccoli, Shelley could with relative ease take up a vegetable-based diet devoid of flesh and elaborate preparations. As others have theorized,[76] the use of food is a way that a person expresses an identity to self and others. Considerations in delineating a personal food system include the salience of food and eating, the extremeness of eating patterns, frequency of eating, body image, concern for health, and such personal attributes as values, emotions, and physiology. An individual's identities, as well as eating behaviors, develop over time and are subject to monitoring, evaluation, and modification. Percy Shelley's personal food system consisted of a small range of "simple fare," eaten sparingly, erratically, and absentmindedly, frequently not at table, and typically in disregard of ordinary mealtime rituals. A vegetable diet was not for his immediate sensory gratification but rather food for thought as he developed his utopian vision, which is as relevant now as it was two centuries ago. He did not always adhere to a restricted diet, however. The reasons for his lapses also obtain among modern vegetarians.

CULINARY CELIBACY: CHALLENGES
AND TRANSGRESSIONS

Hogg writes in his biography of Shelley: "There are . . . contrarieties and contradictions in all schools of philosophers." Shelley, "The Divine Poet, like many other wiser men, used to pass very readily and suddenly from one extreme to the other."[77] Hogg describes meeting Shelley at a "humble inn," where Hogg had just ordered a repast. "I asked for eggs and bacon, but they have no eggs; I am to have some fried bacon," Hogg explained. Shelley "was struck with horror, and his agony was increased at the appearance of my dinner. Bacon was proscribed by him; it was gross and abominable. It distressed him greatly at first to see me eat the bacon." Shelley slowly approached the dish, studying it. "'So this is bacon!' He then ate a small piece. 'It is not so bad either!' More was ordered; he devoured it voraciously. 'Bring more bacon!' It was brought, and eaten. 'Let us have another plate.'" Eventually they exhausted the innkeeper's larder. Shelley "departed with reluctance, grumbling as we walked homewards at the scanty store of bacon, lately condemned as gross and abominable."[78]

Exaggerated by Hogg for comic effect, the account likely contains a grain of truth. Some ex-vegetarians today joke that bacon is "the gateway meat," claiming its aroma, texture, and flavor caused their recidivism.[79] Hogg attributes Shelley's transgression on this and other occasions to an impulsiveness in his personality: "He could follow no other laws than the golden law of doing instantly whatever the inclination of the moment prompted."[80]

An example of Shelley's impulsiveness, writes Hogg, involves his arriving at teatime at the home of poet Robert Southey, who was partaking of "hot tea-cakes heaped up, in scandalous profusion, well buttered, blushing with currants or sprinkled thickly with carraway-seeds [sic] and reeking with allspice," which "shocked [Shelley] grievously. It was a Persian apparatus, which he detested,—a display of excessive and unmanly luxury by which the most powerful empires have been overthrown,—that threatened destruction to all social order." Southey continued eating with obvious enjoyment. After putting his face close to the plate and "curiously" examining the cakes, Shelley "then took up a piece and ventured to taste it, and, finding it very good, he began to eat as greedily as Southey himself," the two men in competition, until none remained. Hogg concludes his account, "Harriet, who told me the tale, added: 'We were to have hot tea-cakes every evening "forever." I was to make them myself, and Mrs. Southey was to teach me.'"[81]

These instances of Shelley's culinary indiscretion involved hunger or curiosity rather than thoughtless abandonment of the vegetable regimen and simple diet that he championed. Although Hogg's report of tea with Southey is a thirdhand narrative embellished with humor, Shelley sometimes did transgress his commitment to a nonflesh diet for several of the reasons that some current vegetarians do. While foodways researchers have largely overlooked such recidivism,[82] the most frequently stated motives are lack of social support, declining health, inconvenience, and cravings for meat.[83]

Shelley's "friends Hogg and Peacock, especially the latter,... did their best to laugh him out of his new system of diet," contended Henry Stephens Salt, vice president of the Vegetarian Society.[84] While they chided him, their bone of contention was his health, about which they were genuinely concerned.

At the end of August 1815, Peacock organized an excursion on the Thames lasting ten days, but Shelley was feeling out of sorts. He had been "living chiefly on tea and bread and butter, drinking occasionally a sort of spurious lemonade, made of some powder in a box." Peacock told him that "if he would allow me to prescribe for him, I would set him to rights." He recommended "three mutton chops, well peppered." Shelley "took the prescription; the success was obvious and immediate. He lived in my way for the rest of our expedition, rowed vigorously, was cheerful, merry, overflowing with animal spirits, and had certainly one week of thorough enjoyment of life."[85]

Like Medwin and Hogg, Peacock relied on a common explanation at the time, blaming Shelley's vegetable diet for his bouts of illness: "When he was fixed in a place he adhered to this diet consistently and conscientiously, but it certainly did not agree with him; it made him weak and nervous, and exaggerated the sensitiveness of his imagination." On the other hand, "While he was living from inn to inn he was obliged to live, as he said, 'on what he could get'; that is to say, like other people. When he got well under this process he gave all the credit to locomotion, and held himself to have thus benefited, not in consequence of his change of regimen, but in spite of it."[86]

To summarize, Shelley sometimes lapsed from his restricted diet because of the intervention of well-meaning friends, inconvenience when traveling, hunger, curiosity, or ill health. A fruitful comparison can be made with two of his friends. Both fellow poet Lord Byron and the barrister and Shelley's future biographer Hogg partook of a vegetable regimen, but without Shelley's convictions and commitment. In addition, both described how they viewed themselves, relating their self-concepts to their eating habits; their behaviors confirm key elements in the model of food choice informing the present chapter. Taken together, their contrasting food styles highlight the nature of Shelley's own personal food system and the ideology he championed.

George Gordon Byron, Sixth Baron Byron (1788–1824), shown in figure 7.4, claimed to be "a leguminous-eating Ascetic."[87] Often he was neither. He was mercurial, perhaps manic-depressive, and a member of a mentally unstable family.[88] His great uncle, "the Wicked Lord," killed his cousin over the best way to hang game. His admiral grandfather, "Foulweather Jack," and his father, "Mad Jack," were rakes; the latter "had an incestuous affair with his own sister Frances."[89] Lord Byron's governess, May Gray, sexually abused him when he was nine. Described by some as extraordinarily handsome, Byron became celebrated in legend. Purportedly at a ball in London a woman fainted at the sight of him, and other women warned their daughters not to cast their gaze upon him. He kept a lock of Lady Caroline Lamb's pubic hair, and one woman, a Mrs. Wherry, cherished his as a memento. He is said to have had at least two hundred women sexually after moving to Venice, Italy, in 1817. One story has it that in 1938 a group of investigators examined the condition of Byron's body in his coffin and discovered a male member "showing quite abnormal development."[90]

Born clubfooted, which he attempted to hide, Byron worried about his teeth and slept with curlers in his hair: "I am as vain of my curls as a girl of sixteen."[91] Bisexual, he was notorious for his compulsive affairs. As a young teen he fell in love with Mary Chaworth (having had a previous passion for his cousins Mary Duff and Margaret Parker), who married another man. In 1813 he had an affair with his half-sister, Augusta Leigh; a daughter, Medora (speculated to be Byron's) was born in 1814, the year that Byron proposed to Annabella Milbank, whom he married in 1815, only to begin a liaison in 1816 with Mary Shelley's stepsister, Claire Clairmont (rumored to be Percy's mistress), who gave birth to their daughter, Allegra. He pursued boys and young men[92] as well as many

Figure 7.4 Portrait of George Gordon Byron, Sixth Baron Byron, in Albanian dress, by Thomas Phillips (1813). © Image: Crown Copyright, UK Government Art Collection, March 2014.

women, most of whom were married; this includes Lady Caroline Lamb, who referred to Byron as "mad, bad, and dangerous to know."[93]

Byron stood five feet eight and a half inches tall. By age eighteen he weighed 202 pounds, his appetite for food competing with other cravings. He devised a weight loss program consisting of "violent exercise, & Fasting, as I found myself too plump," eating only one small meal a day. In July 1811, weighing 137 1/2 pounds, he wrote to his mother that "for a long time I have been restricted to an entire vegetable diet . . . so I expect a powerful stock of potatoes, greens, and biscuits."[94]

If Shelley's "dietary was frugal and independent; very remarkable and quite peculiar to himself," as Hogg observes,[95] then Lord Byron's was unusual too, in his case for cosmetic rather than ideological reasons or owing to gustatory indifference. Often his "terror of getting fat was so great that he reduced his diet to the point of absolute starvation," writes Trelawny.[96] A "highly aberrant eater,"[97] Byron would "exist on biscuits and soda-water for days together, then, to allay the eternal hunger gnawing at his vitals, he would make up a horrid mess of cold potatoes, rice, fish, or greens, deluged in vinegar, and gobble it up like a famished dog," contends Trelawny.[98]

When with Percy Shelley and Mary in Switzerland, Lord Byron's "system of diet here was regulated by an abstinence almost incredible," writes Thomas Moore.[99] "A thin slice of bread, with tea, at breakfast—a light, vegetable dinner, with a bottle or two of Seltzer water, tinged with vin de Grave, and in the evening, a cup of green tea, without milk or sugar, formed the whole of his sustenance. The pangs of hunger he appeased by privately chewing tobacco and smoking cigars." According to Lord Byron's friend, the Countess of Blessington, "Nothing gratifies him so much as being told that he grows thin. This fancy of his is pushed to an almost childish extent: and he frequently asks 'Don't you think I am getting thinner?' or, 'Did you ever see any one so thin as I am, who was not ill?'"[100]

Byron was victim to numerous maladies, including gonorrhea, scarlet fever, constipation, diarrhea, hemorrhoids, convulsions, kidney and liver complaints, severe sunburn, warts, and malaria. He died at age thirty-six while attempting to help the Greeks revolt against the Turks, having suffered an attack of marsh fever; his doctors bled him with leeches and administered laudanum, purgatives, and other nostrums that further weakened him.[101] Although anorexic and bulimic,[102] and given to consuming strange concoctions repugnant to Trelawny, Lord Byron was something of a gourmand, who hosted and was a guest at elaborate dinners (sometimes vomiting after gorging). Like Shelley, he alluded to food and eating in several poems but more in celebration or risibility than condemnation; this included, for example, his last work, *Don Juan*, referred to as "possibly the greatest (and funniest) English poem ever written"[103] and recognized by Shelley as a masterpiece in which "every word has the stamp of immortality."[104]

Shelley's university friend Hogg was a gourmand like Byron and, when the occasion required or "for the mere gratification," a vegetable feeder. In June 1813, Shelley took Hogg to sup with the Newton family, advocates of a natural diet and nudism. Five unclothed children met them at the door. Mrs. Newton "privately practiced nude air bathing three hours a day but failed to convert Hogg who was more susceptible to her 'delightful' vegetable dinners."[105]

Shelley included Hogg in a radical community he established in January 1815 in which everything was shared. Mary Godwin and Percy Shelley composed the central relationship in this experimental commune, but Shelley encouraged intimacies between Mary and Hogg and between himself and Mary's stepsister Claire (who in April 1816 seduced Lord Byron). The ménage also included Peacock, who was torn between his mistress and an heiress. By early 1815 Hogg and a pregnant Mary were exchanging love letters in anticipation of sexual intimacy after the birth of Shelley's and her child, and perhaps they consummated it in April, according to a note by Shelley.[106] Not long before his death, Shelley met Jane Cleveland, who was married to John Johnson, a ship's captain, but living with army officer Edward Williams and calling herself Mrs. Williams. Her music and singing infatuated Shelley, who dedicated several poems to her. After Shelley and Williams drowned while boating, Hogg developed a passion for Jane, the most recent of Shelley's women he pursued; pregnant with his child and needing financial support, she became Hogg's common-law wife in 1827. Hogg died in 1862, corpulent and suffering gout.[107]

A barrister born into wealth, "I was never indifferent to the amenities of life; I had always been accustomed to comfort,—to a certain elegance,"[108] Hogg admits. Because of his closeness to Percy Shelley and the fact that he was an epicure, there exists considerable information about both Shelley's and his food choices and eating experiences. Hogg's *Life of Shelley* (1858) is as much autobiography as biography. It contains numerous references to Hogg's gustatory longings, gratification, and disgust. He scathingly reviewed several culinary efforts. "I know, as well as any man, and to my sorrow, what a bad breakfast is," he insisted, "and I assert with the hard-earned confidence of long and painful experience, that the breakfast at Conway was never surpassed. Vile bread, vile butter, and the vilest tea."[109]

Hogg also railed against a movement dedicated to the consumption of raw food, which once again today, is a fad. "Man should live, they told us, on raw vegetable substances: on salads, apples, peas, beans, and cauliflowers, uncooked; on raw meal, raw carrots, turnips, and potatoes. They rejected the discovery, or the theft, of Prometheus, banishing fire from their kitchens. According to the champions of the extreme party," writes Hogg, attempting to satirize them, "nothing was to be cooked, except that which does not require cookery—water," which was distilled.[110]

On at least one occasion, Hogg's preoccupation with food vied with other appetites. Among the guests at the home of a country clergyman was "a lovely young woman; healthy, comely, fair, and plump." After the visitors departed, the hostess asked Hogg "what I thought of the handsome, well-fleshed girl."

He replied, "I think that she is a beautiful creature!" His hostess said, "She is, indeed, and she is as good as she is beautiful—so useful in a house." Hogg admitted, "I could not take my eyes off her all the evening; I am afraid she would think me rude, but I could not help it! I sat looking at her," he said, "and thinking what delightful jellies she would make."[111]

Principally a flesh eater, Hogg "conformed" to the vegetable diet of Shelley and friends, he writes, "not through faith, but for good fellowship" and as "an agreeable change." Fortunately, the vegetable dinners with the Newton family "were elegant and excellent repasts.... Flesh, fowl, fish, game, never appeared; nor eggs bodily in their individual capacity, nor butter in the gross.... The injunction extended to shell-fish."[112] Indeed, Shelley is reported to have purchased crayfish from a street vendor only to release them into the Thames,[113] which demonstrates his concern over animal welfare.

ARE YOU WHAT YOU EAT? OR, DO YOU EAT WHAT YOU ARE?

At his first meeting of the Shelley Society for which he served as secretary, George Bernard Shaw announced, "I am, like Shelley, an atheist, a socialist, and a vegetarian."[114] In London at the end of the nineteenth century, Shaw was able to dine at a number of vegetarian restaurants. Meals devoid of animal products could not always be ensured a century earlier, however, owing to ridicule by flesh eaters, inconvenience when traveling, hunger, or ignorance of how the food was prepared. Writing in the third person in *An Essay on Abstinence from Animal Food, as a Moral Duty* (1802), which Percy Shelley had read,[115] Joseph Ritson brags that he had abstained from meat since 1772, when he was nineteen years old. He writes that he:

> adhere'd to a milk and vegetable diet, haveing, at least, never tasted, dureing the whole course of those thirty years, a morsel of flesh, fish, or fowl, or any thing *to his knowledge* prepare'd in or with those sub-stances or any extract thereof, *unless on one occasion, when tempted, by wet, cold and hunger,* in the south of Scotland, he venture'd to eat a few potatoes, dress'd under the roast; nothing, less repugnant to his feelings being to be had; *or except by ignorance or imposition; unless, it may be, in eating egs,* which, however, deprives no animal of life, though it may prevent some from comeing into the world to be murder'd and devour'd by others.[116]

The treatment of animals horrified Ritson, like Shelley. There were traditional blood sports such as cock throwing, cock fighting, and bull baiting. Creatures destined for the table were often raised in pain and killed in agony. Battery farming was underway by the Elizabethan era. In some instances so many swine were confined in a pen that they had no room to turn over. Cattle might be kept in "an ox-house," not stirring until slaughtered. Poultry and game birds were frequently confined in darkness, even blinded. Some housewives fattened geese by nailing the webs of their feet to the floor. To make their meat white, calves, pigs, and fowl were drained of blood by being stuck in the neck, the wound then staunched so they would linger for another day.[117]

A German visitor, Frederick Gerstäcker, described the sight at London's Smithfield market, which contained 4,100 cattle, 30,000 sheep, and unnumbered pigs and calves crammed into the space. The butchers were:

wading in blood and covered with it all over. Between them lay the skulls and bones, strewed about in wild confusion; the entrails, which were afterward loaded upon waggons [sic] and carried off; and beyond . . . the unborn calves were lying, in a heap of perhaps thirty or forty; near which, boys standing up to their shoulders in blood, were engaged in stripping off the skin of the largest and most matured ones.[118]

As Ritson noted, "Many ranks of people, whose ordinary diet was, in the last century, prepare'd allmost entirely from milk, roots and vegetables, now require, every day, a considerable portion of the flesh of animals."[119] "Except for the poor . . . it is estimated that on average 147 ½ pounds of meat were consumed per annum per head. England had become the most carnivorous country in Europe and Europe led the world in meat consumption."[120]

Several food-related beliefs, images, and symbols in the eighteenth and nineteenth centuries persist. A recurrent metaphor is that of meat eating as ingesting a "burnt corpse" that defiles the temple of the body. As Thomas Tryon (1691) put it,[121] those devouring meat are "*making themselves the Sepulchres of the dead Bodies of Beasts,*" an image not uncommon among vegetarians today.[122] One of the beliefs past and present is that the characteristics of food are transferred to the eater, a form of symbolic osmosis or magical transference.[123] In the words of William Smellie (1790),[124] those who are "pampered with a variety of animal food, are much more choleric, fierce and cruel in their tempers than those who live chiefly on vegetables." Ritson phrased it simply as "the use of animal food makes man cruel and barbarous."[125] Or, as Lord Byron commented "in a grave tone of inquiry" to his omnivorous dining companion, the Irish poet Thomas Moore, "Moore, don't you find eating beef-steak makes you ferocious?"[126]

Meat has long connoted aggression, strength, and power as well as dominance, particularly men over women and man over nature. In their diets, Joseph Ritson and the physician George Cheyne replaced red meat with milk, associated in their thinking with women, motherhood, and nurturance. Debate continues over whether meat eating or a vegan diet leads to illness and which regimen prevents and cures disease, but for many omnivores in Shelley's day animal food was medicinal. Recall Peacock's "prescription" to Shelley of "three mutton chops, well peppered," the eating of which resulted in his "overflowing with animal spirits." Shelley could not swallow such claims about the beneficial effects of meat, however, holding firmly to the notion that a vegetable diet was superior by citing the "gentle feelings, rising from . . . [a] meal of roots" and observing of Newton's five vegetarian children that "their dispositions are . . . the most gentle and conciliating."[127]

Henry Stephens Salt (1851–1939), social reformer and vice president of the Vegetarian Society, wrote in his monograph on Shelley,[128] "The importance of a man's dietetic tastes and habits in their bearing on his intellectual development and moral character is too often overlooked or underestimated by critics and biographers." In regard to Byron, Hogg, and Shelley, there certainly seems to be a correlation between character and alimentation, although ascertaining the relationship invokes the questions: Which came first, the chicken or the egg? Are you what you eat? Or, do you eat what you are?

Lord Byron remarked, "What I think of myself is, that I am so changeable, being everything by turns and nothing long, I am such a strange mélange, that it would be difficult to describe me."[129] Celebrated for his poetry, renowned for prodigious feats of riding and swimming, and notorious for his sexual escapades, he was a master at self-promotion and manipulating his image (including having his portrait painted in a colorful Albanian folk costume). Obsessed with his appearance and in "terror of getting fat," he starved himself on crackers and soda water, gorged and purged, or whipped up a "horrid mess" of cold vegetables, fish, and rice "deluged in vinegar." An erratic eater, his alimentary behavior was as frenzied as his other activities, including his sex life.

Hogg, a specialist in law, a flesh eater, and a self-proclaimed epicure given to gluttony, occasionally dined on vegetables to ingratiate himself with the Pythagoreans, especially Shelley, and as "an agreeable change." Regarding his self-presentation he writes, "So long as I observed the vegetable rule myself, I observed it very exactly . . . because my mind was naturally disposed for precision and strictness."[130] In his biography of Shelley he portrays the poet as "impulsive" and himself as the rational prop for him to lean on. Hogg derides the "bloodless church" and its "votaries" opposed to killing and eating animals and scorns "Joe" Ritson for calling "sheep, oxen, and pigs 'our fellow creatures.'"[131] Research exploring the attitudes and eating behavior of current omnivores and vegetarians indicates a propensity of the former, like Hogg, to emphasize "self-control and rationality," "endorse hierarchical domination," and place "greater emphasis on social power . . . whereas those tending toward veganism or vegetarianism," such as Shelley, value "equality, peace, and social justice."[132]

Percy Shelley is the only one of the three friends to adhere to a vegetable regimen and to do so with more consistency than did the manic, bulimic Lord Byron, who used the diet to lose weight, and Hogg, who mocked vegetarian beliefs but partook of the food as culinary diversion or to ingratiate himself socially. Of the major considerations people weigh in food choice decisions,[133] Shelly emphasized health and, prior to inheriting £1,000 per annum, cost; Lord Byron seemed more interested in convenience, image, and managing relationships; and Hogg held taste or sensory perceptions as the primary concern.

When Shelley lapsed from his simple diet, it was usually because of hunger, illness, inconvenience, or the intercession of friends. Living "out of the ordinary world and in a world of ideas," the poet had little interest in food for his personal sustenance but realized that a way to peoples' minds is through their stomachs. His vision was of a world of equality and spirituality, achieved by recognizing that the violence sustaining alimentation inures us to the violence pervading society. "The butchering of harmless animals cannot fail to produce much of that spirit of insane and hideous exultation in which news of a victory is related although purchased by the massacre of a hundred thousand men," he writes.[134]

This "spare, weakly" "beardless boy" carving a bit of broccoli as if it were "the substantial wing of a chicken" influenced, through his poems and prose, innumerable writers and reformers, including one of the world's most famous vegetarians and advocates of nonviolence: Mahatma Gandhi.[135] In 1888, Gandhi went to England from India to study law. He stumbled upon a vegetarian restaurant, where he read Shelley's work and Henry Salt's A Plea for Vegetarianism, two writers who fused abstinence from animal flesh with much greater social reforms; he joined the London Vegetarian Society and was elected to its executive committee. A political ethicist and anti-colonial nationalist, Gandhi ultimately led the campaign for India's independence from British rule, inspiring other movements for civil rights and freedom around the world.

Chapter 8

WHAT THE TWO PRESIDENTIAL
FINALISTS ATE IN 2016, AND
WHY IT'S IMPORTANT

"Between now and Election Day, candidates for public office will remind us how impossible it is to separate politicking from eating," wrote a reporter in regard to the 2012 US presidential race; "food is everywhere on the campaign trail."[1] With respect to the 2016 race for the top-level office, another journalist contended, "Never before have politicians' diets come under such scrutiny."[2] Regarding the 2020 presidential election, a commentator observed, "Scrutinizing candidates for how they eat has almost become a national political pastime."[3] Several hundred news articles, op-ed pieces, and blogs attest to these claims, although scholars appear not to have studied the matter.[4]

At the end of April 2020, when the COVID-19 pandemic had caused the death of nearly 50,000 Americans and within three months would kill 100,000 more, President Trump reportedly felt increasingly isolated, embattled over charges of incompetence and lack of empathy, and panicked that he would lose the November election to Joe Biden. At night, while watching TV in the private dining room of the Oval Office, comfort food was readily available for him. Selections included such favorites as french fries and Diet Coke.[5]

In this chapter, I address the question of how the professed culinary choices of political candidates relate to their character and values, but in ways differing substantially from the poets, barrister, and others in the preceding chapter. I focus on the two final contenders in 2016 for the presidency of the United States, namely, Hillary Rodham Clinton and Donald J. Trump. Although their personalities and politics conflict, both utilized food symbolically as expressions of who they are and in efforts to garner votes.[6]

POLITICS ON A PLATE: ALIMENTATION AND
THE PRESENTATION OF SELF

Donald J. Trump: A Burgers-and-Pizza Kind of Guy

Of the scores of articles I have analyzed regarding food and politicking in the 2016 election, slightly more than one-fourth concern Donald J. Trump, seen on the left in figure 8.1, sometimes along with other politicians. Known to some as the "fast-food president,"[7] he has been photographed on his private jet behind a bucket of Kentucky Fried Chicken and quoted often regarding his predilection for mass-produced or processed fare. As Donald Trump, Jr., explained about his family and father, "I always say that we're blue-collar Americans who've been very blessed by success." He added, "My dad isn't the type who puts on a tuxedo and eats caviar. He's a burgers-and-pizza kind of guy."[8]

On Trump's airplane during the 2015–2016 campaign, "there were four major food groups: McDonald's, Kentucky Fried Chicken, pizza, and Diet Coke."[9] Snacks in the plane's cupboards and later in the White House included pretzels, potato chips, Vienna Fingers, and Oreo cookies. After cinching his

Figure 8.1 President Donald J. Trump shaking hands with his Russian counterpart Vladimir Putin at the summit between Russia and the United States in Helsinki, 16 July 2018. Photo by RIA Novosti. Courtesy of www.kremlin.ru.

nomination as the Republican candidate for president in May 2016, Trump posted an Instagram of himself celebrating with a bottle of Diet Coke, a Big Mac, french fries, and four Heinz ketchup packets.[10] Staff members have contended that if not eating with others, Trump typically retired to his White House bedroom to watch three TV screens and eat burgers.[11]

During a tour of Asia in November 2017, Trump avoided sushi by a renowned chef when dining with Japan's prime minister Shinzo Abe in favor of steak and chocolate sundaes; the following day he lunched on a burger.[12] At an event in January 2019, Trump fêted the Clemson University football players and coaches (and another team in March) with a state dinner of three hundred fast-food items from dollar menus, including McDonald's Quarter Pounders, Big Macs, and Filet-O-Fish sandwiches along with fries, packets of dipping sauce for Chicken McNuggets, Wendy's wraps, and Domino's pizzas. "We have everything that I like," he said.[13]

Trump's supporters contend that his predilection for American fast food demonstrates his "authenticity."[14] Why has he dined on such provisions so often, whether as regular meals or in triumph, celebration, or meetings with heads of state?

Factors often cited for Trump's food habits, based largely on his own explanations, are "speed, efficiency and, above all else, cleanliness."[15] Trump told a reporter that he opted for fast food precisely because "it's quick,"[16] which correlates with his alleged unwillingness to concentrate on matters, proneness to distraction, and disinterest in details. In regard to safety and cleanliness, "One bad hamburger, you can destroy McDonald's," said Trump. "One bad hamburger and you take Wendy's and all these other places and they're out of business. I like cleanliness, and I think you're better off going there than maybe some place that you have no idea where the food is coming from."[17] With respect to safety, one writer contends that Trump has "a longtime fear of being poisoned, one reason why he liked to eat at McDonald's." Trump's logic was that "nobody knew he was coming and the food was safely premade."[18]

In regard to hygiene, Trump has claimed to be "very much of a germaphobe,"[19] although ironically he steadfastly refused to wear a mask during the COVID-19 pandemic and then contracted the virus in early October 2020. He has called the custom of shaking hands "barbaric. . . . I happen to be a clean hands freak. I feel much better after I thoroughly wash my hands, which I do as much as possible."[20] Consequently, he prefers drinking some of his dozen Diet Cokes each day through a straw rather than in a glass, eating pizza and fried chicken with a fork, and avoiding the public coming too close to him, which limited the number of times he took part in meet-and-greet events at local venues while campaigning.[21] Trump reportedly refused to eat from previously opened packages in his store of favorite snacks.[22] His claim of fearing germs is questionable, however, if the description of his sexual encounter with pornographic actor Stormy Daniels (Stephanie Clifford) is accurate; she insists that he did not wear or "even mention a condom."[23] Moreover, during his early press conferences concerning the coronavirus pandemic, he proffered a handshake with business and medical people bunched together onstage despite warnings to avoid close contact.

An additional reason for Trump's alimentary choices is that "I think the food's good."[24] "It's great stuff."[25]

The question arises as to what other reasons could explain Trump's partiality for chain outlets' burgers, fried chicken, and pizza that he finds delicious and reportedly consumes routinely. More fully accounting for Trump's penchant requires speculating about how his temperament, self-presentation, and "personality style"[26] might bear on his food preferences.

One possibility is that Trump's culinary affinity is linked to his tremendous sense of disgust that is "so ever-present and deeply felt"[27] and that is evident in his aversion to shaking hands, rarely eating in public, and attacking campaign rival John Kasich's etiquette ("I've never seen a human being eat in such a disgusting fashion"). He also has expressed repugnance at women he dislikes (calling them "fat pigs," "dogs," "slobs," and "disgusting animals"), individuals' bodily functions (Hillary Clinton's bathroom break during a debate, which is "too disgusting . . . let's not talk" about it; an attorney interrupting a deposition to pump breast milk: "disgusting"; Marco Rubio's "disgusting" sweat), and particular sociocultural groups, including Muslims, Mexicans, and people from "shithole countries."

Trump's sense of disgust and anxiety about contamination inform his desire to "Make American Great Again," writes Michael Richardson, that is, a nostalgic return to an era before the present one of "uppity women, black activism, [and] non-white immigrants" that have "dirtied the body politic"; it is "nostalgia for an era of sameness."[28]

Media commentaries dwell on what Trump habitually ingests, not what foods he finds repugnant apart from Japanese and Korean specialties on his Asia trips when he met with Shinzo Abe and Kim Jong Un and for which he substituted steak and chocolate desserts.[29] Moreover, reports do not connect his rejection of several ethnic groups in America to also denouncing their traditional foods, but neither does he eat them.

A seeming exception to avoiding ethnic cuisine is a picture of him posing with a taco salad even though he repeatedly railed against immigrants and defended constructing a wall between the United States and its southern border.[30] On 5 May 2016, Trump tweeted a photo of himself seated in an office, smiling broadly, a fork poised in his right hand above a taco bowl, and his left thumb pointing up; no photo has appeared of him actually tasting the Mexican dish. The tweet reads: "Happy #CincoDeMayo! The best taco bowls are made in Trump Tower Grill. I love Hispanics!" Former Florida governor Jeb Bush, who ran against Trump in the 2016 primary, dubbed Trump's tweet "insensitive" and compared it to "eating a watermelon and saying, 'I love African-Americans.'"[31] Other critics charged Trump with attempting to "cover up his overt racism,"[32] "appease the Latin vote,"[33] and promote his business interests.

A hypothesis that ties Trump's repugnance at selected others to the cuisine associated with them seems possible. With the data available, however, it cannot be sufficiently tested and confirmed.

Another hypothesis to account for Trump's food choices, also provisional, is even more likely. This interpretation derives from the realization that Trump's gustatory preference is obviously for quintessential "American comfort food."

For many, comfort food consists of items that are highly caloric with an abundance of fat, carbohydrates, and sugar; it is warm, exudes a satisfying aroma, and pleasantly fills the stomach while providing a sense of well-being. Think of Trump's order of "two Big Macs, two Filet-O-Fish, and a chocolate malted"[34] containing 2,700 calories by McDonald's count. Often mentioned also as comfort food are potato chips, pie, cookies, and ice cream,[35] all of which Trump favors to the extent of selfishly demanding two scoops of ice cream on his cake while his guests receive only one.[36] Even the ketchup that he douses liberally on burgers and overcooked steaks is sweet with its four grams of sugar per tablespoon.

Why would Trump so often require comforting? What compels such a need?

Numerous labels have been applied to Trump, such as racist, bigot, misogynist, xenophobe, bully, and liar (while president, he made more than thirty thousand false and misleading claims).[37] The most frequently mentioned term is "narcissist." One journalist during the COVID-19 pandemic called Trump the "Me President," writing that "the president made clear that the paramount concern for Trump is Trump" and that "Trump has always had a me-me-me ethos, an uncanny ability to insert himself into the center of just about any situation."[38] The charge has been stated or implied by political pundits, psychologists, and even several psychiatrists, who have ignored or challenged the American Psychiatric Association's tenet of not diagnosing public figures without having personally examined them or revealing their diagnosis. Trump has acknowledged his narcissism in print and interviews by noting that he has a "very large ego," that "a narcissist does not hear the naysayers," and that successful alphas (like him) "display a single method determination to impose their vision on the world, and a rational belief in unreasonable goals, bordering at times on lunacy."[39]

In writing about Trump, commentators refer to psychopathy,[40] the dark triad of narcissism, Machiavellianism,[41] and NPD, or narcissistic personality disorder.[42] NPD is characterized by an attitude of grandiosity or exaggerated feelings of self-importance, a lack of empathy for others, and excessive need for continual admiration, all of which have been said of Trump. Additionally, such a person usually exhibits insecurity, an intolerance of criticism, and a fragile self-concept,[43] which again, have all been attributed to Trump.

George Conway, in an *Atlantic* article titled "Unfit for Office" (3 October 2019), draws on psychiatric literature to refer to Trump's "malignant narcissism," which combines extreme narcissism and sociopathy. Conway quotes the *Diagnostic and Statistical Manual of Mental Disorders* (*DSM*), "Vulnerability in self-esteem makes individuals with narcissistic personality disorder very sensitive to 'injury' from criticism or defeat." In addition, "criticism may haunt these individuals and may leave them feeling humiliated, degraded, hollow and empty."[44]

In *Trump on the Couch*, clinical psychiatrist and physician Justin A. Frank refers to uncertainty, anxiety, and insecurity on at least fifty pages. These feelings are manifested in Trump's claiming himself a victim under attack from all sides, bestowing derisive nicknames on others he views as threatening, engaging in sexist remarks and behavior, and so on. One technique for bolstering self-esteem by those afflicted with NPD is to recover "the security of predictability that comes through repetition."[45] Consistently eating the same food in similar circumstances apparently provides that certainty: "The orchestrating and timing of Mr. Trump's meals was as important as any other aspect of his march to the presidency," write a pair of former campaign staff members; his team devoted exhaustive efforts to ensuring that hot fast food from McDonald's or other chains was delivered to Trump's plane just as he departed for each of his rallies.[46] Recall, too, his fêting first one and then another football team by feeding them with "everything that I like," that is, fast food.[47]

Merriam-Webster's eleventh ed. *Collegiate Dictionary* notes that comfort food usually has a "nostalgic or sentimental appeal." In addition to his penchant for fast food, Trump has declared that he favors meatloaf, specifically his mother's; she did "a great job," he wistfully reminisced on Martha Stewart's TV show in 2005.[48] According to the show's host , who assembles them for Trump and his wife, Melania, "Donald loves meatloaf sandwiches."[49] Chefs at his Mar-a-Lago club, his getaway from the White House, prepare meatloaf for him based on the family recipe; his sister, Maryanne, serves it to him on his birthday.[50]

Further, the *Oxford English Dictionary* contends that comfort food is "food that . . . affords solace." Acknowledging that he lacks close friends to console him, Trump might turn to comfort food when his self-esteem is particularly vulnerable. In the words of one scholar who refers to other experts, "When forming relationships with actual people is not possible, the need to avoid loneliness may lead individuals to seek social surrogates taking the form of . . . comfort food."[51]

Consuming comfort food has been shown to be motivated or accompanied by feelings of nostalgia, indulgence, convenience, physical satisfaction, and relief from stress or loneliness, among other factors. Trump's food choices, as he claims, probably do result in part from his concerns about cleanliness, consistency, and efficiency (not to mention his support of large corporations). They also might relate, however, to the fact that he chooses what seems to be "comfort food," which in turn could be linked to psychosocial needs in someone like Trump, who is said to possess extreme narcissistic traits. This is not to contend that Trump necessarily feels insecure or has a fragile self-concept, although commenters increasingly suggest that the frequency and content of some of his outbursts indicate that he does.

The hypothesis connecting Trump's culinary penchant to his temperament, therefore, seems to have considerable merit. Trump's final competitor in the 2016 presidential election was Hillary Clinton. Her food choices, too, are linked to her character, values, and politics.

Hillary Rodham Clinton: Cookies and Teas, Spices and Boba

The cuisine preferences of Hillary Rodham Clinton, who is shown in figure 8.2, have been diverse, often global, and frequently local, regional, and/or ethnic American. Although noted for guarding her privacy, evidence indicates that sometimes she used food in efforts at impression management by emphasizing the consumption of certain items, emphatically avoiding other food, and seeking to appear to the public as a particular persona. More than once Clinton manipulated food symbolism for political gain.

The majority of executive chefs at the White House since John F. Kennedy became president in 1961 were classically trained Europeans. Hillary Clinton sought to revamp the food, choosing more low-fat, American, and global dishes over French-inspired creations. Led by Alice Waters, the owner of Chez Panisse in Berkeley, California, a group of American chefs sent a letter

Figure 8.2 Former Secretary of State Hillary Clinton speaking with supporters at a campaign rally at the Intramural Fields, Arizona State University, in Tempe, Arizona, 2 November 2016. Photo by Gage Skidmore.

to the Clintons in December 1992, urging them to find a chef who would promote American cooking that highlighted local ingredients and organic food.[52] In 1994, Hillary Clinton chose Walter Scheib as chief cook out of the four thousand applicants and five finalists for the job. Born in Oakland, California, he was the head chef at the Greenbriar in West Virginia. His audition lunch consisted of pecan-crusted lamb in morel sauce and red-curried sweet potatoes. Lamb, he discovered, is a preference of the then-first lady, along with spicy flavors.[53]

According to several reports, Hillary Clinton favored hummus, a fact that was exposed when her hacked personal emails were made public in 2016, along with fish, vegetables, stir fry with tofu, salmon, and the flavors of India and Mexico.[54] Snacks consisted of soy-based Boca Burgers, Dove ice cream bars, and mocha cake[55]; allegedly, she consoled herself with the cake after her husband's affair with Monica Lewinsky came to light.[56] From her years of retail politicking on the campaign trail, she compiled a list of eating spots she fancied, particularly in New York City.[57] In her bid for the presidency in 2008, however, she "relied on junk food to see us through; I remember a lot of pizza with sliced jalapeños delivered right to the plane."[58] She altered her diet eight years later, she writes in *What Happened*, asking friends for more healthful snack recommendations. "Shipments of canned salmon, as well as Quest and Kind protein bars, arrived at my house, which we lugged onto the plane. . . . When the Quest bars got cold, they were too hard to eat, so we sat on them for a few minutes to warm them up."[59] Elizabeth Rivalsi, a trained nutritionist in Queens, New York, prepared for Clinton and her staff chicken tenders made with almond flour, salmon salad, and poblano pepper soup. Clinton writes,[60] "As you can tell, we took eating seriously. Someone once asked what we talked about on long flights. 'Food!' we chorused. It's funny how much you look forward to the next meal when you're living out of a suitcase."

That Hillary Clinton took eating seriously, in regard to not only its hedonic qualities but also its political implications, is apparent in numerous instances of impression management and symbol manipulation. Interviewed by Marian Burros on 29 January 1993 shortly after entering the White House as first lady, she said, "We're trying to get a kitchen cabinet, so to speak, of people who will advise us about new menus. . . . Asking people for their advice, whether it's about policy or food, is a way to give even more people a feeling of inclusion," that is, identification with and support for her. As another political gambit, Clinton claimed, "We are big broccoli eaters," alluding to George H. W. Bush's maligning of broccoli and the bruhaha his remarks created, without actually naming him or noting that her husband, Bill Clinton, had just defeated him in the presidential election. "We do a lot of vegetables and a lot of fiber and a lot of fruit."[61]

In the same interview, Hillary Clinton defended her husband, whose appetite for hamburgers, french fries, chicken enchiladas, steaks, and barbecue was notorious (until his heart surgeries in 2004 and 2010); at a campaign stop in New Hampshire, he reportedly was working his way through a dozen doughnuts until an aide halted him.[62] Legendarily, Bill Clinton's food habits were satirized in a skit on *Saturday Night Live*.[63] "You know he gets an unfair rap," insisted his wife. "An occasional trip to a fast-food restaurant is not the worst of all possible sins."[64] Countering the public's image of a president undisciplined in his food habits and by extension other aspects of his life, the first lady contended that a "typical Clinton family meal" would consist of broiled chicken breasts, steamed fresh vegetables, rice, a green salad, fruit, and iced tea. If dessert were served, it likely would be fruit based, she declared, although over the years she often professed a love of cheesecake. Moreover, the whole litany sounds more like what a devoted, health-conscious spouse is expected to say than a description of a repast truly served often.

As a condition of her interview with Burros in February 1993, Hillary Clinton insisted that she would "answer only questions about her entertaining style,"[65] not about politics or helping shape policy. A likely reason she wanted to avoid political issues is that eleven months earlier during Bill Clinton's first run for the presidency, "I stumbled. . . . I hadn't tamed my tongue."[66] On 16 March 1992, at the Busy Bee Cafe in Chicago, a journalist queried her about the charge by former California governor Jerry Brown that as Arkansas's governor Bill had funneled business to Hillary's legal firm in Little Rock. She also had to defend her role as prospective adviser on health care policy if Bill became president.

The attack on her job and power "really got under my skin," writes Hillary. "'I suppose I could have stayed home and baked cookies and had teas,' I told the press in exasperation, 'but what I decided to do was pursue my profession'" simultaneously with her husband's pursuit of his.[67] "Suddenly," she writes, "I was in the middle of a full-blown political firestorm, with self-righteous moralists saying I had insulted American mothers."[68] Beginning to realize, with the help of her staff, that her remark implied she favored exerting power in a stereotypically man's world over performing domestic tasks in a woman's domain, Clinton added defensively, "The work that I have done . . . has been aimed . . . to assure that women can make choices . . . whether it's full-time career, full-time motherhood, or some combination."[69]

Hillary Clinton has long been a polarizing figure in American politics, especially among men.[70] According to a Pew research report, a month after her cookies and teas remark, unfavorable views of her jumped fourteen points. Such words as "cold," "bossy," "calculating," "overly ambitious," and "intimidating" characterized her often in articles, blogs, and op-ed pieces.[71] In a Pew survey of one-word descriptions applied to her, the top positive ones were "strong" and "intelligent" while the most frequently used negative words were "dishonest" and "a derogatory term for women that rhymes with rich."[72]

I argue that Bill Clinton's campaign slogan in the early 1990s also contributed to the image of his wife's exercising political power rather than performing a traditional domestic role focused on the household. Bill's catchphrase was "Two for one" or "Buy one, get one free," that is, the Clintons would share power and policy making.[73] Hillary allegedly had her own slogan, one that invoked both political and culinary references: "If you vote for my husband, you get me; it's a two-for-one, blue-plate special."[74] During her bid for the presidency in 2008, a Facebook group called themselves "Stop Running for President and Make Me a Sandwich."[75]

Shortly after Clinton's controversial cookies and teas comment, a staff member at *Family Circle* saw an opportunity to hold a cookie bake-off between Barbara Bush, the first lady in the preceding presidency, and Hillary Clinton. Many times Clinton had been quoted as saying she avoids work in the kitchen: "I'm a lousy cook, but I make pretty good soft scrambled eggs." In the interview with Burros, however, Clinton claimed to have been baking chocolate chip cookies for years, "since she and her brothers competed to see who could produce the largest on Christmas."[76]

A commentator wrote, "By the time of the Democratic convention [late July 1992], the official Hillary makeover was complete—now it was all loving wife and devoted mother."[77] Having stepped outside the traditional bounds of womanhood and the customary role of the first lady, Hillary Clinton "had to pay a price": having to participate in a cooking contest.[78]

While using food for the political purpose of generating a more "feminine" persona, Clinton ironically did it aggressively, telling a group of congressional wives at a tea in her honor that she was "going all out to win": "'Join with me in the first real effort of the election year,' she said. 'Try my cookies. I hope you like them, but like good Democrats vote for them anyway.'"[79] Her version, made with oatmeal and shortening, won against Barbara Bush's, made without oatmeal but with butter.

Hillary Clinton's bragging about eating spicy food while running for office furthered her image in ways that contradicted each other. She stated her belief that consuming hot peppers would boost her immune system on the physically demanding campaign trail. Eating a raw jalapeño every morning, carrying a bottle of hot sauce in her purse for culinary emergencies, and partaking of spicy dishes at many meals explained why "I'm so healthy, and I have so much stamina and endurance."[80] On the one hand, this was a good point to make in an arena where her 2016 presidential rival Donald Trump boasted about his vigor and denigrated "low-energy Jeb" Bush.[81] But devouring hot peppers long has had strong cultural associations with masculinity, daring, and displays of strength,[82] that is, the intimidating image, especially held by many men, that plagued Hillary Clinton since 1992 when she announced her dietary predilection.[83]

While engaged in retail politics, Hillary Clinton rarely ate in public, owing to the risk of an unflattering food photo, whether as a candidate or as a woman who stereotypically was expected to eat small portions daintily and with restraint. At the Iowa State Fair, she took only two bites of a pork chop on a stick, finishing the remainder privately on her airplane.[84] At a campaign event at Junior's in Brooklyn, she eyed a slice of strawberry cheesecake. She said to reporters, "I learned early on not to eat in front of all of you. I'm sitting here just pining. Pining for a bite!"[85] In a skit with Clinton at the Carnegie Deli, Stephen Colbert, who hosts *The Late Show* demonstrated how she should eat one of her favorites: he delicately cut a small piece off the point of the cheesecake with his fork and then grabbed the rest and shoved it in his mouth.[86]

In an effort to connect to the values of a local community and demonstrate cultural sensitivity, as political candidates typically aspire to do,

Clinton visited Kung Fu Tea in downtown Flushing, Queens during her 2016 campaign. She partook of boba, or bubble tea, a popular Taiwanese tea-and-milk-based drink containing tapioca balls. Pausing between sentences to imbibe the drink through a straw, Clinton remarked, "Oh, that's good . . . I've never had chewy tea before . . . I love it . . . Energy . . . That's 24 hours . . . That's great."[87] Her one gaffe, which produced a number of negative tweets, was that of referring to the beverage as "chewy tea."

CONCLUSION: FOOD, VALUES, AND IMPRESSION MANAGEMENT

Hillary Clinton's willingness to try boba tea, popular throughout Asia and among many Asian Americans, illustrates themes with which I began this section: that she possesses diverse culinary tastes, is noted for her inquisitiveness and openness to experiences,[88] and, aware of the symbolic values of foods in political campaigning, has used food and beverages for purposes of impression management.

Hillary Rodham Clinton has long been cognizant of identity and the presentation of self. "Since Xmas vacation, I've gone through three and a half metamorphoses and am beginning to feel as though there is a smorgasbord of personalities spread before me," Hillary Rodham wrote to a friend in April 1967 while a student at Wellesley.[89] At the time she was undergoing political transformation from the Republican "Goldwater girl" identity consistent with her father's rigid conservatism to that of a liberal antiwar activist who volunteered on Democratic senator Eugene McCarthy's presidential campaign in New Hampshire. In addition, while in college on a movie date she reportedly told her companion, "I want to be president of the United States. . . . I guess you'd say I'm a goal-oriented person."[90]

Despite having to overcome sexism throughout her political career, to juggle between a leadership role in politics and one of domesticity, and to combat being called, like some other women in power, "divisive, untrustworthy, unlikable, and inauthentic,"[91] Hillary Rodham Clinton almost achieved her college goal of becoming president. She won the popular vote, but "The Donald" gained victory through the electoral college. In the final analysis, though, despite their differences, Clinton's and Trump's food choices were significant in revealing their link to character, values, and politics.

Albeit important in how alimentary preferences relate to personality, there are other food aspects to political campaigns. The next chapter explores several of these connections.

Chapter 9

GAFFES, GIBES, AND GENDER ON THE CAMPAIGN TRAIL

Touting the slogan "Nothing Compares," the Iowa State Fair attracts more than one million visitors during eleven days in August. Hence, it is a place that can make or break a presidential candidate during an election cycle.

The fair boasts having nearly two hundred food booths. The wide range of edible offerings in 2015 included seventy-five items on a stick (eighty in 2018 and eighty-two in 2019), such as caprese salad, fruit, Cajun chicken, egg, teriyaki beef, corn on the cob, chocolate-covered banana, chocolate-dipped almond pretzel with salt, chocolate-covered cheesecake, and apple pie. Among the deep-fried foods on a stick were nacho balls, fruit kabobs, peanut butter and jelly, pineapple, Twinkies, brownies, chocolate-covered cheesecake, chocolate-dipped strawberries, pumpkin-spice funnel cake, and cherry pie.[1]

In addition to politicking from the soapbox as well as meeting, greeting, and mingling with fairgoers, the office seekers can gaze upon the life-size butter cow. A traditional exhibit since 1911,[2] the six hundred pounds of sculpted butter is enough to slather on nineteen thousand slices of toast. After the fair closes, the cow and discarded cooking grease are turned into soap, tires, and biodiesel.[3]

Many office seekers endorse the notion, attributed to Congressman "Tip" O'Neill in 1935, that "all politics is local."[4] This idea informs "retail politics," that is, the custom of a candidate visiting the state fair in Iowa, for example, and stopping at neighborhood eateries in an effort to appeal personally for voters' endorsement.[5] The benefits of retail politics are assumed to be that members of the electorate will feel more involved with the office seeker and also that interacting with and asking questions of the candidate will produce a belief among prospective voters that their concerns matter. It has been debated, however, that such appearances are a crucial and effective means of generating support.[6]

Mingling with prospective constituents in the presence of food or drink, as depicted in figure 9.1, is not new in political campaigning but has existed since colonial days in America.[7] In the late 1700s and early 1800s, some politicians dispensed rum, beer, and cider to voters as incentive or reward for their support,[8] turned "stump speeches" into all-day events complete with food and libations, and by the twentieth century held barbeques like those hosted by senator and then-president Lyndon B. Johnson to promote his regional identity as a Texan and lend a mood of informality to events.[9]

In this chapter I first discuss retail politics: its nature, principal stakeholders, and an important food-related venue where campaign politicking always occurs. Although retail politics is common in every election, I focus on the 2016 presidential race in which contenders' food habits loomed large in the press but focus on elements other than the relationship between the two finalists' food choices and personality in the preceding chapter. Instead, I explore politicians' gaffes, insults, and body image as well as food purveyors naming items in honor or ridicule of contestants. The discussion reveals further how those running for office use and sometimes abuse food and eating during their campaigns.

Figure 9.1 Hillary Clinton at Kirkwood Community College, Monticello, Iowa, 14 April 2015, exemplifying "retail politics." Photo by Michael Davidson for Hillary for America.

MEET-AND-GREETS

Because whistle-stop campaigning requires considerable time and energy, some candidates add other venues. Early in his attempt to win the election, for example, Donald J. Trump spoke at intimate meetups but later relied on rallies, TV interviews, and Twitter; in addition, allegedly he did not enjoy riding in buses or shaking hands with people.[10] Engaging in political fund-raisers is another strategy. Former Arkansas governor and 2016 presidential hopeful Mike Huckabee, however, defended a grassroots approach when he heard that several competitors attended expensive fundraising dinners in Georgetown and Manhattan. "The fact is, if you want to know America and lead America, you better know who the people of America are, and they're the folks coming to the state fair, not the folks who can afford $30,000 for a ticket to a fundraiser," said Huckabee, who was sampling a pork chop on a stick amid the crowds at the Iowa State Fair.[11]

Stakeholders in Retail Politics

Three sets of stakeholders are involved in politicking at eateries. One is the restaurant owner(s) and employees. "Politicians frequent diners because they appear to embody admirable American values. Not only a warm welcome, but also hard-scrabble self-sufficiency"[12]; that is, these are "mom-and-pop" businesses with sentimental appeal that food conglomerates lack. Some eateries, like Lindy's in Keene, New Hampshire, are such a traditional "must stop" on the campaign trail that they posted snapshots of George W. Bush, Bob Dole, Barack Obama, and others. Lindy's slogan is "Where the Politicians Meet the Real People." Contended Nancy Petrillo, who runs Lindy's, "This is the perfect place to talk to voters. . . . Some of our customers get to have real conversations with candidates in just a few minutes. That doesn't happen anywhere else," such as town halls and rallies.[13]

People eating at these small-scale establishments also have a stake. "I've been at events where the candidates are on a stage and we're far back in the audience and there's no chance to ask a question," said one customer. "Here, we can talk to them up close and look them in the eye."[14] Remarked another, "You get a good idea of what these candidates are like by meeting them and seeing how they interact with the public. But I'm not naïve—all of them are going to be super-nice and pleasing because they are trying for the most important seat in the country."[15]

In addition to asking questions of the candidate, diners often want auto-graphs and photos of themselves meeting with potentially the next president.

As Thomas Wood remarks, "attendance at candidate visits is a key way that Americans bring the glamour of a presidential campaign into their own lives."[16] The same holds true at some fairs; for instance, one attendee exclaimed, "You get to meet the next president. You don't know who it's going to be but you get to meet the next president."[17]

Politicians comprise the third set of stakeholders in retail politics. For them, fairs and neighborhood eateries provide ready access to prospective voters representing a wide range of age groups in personable settings.[18] According to one journalist,[19] coffee shops and diners as well as fairs are places in which "handshakes still matter," where "politicians can mingle with 'average Americans,'" and where "unscripted moments do happen every day with the candidates." US Senator Lindsey Graham, whose parents ran a bar in South Carolina in which he worked, said, "I love meeting people at diners. . . . Usually, when people are eating they are in a good mood. And I like to eat. That's one of the biggest assets of my campaign: I'm a good eater."[20] In 2015, Graham was politicking and eating not only at diners but also at a key fair for politicians.

Pork Politics: The Iowa State Fair

Among the presidential contenders at Iowa's state fair in 2015 were thirteen Republicans and five Democrats along with Iowa's governor, lieutenant governor, and US congressional members. Donald Trump arrived theatrically by helicopter sporting a red baseball cap with the slogan "Make America Great Again" and wearing white shirt, shoes, and slacks and a blue blazer in the sweltering heat; he offered free helicopter rides to several youngsters, declaring: "I love children. I love Iowa."[21] Hillary Clinton shook hands with a few fairgoers and waved at others. Both Trump and Clinton avoided pitching politics from the *Des Moines Register*'s Soapbox but several other candidates took advantage of the prospect to speak for twenty minutes despite the risk of hostile responses from the crowd.[22]

Many of the candidates for office cook, serve food and beverages to visitors, and eat among the fairgoers. Reportedly, one saying about the food is, "If you can find it at the Fair, you can find it on a stick."[23] Popular are supersized deep-fried bacon-wrapped corn dogs and, among many of the politicians, a pork chop on a stick. Flipping pork chops at a grill at the Iowa Pork Producers Association's tent while talking to the press and public, office seekers donned a red apron with their name printed on it in white letters. Among the campaigners at the grill in 2015 were Jeb Bush, Chris Christie, Ted Cruz, Carly Fiorina, Lindsey Graham, Marco Rubio, Scott Walker, and Rick Santorum (who also bagged doughnuts at another tent).

At least nine candidates were photographed with a pork burger or, more often, a grilled chop on a stick while being questioned by the press and socializing with prospective voters. They consisted of Jeb Bush, Hillary Clinton, Ted Cruz, Carly Fiorina, Mike Huckabee, John Kasich, Martin O'Malley, Donald Trump, and Scott Walker but not Ben Carson, who, as a Seventh-day Adventist, is a vegetarian. Democrat Martin O'Malley, former governor of Maryland, said, "I had a pork chop on a stick today, and it was awesome."[24] Known for eating substantial amounts of food at stops on the campaign trail, John Kasich bragged as he left the soapbox that he had already consumed three pork chops and an ear of corn with more to come, including ice cream. In her book about the 2016 election, *What Happened*, Hillary Rodham Clinton writes that Nick Merrill, her campaign spokesman, "handed me a pork chop on a stick, which I devoured. When we got back to the plane, I told him, 'I want you to know that I did not eat that pork chop on a stick because it is politically necessary. I ate that pork chop on a stick because it was delicious.'"[25]

The Iowa State Fair is particularly important in the link between eating and political campaigning. Over the course of a week and a half, it attracts hundreds of thousands of visitors to its agricultural and craft exhibits, and scores of food booths make it appealing to candidates, who can meet and greet members of the electorate in a personable, entertaining setting as they stroll the grounds, often with food or beverage in hand.

The fair, secondly, provides the opportunity for presidential contenders to hobnob with other politicians, particularly office holders from Iowa, for whatever mutual benefits might accrue. Press photos in *BuzzFeed*, the *National Journal*, and the *Des Moines Register*, for example, show the state's governor Terry Branstad variously hugging John Kasich, standing beside Chris Christie in front of the tent of the Pork Producers Association, and posing with Jeb Bush; both Bush and Branstad sport red aprons and munch on a pork chop at the tent.[26]

In other photos Marco Rubio mans the pork chop grill with US Representative David Young from Iowa and ambles along the path in a cow barn with Charles Grassley, then-chairman of the US Senate Judiciary Committee, owner of a 750-acre farm in Iowa, and perennial attendee at the fair. According to a reporter, people every few yards stopped to shake Grassley's hand, take a selfie, or tell him how great he is. "The senator has an uncanny ability for remembering people he meets at the fair—where he met them last year, what they were doing at the time, what they talked about."[27] Grassley put on an apron and filled glasses for diners as he walked from table to table in the Iowa Pork Producers tent. "An aide explains he prefers pouring iced tea over grilling pork because he likes to talk to fairgoers as much as they enjoy talking to him."[28] At the end of the day, Grassley's wife, Barbara, and he sat down to plates of sizable pork chops sans salad or sides.

The third significance of politicians campaigning at the fair, and flipping pork chops or eating them, is that Iowa's inventory of pigs and sales of pork place it top in the nation. The state produces nearly three times as many hogs as North Carolina and Minnesota, which rank second and third in the country. Moreover, the Iowa caucuses are the first voting event during presidential and midterm election seasons; hence, they serve as an indicator of how a candidate might do in later contests. It behooves campaigners, therefore, to attend the Iowa State Fair, where they can glad-hand visitors, pitch their politics, and even eat pork on a stick as, in Hillary Clinton's words, "politically necessary."

GAFFES, GIBES, AND GENDER ON THE CAMPAIGN TRAIL

Masculine, Feminine, Elite, and Effete

According to widespread provisioning mythology in the United States historically and even today, many foodstuffs, the size of portion, and one's decorum bear the mark of gender. A hegemonic masculinity associates men with robust amounts of red meat consumed gustily and women with the more delicate and healthful chicken, fish, vegetables, and soup eaten gracefully. While campaigning, for instance, John Kasich was often photographed at diners surrounded by numerous platters of pasta and subs, his head bent over a plate and hands pushing a sandwich into his mouth. Chris Christie, not noted as a fan of vegetables,[29] reportedly merely picked at the cucumbers, lettuce, and green beans on his plate. Donald Trump's herbivorous intake consisted mostly of lettuce and tomato on his burgers and potato with his steak that, according to his manservant for thirty years, "would rock on the plate, it was so well done."[30] In contrast, Hillary Clinton was noted for consuming a range of vegetables and soups. To Clinton's detriment at times, her daily intake of raw jalapeños was likely interpreted as a sign of social aggression, especially among some men for whom she was seen as assuming a male prerogative.

More subtlety, women have been viewed as controlling their husband's alimentary behavior, resulting in the men sneaking stereotypically masculine food to restore their privilege. When Bill Clinton was alone for dinner, he sometimes canceled the healthful meal advocated by Hillary and requested the chef to raid a secret stash of prime meat and prepare a twenty-four-ounce porterhouse steak with fried onion rings. On the campaign trail, Barack Obama opted for a beefy cheeseburger instead of Michelle's leaner turkey burger.[31] At the Iowa State Fair in 2015, Mike Huckabee told reporters he would have eaten the whole pork chop on a stick had his health-conscious wife not taken it from him.[32]

Sometimes campaigners are accused of elitism and being out of touch with the "average American" voter. This is particularly the case when they make a culinary gaffe in the eyes of their local audience or some reporters. When California gubernatorial candidate Meg Whitman, former eBay CEO, was served a chili dog at Philliedog in Bakersfield, she cut it "into quarters with a plastic knife and took a bite, pinky finger extended."[33] Mitt Romney in 2012 was mocked for ordering a "sub" in hoagie country and then in the South for referring to cheese grits as "cheesy grits."[34]

Moreover, the food choices of or comments by a man on the campaign trail might be taken as signaling his degree of masculinity or femininity: "Male politicians make a point of being photographed scarfing down fattening foods . . . in order to avoid the appearance of being health conscious and therefore effeminate."[35] In 2008, Barrack Obama asked a group of Iowa farmers, "Anybody gone into Whole Foods lately and seen what they charge for arugula?" Many in the room were not familiar with the leafy green, and Whole Foods had no stores in the state.[36] Obama was derided for his comment, not only for its seeming snobbery but also "because it made him appear effeminate," picking daintily at a salad. Supposedly, Obama countered his faux pas by sometimes claiming a preference for fried foods and cheeseburgers on the road.[37] Similarly, in his 2004 bid for the presidency, John Kerry committed a notable gaffe by requesting Swiss cheese rather than the traditional Cheez Whiz on his Philly cheesesteak at Pat's King of Steaks in South Philadelphia; he then "made matters worse by delicately nibbling at it as if it were tea toast."[38]

Blunders

Candidates involved in retail politicking face the hazard of committing a food-related faux pas and must contend with the consequences, one of which is an enduring blemish on character or reputation. Hillary Clinton's cookies and teas comment has continued to be repeated in the media since she uttered it in 1992. In 1972, Democratic presidential candidate George McGovern's running mate Sargent Shriver, the founding director of the Peace Corps, "made a huge gaffe on the campaign trail while visiting a bar near a steel mill in Youngstown, Ohio. Locals ordered Pabsts, Schlitzes or Buds.

Mr. Shriver called out, 'Make mine a Courvoisier!'" (a brandy) reads a passage in his obituary thirty-nine years later.[39] In his bid for a second term as president in 1976 against Jimmy Carter, the campaigning Gerald Ford was met by the mayor of San Antonio, Texas, who offered him a tamale. Unfamiliar with tamales, Ford bit into it without, however, removing the corn husk wrapper. Mike Huckabee, a 2016 contender for the presidency, has insisted that Ford's blunder became a media focal point for days; certainly the event has been referred to often since it occurred. "To this day I am convinced that it was that gaffe with the tamale that cost him the state of Texas," Huckabee said. "Carter won Texas and Carter won the presidency, and it may have been a tamale that did it."[40]

Food-related remarks and the act of eating pose risks, and so does food preparation. During the 2008 presidential campaign, Mitt Romney participated in the Iowa State Fair's custom of political candidates flipping pork chops at the Pork Producers Association's tent. He inadvertently flicked the meat onto the ground. Citing the traditional "five-second rule," he retrieved the errant chop and placed it back on the grill despite admonitions to "leave it, leave it." Some onlookers booed, and some said "Eeeewwww!" One grill attendant tossed the pork chop into a trashcan.[41]

Any food blunder or perceived peculiarity in eating may result in criticism and even mockery of the political candidate. "If you're too dainty that'll hurt you and if you're a pig that'll hurt you," maintains Mike Huckabee; "you have to find the sweet spot." In sum, "Everything you do can and will be used against you."[42]

Sarcasm, Slurs, and the Right to Refuse Service

At 598 by mid-2019, Donald Trump held the record for the number of people, places, and things he had insulted[43]; this includes rivals in the 2016 presidential election, whose food choices he derided. He labeled Bush, who was adhering to the Paleo diet to lose weight, "low-energy Jeb." On several occasions Trump demeaned an overweight Chris Christie, particularly in regard to his predilection for sweets. Trump singled out Ohio governor John Kasich, mocking the quantity of food he ingested as well as castigating his table manners. "I've never seen a guy eat like this," Trump declared at a rally in Rhode Island. "Did you see him? He has a news conference all the time when he's eating. I have never seen a human being eat in such a disgusting fashion," said Trump. "I'm always telling my young son Barron, I'm saying, and I'm always with my kids—all of them—I say, 'Children! Small little bites! Small!'" He continued, "This guy takes a pancake and he's shoving it in his mouth. It's disgusting. Do you want that for your president? I don't think so. I don't think so. . . . Honestly," said Trump regarding the pancake event that in fact did not occur, "it's disgusting."[44] Speaking to another group near Philadelphia hours later, Trump persisted in disparaging Kasich: "I've never seen anything like it. . . . It's pouring out of his mouth! And the cameras are on him. That's not presidential, I can tell you."[45]

Portraying Kasich as uncouth, "a slob, a low life, [and] a 'subhuman,'" Trump's contemptuous remarks were efforts at crude and cruel humor to which crowds of supporters responded with cheers, laughter, and boos.[46] Trump's performance seemed intended to produce feelings of revulsion and loathing in his audience toward Kasich, and therefore hostility toward the governor as a presidential candidate.[47]

Noteworthy is that Trump's slurs came a day after Ohio governor John Kasich announced an alliance with Senator Ted Cruz from Texas to consolidate anti-Trump voters by ceding forthcoming primary contests to each other. Kasich and Cruz were hopeful of denying Trump the Republican presidential nomination.[48] Trump struck back, attacking Kasich's etiquette at table rather than challenging him on policy matters or his record in the Senate.

Restaurants are an arena for politics for campaigners, customers, and staff. Owners approve or deny the premises for candidates to engage in retail politicking. Some have banned customers sporting clothing promoting a particular politician; a chef in the San Francisco Bay area, for instance, barred anyone wearing a Trump cap with the acronym MAGA (Make America Great Again).[49] The owner of a restaurant in Lexington, Virginia, requested that Trump's press secretary, Sarah Huckabee Sanders, and her dinner party leave because her staff and she disapproved of Trump's political positions.[50]

In addition to concerns about what to eat, how to eat, and where to eat, there are other aspects of foodways and politics. One is politicians eating less.

Weighing In and Shaping Up

The fattest US president was William Howard Taft who, at six feet in height, weighed a portly 350 pounds. According to legend, on at least one occasion he had to be pried out of his bathtub.[51] When Taft presided in the White House in the early twentieth century, being hefty symbolized to some people social status and power. A more recent cult of thinness and fat phobia in the United States stigmatizes the overweight body. Several politicians hold the belief that such a negative attitude will hurt their appeal to voters. Eating less food, or different food, is a means of presenting a thinner body, one that is believed to prepare the campaigners for the rigors of running and symbolizes restraint.

Jeb Bush was among those dieting before or during a political campaign. He lost forty pounds on the Paleo diet by avoiding dairy, starches, and refined sugars and opting instead for salads and grilled-chicken lunches along with nuts for snacks. His slenderizing effort "was widely interpreted as a strong sign that he was really serious about running this time, [and] a demonstration of discipline." However, "I'm always hungry," said Bush.[52] At a "politics and pies" event in New Hampshire in mid-April 2015, he lost his resolve. "Suddenly he was holding a plate with a slice of blueberry pie on it. 'To hell with the diet,' he said as he dove in. 'Where are the french fries?'"[53] Often he declined offers of food at local stops on grounds that the diet came first, which might have made him appear aloof, alienating him from some prospective voters.

Chris Christie and Mike Huckabee were among other campaign dieters. The New Jersey governor had lap-band surgery to reduce the size of his stomach; he lost eighty-five pounds. "I'm not nearly as interested in food as I used to be," Christie said. "But that hasn't all of a sudden made me a huge vegetable fan."[54] Huckabee dropped 110 pounds in fifteen months. "If you're really overweight, some people just look at you and immediately sort of write you off," he said. "They just assume you're undisciplined." The former Arkansas governor described himself as a "recovering food addict."[55]

With respect to candidates slimming down in their run for the presidency, Donald Trump is an exception, although he did say, "The one thing I would like to do is be able to drop 15, 20 pounds."[56] His habit of scraping off the cheese and toppings from pizza to eat and ignoring the dough often was described in the press. Trump explained, "I like to not eat the crust so we can keep the weight down at least as good as possible."[57] Overweight at the beginning of his campaign, he was obese as president by mid-February 2019, weighing 243 pounds or more and having a body mass index of about 33.[58]

Regarding exercise, Trump voiced several unusual notions. "I never thought it [until now], but speaking is almost a form of exercise," he said.[59] Further, Trump subscribes to a "battery theory" concerning the effect of exercise. Like a battery, the human body contains a finite amount of energy that exertion depletes. Work or working out, he also insists, is harmful in leading to injury and the need for joint replacements.[60] Although he golfs, Trump rides around the course in a cart rather than walking.

Hillary Clinton, in contrast to Trump, maintained a regimen of yoga, water aerobics, and other exercise.[61] Body image assumes far greater importance for women in politics than for men. "I've never gotten used to how much effort it takes just to be a woman in the public eye," Clinton writes. "I once calculated how many hours I spent having my hair and makeup done during the campaign. It came to about six hundred hours, or twenty-five days!"[62] Whether slender or plump, a woman in the spotlight may be subjected to misogynistic remarks. Numerous jokes circulating orally and in tweets have appeared regarding Hillary Clinton's anatomy, particularly commenting on smaller breasts and thicker thighs than some people consider ideal.[63] Although Trump as a fat man has garnered a degree of ridicule, a fleshy woman is likely to face much more prejudice as a political candidate.

Naming Dishes: Honor and Ridicule

Some restaurant owners play a role in campaign politics by labeling a dish or product for a candidate. They know the politics of their customer base. They also have their own political affiliation and contestant preference. In an election year, food purveyors can capitalize on the campaigns just as they do at other times with special promotions; in this case, paying tribute to or showing disdain for a contender for office.

During the 2016 election year, a restaurant in Winterset, Iowa, honored Donald Trump with a "No-Nonsense" burger. The eatery devoted 128 words on the menu to explaining the symbolism of ingredients. The account states that, like Trump, the Trump Burger is "all business," it tops one-third pound of hamburger with a half-pound of ham for the "man who likes to ham it up," shredded cheese crowns the sandwich, just like Trump "continues to shred the competition," and the addition of grilled onions represents "all the tears from political pundits who can't figure Trump out." In sum, "We're making the hamburger great again with the Trump burger."[64]

Rather than honor a candidate, some restauranteurs ridicule him or her by using a pile of machine-processed meat. For instance, a diner in Washington, DC, created the Trump Sandwich, which is full of bologna; "just like Trump," said the owner.[65] A pub and grill in Binghamton, New York, sold the Hillary Special, consisting of a hard roll packed with a full pound of bologna.[66] Another eatery offered a Marco Rubio sandwich, dubbed the Cuban Heel, that included shredded Spam and sliced bologna.[67]

In one instance, a restaurant struck a politician's name from its burger. A gourmet eatery had concocted an expensive and "decadent" sandwich featuring Angus beef, an egg sunny-side up, award-winning cheese, balsamic onions, sautéed mushrooms, tomato, truffle aioli, and lettuce tossed in a black currant-shiraz reduction sauce. "We thought, who is pompous, only wants the *best* ingredients, and very full of himself? There was only one answer: Donald Trump," said one of the co-owners. "[We] knew Donald Trump was an arrogant, ignorant joke and we named . . . [The Donald] after him to get a laugh! We didn't know until now the extent of his disturbing, bigoted, fascist and misogynist ideologies." On their Facebook page they add, "Now we absolutely want NO association with his name in any way shape or form. Donald, you're fired!"[68]

While restaurants typically name burgers for candidates, a manufacturer of another popular food item designated it in honor of a friend from Vermont running for president in 2016 (and later in 2020). Ben Cohen, cofounder of Ben & Jerry's, unveiled the limited-edition ice cream flavor called Bernie's Yearning. A thick disk of chocolate covered the top, representing the majority of economic gains that went to the top 1 percent of the population since the recession ending in 2009. Beneath it symbolically lies everyone else. Instructions on the pint container directed the eater to whack the chocolate disk into small pieces and then mix them with the rest of the ice cream. The carton's lid proclaimed: "Open Joyfully. Political Revolution Inside."[69]

CONCLUSION: FOOD IN POLITICAL CAMPAIGNS

Foodways are inseparable from campaigning for office. News articles often report on one or another aspect of the eating habits of candidates. Early in the 2020 presidential race, for example, several articles appeared about Senator Kirsten Gillibrand, who faced a dilemma at a chicken and waffles restaurant. Wanting to avoid an embarrassing gaffe at a roundtable meeting with a group of African American business leaders in South Carolina, she puzzled over how to eat the fried chicken on her plate. The owner of the chicken and waffles restaurant advised Gillibrand to put down her fork and use her fingers like the other diners.

In another instance in 2020, Minnesota's senator Amy Klobuchar fed her recipe for the state's "hot dish" to gatherings that her campaign called Hot Dish House Parties. The church supper staple is a "great unifier—just like Amy" read the invitation. Klobuchar's oven-based dish contains ground beef, cream of mushroom and cream of chicken soups, garlic, cheese, and onion with Tater Tots on top; it continues a Midwestern tradition from the 1950s, like green bean casserole,[70] of relying on commercial, canned products in home cooking.

The custom of retail politics, whether demonstrably effective or not, will continue as it did in the 2020 presidential election because local eateries and fairs are places where candidates are able to talk directly to prospective voters, members of the electorate can ask the runners for office-specific questions, and many politicians believe that shaking hands with "average Americans" still matters. Candidates who meet, greet, and mingle with voters face the prospect, however, of committing food-related gaffes, whether by referring to a dish with the wrong name, eating an unfamiliar food incorrectly, or consuming an item that marks the politician as elitist, out of touch, or too masculine or feminine according to provisioning mythology.

A political contender in the future might disparage a rival's food choice or etiquette. Predictably, body image and impression management will concern a number of political candidates in forthcoming campaigns; they know that some of the public will judge their physical fitness to run for office, which in turn involves the quantity, quality, and frequency of what they ingest. Finally, some restauranteurs will capitalize on the election cycle by naming food items in honor or ridicule of a candidate in order to express their own values and appeal to a particular customer base. In future elections, other links between foodways and politicking might become evident, but many of those discussed in this chapter surely will be manifested as well.

Unfortunately, what also will continue is feeding prisoners with unfair fare resulting in illness both physical and mental. Food of poor quality increases healthcare costs, resentment, and efforts to subvert the system. There are, however, several solutions to providing more healthful meals that also satisfy other needs, as I discuss in chapter 10.

Chapter 10

MUST PRISON FOOD SICKEN BODIES AND MINDS?

"The first thing an inmate wants to know when he comes to jail is how can I get out of here, legally or otherwise," said Kevin McDonough, the warden at Cuyahoga County Jail in Cleveland, Ohio. "And when they figure out they're not going anywhere, they want to know what's for dinner."[1]

Tito David Valdez, Jr. describes his introduction to meals when he began his sentence at the New Folsom State Prison in Represa, California.[2] During meal release only sixteen convicts at a time were permitted to enter the dayroom from their cells. A guard kept a rifle pointed at them, ready to break up a fight by firing a bullet into an inmate's leg. Moving down the chow line, the men picked up plastic trays and a plastic mug for cold water, received Monday night's meal, and sat down four to a table.

"Hungry, my mouth watering, I grabbed a plastic state-issued fork and cut one piece off the chicken patty, tasting it," recalls Valdez. I couldn't help but spit it out into my napkin. Fuck! That shit is nasty. What is it?" Another inmate replied, "It's mystery meat. My homie says that shit comes in a box that says, 'For institutional use only.' He says that the stray cats that come around don't even eat it. That's why I always ask for extra rice."

"There wasn't much to the dinner," continues Valdez. "Mashed potatoes and gravy, a thin slice of cornbread, and Jello [sic] for dessert. I was still hungry." The men were given seven minutes in which to eat. Tuesday night's offering was Chicken Alfredo. "I expected something like a dish from the Olive Garden in San Luis Obispo. Turned out to be watered-down noodles with chopped up mystery meat." The Wednesday night meal consisted of Chicken à la King: "Looked exactly like the night before." Thursday's dinner was Chicken Adobo. Friday night it was Kung Poo [sic] chicken. Saturday night chicken wings were served. Dinner on Sunday was chicken quarters.

Prison food tends toward the monochromatic, bland, and monotonous: instant mashed potatoes, white rice, beige oatmeal, soy-extended chicken, soggy vegetables, and little seasoning.[3] His freedom taken away, Bernardino Muniz, a prisoner at the Oregon State Penitentiary, said, "The food shouldn't be part of the punishment. . . . We're still human beings, and we care about what we eat."[4]

Several American jails and prisons released inmates during the 2020 COVID-19 pandemic, reducing somewhat the number from a high in 2016 of 2.3 million people. However, to combat other illnesses, both physical and mental, the incarcerated have had to launch lawsuits charging violation of constitutional rights regarding unacceptable fare, mount hunger strikes and boycotts over contaminated or inadequate amounts of food, and participate in violent uprisings over their treatment, including food. "Any corrections officer will tell you that when inmates don't get fed right, that's where the riots start," remarked a former corrections officer in Florida.[5]

This chapter, like chapter 5 on prisoners' last meals and chapter 6 concerning pork bans, involves food among the incarcerated. It differs, however, in setting forth the application of concepts in food studies to address issues in this segment of society; the next chapter also deals with applied food studies to changing practices, namely, diabetes counseling and education. The ultimate question in the present chapter about prisons is, how do you revamp policy so that inmates are properly fed, uprisings are averted, and illnesses prevented? Finding the answers requires first a review of some of the ways that institutions punish through food and an exploration of how prisoners resist in order to regain a sense of identity and agency. Then it will be possible to consider methods of transforming prison policy and practice to emphasize a rehabilitative rather than solely punitive function.

ADDING FOOD TO THE PAINS OF IMPRISONMENT

Although standards for prison diet have been devised and distributed by several health, correctional, and government agencies, whether state prisons and local jails follow these guidelines is voluntary; they commonly do in the best facilities and commonly do not in the worst. Whether standards are subscribed to or not, control over food rests with the correctional center, not with its inmates. Prison food thus becomes a constant reminder and primary symbol of one's loss of choice, autonomy, and agency.

Food as domination and manipulation runs the gamut from type of fare to nutritional content, preparation, service, and the form of eating utensils with which it is consumed. The menu of the federal BOP stipulates three thousand calories a day, of which 13 percent are from protein, 30 percent from fat, and 57 percent from carbohydrates.[6] Many jails and state prisons diverge from these guidelines, providing more or fewer calories or the wrong kind.

The dietician for the Maricopa County Jail in Arizona claimed that detainees received 2,400 to 2,500 calories a day but submitted only vague menus and did not know what prisoners were actually fed.[7] The calorie provision is not always differentiated by sex and age categories. Also, some of the calories are "empty," such as Jell-O, a cheap, pervasive dessert that boosts the calorie count through sugar, and margarine, which is added to soup and slathered on peanut butter sandwiches in order to add as many as three hundred calories to achieve the desired number.[8] Writing about a lunch to which he was subjected at the Westville Correctional Facility in Indiana, Kevin Pang remarks: "The fish patty sits atop three slices of white bread—two to make a sandwich, and the extra slice presumably to meet the 2,500 to 2,800 daily calories as recommended by the American Correctional Association for adult males under fifty."[9] As the authors of a National Research Council study indicate, "The nutritional value of prison meals is far from ideal because energy-dense (high-fat, high-calorie) foods are common."[10] Repetition of dishes also prevails, and reliance on processed and packaged foods is all too common: "Hot dogs, hot dogs, hot dogs," complained a prisoner in Texas about the kind of food served.[11]

The era of feeding prisoners gruel or bread and water has (largely) passed in Western countries,[12] but the role of food—including its absence or its presence in inedible condition—in punishment continues. Some of the most publicized examples of abuse involved Joe Arpaio, who proclaimed himself "America's toughest sheriff"[13] and was in charge of what others call "the harshest jail system in the US,"[14] namely, Maricopa County Jail in Phoenix, Arizona. A year after he was elected, he opened an infamous "tent city" by purchasing surplus army tents to hold two thousand pretrial detainees; in summer, the temperature inside soared to 120–130 degrees. He eliminated coffee because it lacks nutritional value and is expensive (thus saving the county a projected $94,000 per year). Arpaio prohibited a hot lunch; fed inmates only twice a day; eliminated salt, pepper, and ketchup; and introduced a steady diet of bologna sandwiches (at a cost savings of $1 million a year). Arpaio lowered calories from 3,000 to 2,500 per day, telling inmates: "Do you hear me? You're too fat. I'm taking away your food because I'm trying to help you."[15] He boasted that he saved the county $300,000 a year by cutting food prices to less than the expenditure for dog food. In 2008 and again in 2010, a federal judge ruled that the Maricopa County Jail violated the Eighth Amendment to the Constitution, which prohibits cruel and unusual punishment: holding them in cells that endangered their health from the heat and feeding them moldy bread, rotten fruit, tainted bologna, and other contaminated fare. On

25 August 2017, however, President Trump pardoned Arpaio of a contempt of court conviction and any not-yet-charged offenses.[16]

Food might be quite filling and nourishing but intentionally disgusting. Inmates who act in an unruly manner may be given a "dietary adjustment," "behavior modification," or "disciplinary" loaf also known as "nutraloaf." It consists of vegetables and dehydrated items, yesterday's meal mashed up, or even pulverized salad, spaghetti with tomato sauce, green beans, white bread, a cookie, and coffee or Kool-Aid. At about one thousand calories, it is considered "nutritious." Served to a prisoner daily for a week, this "suicide loaf" has a mushy texture and a bland taste and often exudes an overpowering aroma of spinach.[17] It is dished up on a sheet of paper and eaten with the hands.[18] Owing to its potential impact on the digestive system, several state prison systems have banned the loaf.[19]

The regular fare behind bars, often lacking seasonings, spices, and condiments and frequently consisting of soy-extended casseroles, goulash, and sloppy joes, is not appetizing to many. It also mistreats individuals by depriving members of ethnic and regional populations of culturally suitable food, which is a potent form of identity.

Sometimes it is a matter of ignorance that renders prison food harmful and thus punitive. Meals with high salt content and salads with a high-fat content, which are neither healthful nor appropriate for those with certain medical conditions, are served in prisons owing to a reliance on processed food. Often no thought is given to the different caloric needs of the sex, age, medical condition, and activity level of incarcerated individuals, making these meals a form of ill treatment.

Although the word "punishment" connotes inflicting sanction as retribution for an offense, it also means treating someone in an unfair or harsh way. In addition, regardless of what was or was not intended by an act, there is the matter of how it is interpreted by the affected individual. For example, writing about the Thanksgiving dinners he endured over his eleven years in prison, Daniel Genis notes: "I had just a few minutes to eat slimy turkey roll off a plastic tray, rushed along by guards eager to get home for their holiday meal. Thanksgiving in prison was a meal that implied I deserved no better."[20]

Neglecting or disregarding the quality or condition of food and the state of facilities is also insidious. Inspectors found maggots on serving trays and kitchen floors in a correctional facility in Florida,[21] as well as along the food service line at one facility in Michigan and in potatoes being peeled at another.[22] Inmates in a county jail in Florida found cockroaches in their food.[23] At Florida's Santa Rosa Correctional Institution, chili kept at the wrong temperature sickened 277 prisoners.[24]

In a study of outbreaks between 1998 and 2014, the US Centers for Disease Control and Prevention found that correctional inmates are more than six times as likely to suffer from a food-related illness than the general population.[25] More than one hundred prisoners in Wisconsin fell ill from toxic food, twenty-seven inmates in Colorado suffered bloody diarrhea owing to *E. coli*, and salmonella poisoned nine inmates in Tennessee and another 528 in Arkansas. In many instances, the culprit was chicken, usually in a casserole that had been prepared or stored improperly.[26]

To those confined in the "cross-bar hotel," the pervasiveness of soy in their food is yet another punitive measure, one that makes many of them ill with abdominal pain, skin ailments, enlarged breasts, and thyroid disorders. Some prisoners insist they cannot tolerate a soy-based diet, such as the one introduced in Illinois resulting in complaints by more than two hundred inmates of digestive turmoil. The governor justified a diet of soy in order to lower costs, although political payback was suggested in that the main supplier of soy products to Illinois prisons contributed heavily to his campaign.[27] A convict in Florida sought class-action status against the Department of Corrections for feeding inmates soy-loaded dishes on the grounds that he and many others suffer severe allergies or intolerances to this legume-based food. The only alternative entrée offered was another legume, either dried beans or peanut butter.[28]

Whether or not it is harmful to some and healthful for others, the increased reliance on soy is one result of frequent efforts at cost cutting. In many facilities, the traditional "three hots and a cot" have become only one or two hot meals, if that many, consumed standing up in an overcrowded cell. Meals have been trimmed from three to two on weekends and holidays or on days when inmates are not working, a cutback that contributed to a dramatic increase in prisoner assaults in Georgia.[29] Milk tends to be available only at breakfast but not every day in some facilities. Water, an artificial fruit drink, or a beverage resembling Kool-Aid is provided at other meals. A Minnesota state representative proposed a "brunch bill" that would reduce food service to two meals a day on weekends. "We have to make sure the rapists and murderers sacrifice like everyone else," he said. He was thwarted in cutting prisoners' desserts when he learned from the Department of Corrections that Jell-O costs a fraction of what a replacement item of equal caloric value would, and therefore expenditures would actually increase by half a million dollars a year.[30]

Numerous states had opted for privatizing on the promise of reduced expenses, but the arrangement has had problems, and several states and the federal system have been phasing out for-profit facilities owing to cost as well as prisoner safety and health concerns.[31] In Florida, a food service provider was charged with sanitation violations, low food quality, and inadequate portion size, as well as failing to provide a sufficient number of meals. Among the alleged infractions: a supervisor ordered workers to soak spoiled chicken in vinegar and water to remove the smell, pans of refrigerated food had their dates altered, a spaghetti dinner was prepared using chili con carne from the previous week and creamed chipped beef from the day before, meat was undercooked, and jelly was heated in place of pancake syrup. Prisoner complaints rose; inmates staged a one-day food strike.[32]

At one Michigan jail, inmates filed suit against the county and the company that sickened 250 with spoiled chicken tacos. In another Michigan facility, prisoners were fed food retrieved from the trash; at another, food partially eaten by rodents was given to prisoners; and at yet another lockup, inmates outraged over the low quality and inadequate quantity of food were sprayed with tear gas to stave off an incipient riot.[33]

Faced with smaller portions, reduction in calories, fewer hot meals, no lunch, greater amounts of processed food, more soy, added rice and pasta, little if any milk or fresh fruit, and a high rate of food-borne illnesses from spoiled food and lack of safeguards, prisoners view cost cutting and its results as mistreatment—a kind of retribution and, hence, punishment through food. The most popular refrains by officials in the news are that regardless of slashed food budgets, the meals are "nutritious" (they allegedly contain a certain number of calories, even if empty ones) and that if inmates "don't like the food, they should stay out of jail."[34]

COPING

"The food is awful; it's like an extra form of punishment," remarked a woman inmate.[35] Some prisoners internalize their resentment, enact violence against themselves, or employ other coping mechanisms. Complaining often and vociferously about the monotony, blandness, and repetitiveness of the food is one means of resistance.[36]

Because of the unappetizing fare, some inmates' emotional response is to not eat.[37] Bingeing or bulimia, precipitated by frustration, irritation, or anger over their inability to make decisions about diet, is common among female prisoners.[38] "I need my eating disorder," remarked one woman. "It's the only thing I have any control over and it takes the pain away from whatever they want to do or threaten to do."[39] Wresting control of food intake, even by starving herself, was a way of taking charge of her body.

Other inmates have endeavored to combat feelings of suffering by rejecting the prison fare in favor of chocolates, cookies, and chips from the canteen.
"I am a comfort eater," admitted one woman. Another said: "You've got to get
solace somehow . . . so I eat. I eat the sweets because the dinner's disgusting,
but also because it makes me feel better, cheers me up."[40]

Those employed in various lockups and at different kinds of jobs earn as
little as a dollar a day; canteen items ("zoom zooms") usually cost the market rate, however.[41] There are also limitations on how much one can spend
weekly or monthly at the commissary (the "A&P store") and how frequently
purchases may be made. Cookies and candies ("wham-whams" or "zu-zus")
are popular items for comfort eaters. So are honey buns. Craved, and consumed avidly for their 680 calories, 51 grams of sugar, and 30 grams of fat,
they also are used to fashion cakes for cellmates' birthdays or to celebrate
forthcoming release from prison.[42] Special occasions such as birthdays and
annual holidays are particularly significant in prison, given their symbolic
role and association with favorite foods, religious customs, and relationships
with family and friends, which are part and parcel of an individual's identity.[43]

In minimum security prisons or honor wings, inmates might have
a microwave in the centralized dayroom, or they prepare dishes in their
cubicles as best they can. "Here is what I had for dinner last night," writes
Erin George in the Fluvanna Correctional Center for Women: "potato soup
sprinkled with croutons, chicken salad and peanut tortilla rolls, and, for
dessert, a rich chocolate cake with fudgy icing."[44] It was prepared in her
cellblock with friends, not in the Center's kitchen or served in the chow
hall that offered only "an unbreaded square of fish . . . unpeeled semiraw
carrots, a third of a cup of steamed rice, and about twelve long-past-their-
prime grapes."

Cooking in a cell requires considerable ingenuity and resourcefulness. A
"hotstick" or "stinger" is essential, whether a commercially available immer-
sion heater or one cobbled together in prison from a foot of electrical wiring
with a plug at one end and a bared loop at the other.[45] Inmates also warm
food by putting it on a lightbulb or radiator, wrapping it in a trash bag around
hot water pipes, gripping it over a candle made from shortening, fashioning a
skillet out of a metal plate held over a toilet filled with burning paper, or (in
women's prisons) heating bags of chili with flatirons and cooking burritos
with blow-dryers.[46] They construct a steam cooker out of Tupperware and
a stinger, turn an empty potato chip bag into a warming pot, and make a
fry station using a trash can, a stinger, and vegetable oil purloined from the
kitchen.[47] They create multipurpose tools by utilizing a plastic coffee cup as a
device for mixing, measuring, rolling, and cutting bread rounds; turning the

bowl of a plastic spoon inside out to serve as a knife for shaving chocolate, peeling apples, and spreading icing; and using plastic-covered magazines as a base for making pies.[48]

At night, some of the inmates create a "spread," "cook-up," or "break" for themselves or for cellmates and others. Ingredients, most of which come from the canteen, feature instant ramen noodles, hot water, and flavorings. A recipe on prisontalk.com calls for a combination of one bag of crushed noodle soup, another bag of pounded corn chips, and a third of smashed BBQ potato chips in a plastic bag, to which one and a half cups of hot water are added, and then the ingredients are mixed thoroughly, the bag is sealed, and a towel or a bunch of newspapers is wrapped around the container. Other additions consist of spicy dill pickles, canned or packaged meat (tuna, jerky, Slim Jims, or teriyaki sausage sticks), mayonnaise, Doritos, pork rinds, flavored popcorn, crushed Hot & Spicy Cheez-it crackers, Tabasco, or jalapeños.

Entrées prepared in cells include such items as zesty tuna tacos, po' man's burritos, and jailhouse pizza. The last might be composed of peanut butter crackers for the crust[49] or ramen noodles that are covered with pizza sauce, cheese spread, summer sausage, and corn chips.[50] Rehydrated potato chips in a warming pot become mashed potatoes or a tasty potato soup with the addition of crushed cheese curls, evaporated milk, and thinned onion dip.[51] Baklava can be made by using flour tortillas layered with peanut butter, honey, banana, and peanuts.[52] Many dishes are traditional, such as dope-fiend sandwich, consisting of two Grandma's brand peanut butter cookies with a smashed Snickers bar between them (and so named because drug addicts entering prison often crave sweets).[53]

A group of prisoners at the Washington State Penitentiary in Walla Walla published *The Convict Cookbook*, which grew out of a social skills class helping inmates ease the transition from prison to the free world. One of the compilers, Rick Webb, writes: "Cell cooking gives us variety and spice, as well as the ability to exercise some independence and control over our lives."[54] Six women incarcerated in Gatesville, Texas, assembled two hundred recipes in their volume *From the Big House to Your House: Cooking in Prison*. The authors write: "While there isn't much freedom to be found when incarcerated, using the commissary to cook what you want offers a wonderful avenue for creativity and enjoyment!"[55]

Making spreads offers a small measure of control in inmates' lives, diversion, and flavorful alternatives to institutional food. "Most of the time we make spread because we don't want to eat what the institution is serving and it's a way of getting full at night," said an inmate at the San Francisco County Jail.[56] Some prisoners prepare a personal spread, but often it is a community event with collective contributions and final sharing. In addition to providing culinary variety and satisfying flavors, spreads establish social relationships, contribute to the development of noncriminogenic personalities, and create a degree of agency, autonomy, and independence in a controlled environment. A spread may also reinforce bonds, exhibit who has access to resources, reflect social status, highlight ingenuity, or be used to curry favors.[57] As Sing Sing inmate John Mandala writes about spreads: "A unique bond of trust, respect and friendship is evident, which brings back pleasant memories of home and time shared in the kitchen or at the dinner table. This is an important process towards transformation of men who will someday be returned to society."[58]

CHANGING FOOD POLICIES AND PRACTICES

Many of those who are captives of the kitchen in institutions such as schools, hospitals, and prisons can be counted on to complain about the fare over which they have little or no control. Some jails and prisons, particularly smaller ones, do in fact turn out better cuisine than others and are praised for their efforts. All too often, though, prisoners must sue, riot, or subvert the system to gain access to proper food and restore a sense of self.

The operations manager for the state prison in Oregon contends that 97 percent of the institution's population eventually will be released. Substandard meals in prison, he said, will produce substandard human beings. "We could either send them back more angry," he noted, "or more inclined toward law-abiding behavior."[59] The assistant superintendent at Vermont's Swanton prison expressed a similar sentiment when he remarked: "If we released someone to the community, and this experience [the food given them in prison] had been nothing but punishment, they'd be at a greater risk."[60] Moreover, a deficient diet in prison that results in poor eating habits and chronic illness becomes a community health problem after that individual is released.

Four changes in policies and practices might in the future solve or avert certain problems apparent in the present. Each is based on the experiences and understandings of those closest to prisoners and their food.

Upgrade Prison Diets

First, improve rather than diminish the quality of prison fare (as well as increase the quantity), for adequate nutrition is a fundamental human right and essential to good health. Reviews of menus in correctional facilities often find considerably higher levels of cholesterol, sodium, and sugar and lower levels of fiber and vitamins than recommended by dietary guidelines. As the food service manager at a county jail said: "The more fresh fruits and vegetables they eat, the less likely they are to get sick, and this cuts down on our medical expenses."[61] According to a study in Washington State, prison food expenditures hover around 4 percent of the cost of incarcerating a person, while health care expenses constitute about 19 percent.[62]

A number of studies indicate that inmates become significantly less violent when put on a diet rich in vitamins and the omega-3 fatty acids found in fish such as salmon.[63] Whether or not this diet affects behavior so dramatically, simply providing more and better food has instrumental value in promoting long-term health status[64] as well as staving off discontent.[65]

Increase Prisoner Participation in Food Choice and Preparation

The federal BOP and some state prisons undertake an annual survey to find out what food inmates desire, which items in the current diet appeal most, and what selections they despise, in order to reduce waste, complaints, and unrest. These surveys, however rudimentary, are a form of increasing prisoner participation in decision making that directly affects their lives and well-being, which is the second proposal for changing prison food policy and practice.

Several other methods of including prisoners in food selection, preparation, and service have been utilized in a few instances; they warrant further development and implementation on a broader scale. One involves having "caterers inviting local religious leaders into their kitchens; observing religious festivals by preparing special meals; and involving religious and ethnic minority prisoners in kitchen work."[66] Creating special meals at holidays is admirable but not sufficient, owing to their infrequency.

A greater advance in participation occurred in some penal institutions, where ethnic identity-based groups gained official approval to coordinate monthly orders of culturally appropriate foods to prepare. Thus they accessed food of their liking that was not normally available, prepared it as they desired, enjoyed a social meal outside of the regular dining area, and, in the process, were enabled "to engage with the construction and maintenance of their identities."[67]

An even more unorthodox approach than monthly ethnic meals occurred at a medium-security prison in which each wing had a "self-cook" or "self-catering" area equipped with grills, ovens, and gas rings, as well as sinks and storage cupboards—not just a microwave that dozens of inmates must jostle one another to use. The facility "buzzed with activity as the men prepared meals to supplement or substitute for prison-provided meals."[68] The preparation and sharing of food had a salubrious effect on race and ethnic relations, validated cultural identities, provided "welcome relief from the sterile anomie of prison life in the novel bonhomie," and helped individuals "transcend the dehumanizing and mortifying conditions of their incarceration."[69]

Teach about Food as Part of Rehabilitation

In addition to improving the diet and increasing the participation of prisoners in decision making and food preparation, a third proposal is to bolster the rehabilitative function of imprisonment, restoring what has been largely superseded by other purposes. US penal theory includes rehabilitation as well as punishment, incapacitation, and deterrence as the intent of confinement.[70] Specialists and much of the public now believe the emphasis should be on reintegrating prisoners into society through, for example, educational and vocational programming.

Like food service, however, educational programs often have been targeted for cost cutting. Another problem is that most of those working in the kitchen are inmate volunteers not required to have previous cooking experience (but motivated by a desire for extra or better food) and not taught skills for employment after prison. At the Swanton facility in Vermont, however, administrators recruit trained food service professionals to instruct inmates, who are then certified through the National Restaurant Association; the prison also has a restaurant management program.[71] Funded by the US Department of Education, Boston's Suffolk County House of Correction for Women conducted a three-year project to teach prisoners how to prepare and eat more healthful meals. Graduate students in physical therapy at Simmons College taught the women what foods to choose from the commissary, how to decipher nutrition labels, and how to differentiate fats, proteins, and carbohydrates. The inmates' newly acquired knowledge was more appropriate after release, however, because they were not allowed to prepare food in prison, where instead they received large amounts of bread, rice, and cake.[72]

Alter Perceptions of the Incarcerated through Food Production

"I'm so fed up with crime, it wouldn't bother me if they just got bread & water," writes one person in the comments section appended to a news article about eating behind bars.[73] "People are in prison, where the primary purpose is to punish them," writes another. "These people are in prison for a reason," contends a third; "let them eat this crap and be grateful for it." Such remarks resonate with the findings of an NBC television poll as long ago as the 1990s "that 82 percent of Americans say life in prison is too easy."[74] Those in jails and prisons increased more than 400 percent after 1980. Policies such as mounting a "war on drugs" and being "tough on crime" paved the way for mass incarceration. Mandatory sentencing added to the climbing rates. "Three strikes and you're out" was voted in, parole violators were subjected to the practice of "trail 'em, nail 'em, and jail 'em," and ever more "supermax" facilities were built.

Recent years have witnessed changes in attitudes among politicians and the public, however. A Pew poll found that most Americans are weary of battling drug use with stiff sentences; 67 percent of respondents indicated that the government should focus on treating, not punishing, drug users, and 63 percent wanted to set aside minimum sentencing for drug crimes. In late 2021, the medical use of cannabis was legal in thirty-six states, four US territories, and the District of Columbia, and the recreational use of cannabis was legal in eighteen states (and Guam, the Northern Mariana Islands, and the District of Columbia) and decriminalized in thirteen other states (and the US Virgin Islands). Several presidential candidates in 2020 were advocating numerous reforms, including shifting away from tough-on-crime policies, canceling mandatory minimum sentences for drug offenses, advocating mental health and substance abuse counseling, reversing mass incarceration policies, shortening probation terms for most felonies, proposing prison work programs, and requiring a federal prison reentry education program.

Less often mentioned in the news is that an increasing number of correctional facilities have launched gardening programs, reminiscent of what existed in American prisons until recent decades, to provide fresh produce, improve the nutritional intake of inmates, reduce costs, teach employable skills, donate to food banks, and enhance relations with communities, resulting in altered perceptions about inmates.

Dating back to 1982, a counselor and a sheriff at the San Francisco County Jail established the Horticulture Program to teach inmates not only agricultural practices but also life lessons and skills. A decade later, the counselor, Catherine Sneed, founded the Garden Project at the same facility. It provides job training, employment, and support to ex-inmates while also "fostering positive relations with the communities from which convicts come."[75] Recidivism, which has run as high as 66 percent nationally, reportedly dropped to 24 percent among participants in the project.[76]

The garden program at the California Institution for Women in Corona grows produce for prison and hospital kitchens and establishes connections between the women inmates and the outside community. The Gardening Project at Ohio's Sandusky County Jail began as a way to cut costs, but its 1.5 acres produced enough vegetables to donate to food pantries and soup kitchens; whether entirely because of this enterprise or owing to multiple reasons, the recidivism rate among participating inmates declined from 40 percent to 18 percent. Other programs have developed, including at Washington's McNeil Island Corrections Center, San Quentin Prison, and Wisconsin's twenty-eight adult correctional institutions.[77] The recidivism rate in most instances is considerably lower than that achieved through literacy or vocational training, although these programs should be funded along with those involving inmates in the production and preparation of food.

FOOD MATTERS BEHIND BARS

Most reviews of how to improve food in carceral settings advocate administrative and technological changes, such as training staff in basic food safety standards, replacing outdated equipment with space- and labor-saving machinery, and providing more oversight of preparation, storage, and service. While not to gainsay such recommendations, they neglect the extranutritional meanings people attribute to food and other issues dealt with in this book. What is also needed, therefore, is specialists in food studies who can contribute substantially to inmates' physical well-being, mental health, relationships with one another and correctional staff, and sense of control over their lives in prison.

One way a food studies or foodways professional can introduce changes beneficial to inmates, like serving culturally appropriate foods or allowing the inmates to occasionally cook for themselves, is to develop participatory action projects involving staff together with a council composed of inmate-elected representatives from the major ethnic and racial groups—a practice with precedence in a few institutions.[78] A consultant knowledgeable about the importance of food traditions and symbolism can enable communication between the parties to effect more appropriate food choice, preparation, and service.

Another area of outreach is youth training programs. The Harvest Kitchen Program in Rhode Island, for example, provides a twenty-week culinary and job readiness training program for youth in the Division of Juvenile Corrections, who produce preserved foods using ingredients sourced from local farmers. The program teaches young offenders about the basics of food preservation, weights and measurements, food ordering, nutrition, kitchen safety, and so on.

Incorporating a foodways orientation in this kind of program would greatly enrich it, helping to integrate the youth into their communities. A specialist in foodways might have the youth meet and interview local residents engaged in a variety of traditional occupations and food-related activities. The foodways coordinator could help the young people develop knowledge about place-based foods, discuss family recipes, examine locally produced cookbooks, and learn about food preservation and storage methods through time. The young might be guided in talking with one another regarding their own food choices and experiences, for instance, best and worst meals, unusual food eaten, sustenance during hard times, and memories of foods they enjoyed with others. They could be oriented toward greater awareness of or participation in community food events, such as pancake breakfasts, potluck dinners, box socials, church suppers, bake sales, roadside and farmers' markets.

The youth would gain a richer sense of food in their lives; their relationships with others; and the historical, cultural, and social influences on food and their identities. By immersing themselves in matters of family, community, and locale, incarcerated individuals are more likely to achieve a primary goal of rehabilitation programs, namely, shifting self-identity from criminogenic to pro-social and becoming assimilated into the community.

Models for these activities already exist. One is the teacher's guide prepared for the Smithsonian Institution's traveling exhibition *Key Ingredients: America by Food*.[79] A second is the *Michigan Eats* exhibition curated by Yvonne Lockwood, which concerns ethnic, regional, and local foods in the state, Michigan cookbooks and historical kitchen equipment, and food-centered celebrations.[80] Rachelle Saltzman's survey of place-based foods in Iowa can be employed in other geographical areas as well.[81] Marsha Mac-Dowell's "Foodways: A 4-H Folkpatterns Project," available online, provides a large compendium of activities related to a wide range of foodways topics[82]; they can be adapted for use in various circumstances, including existing nutritional and residents' wellness programs in jails and prisons.[83]

In 2013, the museum at the Eastern State Penitentiary in Philadelphia hosted a one-day event for visitors to sample prison food prepared by a catering company owned by a corrections officer.[84] The menu consisted of 1830s fare of salted beef with Indian mush (porridge of cornmeal), items from a 1949 prison menu, and the modern nutraloaf. The press release reads in part: "Visitors will learn how changing correctional philosophies contributed to prison food policies and preparation. Also on view will be sample menus, archival photographs, and reports of the prison fare throughout Eastern State Penitentiary's 142-year operational history." Available at the exhibition was a small booklet by sociologist Norman Johnston titled *Chow: Food and Drink in Eastern State Penitentiary*, which was published by the historic site.[85]

Another way, then, to reach the public regarding foodways issues in correctional institutions is by undertaking projects similar to the one at the Eastern State Penitentiary. The presentation could include interviews with former inmates; historical menus and cookbooks; copies of pages from kitchen logs and prisoner complaint forms; historical equipment for cooking and serving food; food samples offered to visitors at an opening reception; plastic models made to look like the actual dishes from different time periods; and archival photos of kitchen staff preparing food, inmates eating in mess halls, and food trolleys headed for cells; along with printed information about not only prison fare past and present but also its relation to punishment, resistance, health, and identity. Such exhibitions might be installed in former jails and prisons with educational programming, libraries, history museums, and college campus facilities, many of which have had exhibits devoted to other aspects of prison life.

In sum, it is clear that the current system of corrections in the United States is inadequate. The application of foodways research provides ways to improve the culture of carceral institutions and also enhance the well-being of inmates. Among the possible endeavors are those involving foodways curricula in educational programs; gardens and horticulture therapy measures that encompass information about food traditions; and workshops for staff regarding the extranutritional meanings accorded food, the relation of emotional health to foodways, and the importance of identity formation through alimentation. While many issues need to be addressed in reforming corrections policy and practice, the data and suggestions presented here boil down to the fact that in the end, food matters.

Food also matters greatly for people with diabetes, who number in the millions. The emphasis has long been on knowledge transfer, that is, teaching patients about calories, testing blood sugar levels, and eliminating or reducing certain items in their diet. Interviewees tell me they have other concerns that are not addressed. As explored in the next chapter, these issues pertain to the social and symbolic aspects of food and eating.

Chapter 11

WHAT DIABETES
COUNSELING OVERLOOKS

Sitting on a well-worn sofa in the living room of her small apartment in Venice, California, the walls adorned with family photos and religious images, Silvia Herrera[1] lists her relatives with diabetes. They include her mother, an aunt, a nephew, and one brother—all of whom died of complications from the disease—along with another brother, two sisters, a grandson, and a six-year-old niece who are still living. Mrs. Herrera, an émigré from Guadalajara, has diabetes as well. The disorder has also beset Jorge Alvarez and his wife Rosa Alvarez, both from Jalisco, Mexico, who have had diabetes for thirty years and twenty years, respectively. Mr. Alvarez's father and grandfather suffered from diabetes, as did Mrs. Alvarez's father, two of her father's brothers, and two of her older sisters and her younger sister (who died at age sixty-five from the disease). None of Mr. and Mrs. Alvarez's three daughters has diabetes, but two of their four sons were diagnosed with the disease ten and eight years previously at ages thirty-nine and forty-two. A similar situation obtains for many other immigrants and Mexican Americans I have interviewed; they or a spouse or other family members have diabetes. Several have died from it.

Statistics released by the National Institute of Diabetes and Digestive and Kidney Diseases (NIDDK) indicate that more than 34 million Americans suffer from diabetes. Millions more have prediabetes, consisting of impaired fasting glucose and impaired glucose tolerance. The prevalence rate of adult-onset diabetes among Latinx, African Americans, American Indians, and Native Hawaiians is at least twice that of Whites. These ethnic populations experience much higher rates of complications too, such as blindness, amputations, strokes, and heart disease.

Even now, whether for ethnic or for White populations, diabetes counseling overlooks or downplays helping individuals generate insights into their identities and symbolic uses of food. Rather, educational materials and personal guidance stress "knowledge transfer" (conveying information to patients about diabetes and its treatment) along with "skills acquisition" (in taking medications and reading glucose levels). Predictably, assessing the success of programs entails determining "adherence behaviors" (glucose monitoring and taking prescribed medications) and measuring such "physiologic outcomes" as levels of weight, fitness, cholesterol, and blood glucose.

Critics argue that this technological approach is no panacea for changing behavior and maintaining alterations in lifestyle after program completion.[2] They contend that programs are class based and ethnocentric and pathologize the tastes of individuals who lack the right cultural knowledge to eat "properly."[3] Many with diabetes, particularly those identifying as ethnic minorities, complain that nutritional information is not specific to their own traditions or in a language comprehensible to them, publications are bereft of images of people like themselves, and the recipes "are for things I would never eat."[4] The issues of living and coping with diabetes suggest the need to shift from a knowledge model to patient-centered perspectives, self-management, and empowerment.

In order to surmount shortcomings in diabetes counseling and educational programs, particularly among Latinx, it is useful to examine "local knowledge."[5] The model encompasses the traditions, knowledge, beliefs, and practices developed by local communities as adaptive strategies. I employ the notion here to explore ideas among individuals about the causes of diabetes, plant treatments for lowering blood glucose levels, and nonnutritional meanings and uses of food—rituals, symbols, and sources of identity—which dieticians seem to seldom take into account but which render modifications in diet difficult. The concept of local knowledge also includes a person's self-reported challenges to maintaining a recommended dietary regimen that go beyond several mentioned in the literature blaming and stigmatizing the patient. By means of in-depth interviews and other qualitative methods,[6] we can discover people's experiences, understanding, and explanations, like those reported here among Mexican American immigrants in Southern California.

EMOTIONS AND STRESS

With no prompting other than my statement that I wanted to talk about diabetes, most of the twenty-eight individuals I interviewed immediately launched into narratives about stressful life events that caused or exacerbated their disease. Martha Cruz, six months pregnant, came upon her husband's truck in the field, opened the door to greet him, and discovered to her horror a corpse behind the steering wheel. She collapsed from *susto* (fright). She was hospitalized with diabetes, her blood glucose so high that her unborn son's life was in danger.

"In my case," said Yolanda Lopez, "I believe it was *corajes* [fits of anger] . . . I had a lot of problems with a neighbor and we were at each other's throats every day . . . and that was when it developed, I think. . . . I believe it is more about one's character, one's problems, what one goes through. They have much mortification because of family problems and they become diabetics." Several others agreed.

Alicia Gutierrez has experienced a variety of strong emotions that precipitated or aggravated her diabetes, beginning with *susto* and anger after she was stabbed by three youth attempting to steal her purse. Living alone since her husband's death four years earlier, she suffers *tristeza* (deep sadness or depression) that has made her diabetes worse, she said, weeping as she tried to talk about it. Worry (*inquietude* or *preoccupado*) and anxiety (*nervios*) or *ataque de nervios* (an attack of great anxiety) also can aggravate diabetes, which they have done in her case, she said.

Interviewees accepted biomedical hypotheses about the role of genetics, exercise, and diet. A few expressed uncertainty regarding the impact of diet on themselves or others, although many accepted it as a contributing factor, mentioning excessive consumption of sodas, pork, and starchy foods along with obesity and lack of exercise. No one said the illness was God's will, punishment for bad behavior, or fate. Most, however, referred to stressful events and extreme emotional states as precipitating the disorder in themselves or other people, or of making their condition worse.

Ascribing the onset of diabetes to an intense emotional experience affords a reason one person has the disease but other people who have eaten the same kinds and amount of food as that individual and exercised less do not have diabetes. Because type 2 diabetes usually develops slowly over time as the pancreas is stressed, it is initially asymptomatic, and some of its physiological consequences might not seem connected to it. Identifying a sudden provoking factor may provide a sense of a proximate cause of a condition that has existed for a while with no one's awareness of it.

In addition, a growing body of literature concerning laboratory experiments with animals and human beings suggests that intensely felt emotions may indeed be linked to diabetes. Stress has long been suspected of having significant effects on metabolic activity. "Counterregulatory" hormones appear to be released in response to stress, which results in elevated blood glucose levels and decreased insulin action.[7] Such an energy-mobilizing effect (the result of the fight-or-flight response) is beneficial (i.e., of adaptive

importance) in a healthy organism. Stress-induced increases in blood glucose
cannot be adequately metabolized, however, where there is a relative lack of
insulin.[8] In addition, psychological stress has been implicated as a link to
psychoendocrinical pathways that cause insulin resistance.[9]

Medical textbooks as well as publications from the NIDDK have ignored
or minimized the salience of stress to diabetes. Nutrition education programs rarely include stress reduction or relaxation techniques but instead
focus heavily on diet, exercise, adherence to testing blood glucose levels,
and compliance with taking medications.[10] Some medical personnel and
nutrition educators use scare tactics to promote adherence to prescribed
behaviors by warning of severe complications of diabetes (amputations,
blindness), undermining efforts to prevent or forestall these symptoms.[11]
Research on the role of stress in causing high blood glucose levels, making
a patient's condition worse, interfering with efforts to manage the disease
and its symptoms, and contributing to the development of complications
should be discussed in medical texts, included in the training of health care
personnel, and incorporated into educational programs for the public.

FROM CACTUS SALAD TO HORSETAIL TEA

The NIDDK insists that improved glycemic control through diet greatly
benefits people with diabetes. The agency bemoans the fact that more than
half of those known to have this disorder do not receive formal "self-control
training." However, some Latinx utilize certain plants to treat diabetes and
the associated condition of hypertension, thereby exercising a degree of self-
control by participating in the use of traditional remedies.

The few surveys that have recorded information about herbal remedy
use in the United States by Latinx indicate that as many as 91 percent of the
subjects in the studies have employed plant materials in treating diabetes.[12]
In one research project 84 percent of respondents cited herbs as possible
alternative modalities.[13] Among the small number of plants to treat diabetes
that have been documented thus far from Latinx are *nopal* or prickly pear
cactus (the most frequently mentioned in several studies including my own)[14]
along with *sábila* (aloe vera), *maguey* (century plant), *chaya* (vegetable pear),
barbas de elote (corn silk), *lagrimas de San Pedro* (tears of St. Peter), *cola de
caballo* (horsetail), *nispero* (loquat), and *prodigiosa* (brickellbush).

"Nopal, it's good for diabetes and for other things," said Jorge Alvarez.
"I try to give it to my wife by taking off the spines [on the pads] and then

Figure 11.1 Nopal cactus pad with "tuna" (fruit) eaten in salad or made into a "smoothie" for treating diabetes. Photo by the author.

I toast it a bit on the skillet. I think this is the best way of eating the nopal," referring to the plant in figure 11.1. His wife Rosa Alvarez said, "I boil it to make a salad with onion and tomato." Mr. Alvarez also prepares a *licuado* or "smoothie" composed of raw items, which seems to be the common way of consuming cactus: nopal liquefied with *apio* (celery) and *berro* (watercress) along with a small amount of pineapple and apple juice (to reduce the sharp tang of the cactus) and ingested in the morning.

Most people I interviewed tend gardens in which they grow a dozen or more plants having medicinal uses, along with other culinary plants and also those having dual purposes. Adriana Moreno has cultivated the area behind the apartment building where she lives in Venice, but in addition, she has "emergency plants" in hangers and pots on her balcony for times when one of her children wakes up in the middle of the night with an ailment.

A woman in City Terrace[15] tends more than forty plants, and a *curandero* (healer) in Echo Park has eighty. Arturo Sandoval in Culver City grows about 150 plants in his front-, side-, and backyards, which includes some duplicates. He remarked on the pleasure of digging the soil with his bare hands, the prettiness of the plants including *nopal*, the sweetness of the fruit, and the beauty that the flowers and greenery contribute to his home.

Many desert plants eaten as food or medicine, including nopal, aloe vera, and century plant, "contain mucilaginous polysaccharide gums that are viscous enough to slow the digestion and absorption of sugary foods."[16] For instance, aloe gel contains glucomannan, a water-soluble fiber, and nopal "has a high-soluble fiber and pectin content, which may affect intestinal glucose uptake, partially accounting for its hypoglycemic actions."[17] There appears to be increased cellular sensitivity to insulin as well.[18] Therefore, nopal and other desert plants likely reduce blood sugar levels that stress the pancreas (which permanently damages insulin metabolism), or at least they prolong the period over which sugar is absorbed into the blood after one eats.

Other frequently employed remedies for diabetes consist of teas. According to Silvia Herrera, one is made by boiling a handful of *matarique* (Indian plantain) leaves in a liter of water, which is drunk four or five times a day. Yolanda Lopez and Alicia Gutierrez mentioned *nispero* (loquat) tea, using about three leaves per cup. Another remedy combines the leaves of *lagrimas de San Pedro* (tears of St. Peter) and the stems of *cola de caballo* (horsetail), the last of which is seen dried in figure 11.2. "You get a little of each, a cup, like this, like four fingers per cup," explained Carlos Mendez. "You get the water first, boil it for five minutes and then you turn it off [and steep leaves in it]. [You drink it] in the morning and at night."

Figure 11.2 Dried stalks of horsetail used as tea for treating diabetes. Photo by the author.

A study of 31,512 adults found that treatment with a diuretic was not only less expensive but often more beneficial than a calcium channel blocker or an angiotensin-converting enzyme (ACE) inhibitor in protecting against stroke and heart attacks in people with diabetes and those with elevated fasting glucose.[19] Some interviewees were outspoken in their preference for herbal remedies over prescription drugs or advocated complementary rather than alternative use of them. Verónica Mendez summed up this attitude, saying: "If I could find something that's natural I would take it anytime more than the medications. The medications do you good for this, but then they harm you for that. Of course the natural herbs are a very slow process but they work."

Health care professionals tend to overlook or downplay the significance of folk and alternative medicine[20] rather than incorporate it into a plan of care.[21] Several authors of works about diabetes among Latinx consider traditional therapies to be negative health practices, noncongruent cultural beliefs, and dangerous owing to the chance of people using them for the wrong indications and possible interactions with prescription medications.

Few of the interviewees told medical personnel about their ideas of the emotional causes of diabetes or about their using plants as hypoglycemic agents. "They don't believe in them," stated Margarita Mendoza, with whom several others agreed. I asked Jorge Alvarez, too, about his interaction with medical personnel, specifically if he had told his doctor about using *lagrimas de San Pedro* and *cola de caballo*. "Yeah. He is not happy with it." I also mentioned the cactus, to which Mr. Alvarez replied that the doctor told him, "I know you take it but I am not happy about that."

Laboratory studies strongly suggest that several plants appear efficacious in treating diabetes and associated diseases. As the authors of one review of 108 trials involving thirty-six herbs and nine supplements write, medical personnel should "keep an open mind in advising patients who might already be using these."[22] Further, "They should be guided not only by sound clinical judgment, but also by patients' preferences, needs, and values."

Nopal, aloe vera, and other plants are familiar to people who know of their use traditionally in their families and communities. Some individuals prefer "natural medicine" to prescription drugs. Those who cultivate medicinal herbs in their yards appear to derive sensory and aesthetic pleasure from looking at the plants and breaking off a leaf, crushing it, and smelling the aroma as well as making teas and tinctures with them. For everyone I interviewed, growing and utilizing medicinal plants symbolizes self-reliance. When standard interventions fail, including phytomedicine with proven hypoglycemic outcomes in the treatment plan might prove attractive and efficacious.

RITUAL, SYMBOL, AND SACRIFICE

Nonnutritional meanings and uses of food is a third aspect of local knowledge. Individuals convey feelings toward others through offerings of food; rejecting the food may be construed as a rejection of the host. Remarked Gabriela Diaz: "I feel bad when I refuse to eat food that friends offer me. I don't like to explain my health to everybody so I say no thank you, and they say, 'Why don't you like this?'" When Yolanda Lopez goes to someone's home, she admitted: "I eat as if I am not diabetic." Rita Valdez said that most people know she is diabetic but they nevertheless insist that she eat the foods they have prepared, "so I take only a small bite."

That food is gendered impacts the choice of fare. Typically, meat and starches are often considered masculine, while chicken, fish, and fruit are conceived of as feminine, which strongly affects efforts to modify men's diets.[23] Also affecting food choice is the conception of a "proper" meal[24] and the notion of a "complete" meal,[25] whether this includes dessert or some other item. "Desserts: those are my comfort foods," declared Gloria Aguilar. "I do crave my little chocolate," said Elizabeth Castillo. Food often conjures up fond memories. "I know that some of our traditional foods are not full of nutrients but they bring back good memories of childhood and I'm not giving them up just because some researcher says they are bad."[26]

The preparation, service, and consumption of food are fraught with meanings and meaningfulness and serve as a basis for meaning making. Not surprisingly, food is also inextricably bound up with self and self-making, from family, regional, and ethnic identity to personal characteristics. "Yes, I like to cook. And unfortunately, I like *what* I cook!" said Margarita Mendoza. Remarked Elizabeth Castillo: "I am a bread eater; I am a sweet eater. I'm sure that I'm like an alcoholic but with regard to sweets."

Verónica Mendez conceded the impact of diabetes on her eating habits: "It's affected me a lot 'cause I love my tortillas. I don't eat as many vegetables or salads as I would like to because I don't love my salads. . . . I need my beans and my tortillas. I have two friends, they were borderline diabetic . . . one of them lost so much weight. Both of them did it. But they really sacrificed a lot and I said, 'I don't know.' . . . I can sacrifice, but not as much as they did."

As Mrs. Mendez's remark indicates, "sacrifice" means to suffer loss, to give up something cherished, to renounced or surrender for an ideal, a belief, or an end. A number of interviewees bemoaned having to give up rice and beans and other items common to the diets of many Latinx as well as foods specific to the holiday season and being unable to eat what they liked or what was served at family get-togethers. Clearly, clinicians need to pay attention to language in counseling. The use of negative terms such as "give up," "do without," and "cannot eat" may result in feelings of failure and low self-esteem among patients unable to achieve the ideal. This is apparent in metaphors employed by a patient suggesting that he or she is a naughty child, a foolish adult, or beyond redemption. "I mean, it's just . . . we're bad . . . we are," said Elizabeth Castillo, who, with her husband, has struggled often unsuccessfully to control diabetes through diet. "We're just bad, period."

Why people think they must sacrifice foods they have known since childhood, identify with, and prefer has not been explained. Few cookbooks exist for Latinx with diabetes, and recipes in educational materials usually describe American-style foods and eating habits. A notable exception is *Comer Bien Para Vivir Mejor* (Eat Well to Live Better), a booklet distributed some years ago by the California Diabetes Control Program. Teri A. Hall writes: "Fortunately, traditional Mexican foods such as beans, rice, and tortillas lend themselves easily to the high-fiber, low-fat diet recommended for management of diabetes. The *Comer Bien* plan," which she helped develop, "instead of prescribing an unfamiliar eating pattern, illustrates ways to modify methods of preparation of traditional foods (e.g., using less oil or lard, grilling instead of frying)." In addition, "Menus for the high-fiber, low-fat food plan make daily use of beans and tortillas, with frequent use of rice, Mexican cheese (*queso fresco*), avocadoes, tomatoes, and cereals," as well as nopal, used also as a hypoglycemic agent.[27]

To maximize the good that they do, clinicians should understand the impact of customs and symbolism on identity and food choice. One way to achieve this goal might be to draw upon a list of general questions to obtain information from patients.[28] Such queries might include several of the following:

> What are some things that make it difficult for people to treat their diabetes?
> What are some things that help people treat their diabetes?
> Which foods are most difficult to limit or give up from your diet, and why?
> Which foods would be the most difficult to add to your diet, and why?
> How important is eating to your social interactions, and why?
> How do certain foods represent an event?
> How would relationships with family and friends change if you altered your diet?
> How often do you use food as a gift or to celebrate special occasions?

Devising a list of questions is not a recipe for success, however. Clinicians' perspectives need to change from strict adherence to technological and compliance models to approaches that emphasize collaboration, negotiation, and the joint development of treatment plans that the patient can live with, plans that are appropriate to the symbolic significance of food in the patient's daily life, social relations, and self-making. To gain this orientation, health care personnel should identify assumptions in their own system of beliefs, for example, patients who do not practice healthful behaviors do not care about their well-being, biomedicine is "right," traditional beliefs must be changed rather than built upon, people should and will follow instructions given by health practitioners, and adherence failure is the patient's fault and problem.[29] They can also reflect on their own symbolic uses of food socially and emotionally, which may generate greater understanding of and empathy toward patients.[30]

SELF-REPORTED CHALLENGES TO SELF-MANAGING DIABETES

Those with diabetes face many difficulties in attempting the self-management of their condition as articulated by the patients themselves. Self-reported difficulties include being forced to follow a prescribed diet that does not involve traditional foods and customary flavors. "I cannot eat good if I don't have my salsa in my food all the time," insisted Gabriela Diaz. "Tortillas!" exclaimed Rita Valdez, who avoids flour tortillas now but at each meal eats one made of corn. She particularly misses, and often craves, enchiladas, chili rellenos, pozole, and menudo. "What's difficult for me is to give up desserts, and chocolate desserts in particular," admitted Elizabeth Castillo. "It's very difficult for me say, 'Oh, no thank you.'" Added her sister, Gloria Aguilar, "But those are my comfort foods."

Holidays and family get-togethers are especially problematic. Josephina Rivera said: "The day of Thanksgiving . . . that one pie made of pumpkin: I know that I shouldn't eat it, but I get tempted and I take nibbles . . . nibbles." Remarked Margarita Mendoza: "It's just that sometimes when there's a gathering or a party I eat the sweets that are there. I can't help myself and I have them. I don't stick strictly to my diet."

Another concern, however, is financial; not only the cost of food but also prescription drugs. Half a dozen oral medications are prescribed by physicians to treat individuals with diabetes. Many of the people I interviewed are retired; a number have annual incomes of $10,000 or less for the household. The cost of medications overwhelms some budgets; for instance, Alicia

Gutierrez spends $350 per month for them out of her income of $780. Among other health problems, Rafael Mendoza, a retired billing clerk for a trucking company, has a heart condition and his wife, Margarita Mendoza, who had worked in a beauty salon, has diabetes. They live in an apartment. Their annual income is less than $20,000 combined. Medications total $800 per month. How can they afford it? "The pills, we just cut them in half. That's the only way." Like a number of others, they also take a bus from a local senior center to Tijuana, Mexico, where they purchase their medications at half the price charged in the United States.

Yet another hindrance to seeking help for diabetes is the attitude and behavior of some clinicians. Patients remarked on the lack of communication, being rebuked for their traditional ideas and practices, suffering long waits at the office or clinic, and being given short shrift by personnel. Alicia Gutierrez complained that doctors do not take time to listen to or discuss matters with older sick people like her. "They just take tests but they don't tell me why." Francisca Perez was concerned that at least one of her husband's medications caused diarrhea, "but the doctors don't ask or care." Margarita Mendoza complained, "The doctors don't tell me anything. I have a doctor who . . . it's not right to speak of the doctors but . . . she doesn't let me get a word in. She says, 'I don't have time! I don't have time!' She just writes down what the nurse wrote down [the prescriptions] I was low on and she leaves. She doesn't give a chance to talk."

While undoubtedly there are providers desiring to build trusting relationships with Latinx patients, understanding their health beliefs and healing practices, and discovering community resources and support networks, interviewees in my research were not sanguine. Studies indicate that diabetes patients who assess providers positively engaged in self-management tasks more than those holding negative views.[31]

LIVING WITH DIABETES

Those with diabetes are urged to alter long-standing eating habits that involve sensory experiences, extranutritional meanings, and symbolic uses of food. Many find that doing so is exceedingly difficult. Remarked Josephina Rivera: "There are times I see ice cream [sold by vendors] in the streets and my mouth waters, and I say, 'Oh, my God!' I tell my daughters that one day, when I know I am really sick, I am going to eat a really big one, even if I die—but I will die happy. The day will arrive, but not yet. One makes a huge sacrifice. A lot of sacrifice."

Attempting to manage diabetes imposes great demands on patients who must test their blood sugar level several times a day, plan meals that balance food group selections, calculate calories and fat content, schedule exercise in relation to eating, and, in advanced stages of the disease, take medications orally or by injection daily. Local knowledge reveals that diabetes is not only pathophysiological; it is also social, cultural, and psychological. Both clinical practice and public health need to be more fully oriented to these aspects of the disease.

In recent years a number of articles about ethnic beliefs and practices conclude by calling for "culturally sensitive," "culturally appropriate," "culturally competent," and "culturally relevant" health care.[32] What we seem to be dealing with is not necessarily cultural, and not reducible to a patient's ethnicity, but more likely universal experiences and concerns in the human condition.

In conclusion, documents and programs originating with national and state agencies should counsel people in regard to emotional stress, the impact on the family, and the effect on social relations. Training for physicians, nurses, and nutritionists needs to provide information that includes people's use of herbal treatments, the nonnutritional meanings and uses of food, and the psychological and social aspects of diabetes in order for clinicians to better communicate with, guide, and help their patients. Otherwise, those with diabetes will not be adequately equipped to deal with their illness, forestall or prevent complications, and maximize their quality of life.

NOTES

CHAPTER 1. THE LANGUAGE OF FOOD

1. For an overview of the economic consequences of the virus, see William Masters, "COVID-19 Impacts on Agriculture, Food, and Nutrition," *Econofact*, 20 Apr 2020, https://econofact.org/covid-19-impacts-on-agriculture-food-and-nutrition.

2. Noah F. G. Evers, Patricia M. Greenfield, and Gabriel W. Evers, "COVID-19 Shifts Mortality Salience, Activities, and Values in the United States: Big Data Analysis of Online Adaptation," *Human Behavior and Emerging Technologies*, vol. 3 (2021), pp. 107–26.

3. David Mas Masumoto, "*Gochisou* and Brown Rice *Sushi*," *Country Voices: The Oral History of a Japanese American Family Farm Community*, by Masumoto (Inaka Countryside Publications, 1987).

4. Ben Mims, "The Power of a Meal Shared: Gifting Food Is a Win-Win in Times of Hardship," *Los Angeles Times*, 7 Mar 2021, p. F06.

5. Annie Hauck-Lawson, "Hearing the Food Voice: An Epiphany for a Researcher," *Digest—An Interdisciplinary Study of Food and Foodways*, vol. 12 (1992), p. 6. See also Annie Hauck-Lawson, "Foodways of Three Polish-American Families in New York," PhD Dissertation, New York University, 1991. For other references to "food voice," see the section of essays titled "Food, Meaning, and Voice" in Carole Counihan and Penny Van Esterik, editors, *Food and Culture: A Reader* (Routledge, 1997), pp. 11–91; and Diana Pittet, "Food Voice Annotated Bibliography," *Food, Culture & Society*, vol. 7 (2004), pp. 135–45.

6. Lucy M. Long, "Learning to Listen to the Food Voice: Recipes as Expressions of Identity and Carriers of Memory," *Food, Culture & Society*, vol. 7 (2004), pp. 118–22.

7. Dan Jurafsky, *The Language of Food: A Linguist Reads the Menu* (W. W. Norton, 2014), pp. 177–78.

8. See Emily Monaco, "Introducing 'Food Grammar,' the Unspoken Rules of Every Cuisine: Technically, Spaghetti and Meatballs Is Bad Grammar," *Atlas Obscura*, 29 Jan 2021, https://www.atlasobscura.com/articles/do-italians-eat-spaghetti-and-meatballs. Also see Claude Lévi-Strauss, "The Culinary Triangle" (reprinted in Counihan and Van Esterik, editors, *Food and Culture*, 35), who contends that "we can hope to discover for each specific case how the cooking of a society is a language in which it unconsciously translates its structure—or else resigns itself, still unconsciously, to reveal its contradictions."

9. Richard Raspa, "Exotic Foods among Italian-Americans in Mormon Utah: Food as Nostalgic Enactment of Identity," *Ethnic and Regional Foodways in the United States: The Performance of Group Identity*, edited by Linda Keller Brown and Kay Mussell (U of Tennessee P, 1984), p. 191.

10. See the section "Part III: Food as Art, Symbol, and Ritual," *The Food and Folklore Reader*, edited by Lucy M. Long (Bloomsbury, 2015), pp. 157–279; the symbolism and customs in David Wilson and Angus K. Gillespie, editors, *Rooted in America: Foodlore of Popular Fruits and Vegetables* (U of Tennessee P, 1999); and introductions in sections of essays in Michael Owen Jones, Bruce Giuliano, and Roberta Krell, editors, *Foodways and Eating Habits: Directions for Research* (California Folklore Society, 1983).

11. Margaret Visser, *Much Depends on Dinner* (McClelland and Stewart Weidenfeld, 1986), p. 14.

12. See also Melissa Caswell Mason, "You Said a Mouthful: Food and Food-Related Metaphors in Folkspeech," *Folklore and Mythology Studies*, vol. 6 (1982), pp. 29–33; and Mark Morton, "Boning Up on Language," *Gastronomica: The Journal of Food and Culture*, vol. 5 (2005), pp. 6–7.

13. Quoted in Jeremy MacClancy, *Consuming Culture: Why You Eat What You Eat* (Henry Holt, 1992), p. 2.

14. Quoted in Stephen Adams and Barbara Adams, "Thoreau's Diet at Walden," *Studies in the American Renaissance*, vol. 14 (1990), pp. 243–60.

15. Soudi Jiménez, "Defying the Pandemic, Latinos Missing Loved Ones Travel to Their Homelands for the Holiday," *Los Angeles Times*, 24 Dec 2020, https://www.latimes.com /california/story/2020-12-24/latinos-travel-homelands-holiday.

16. Regarding sensations in varied food contexts, see Barbara Kirshenblatt-Gimblett, "Playing to the Senses: Food as a Performance Medium," *Performance Research*, vol. 4 (2014), pp. 1–30.

17. Ernst Cassirer, *An Essay on Man: An Introduction to a Philosophy of Human Culture* (Yale University P, 1944), p. 26.

18. Raymond Firth, *Symbols: Public and Private* (Cornell University P, 1973), p. 20.

19. G. Morgan, P. J. Frost, and L. R. Pondy, "Organizational Symbolism," *Organizational Symbolism*, edited by L. R. Pondy, P. J. Frost, G. T. Morgan, et al. (JAI, 1983), pp. 3–35.

20. See Constance Classen, "Foundations for an Anthropology of the Senses," *International Social Sciences Journal*, vol. 153 (1997), pp. 401–12.

21. L. E. Grivetti, S. J. Lamprecht, H. J. Rocke, et al., "Threads of Cultural Nutrition: Arts and Humanities," *Progress in Food and Nutrition Science*, vol. 11 (1987), p. 269.

22. Norine Dresser, "Multicultural Manners: Sour Taste," *Los Angeles Times*, 13 Nov 1999, p. B9.

23. John Thorne, "The Fork," *American Wine & Food*, vol. 1 (1987), pp. 1–2.

24. Diane Tye, "Edible Men: Playing with Food at Bachelorette Parties," *Western Folklore*, vol. 77 (2018), pp. 221–48.

25. Tye, "Edible Men," 233.

26. David Bell and Gill Valentine, *Consuming Geographies: We Are Where We Eat* (Routledge, 1997).

27. Yvonne R. Lockwood and William G. Lockwood, "Pasties in Michigan's Upper Peninsula: Foodways, Interethnic Relations, and Regionalism," *Creative Ethnicity: Symbols and Strategies of Contemporary Ethnic Life*, edited by Stephen Stern and John Allan Cicala (Utah State UP), 3–20.

28. Timothy Charles Lloyd, "The Cincinnati Chili Culinary Complex," *Western Folklore*, vol. 40 (1981), pp. 28–40.

29. Lucy M. Long, "Green Bean Casserole and Midwestern Identity: A Regional Foodways Aesthetic and Ethos," *Midwestern Folklore*, vol. 33 (2007), pp. 29–44. Reprinted in Long, *The Food and Folklore Reader*, 191–204.

30. "Giant Hamburger Puts Nebraska Burg on Map," *The Topeka Capital-Journal*, 19 Jul 1989, p. 4-B.

31. Michael Owen Jones, *Corn: A Global History* (Reaktion Books, 2017).

32. Jane Dusselier, "Does Food Make Place? Food Protests in Japanese American Concentration Camps," *Food and Foodways*, vol. 10 (2002), pp. 137–65.

33. Annie Hauck-Lawson, "Hearing the Food Voice," 6–7.

34. John Lancaster, "Incredible Edibles," *New Yorker*, 21 Mar 2011, pp. 64–68.

35. Michelle Huneven, "Meanwhile, Back on the Farm," review of *Up a Country Lane Cookbook* by Evelyn Birkby, *Los Angeles Times*, 1 Sep 1994, p. H11. For the symbolic significance of Jell-O, see Sarah E. Newton, "The Jell-O Syndrome: Investigating Popular Culture/Foodways," *Western Folklore*, vol. 51 (1982), pp. 249–67.

36. Emma-Kate Symons, "Chirac Food Slur Brings Brits to the Boil," *The Australian*, 6 Jul 2005.

37. Alexander A. Robach, *Dictionary of International Slurs (Ethnophaulisms)* (Sci-Art Publishers; reprinted by Maledicta Press, [1944] 1979). See also Simon J. Bronner, *Folklore: The Basics* (Routledge, 2017), pp. 137–38; and LuAnne Roth, "Do the [White] Thing: What Oppositional Gaze Narratives Reveal about Culinary Nationalism and Whiteness," *Western Folklore*, vol. 80 (2021), pp. 81–117.

38. Mario Montaño, "Appropriation and Counterhegemony in South Texas: Food Slurs, Offal Meats, and Blood," *Usable Pasts: Traditions and Group Expressions in North America*, edited by Tad Tuleja (Utah State UP, 1997), 50–67.

39. Gerald V. O'Brien, "Indigestible Food, Conquering Hordes, and Waste Materials: Metaphors of Immigrants and the Early Immigration Restriction Debate in the United States," *Metaphor and Symbol*, vol. 18 (2003), pp. 33–47.

40. Mary Oster, "Woman Charged with Hate Crime for Throwing Pork Chops at Upstate NY Synagogue," *Jewish Telegraphic Agency*, 27 Jan 2020, https://www.jta.org/quick-reads/woman-charged-with-hate-crime-for-throwing-pork-chops-at-upstate-ny-synagogue.

41. Larry Hirschhorn, *The Workplace Within: Psychodynamics of Organizational Life* (MIT Press, 1988), pp. 247–48.

42. Susan Lanser, "Burning Dinners: Feminist Subversions of Domesticity," *Feminist Messages: Coding in Women's Folk Culture*, edited by Joan Newlon Radner (U of Illinois P, 1993), pp. 36–53.

43. For an example in the folkloristic literature, see John Cicala, "Cuscuszu in Detroit, July 18, 1993: Memory, Conflict, and Bella Figura during a Sicilian-American Meal,"

Italian Folk: Vernacular Culture in Italian-American Lives, edited by Joseph Sciorra (Fordham University, 2011), 31–48.

44. Simon J. Bronner, "Manner Books and Suburban Houses: The Structure of Tradition and Aesthetics," *Winterthur Portfolio*, vol. 18 (1983), pp. 61–68.

45. See, for example, Florence E. Baer, "'Give me . . . your huddled masses': Anti-Vietnamese Refugee Lore and the 'Image of the Limited Good,'" *Western Folklore*, vol. 41 (1982), pp. 275–29.

46. George W. Rich and David F. Jacobs, "Saltpeter: A Folkloric Adjustment to Acculturation Stress," *Western Folklore*, vol. 32 (1973), pp. 164–79.

47. Gary Alan Fine, "The Kentucky Fried Rat: Legends and Modern Society," *Journal of the Folklore Institute* 17 (1980), pp. 222–43.

48. Patricia Turner, "Church's Fried Chicken and the Klan: A Rhetorical Analysis of Rumor in the Black Community," *Western Folklore*, vol. 46 (1987), pp. 294–306.

49. David Mikkelson, "Does KFC Use Mutant Chickens?" Snopes, 1 Feb 1999, snopes .com/fact-check/kfc-mutant-chickens.

50. Norine Dresser, "Multicultural Manners: Meal Runs Afoul of Taiwan Custom, *Los Angeles Times*, 22 Aug 1994, p. B5.

51. For an excellent examination of the themes, root metaphors, and symbolic construction of meanings in regard to growing food, see Carolyn P. Egri, "War and Peace on the Land: An Analysis of the Symbolism of Organic Farming," *Studies in Cultures, Organizations and Societies*, vol. 3 (1997), pp. 17–40.

52. See also "Symbol" in Lucy M. Long, editor, *The Food and Folklore Reader* (Bloomsbury, 2015), pp. 161–62.

CHAPTER 2. EATING WHAT YOU ARE, WERE, OR WANT TO BE

1. See, e.g., Warren Belasco, *Food: The Key Concepts* (Berg, 2008); Carole Counihan and Penny Van Esterik, editors, *Food and Culture: A Reader* (Routledge, 1997); Long, *The Food and Folklore Reader*.

2. Felicia Lee, "When Breaking Bread Means Breaking Bonds," *Los Angeles Times*, 23 Nov 2003, http://www.latimes.com/features/printedition/magazine/la-tm-pickyeater 47nov23,1,7126513.story.

3. Eve Conant, "One Way to Fight Invasive Species? Eat Them," *National Geographic*, 23 Dec 2020, https://www.nationalgeographic.com/travel/features/eating-invasive-species -on-a-road-trip-across-the-southern-us/#close.

4. Alan Beardsworth and Teresa Keil, "The Vegetarian Option: Varieties, Conversions, Motives and Careers," *The Sociological Review*, vol. 40 (1992), pp. 253–93.

5. Thomas M. Dunn and Steven Bratman, "On Orthorexia Nervosa: A Review of the Literature and Proposed Diagnostic Criteria," *Eating Behavior*, vol. 21 (2016), pp. 11–17.

6. Irene Pearson, "The Social and Moral Roles of Food in *Anna Karenina*," *Journal of Russian Studies*, vol. 48 (1984), pp. 10–19.

7. Elizabeth Adler, "Creative Eating: The Oreo Syndrome," *Western Folklore*, vol. 40 (1981), pp. 4–10.

8. Such concerns today were propagated during the 1960s by the counterculture protest against the food industry establishment; see Jill Dubisch, "You Are What You Eat: Religious Aspects of the Health Food Movement," *Folk Groups and Folklore Genres: A Reader*, edited by Elliott Oring (Utah State UP, 1989), 124–35.

The evils were numerous: the high sugar content of popular breakfast cereals (according to *Esquire*'s "Dubious Achievement Awards" in 1972, Wheaties, "the breakfast of champions," ranked thirtieth in a field of sixty, falling in nutritional value behind Apple Jacks, Clackers, Froot Loops, and other sugar-laden products), heavy doses of additives and preservatives in processed foods that already had lost much of their nutritive value (a classic example of additives is "lemon cream pie" that contains neither lemon nor cream), the overuse of chemical fertilizers, the reliance on hormones and antibiotics to stimulate animal growth, and the proliferation of pesticides which continues to be a problem ("Sure, it's going to kill a lot of people, but they may be dying of something else anyway," allegedly remarked Othal Brand, member of a Texas pesticide review board, regarding chlordane).

A system of symbols that binds beliefs and behaviors includes a romantic ideal of returning to nature or a "golden age" signified by homemade bread, home-canned produce, and other forms of subsistence, preference for frozen yogurt over ice cream, wheat germ sprinkled on cereal, sprouts on whole grain bread, vegetable and fruit juice in place of sodas, and raw and coarse foods rather than processed and refined ones. See R. P. Fleshman, "Symposium on the Young Adult in Today's World: Eating Rituals and Realities," *The Nursing Clinics of North America*, vol. 8 (1973), pp. 91–104; and Suzanne Waldenberger, "Our Daily Bread: A Look at Bible Breads," *The Digest: An Interdisciplinary Study of Food and Foodways*, vol. 15 (1995), pp. 17–19.

Sugar has been one of the most powerful condensed symbols for colonialism, slavery, industrial capitalism, and globalization. It is also drawn upon to explain youth violence through addiction and hyperactivity and serves as a class-based emblem of what's wrong with welfare programs because the poor spend their food stamps on soft drinks and sweets. See Elisabeth Walker Mechling and Jay Mechling, "Sweet Talk: The Moral Rhetoric of Sugar," *Central States Speech Journal*, vol. 34 (1988), pp. 19–32; and Sidney W. Mintz, *Sweetness and Power: The Place of Sugar in Modern History* (Elisabeth Sifton Books/ Viking, 1985).

The Twinkie defense became a metaphor for the evils of sweets and junk food. The attorney defending former San Francisco supervisor Dan White on trial for killing Mayor George Moscone and Supervisor Harvey Milk in 1980 mustered the defense that extended the notion of "diminished capacity" to the cycle of stress, depression, consumption of sugar-laden junk food, and ultimate loss of self-control (the jury returned a verdict of manslaughter, not murder); however, many today who have heard of the Twinkie defense think that eating sweets caused White's diminished capacity, which further strengthens the symbolism of the evils of junk food. "Some people say that Twinkies are the quintessential junk food, but I believe in the things," remarked Jimmy Dewar, who named them (inspired by a sign outside St. Louis advertising Twinkle Toes Shoes). I fed them to my four kids, and they feed them to my 15 grandchildren." One son played college football, another professional ball. "Twinkies never hurt them." See Dianne Klein, "Even an Apple a Day Can't Keep Twinkies Away," *Los Angeles Times*, 17 Mar 1991, section V, pp. 1, 3.

9. Jee-Hyun Jeannie Park, "Spam Ways" (unpublished paper, World Arts and Cultures Senior Colloquium, UCLA, 1991).

10. Emily Jenkins, *Tongue First: Adventures in Physical Culture* (Virago, 1999).

11. Carole M. Counihan, *The Anthropology of Food and Body: Gender, Meaning, and Power* (Routledge, 1999), 122–23. See also D. Mori, S. Chaiken, and P. Pliner, "'Eating Lightly' and the Self-Presentation of Femininity," *Journal of Personality and Social Psychology*, vol. 53 (1987), pp. 693–702.

12. Colin Spencer, *The Heretic's Feast: A History of Vegetarianism* (UP of New England, 1995), 280.

13. Robert Hank, "Mass Media and Lifestyle Differentiation: An Analysis of the Public Discourse about Food," *Communication*, vol. 11 (1989), pp. 231–38.

14. Leslie Prosterman, "Food and Alliance at the County Fair," *Western Folklore*, vol. 40 (1981), pp. 81–90. In regard to religious values and ideology, see Caroline Walker Bynum, *Holy Feast and Holy Fast: The Religious Significance of Food to Medieval Women* (U of California P, 1987).

15. Carol J. Adams, *The Sexual Politics of Meat: A Feminist-Vegetarian Critical Theory* (Polity; Continuum, 1990); Jonathan Deutsch, "'Please Pass the Chicken Tits': Rethinking Men and Cooking at the Urban Firehouse" *Food and Foodways*, vol. 13 (2005), pp. 91–114; Deborah Dale Heisley, "Gender Symbolism in Food," PhD dissertation, Northwestern University, 1990; Harriet Bruce Moore, "The Meaning of Food," *American Journal of Clinical Nutrition*, vol. 5 (1957), pp. 77–82; J. Twigg, "Vegetarianism and the Meanings of Meat," *The Sociology of Food and Eating,* edited by A. Murcott (Gower, 1983), 18–30; Richard Wik and Persephone Hintlian, "Cooking on Their Own: Cuisines of Manly Men," *Food & Foodways*, vol. 13 (2005), pp. 159–68.

16. Marshall Sahlins, *Culture and Practical Reason* (U of Chicago P, 1976).

17. Heisley, "Gender Symbolism," 9.

18. Heber Rodrigues, Carlos Goméz-Corona, and Dominique Valentin, "Femininities & Masculinities: Sex, Gender, and Stereotypes in Food Studies," *Current Opinion in Food Science*, vol. 33 (2020), p. 159.

19. For two of the few works on the eating behavior of transgender individuals, see Nevin Cohen and Kristen Cribbs, "The Everyday Food Practices of Community-Dwelling Lesbian, Gay, Bisexual, and Transgender (LGBT) Older Adults," *Journal of Aging Studies*, vol. 41 (2017), pp. 75–83; and Whitney Linsenmeyer, Rabia Rahman, and Daniel B. Stewart, "The Evolution of a Transgender Male's Relationship with Food and Exercise: A Narrative Inquiry," 19 Oct 2020, https://www.tandfonline.com/doi/full/10.1080/15401383.2020.1820924.

20. Adams, *Sexual Politics*; Twigg, "Vegetarianism and the Meanings of Meat."

21. Joseph Ritson, *An Essay on Abstinence from Animal Food, as a Moral Duty* (Richard Phillips, 1802); reprinted in *Radical Food: The Culture and Politics of Eating and Drinking 1790–1820*, edited by Timothy Morton (3 vols., Routledge, 2000), vol. I, pp. 171–273. Page citations are to the Morton edition.

22. Twig, "Vegetarianism and the Meanings of Meat."

23. Carol Nemeroff and Paul Rozin, "'You Are What You Eat': Applying the Demand-Free 'Impression' Technique to an Unacknowledged Belief," *Ethos*, vol. 17 (1989), pp. 50–63.

24. Gerald Carson, *Cornflake Crusade* (Rinehart, 1957); Gerald Carson, "Graham: The Man Who Made the Cracker Famous," *New-England Galaxy*, vol. 10 (1969), pp. 3–8;

John P. Coleman, "Casting Bread on Troubled Waters: Grahamism and the West," *Journal of American Culture*, vol. 9 (1986), pp. 1–8; Spencer, *Heretic's Feast*.

25. Michael W. Allen, Marc Wilson, Sik Hung Ng, et al., "Values and Beliefs of Vegetarians and Omnivores," *The Journal of Social Psychology*, vol. 140 (2000), pp. 405–22; and Malcolm Hamilton, "Eating Death: Vegetarians, Meat, and Violence," *Food, Culture & Society*, vol. 9 (2006), pp. 155–77.

26. Lean Leneman, "The Awakened Instinct: Vegetarianism and the Women's Suffrage Movement in Britain," *Women's History Review*, vol. 6 (1997), pp. 271–87.

27. Christine Kenyon Jones, "'Man Is a Carnivorous Production': Byron and the Anthropology of Food," *Prism(s)*, vol. 6 (1998), pp. 41–58.

28. Deutsch, "Please Pass the Chicken Tits," 105.

29. Jeffrey Sobal, "Men, Meat, and Marriage: Models of Masculinity," *Food and Foodways*, vol. 13 (2005), pp. 135–58.

30. Ramiro Fernandez Unsain, Mariana Dimitrov Ulian, Priscila de Morais Sato, et al., "'Macho Food': Masculinities, Food Preferences, Eating Practices History and Commensality among Gay Bears in São Paulo, Brazil," *Appetite*, vol. 144 (Sep 2019), pp. 1–7.

31. Pamela R. Frese, "Food and Gender in America: A Review Essay," *Food & Foodways*, vol. 5 (1992), pp. 205–11.

32. Elaine Showalter, *The Female Malady: Women, Madness, and English Culture, 1830–1980* (Pantheon Books, 1985).

33. Joan Jacobs Brumberg, *Fasting Girls: The Emergence of Anorexia Nervosa as a Modern Disease* (Harvard UP, 1988).

34. Heisley, "Gender Symbolism in Food"; and Gun Roos and Margareta Wandel, "'I Eat Because I'm Hungry, Because It's Good, and to Become Full': Everyday Eating Voiced by Male Carpenters, Drivers, and Engineers in Contemporary Oslo," *Food and Foodways*, vol. 13 (2005), pp. 169–80.

35. M. Kerr and N. Charles, "Servers and Providers: The Distribution of Food within the Family," *The Sociological Review*, vol. 34 (1986), pp. 115–57. See also Marjorie Devault, "Conflict and Deference," *Food and Culture: A Reader*, edited by Carole Counihan and Penny Van Esterik (Routledge, 1997), pp. 180–99.

36. In regard to what and how we eat related to personal characteristics, I am greatly influenced by ideas in Carole A. Bisogni, Margaret Connors, Carol M. Devine, et al., "Who We Are and How We Eat: A Qualitative Study of Identities in Food Choice," *Journal of Nutrition Education and Behavior*, vol. 34 (2002), pp. 128–40.

37. Margaret Tailberi Flynn, "Dining with Samuel Pepys in Seventeenth Century England," *American Dietetic Association Journal*, vol. 20 (1944), pp. 434–40; David Mas Masumoto, "*Gochisou* and Brown Rice *Sushi*," *Country Voices: The Oral History of a Japanese American Family Farm Community* (Inaka Countryside Publications, 1987); Spencer, *Heretic's Feast*, 280.

38. Frances Trollope, *Domestic Manners of the Americans* (Alfred A. Knopf, [1832] 1949), p. 297. On tourists' reactions to foodways in two Canadian provinces, and issues of identity, class, morality, and civic responsibility, see Holly Everett, "Vernacular Health Moralities and Culinary Tourism in Newfoundland and Labrador," *Journal of American Folklore*, vol. 122 (2009), pp. 28–52.

39. Arthur M. Schlesinger, Sr., "A Dietary Interpretation of American History," *Massachusetts Historical Society Proceedings*, vol. 68 (1944–47), pp. 199–227.

40. "Eating to Win," *Los Angeles Times*, 7 Feb 1991; see also Michael Rosen, "Breakfast at Spiro's: Dramaturgy and Dominance," *Journal of Management*, vol. 11 (1985), pp. 31–48.

41. Nathan Fenno and David Wharton, "UCLA Football Remains Success-Starved, but No Program Is Eating Richer," *Los Angeles Times*, 27 Oct 2020, https://www.latimes.com /sports/ucla/story/2020-10-27/ucla-chip-kelly-food-costs-college-football.

42. Sarah E. Newton, "The Jell-O Syndrome: Investigating Popular Culture/Foodways," *Western Folklore*, vol. 51 (1992), pp. 249–67.

43. Gerald Sussman, "Welcome to the Cooking of Provincial New Jersey: Twenty-One Cuisines, One Great Taste," *National Lampoon* (Jun 1974), pp. 57–63.

44. Ernest Mickler, *White Trash Cooking* (Ten-Speed Press, 1986). See also Robley Evans, "'Or Else This Were a Savage Spectacle': Eating and Troping Southern Culture," *Southern Quarterly*, vol. 30 (1992), pp. 141–49.

45. Lucy M. Long, "Green Bean Casserole and Midwestern Identity: A Regional Foodways Aesthetic and Ethos," *Midwestern Folklore*, vol. 33 (2007), pp. 29–44. Reprinted in Long, *The Food and Folklore Reader*, 191–204.

46. Long, "Green Bean Casserole," 29.

47. Long, "Green Bean Casserole," 37.

48. V. I. Clendenen, C. P. Herman, and J. Polivy, "Social Facilitation of Eating among Friends and Strangers," *Appetite*, vol. 23 (1994), pp. 1–13; Robert C. Klesges, Diane Bartsch, J. Derrick Norwood, et al., "The Effects of Selected Social Environmental Variables on the Eating Behavior of Adults in the Natural Environment," *International Journal of Eating Disorders*, vol. 3 (1984), pp. 35–41.

49. Mary Kreuger, "Women, Sensuality, and Stigma," *Digest: An Interdisciplinary Study of Food and Foodways*, vol. 19 (1999), pp. 10–11; and D. Mori, S. Chaiken, and P. Pliner, "'Eating Lightly' and the Self-Presentation of Femininity," *Journal of Personality and Social Psychology*, vol. 53 (1987), pp. 693–702.

50. See such works by folklorists as Charles Camp, *American Foodways: What, When, Why and How We Eat in America* (August House, 1989); Susan Kalčik, "Ethnic Foodways in America: Symbol and the Performance of Identity," *Ethnic and Regional Foodways in the United States: The Performance of Group Identity*, edited by Linda Keller Brown and Kay Mussell (U of Tennessee P, 1984), pp. 37–65; Yvonne R. Lockwood and William G. Lockwood, "Continuity and Adaptation of Arab-American Foodways," *Arab Detroit: From Margin to Mainstream*, edited by Nabeel Abraham and Andrew Shryock (Wayne State UP, 2000), pp. 515–49; Lucy M. Long, editor, *Ethnic American Food: A Cultural Encyclopedia* (2 vols., Rowman and Littlefield, 2015); and J. Sanford Rikoon, "Ethnic Food Traditions: A Review and Preview of Folklore Scholarship," *Kentucky Folklore Record*, vol. 28 (1982), pp. 12–25. Also see essays in Theodore C. Humphrey and Lin C. Humphrey, editors, *"We Gather Together": Food and Festival in American Life* (UMI Research Press, 1988). See also Don Yoder's articles about particular ethnic and regional food items: "Schnitz in the Pennsylvania Folk-Culture," *Pennsylvania Folklife*, vol. 12 (1961), pp. 44–53; "Sauerkraut in the Pennsylvania German Folk-Culture," *Pennsylvania Folklife*, vol. 12 (1961), pp. 56–69; and "Pennsylvanians Called It Mush," *Pennsylvania Folklife*, vol. 13 (1962–1963), pp. 27–49.

51. James Griffith, "We Always Call It 'Tucson Eat Yourself': The Role of Food at a Constructed Festival," Humphrey and Humphrey, editors, "*We Gather Together*," 219–34; and Richard Kurin, *Reflections of a Culture Broker: A View from the Smithsonian* (Smithsonian Institution Press, 1997).

52. Susan Auerbach, "The Brokering of Ethnic Folklore: Selection and Presentation Issues at a Multicultural Festival," *Creative Ethnicity: Symbols and Strategies of Contemporary Ethnic Life*, edited by Stephen Stern and John Allan Cicala (Utah State UP, 1991), 225–38.

53. Sabina Magliocco, "Playing with Food: The Negotiation of Identity in the Ethnic Display Event by Italian Americans in Clinton Indiana," *Studies in Italian American Folklore*, edited by Luisa Del Giudice (Utah State UP, 1993), 107–26. Regarding heritage foods in the United States and Western Europe, see Ronda L. Brulotte and Michael A. Di Giovine, editors, *Edible Identities: Food as Cultural Heritage* (Ashgate, 2014).

54. Carol M. Devine, Jeffery Sobal, Carole A. Bisogni, et al., "Food Choices in Three Ethnic Groups: Interactions of Ideals, Identities, and Roles," *Journal of Nutrition Education*, vol. 31 (1999), pp. 86–93; and Gill Valentine, "Eating in: Home, Consumption and Identity," *The Sociological Review*, vol. 47 (1999), pp. 491–524.

55. Jack Kugelmass, "Green Bagels: An Essay on Food, Nostalgia, and the Carnivalesque," *YIVO Annual*, vol. 19 (1990), pp. 57–80; Yvonne R. Lockwood and William G. Lockwood, "Continuity and Adaptation of Arab-American Foodways," *Arab Detroit: From Margin to Mainstream*, edited by Nabeel Abraham and Andrew Shryock (Wayne State UP, 2000), pp. 515–49; and Richard Raspa, "Exotic Foods among Italian Americans in Mormon, Utah: Food as Nostalgic Enactment of Identity," *Ethnic and Regional Foodways in the United States*, edited by Linda Keller Brown and Kay Mussel (U of Tennessee P, 1984), pp. 185–94. For studies regarding the nostalgia that seemingly sustains food-centric films and/or ethnic-themed restaurants, see Diane Negra, "Ethnic Food Fetishism, Whiteness, and Nostalgia in Recent Film and Television," *Velvet Light Trap*, vol. 62 (2002), pp. 15–77; and Davide Girardelli, "Commodified Identity: The Myth of Italian Food in the United States," *Journal of Communication Inquiry*, vol. 28 (2004), pp. 307–24.

56. Delores C. S. James, "Factors Influencing Food Choices, Dietary Intake, and Nutrition-Related Attitudes among African Americans: Application of a Culturally Sensitive Model," *Ethnicity & Health*, vol. 9 (2004), pp. 349–67.

57. Robert A. Georges, "You Often Eat What Others Think You Are: Food as an Index of Others' Conceptions of Who One Is," *Western Folklore*, vol. 43 (1984), p. 256.

58. Zoot Suit: The Play and the Promise, KCBS-TV, Los Angeles, 1982.

59. Valentine, "Eating in." For a study of female friends, family members, and peers celebrating an event with food and drink, see Tye, "Edible Men," pp. 221–48.

60. Elinor Ochs, Clotilde Pontecorvo, and Alessandra Fasulo, "Socializing Taste," *Ethnos*, vol. 61 (1996), pp. 7–46. Of related interest is Peter Jackson and Angela Meah, "Taking Humor Seriously in Contemporary Food Research," *Food, Culture & Society*, vol. 22 (2019), pp. 262–79.

61. Stephen Adams and Barbara Adams, "Thoreau's Diet at Walden," *Studies in the American Renaissance*, vol. 14 (1990), pp. 243–60; Caroline Giles Banks, "'Culture' in Culture-Bound Syndromes: The Case of Anorexia Nervosa," *Social Science & Medicine*,

vol. 34 (1992), pp. 867–84; and Hilde Bruch, *The Golden Cage: The Enigma of Anorexia Nervosa* (Vintage, 1978).

62. G. Chapman and H. Maclean, "'Junk Food' and 'Healthy Food': Meanings of Food in Adolescent Women's Culture," *Journal of Nutrition Education*, vol. 25 (1993), pp. 108–13.

63. Susan Bordo, "Reading the Slender Body," *Body Politics*, edited by M. Jacobus, E. F. Keller, and S. Shuttleworth (Routledge, 1990), pp. 83–112.

64. Arthur A. Berger, "Soft Drinks and Hard Icons," *Icons of Popular Culture*, edited by Marshall Fishwick and Ray B. Browne (Bowling Green University Popular Press, 1970), p. 433.

65. Mintz, *Sweetness and Power*, 211.

66. D. Battaglia, "Problematizing the Self: A Thematic Introduction," *Rhetorics of Self-Making*, edited by Battaglila (U of California P, 1995), pp. 1–15; and Bisogni et al., "Who We Are."

67. Michael Holroyd, *Bernard Shaw* (5 vols., Chatto & Windus, 1988), vol. I: *1856–1898, The Search for Love*, 93.

68. Carson, *Cornflake Crusade*.

69. Bisogni et al., "Who We Are."

70. L. Ryan Smart and Carole A. Bisogni, "Personal Food Systems of Male College Hockey Players," *Appetite*, vol. 37 (2001), pp. 57–70.

71. Michael Owen Jones, "'Tradition' in Identity Discourses and an Individual's Symbolic Construction of Self," *Western Folklore*, vol. 59 (2000), pp. 115–41.

CHAPTER 3. WHAT'S DISGUSTING, WHY, AND WHAT DOES IT MATTER?

1. Charles Darwin, *The Expression of Emotions in Man and Animals* (U of Chicago P, [1872] 1965), pp. 256–57.

2. Paul Dickson, *Chow: A Cook's Tour of Military Food* (New American Library, 1978). See also Trish Hall, "Few People Will Eat Whatever Crawls onto the Plate," *New York Times*, 30 Oct 1991.

3. Claire Palmerino, "Pleasing the Palate: Diet Selection and Aversion Learning," *Western Folklore*, vol. 40 (1981), pp. 19–27.

4. Paul Rozin and April E. Fallon, "A Perspective on Disgust," *Psychological Review*, vol. 94 (1987), pp. 23–41; Paul Rozin, April E. Fallon, and M. Augustoni-Ziskind, "The Child's Conception of Food: The Development of Contamination Sensitivity to 'Disgusting' Substances," *Developmental Psychology*, vol. 21 (1985), pp. 1075–79; and Paul Rozin, Linda Millman, and Carol Nemeroff, "Operation of the Laws of Sympathetic Magic in Disgust and Other Domains," *Journal of Personality and Social Psychology*, vol. 50 (1986), pp. 703–12.

5. A. Angyal, "Disgust and Related Aversions," *Journal of Abnormal and Social Psychology*, vol. 36 (1941), pp. 393–41; and Rozin, Millman, and Nemeroff, "Operation of the Laws of Sympathetic Magic."

6. For other examples, see Frederick J. Simoons, *Eat Not This Flesh: Food Avoidances from Prehistory to the Present* (2nd rev. ed., U of Wisconsin P, 1994).

7. Simon J. Bronner, "The Paradox of Pride and Loathing, and other Problems," *Western Folklore*, vol. 40 (1981), pp. 115–24.

8. Angyal, "Disgust and Related Aversions."

9. Charles Perry, "Hey, We'll Just Call It Sewsage," *Los Angeles Times*, 30 Dec 1993.

10. William Ian Miller, *The Anatomy of Disgust* (Harvard UP, 1997).

11. Angyal, "Disgust and Related Aversions"; Sigmund Freud, "The 'Uncanny,'" *Collected Papers* (Basic Books, 1959), vol. 4.

12. Miller, *The Anatomy of Disgust*, 50; see also 19, 40–41, 42, 49, 60, 106.

13. Rozin et al., "Operation of the Laws of Sympathetic Magic."

14. Miller, *Anatomy of Disgust*, 14.

15. J. G. Bourke, *Scatological Rites of All Nations* (W. H. Lowdermilk, 1891).

16. *Salamanders—A Night at the Phi Delt House*. Produced and directed by Ken Thigpen. 13 min. (Documentary Educational Resources, 1982).

17. Miller, *Anatomy of Disgust*, 137.

18. Tracy Crowe McGonigle, "Party Plans: Let Them Eat Snake," *Los Angeles Times*, 22 Oct 1997.

19. Kristin Kendle, "8 Weird Facts about Seattle's Gum Wall," Trip Savvy, 4 Jun 2019, https://www.tripsavvy.com/weird-facts-about-seattles-gum-wall-4134249; and Karin Vandraiss, "Seattle's Gum Wall to Be Completely Scrubbed," *Seattle Met*, 3 Nov 2015, https://www.seattlemet.com/news-and-city-life/2015/11/seattle-gum-wall-to-be -completely-scrubbed.

20. Charles Perry, "The Other, Other, Other White Meat," *Los Angeles Times*, 15 Dec 1994.

21. Charles Perry, "Tastes Just Like Chicken!" *Los Angeles Times*, 1 Sep 1994.

22. Daniel Boffey, "Edible Insects Set to Be Approved by EU in 'Breakthrough Moment,'" *The Guardian*, 3 Apr 2020, https://www.theguardian.com/environment/2020 /apr/03/insects-likely-approved-human-consumption-by-eu.

23. "Chile: Deliverance," *Newsweek*, 8 Jan 1973, p. 27.

24. Rudolph M. Bell, *Holy Anorexia* (U of Chicago P, 1985); Caroline Walker Bynum, *Holy Feast and Holy Fast: The Religious Significance of Food to Medieval Women* (U of California P, 1987); and Rebecca J. Lester, "Embodied Voices: Women's Food Asceticism and the Negotiation of Identity," *Ethos*, vol. 23 (1995), pp. 187–222. For contemporary examples, see Caroline G. Banks, "The Imaginative Use of Religious Symbols in Subjective Experiences of Anorexia Nervosa," *Psychoanalytical Review*, vol. 84 (1997), pp. 227–36.

25. Bynum, *Holy Feast and Holy Fast*; and Miller, *The Anatomy of Disgust*.

26. Mary O. Douglas, *Purity and Danger: An Analysis of the Concepts of Pollution and Taboo* (Routledge; Kegan Paul, 1966); and Simoons, *Eat Not This Flesh*.

27. C. V. Riley, "Locusts as Food for Man," *Proceedings of the American Association for the Advancement of Science* (1876), pp. 208–14. C. W. Schwabe, *Unmentionable Cuisine* (UP of Virginia, 1981).

28. Boffey, "Edible Insects."

29. Stephen Bayley, *Taste: The Secret Meaning of Things* (Pantheon Books, 1991), 198.

30. Quoted in John Sutherland, *Orwell's Nose: A Pathological Biography* (London: Reaktion Books, 2016), p. 241.

31. Miller, *Anatomy of Disgust*, 170.

32. Lenny R. Vartanian, Tara Trewartha, and Eric J. Vanman, "Disgust Predicts Prejudice and Discrimination toward Individuals with Obesity," *Journal of Applied Social Psychology*, vol. 46 (2016), pp. 369–75.

33. Miller, *Anatomy of Disgust*, 168.

34. Hilde Bruch, *Conversations with Anorexics*, edited by Danita Czyzewski and Melanie A. Suhr (Basic Books, 1988), pp. 120–21.

35. Miller, *Anatomy of Disgust*, 121.

36. Aimee Liu, *Solitaire* (Harper and Row, 1979), vii–viii.

37. Arthur M. Schlesinger, Sr., *Learning How to Behave: A Historical Study of American Etiquette Books* (Macmillan, 1946), p. 51; see also Simon J. Bronner, "Manner Books and Suburban Houses: The Structure of Tradition and Aesthetics," *Winterthur Portfolio*, vol. 18 (1983), p. 44.

38. Charles Darwin, *The Descent of Man* (2nd ed., A. L. Burt, 1874), p. 707.

CHAPTER 4. "STRESSED" SPELLED BACKWARD IS "DESSERTS": SELF-MEDICATING MOODS WITH FOODS

1. Elaine Paravati, Esha Naidu, and Shira Gabriel, "From 'Love Actually' to Love, Actually: The Sociometer Takes Every Kind of Fuel," *Self and Identity*, vol. 19 (2020), p. 3.

2. Paravati et al., "From 'Love Actually' to Love, Actually," 15.

3. Larry Bleiberg, "Why Maui Does Banana Bread Best," 21 Apr 2020, http://www.bbc.com/travel/story/20200420-banana-bread-the-internets-most-searched-for-recipe.

4. "A Nation Turns to Comfort Food," *ABC News*, 7 Nov 2006, http://abcnews.go.com/US/story?id=92217&page=1.

5. Bret Thorn, "Seeking Comfort, Diners Indulge in Feel-Good Fare," *Nation's Restaurant News*, vol. 35 (2001), p. 32.

6. For these and similar examples in this chapter, see such websites as Cafepress.com, Zazzle.com, Facts-about-chocolate.com, and Jokes.com.

7. Julie L. Locher, William C. Yoels, Donna Maurer, et al., "Comfort Foods: An Exploratory Journey into the Social and Emotional Significance of Food," *Food and Foodways*, vol. 13 (2005), pp. 273–97; and Brian Wansink, Matthew M. Cheney, and Nina Chan, "Exploring Comfort Food Preferences across Age and Gender," *Physiology & Behavior*, vol. 79 (2003), pp. 739–47.

8. Locker et al., "Comfort Foods"; Wansink et al., "Exploring Comfort Food Preferences."

9. Karlene Lukovitz, "Does Meaning of 'Comfort Foods' Vary by Age?" 31 Jul 2009, http://www.mediapost.com/publications/article/110781/does-meaning-of-comfort-foods-vary-by-age.html#axzz2Leodj8ws.

10. Brad Japhe, "Japanese Comfort Food at Del Rey Kitchen from Satoru Yokomori and Michael Yee," *LA Weekly*, 10 Nov 2014, http://m.laweekly.com/squidink/2014/11/10/japanese-comfort-food-at-del-rey-kitchen-from-satoru-yokomori-and-michael-yee. Among the dishes served are *nankotsu* (bite-sized pieces of deep-fried chicken cartilage)

and *itameshi* pasta (a spaghetti hybrid infused with umami-rich flavors of such items as shaved *bonito, nori,* and *ponzu* butter).

11. For studies of rat behavior, see Mary F. Dallman, Susan F. Akana, Susanne E. la Fleur, et al., "Chronic Stress and Obesity: A New View of 'Comfort Food,'" *Publications of the National Academy of Sciences,* vol. 100 (2003), pp. 11696–701; and Jen-Chieh Chuang, Mario Perello, Ichiro Sakata, et al., "Ghrelin Mediates Stress-Induced Food-Reward Behavior in Mice," *Journal of Clinical Investigation,* vol. 121 (2011), pp. 2684–92. For observations of primates, see Marilyn Arce, Vasiliki Michopoulos, Kathryn N. Shepard, et al., "Diet Choice, Cortisol Reactivity, and Emotional Feeding in Socially Housed Rhesus Monkeys," *Physiology & Behavior,* vol. 101 (2010), pp. 446–55; John Tierney, "Comfort Food, for Monkeys," *New York Times,* 20 May 2008, http://www.nytimes.com/2008/05/20 /science/20tier.html; and M. E. Wilson, J. Fisher, A. Fischer, et al., "Quantifying Food Intake in Socially Housed Monkeys: Social Status Effects on Caloric Consumption," *Physiology & Behavior,* vol. 94 (2008), pp. 586–94.

12. Carl T. Hall, "'Comfort Food' Research Finds Medicinal Effect/High-Fat Fare Helps Rats in Dealing with High Stress Levels," *San Francisco Gate,* 9 Sep 2003, http://www .sfgate.com/health/article/Comfort-food-research-finds-medicinal-effect-2573565.php; and A. Tomiyama, Mary F. Dallman, and Elissa S. Epel, "Comfort Food Is Comforting to Those Most Stressed: Evidence of the Chronic Stress Response Network in High Stress Women," *Psychoneuroendocrinology,* vol. 36 (2011), pp. 1513–19.

13. Julie Wan, "Fat Might Be the Sixth Basic Taste," *Washington Post,* 4 Jun 2012, http:// articles.washingtonpost.com/2012-06-04/national/35462005_1_fat-taste-nada-abumrad -meatiness. See also Gary Wenk, "Why Does Fat Taste So Good? The Importance of Fat-Tasting Proteins on the Tongue," *Psychology Today,* Jan 2012, http://www.psychologytoday .com/blog/your-brain-food/201201/why-does-fat-taste-so-good. Both authors report on recent research concerning CD36, which was discovered by Nada Abumrad. See Marta Yanina Pepino, Latisha Love-Gregory, Samuel Klein, et al., "The Fatty Acid Translocase Gene CD36 and Lingual Lipase Influence Oral Sensitivity to Fat in Obese Subjects," *Journal of Lipid Research,* vol. 53 (2012), pp. 561–66.

14. Kikunae Ikeda, a chemistry professor at Tokyo's Imperial University, discovered umami in the early twentieth century. The name of the taste is derived from the Japanese word *umai* (delicious). See Bernd Lindemann, Yoko Ogiwara, and Yuzo Ninomiya, "The Discovery of Umami," *Chemical Senses,* vol. 27 (2002), pp. 843–44.

15. Lucas Van Oudenhove, Shane McKie, Daniel Lassman, et al., "Fatty Acid–Induced Gut-Brain Signaling Attenuates Neural and Behavioral Effects of Sad Emotion in Humans," *Journal of Clinical Investigation,* vol. 121 (2011), pp. 3094–99.

16. Drew Harwell, "Honey Buns Sweeten Life for Florida Prisoners," *Tampa Bay Times,* 2 Jan 2011, http://www.tampabay.com/features/humaninterest/honey-buns-sweeten-life -for-florida-prisoners/1142687.

17. Joel Stein, "You Eat What You Are," *Time,* 18 Oct 2007, http://www.time.com/time /magazine/article/0,9171,1673252,00.html.

18. Bookgirl, 2002, http://www.prisontalk.com/forums/archive/index.php/t-150289.html.

19. Catrin Smith, "Punishment and Pleasure: Women, Food and the Imprisoned Body," *The Sociological Review,* vol. 50 (2002), p. 204.

20. Carole M. Counihan, *The Anthropology of Food and Body: Gender, Meaning, and Power* (Routledge, 1999), 120.

21. Locher et al., "Comfort Foods."

22. Locher et al., "Comfort Foods," 287.

23. Wan Shen, Lucy M. Long, Chia-Hao Shin, et al., "A Humanities-Based Explanation for the Effects of Emotional Eating and Perceived Stress on Food Choice Motives during the COVID-19 Pandemic," *Nutrients*, vol. 12 (2020), p. 10, https://www.mdpi.com/2072 -6643/12/9/2712/htm.

24. Shen et al., "Humanities-Based Explanation," 11.

25. Locher et al., "Comfort Foods."

26. Jordan D. Troisi and Shira Gabriel, "Chicken Soup Really Is Good for the Soul: 'Comfort Food' Fulfills the Need to Belong," *Psychological Science*, 2 May 2011, http://pss .sagepub.com/content/early/2011/05/02/0956797611407931.

27. Michael Owen Jones, "The Proof Is in the Pudding: The Role of Sensation in Food Choice as Revealed by Sensory Deprivation," *Exploring Folk Art: Twenty Years of Thought on Craft, Work, and Aesthetics*, by Jones (UMI Research Press, 1987), 99.

28. Troisi and Gabriel, "Chicken Soup."

29. Gill Valentine and Beth Longstaff, "Doing Porridge: Food and Social Relations in a Male Prison," *Journal of Material Culture*, vol. 3 (1998), p. 139. For an example of emotion evoked by memory of a food's preparer, see Jillian Gould, "Hungry for My Past: Kitchen Comfort with Fried Bread and Eggs," *Comfort Food Meanings and Memories*, edited by Michael Owen Jones and Lucy M. Long (UP of Mississippi, 2017), pp. 99–114.

30. Daniel E. Slotkin, "What's Your Comfort Food?" 25 May 2012, http://learning.blogs .nytimes.com/2012/05/25/whats-your-comfort-food/?_r=1&apage=2#comments.

31. Laurette Dubé, Jordan L. LeBel, and Ji Lu, "Affect Asymmetry and Comfort Food Consumption," *Physiology & Behavior*, vol. 86 (2005), pp. 559–67.

32. Unilever. See also Levitan and Davis, "Emotions"; Weingarten and Elston, "Food Cravings"; and Wansink et al., "Exploring Comfort Food."

33. Weingarten and Elston, "Food Cravings."

34. Benford and Gough, "'Unhealthy' Practices"; Parker et al., "Mood State"; and Rogers and Smit, "Food Craving."

35. Paulette Wood and Barbra D. Vogen, "Feeding the Anorectic Client: Comfort Foods and Happy Hour," *Geriatric Nursing*, vol. 19 (1998), p. 192

36. Wood and Vogen, "Feeding the Anorectic Client," 193.

37. Wood and Vogen, "Feeding the Anorectic Client," 194.

38. Sandip Roy, "There's Lead in My Grasshopper Snack: Environmental Problems Cross Borders," *New America Media*, 3 Apr 2007, http://news.newamericamedia.org/news /view_article.html?article_id=93856b1c427e995ccdb2aca6cdd5 b303.

39. James I. Grieshop, "The *Envios* of San Pablo Huixtepec, Oaxaca: Food, Homes, and Transnationalism," *Human Organization*, vol. 65 (2006), p. 404.

40. Grieshop, "*Envios*," 405.

41. Lucy M. Long at the Center for Food and Culture, which she founded at Bowling Green State University, undertook an oral history project documenting ways in which people were finding both comfort and discomfort through food and foodways activities

during the COVID-19 pandemic. The Center hosted a virtual symposium on 23 Sep 2020, inviting participants to contribute questions and comments as well as photographs of their own experiences; results of her research likely will be published in 2022. In regard to food discomfort in films, see LuAnne Roth, "Comfort (and Discomfort) Food: Social Surrogacy and Embodied Memory in Real and Reel Time," *Comfort Food Meanings and Memories*, edited by Michael Owen Jones and Lucy M. Long (UP of Mississippi, 2017), pp. 182–211.

42. Michael Owen Jones, "Latina/o Local Knowledge about Diabetes: Emotional Triggers, Plant Treatments, and Food Symbolism," *Diagnosing Folklore: Perspectives on Health, Trauma, and Disability*, edited by Trevor J. Blank and Andrea Kitta (UP of Mississippi, 2015), pp. 97–103.

43. Margaret A. Handley, Kaitie Drace, Robert Wilson, et al., "Globalization, Binational Communities, and Imported Food Risks: Results of an Outbreak Investigation of Lead Poisoning in Monterey County, California," *American Journal of Public Health*, vol. 97 (2007), pp. 900–906.

44. Roy, "There's Lead in My Grasshopper Snack."

45. Willa Michener and Paul Rozin, "Pharmacological Versus Sensory Factors in the Satiation of Chocolate Craving," *Physiology & Behavior*, vol. 56 (1994), pp. 419–22.

46. Teresa L. Dillinger, Patricia Barriga, Sylvia Escarcega, et al., "Food of the Gods: Cure for Humanity? A Cultural History of the Medicinal and Ritual Use of Chocolate," *Journal of Nutrition*, vol. 130 (2000), pp. 2057S–72S.

47. Dillinger et al., "Food of the Gods." See also Parker et al., "Mood State Effects."

48. D. Barthel, "Modernism and Marketing: The Chocolate Box Revisited," *Theory of Culture and Society*, vol. 6 (1989), pp. 429–38; Rebecca Benford and Brendan Gough, "Defining and Defending 'Unhealthy' Practices: A Discourse Analysis of Chocolate 'Addicts'' Accounts," *Journal of Health Psychology*, vol. 11 (2006), pp. 427–40; Peter J. Rogers and Hendrick J. Smit, "Food Craving and Food 'Addiction': A Critical Review of the Evidence from a Biopsychosocial Perspective," *Pharmacology, Biochemistry & Behavior*, vol. 66 (2000), pp. 3–14; and H. E. Yuker, "Perceived Attributes of Chocolate," *Chocolate: Food of the Gods*, edited by Alex Szogyi (Greenwood Press, 1997), pp. 35–43.

49. Michener and Rozin, "Pharmacological"; see also Debra A. Zellner, Ana Garriga-Trillo, Soraya Centeno, et al., "Chocolate Craving and the Menstrual Cycle," *Appetite*, vol. 42 (2004), pp. 119–21.

50. Michener and Rozin, "Pharmacological"; Parker et al., "Mood State"; and P. Rozin, E. Levine, and C. Stoess, "Chocolate Craving and Liking," *Appetite*, vol. 17 (1991), pp. 199–212; see also H. P. Weingarten and D. Elston, "Food Cravings in a College Population," *Appetite*, vol. 17 (1991), pp. 167–75 regarding magnesium.

51. Weingarten and Elston, "Food Cravings in a College Population."

52. Rogers and Smit, "Food Craving."

53. Zellner et al., "Chocolate Craving."

54. D. A. Zellner, A. Garriga-Trillo, E. Rohm, et al., "Food Liking and Craving: A Cross-Cultural Approach," *Appetite*, vol. 33 (1999), pp. 61–70.

55. Scott Parker, Niveen Kamel, and Debra Zellner, "Food Craving Patterns in Egypt: Comparisons with North America and Spain," *Appetite*, vol. 40 (2003), pp. 193–95.

56. Michener and Rozin, "Pharmacological"; Rozin et al., "Chocolate Craving"; and D. Benton and R. T. Donohoe, "The Effects of Nutrients on Mood," *Public Health Nutrition*, vol. 2 (1999), pp. 403–9.

57. Parker et al., "Mood State."

58. Weingarten and Elston, "Phenomenology," 239.

59. Rogers and Smit, "Food Craving," 6.

60. Benford and Gough, "'Unhealthy' Practices," 436.

61. Rogers and Smit, "Food Craving."

62. Rogers and Smit, "Food Craving."

63. Weingarten and Elston, "Phenomenology."

64. Hank Ketcham, "Dennis the Menace [cartoon]," *Los Angeles Times*, 18 Jun 2013, p. D6.

65. Benford and Gough, "'Unhealthy' Practices," 433.

66. Indeed, the survey reported in "Exploring Comfort Food," by Wansink et al., found that, contrary to popular belief, 86 percent of respondents consumed comfort food as reward in contrast to 36 percent who used it as therapy when depressed.

67. Benford and Gough, "'Unhealthy' Practices," 434.

68. Barthel, "Modernism and Marketing."

69. Mary M. Boggiano, Bulent Turan, Christine R. Maldonado, et al., "Secretive Food Concocting in Binge Eating: Test of a Famine Hypotheses," *International Journal of Eating Disorders*, vol. 46 (2012), pp. 212–25.

70. Rogers and Smit, "Food Craving," 6.

71. Parker et al., "Mood State."

72. Weingarten and Elston, "Phenomenology."

73. Chuang et al., "Ghrelin Mediates."

74. Edward Leigh Gibson, "Emotional Influences on Food Choice: Sensory, Physiological and Psychological Pathways," *Physiology & Behavior*, vol. 89 (2006), pp. 53–61.

75. Jayanthi Kandiah, Melissa Yake, James Jones, et al., "Stress Influences Appetite and Comfort Food Preferences in College Women," *Nutrition Research*, vol. 26 (2006), pp. 118–23; see also Wansink et al., "Exploring Comfort Food."

76. Troisi and Gabriel, "Chicken Soup."

77. Elisabeth Rozin, *Ethnic Cuisine: The Flavor Principle Cookbook* (Stephen Greene, 1983).

78. Robert A. Georges and Michael Owen Jones, *Folkloristics: An Introduction* (Indiana UP, 1995).

79. Humphrey, "Traditional Foods?"

80. Benjamin D. Steiner, William J. Bowers, and Austin Sarat, "Folk Knowledge as Legal Action: Death Penalty Judgments and the Tenet of Early Release in a Culture of Mistrust and Punitiveness," *Law & Society Review*, vol. 33 (1999), pp. 461–506.

81. Anne Marie Helmenstine, "Does Eating Turkey Make You Sleepy? Tryptophan & Carbohydrate Chemistry," http://chemistry.about.com/od/holidaysseasons/a/tiredturkey .htm.

82. Simon N. Young, "How to Increase Serotonin in the Human Brain without Drugs," *Journal of Psychiatry and Neuroscience*, vol. 32 (2007), pp. 394–99.

83. Giovanni Cizza and Kristina I. Rother, "Was Feuerbach Right: Are We What We Eat?" *Journal of Clinical Investigation*, vol. 121 (2011), pp. 2969–71.

84. Erika Brady, "Preface," *Healing Logics: Culture and Medicine in Modern Health Belief Systems*, edited by Erika Brady (Utah State UP, 2001), vii.

CHAPTER 5. LAST MEALS AND THE CRUTCH OF RITUAL

1. For examples of the few works on the subject, see Bill Crawford, *Texas Death Row: Last Words, Last Meals, Last Rites* (Penguin, 2008); Doug Duda, "Eat like There's No Tomorrow and Other Lessons Learned from Last Meals, *Food and Morality: Proceedings of the Oxford Symposium on Food and Cookery* (Prospect Books, 2007), 103–8; Kevin M. Kniffen and Brian Wansink, "Death Row Confessions and the Last Meal Test of Innocence," *Laws*, vol. 3 (2014), pp. 1–11; Daniel LaChance, "Last Words, Last Meals, and Last Stands: Agency and Individuality in the Modern Execution Process," *Law & Social Inquiry*, vol. 32 (2007), pp. 719; L. R. Ross, "The Meaning of Death: Last Words, Last Meals," in *Who Deserves to Die*, edited by Austin Sarat and Karl Shoemaker (U of Massachusetts P, 2011), pp. 176–206; Eline van Hagen, "'A Salisbury Steak Is Not a Steak, It's Ground Beef.' The Significance, Messages and Symbolism of Final Meals on Death Row," *Appetite*, vol. 144 (2020), https://www.sciencedirect.com/science/article/abs/pii/S0195666319302703; and Brian Wansink, Kevin M. Kniffin, and Mitsuru Shimizu, "Death Row Nutrition: Curious Conclusions of Last Meals," *Appetite*, vol. 59 (2012), pp. 837–43.

2. Jan Bremmer, "Scapegoat Rituals in Ancient Greece," *Harvard Studies in Classical Philology*, vol. 87 (1983), pp. 299–320.

3. Marc Zvi Brettler and Michael Poliakoff, "Rabbi Simeon ben Lakish at the Gladiator's Banquet: Rabbinic Observations on the Roman Arena," *Harvard Theological Review*, vol. 83 (1990), pp. 93–98.

4. C. Calvert, "A Brief Account of Criminal Procedure in Germany in the Middle Ages," *A Hangman's Diary, Being the Journal of Master Franz Schmidt, Public Executioner of Nuremberg, 1573–1617*, edited by Albrecht Keller, trans. C. Calvert and A. W. Gruner (Philip Allan, 1928), pp. 1–71, 36.

5. V. A. C. Gatrell, *The Hanging Tree: Execution and the English People 1770–1868* (Oxford UP, 1994); Robert Johnson, *Death Work: A Study of the Modern Execution Process* (2nd ed., Wadsworth, Thomson, 1990); and Philip Smith, "Executing Executions: Aesthetics, Identity, and the Problematic Narratives of Capital Punishment Ritual," *Theory and Society*, vol. 25 (1996), pp. 235–41.

6. Johnson, *Death Work*, 12.

7. This newspaper and others cited later were accessed from http://chroniclingamerica .loc.gov/lccn/sn82016187/and www.newspaperarchive.com.

8. Beth Kassab, "Wuornos Attracts Interest until End," *Orlando Sentinel*, 7 Oct 2002, http://articles.orlandosentinel.com/2002-10-07/news/0210070307_1_wuornos-serial -killers-female-serial; KRT, "Florida Executes 'Damsel of Death,'" *Sydney Morning Herald*, 11 Oct 2002, http://www.smh .com.au/articles/2002/10/11/1034222548910.html; and Ron Word, "Florida Executes Female Serial Killer," *St. Petersburg Times*, 9 Oct 2002.

9. John Stossel, "How True Is 'Monster'"? *ABC News*, 13 Feb 2004, http://abcnews.go
.com/2020/GiveMeABreak/story?id=124320&page=1.

10. Katherine Ramsland, "Gary Gilmore," Crime Library, n.d., http://www.crimelibrary
.com/notorious_ murders/mass/gilmore/begin_7.html.

11. snltranscripts.jt.org.

12. David Greene, "In the Immortal Words of Gary Gilmore and NIKE, '[Just] Do It,'"
Entertainment Agent Blog, 10 Jun 2010, entertainmentagentblog.com/2010/06/20/in-the
-immortal-words-of-gary-gilmore-and-nike-just-do-it.

13. deathpenaltyinfo.org.

14. The source of these counts is 245 final meal requests (65 of the 310 inmates declined
food) between 7 Dec 1982 and 10 Sep 2003, listed by the Texas Department of Criminal
Justice at the online site web.archive.org. David Shaw states that there were 314 executions
since 1982. By Shaw's count, 111 death row inmates ordered fries, 85 requested hamburgers,
54 wanted steak (none was honored after 1993; see statements by Brian Price, who prepared last meals), 56 asked for ice cream (and another 19 requested milk shakes), and 50
opted for chicken (mostly fried); see David Shaw, "What Would You Have for Your
Last Meal?" *Los Angeles Times*, 14 Jan 2004, http://articles.latimes.com/2004/jan/14/food
/fo-matters14.

In 1998, Sam Howe Verhovek, referring to the 144 men executed by Texas over
the previous fifteen years, notes that "Burgers top the entrees. Twenty-two men chose
double cheeseburgers, 15 opted for single cheeseburgers, 9 for hamburgers. Next most
popular were steaks, typically T-bones, with 27 requests, and eggs (10 requests, most for
scrambled). Most desired overall is a side of French fries (56 requests). Ice cream is the
most popular dessert (21 requests), Coca-Cola the most popular beverage (13, just edging
out 12 requests for iced tea). And 24 inmates declined any last meal at all." See Sam Howe
Verhovek, "Word for Word/Last Meals: For the Condemned in Texas, Cheeseburgers without Mercy," *New York Times*, 4 Jan 1998, http://www.nytimes.com/1998/01/04/weekin
review/word-for-word-last-meals-for-the-condemned-in-texas-cheeseburgers-without
-mercy.html. At least in Texas, then, burgers and fries head the list, followed by steak and
chicken.

15. Francie Grace, "Cost Cutters Slash Prison Food Budgets," CBS News, 14 May 2003,
http://www.cbsnews.com/stories/2003/05/14/politics/main553785.shtml.

16. Food Service Director, 15 Oct 1999, http://www.allbusiness.com/retail-trade/eating
-drinking-places/4177194-1.html.

17. Alex Hannaford, "Confessions of a Death Row Chef," *Observer [UK]*, 14 Mar 2004,
http://www.guardian.co.uk/lifeandstyle/2004/mar/14/foodanddrink.features12/print.

18. Hannaford, "Confessions."

19. Shaw, "What Would You Have?"

20. Brian Price, "Last Supper," *Legal Affairs*, Mar/Apr, 2004, http://www.legalaffairs.org
/issues/March-April-2004/feature_price_marapr04.msp.

21. Shaw, "What Would You Have?"

22. Verhovek, "Word for Word/Last Meals."

23. Brian Price, *Meals to Die For* (Dyna-Paige Corporation, 2004), 15.

24. Price, "Last Supper."

25. Jennifer G. Hickey, "Dining In with Capital Punishment," Insight on the News, 17 (28 May 2001), p. 24.

26. Price, "Last Supper."

27. These counts are based on profiles in Price's *Meals to Die For*, which lists the educational level of 212 inmates, for 16 of whom, however, the information is not known. In regard to 10 individuals, it is not possible for me to determine if money, vehicles, or other stolen objects were involved, so I based figures on 202 people, of whom 135 benefitted materially. The examples, in order, are Richard Donald Foster, Glen Charles McGinnis, and Earl Carl Heiselbetz, Jr. (Price, "Last Supper") and James David ("cowboy") Autry; for Autry, see Michael S. Serrill, "Thirty-One Minutes from Death," *Time*, 17 Oct 1983, http://content.time.com/time/magazine/article/0,9171,952204,00.html.

As often noted, the inmates have come from impoverished backgrounds. San Quentin warden Clifton Duffy remarked: "It seems to me the death penalty is a privilege reserved for the poor"; see Mark Dow, "'The Line between Us and Them': Interview with Warden Donald Cabana," in *Machinery of Death: The Reality of America's Death Penalty Regime*, edited by David R. Dow and Mark Dow (Routledge, 2002), pp. 175–91. Cabana's remark was echoed by John Spenkelink, electrocuted in Florida on 25 May 1979, who said: "Capital punishment: them without the capital get the punishment," http://crime.about.com/od/history/qt/lstwrds_spnklk.htm.

28. Price, *Meals to Die For*, 311, 320, 337; and Serrill, "Thirty-One Minutes from Death."

29. The inmate was not served the chitterlings, however; see Price, *Meals to Die For*, 309.

30. Thomas Adler, "Making Pancakes on Sunday: The Male Cook in Family Tradition," *Western Folklore*, vol. 40 (1981), pp. 45–54; Elizabeth Fakazis, "Esquire Mans the Kitchenette," *Gastronomica*, vol. 11 (2011), pp. 29–39; and Deborah Dale Heisley, "Gender Symbolism in Food" (PhD dissertation, Northwestern University, 1990).

31. deathpenaltyinfo.org.

32. For particulars, see http://deathpenaltyinfo.org/women-and-death-penalty.

33. Hannaford, "Confessions."

34. "Oklahoma Executes Third Woman This Year," Community of Sant Egidio, 5 Dec 2001, SantEgidio.org/pdm/news/08_12_01_c.htm.

35. Sydney P. Freedberg, "The 13 Other Survivors and Their Stories Series: Freed from Death Row," *St. Petersburg Times*, 4 Jul 1999, p. 10A, http://pqasb.pqarchiver.com/sptimes/access/42911235.html?FMT=ABS&FMTS=ABS:FT&date=Jul+4%2C+1999&author=SYDNEY+P.+FREEDBERG&pub=St.+Petersburg+Times&edition=&startpage=10.A&desc=The+13+other+survivors+and+their+stories+Series%3A+FREED+FROM+DEATH+ROW.

36. Hickey, "Dining in with Capital Punishment."

37. Abbie VanSickle, "Condemned Can Make Big Deal Out of Last Meal," *Indianapolis Star*, 13 Jun 2003, http://www.indystar.com.

38. Shannon Tan, "Joseph Trueblood Put to Death; Relatives of Ex-Girlfriend, 2 Children Waited for Call, Closure," *Indianapolis Star*, 13 Jun 2003, http://www.indystar.com; and VanSickle, "Condemned Can Make Big Deal."

39. See reports in Hickey, "Dining In with Capital Punishment"; Josh Poltilove, "Death Row Last Meals Run Gamut from Lobster Tail to Tacos," *Tampa Tribune*, 11 Feb 2009,

http://tbo.com/news/death-row-last-meals-run-gamut-from-lobster-tail-to-tacos-123223;
and Verhovek, "Word for Word/Last Meals."

40. Daryl C. McClary, "Ex-Convicts Claude H. Ryan and Walter Seelert Kill Lewis
County Deputy Sheriff Seth R. Jackson on 7 Apr 1937," HistoryLink, 18 Sep 2007, http://
www.historylink.org/index.cfm?DisplayPage=output.cfm&file_id=8239.

41. Carla Crowder, "Mentally Ill Man Executed for 1998 Killing," *Birmingham News*,
1 Oct 2004, http://www.prisontalk.com/forums/archive/index.php/t-81301.html.

42. Quoted in Dow and Dow, *Machinery of Death*, 188–89.

43. Johnson, *Death* Work, 91.

44. "Last Words on Death Row," CNN, 31 Dec 2007, cnn.com/2007/US/law/12/10/court
.last.words/index.html.

45. Michael Graczyk, "Special Last Meals: Texas Prisons End Special Last Meals for
Inmates Facing Execution," *Huffington Post*, 22 Sep 2011, http://www.huffingtonpost
.com/2011/09/22/special-last-meals-texas-_n_976543.html; Will Oremus, "No More 'Last
Meals' on Texas Death Row," *Slatest*, 22 Sep 2011, http://slatest.slate.com/posts/2011/09/22
/lawrence_brewer_no_more_last_meal_for_texas_inmates_on_death_row.html; and Jim
Forsyth Reuters, "Texas Kills Fancy Last Meal Requests on Death Row," *Los Angeles Times*,
22 Sep 2011, http://www.latimes.com/sns-rt-usa-executionlastmeals1e7811zv-20110
922,0,4272524 .story.

46. Manny Fernandez, "Texas Death Row Kitchen Cooks Its Last 'Last Meal,'" *New York
Times*, 22 Sep 2011, http://www.nytimes.com/2011/09/23/us/texas-death-row-kitchen
-cooks-its-last-last-meal.html.

47. Ashley Fantz, "Executed Man's Last Request Honored—Pizza for Homeless," CNN,
9 May 2007, http://www.cnn.com/2007/US/05/09/execution.pizza/index.html.

48. Price, *Meals to Die For*, 21.

49. Joel Stein, "You Eat What You Are," *Time*, 18 Oct 2007, http://www.time.com/time
/magazine/article/0,9171,1673252,00.html.

50. Hickey, "Dining in with Capital Punishment."

51. Two articles lend support to this interpretation that seeking comfort through food
choice is a major factor accounting for many of the items in last meal requests. In their
studies of the effects of "mortality salience" (preoccupation with one's death), Friese and
Hofmann confirmed that the hypotheses that individuals turn to their own culture and
worldview as a psychological buffer, choosing familiar and therefore comforting food
and beverages over something foreign, and that in high mortality salience, there is often
impaired self-control resulting in increased impulsive behavior; see Malta Friese and
Wilhelm Hofmann, "What Would You Have as a Last Supper? Thoughts about Death
Influence Evaluation and Consumption of Food Products," *Journal of Experimental Social
Psychology*, vol. 44 (2008), pp. 1388–94.

In "Death Row Nutrition," a team of three researchers analyzed the contents of 193 last
meal orders of prisoners in several states, executed between 2002 and 2006. They found
that the average number of calories in a last meal request was 2,756 (in four instances, it
was 7,200 or more), which is greater than the 2,200 to 2,400 recommended for sedentary
males for an entire day. The most frequent items asked for were meat (83.9 percent), fried
food (67.9 percent), desserts (66.3 percent), and soft drinks (60 percent). In regard to

starches and grains, 40.9 percent of requests were for french fries, 20.7 percent for other potato sides, and 17.1 percent for bread. Nuts appeared in only one of the orders, and yogurt, tofu, and specifically vegetarian meals were not requested at all. Their findings "are consistent with studies of how food is used to mediate feelings of stress and distress," that is, a craving for or overindulgence in fats and carbohydrates—high caloric food consumption—when an individual is under duress and the future appears bleak. See Wansink et al., "Death Row Nutrition."

52. I based the calculations on data in Malone's MA thesis concerning the last words of 355 prisoners executed in Texas from 7 Dec 1982 to 16 Nov 2005, and the final meal requests of 310 inmates from 7 Dec 1982 to 10 Sep 2003, on the archived list issued by the Texas Department of Criminal Justice (web.archive.org). Usable records that contain both last words and final meals total 237. I coded the data into six themes evident in last words ("no last words," "innocence," "remorsefulness," "resignation," "bravado," and "defiance") and four categories of last meal requests ("no food requested," "light meal or snack," "normal meal," and "excessive"). See Dan F. Malone, "Dead Men Talking: Content Analysis of Prisoners' Last Words, Innocence Claims and News Coverage from Texas' Death Row," MA Thesis, U of North Texas, 2006. For other efforts at thematic analysis, see Linda Ross Meyer, "Rituals of Death: The Meaning of Last Words and Last Meals," 2008, http://papers .ssrn.com/s013/papers.cfm?abstract_id=1480686; and Stephen K. Rice, Danielle Dirks, and Julie J. Exline, "Of Guilt, Defiance, and Repentance: Evidence from the Texas Death Chamber," *Justice Quarterly*, vol. 26 (2009), pp. 295–326.

53. Quoted in a review by David D. Perlmutter of Jacquelyn C. Black, *Last Meal* (Common Courage Press, 2003) in *Contemporary Justice Review*, vol. 8 (2005), pp. 337.

54. Dina R. Hellerstein, "What Do We Gain by Taking These Childlike Lives?" *New York Times*, 30 Mar 1997, http://www.deathpenaltyinfo.org/node/656; Michele Orecklin, "Should John Penry Die?" *Time* (27 Nov 2000), p. 76, http://www.time.com/time/maga zine/article/0,9171,998589,00.html.

55. Laura Mansnerus, "Damaged Brains and the Death Penalty," *New York Times*, 21 Jul 2001, http://www .nytimes.com/2001/07/21/arts/damaged-brains-and-the-death-penalty .html?scp=1&sq=laura%20 mansnerus%20damaged%20brains&st=cse.

56. Jack Reynolds, "Retarded Last Meals for Texas' Death Row Inmates," Exiled Online, 17 Jan 2010, http://exiledonline.com/retarded-last-meals-for-texas-death-row-inmates.

57. Hellerstein, "What Do We Gain?"

58. "Executing Mentally Impaired Prisoners Is Unjust and Cruel," *Dallas Morning News*, 22 Nov 1988, http://www.fdp.dk/uk/ment.htm [reprint of an editorial].

59. Bob Greene, "They Didn't Get to Choose Their Last Meals," *Jewish World Review*, 12 Jun 2001, http://www.jewishworldreview.com/bob/greene061201.asp.

60. Graczyk, "Special Last Meals"; and Oremus, "No More 'Last Meals.'"

61. Quoted in Fernandez, "Texas Death Row Kitchen."

62. From a poem by Jeanne Nail Adams, quoted in Lonnie Yoder, "The Funeral Meal: A Significant Funerary Ritual," *Journal of Religion and Health*, vol. 25 (1986), p. 149.

63. Quoted in Russell F. Canan, "Burning at the Wire," *Facing the Death Penalty: Essays on a Cruel and Unusual Punishment*, edited by Michael L. Radelet (Temple UP, 1989), p. 75.

64. *Last Supper*, directed by Mats Bigert and Lars Bergstrom (SVT, Kultur & Samhalle, 2005), DVD, 58 min.

65. Tony Karon, "Why We're Fascinated by Death Row Cuisine," *Time*, 10 Aug 2000, http://www.time.com/time/nation/article/0,8599,52337,00.html.

66. LaChance, "Last Words," 719.

67. Terri J. Gordon, "Debt, Guilt, and Hungry Ghosts: A Foucauldian Perspective on Bigert's and Bergstrom's *Last Supper*," *Cabinet Magazine Online*, 2006, http://www.cabinet magazine.org/events/lastsuppergordon.php.

68. Price, "Last Supper."

69. Mona Lynch, "The Disposal of Inmate #85271," *Studies in Law, Politics, and Society*, vol. 20 (2000), pp. 3–34.

70. Johnson, *Death Work*, 106.

71. Helen Prejean, *Dead Man Walking: An Eyewitness Account of the Death Penalty in the United States* (Random House, 1993), p. 87.

72. Price, "Last Supper."

73. Stuart Banner, "The Death Penalty's Strange Career," *Wilson Quarterly* 26 (2002), pp. 70–82.

74. Quoted in Dow and Dow, *Machinery of Death*, 189.

75. Johnson, *Death Work*, 90.

76. Johnson, *Death Work*, 90.

77. Richard J. Bonnie, "Dilemmas in Administering the Death Penalty: Conscientious Abstention, Professional Ethics, and the Needs of the Legal System," *Law and Human Behavior*, vol. 14 (1990), pp. 67–90; Markus Dirk Dubber, "The Pain of Punishment," *Buffalo Law Review*, vol. 44 (1996), pp. 45–611; and Lynch, "Disposal of Inmate #85271."

78. See, e.g., statements on lawfreefaq.com.

79. Canan, "Burning at the Wire."

80. Herb Haines, "Flawed Executions, the Anti-Death Penalty Movement, and the Politics of Capital Punishment," *Social Problems*, vol. 39 (1992), p. 126.

81. Quoted in Dow and Dow, *Machinery of Death*, 189.

82. Margaret Visser, *Much Depends on Dinner* (McClelland and Stewart Weidenfeld, 1986), 12.

CHAPTER 6. PORK BANS REAL AND RUMORED: FEAR, BIGOTRY, AND LOST IDENTITY

1. Lisa Rein, "Finally, the Government Has Decided to Eliminate Pork—from the Menu in Federal Prisons," *Washington Post*, 9 Oct 2015, washingtonpost.com/news/federal-eye /wp/2015/10/09/finally-the-government-has-decided-to-eliminate-pork-from-the-menu -in-federal-prisons/?utm_term=.eb2e8991a4bb.

2. These include Gina Cassini, "Obama Forced to Reverse His Sharia Prison Pork Ban after National Outrage," *Top Right News*, 17 Oct 2015, toprightnews.com/obama-forced -to-reverse-his-sharia-prison-pork-ban-after-national-outrage; Sandy Fitzgerald, "Federal Prison Pork Ban Revoked," *Newsmax*, 16 Oct 2015, newsmax.com/Newsfront

/federal-prison-pork-ban/2015/10/16/id/696612/#ixzz4Lwp7eOf4; Bill Hanna, "Inmates, Industry Decry Feds Pulling Pork from Menus," *Fort Worth Star-Telegram*, 6 Oct 2015, star-telegram.com/news/local/community/fort-worth/article37990749.html#storylink =cpy; Rein, "Finally"; Lisa Rein, "After Firestorm, Pork Roast Is Back on the Menu at Federal Prisons," *Washington Post*, 16 Oct 2015, washingtonpost.com/news/federal-eye /wp/2015/10/16/after-firestorm-pork-roast-is-back-on-the-menu-at-federal-prisons; Lisa Rein, "The (Half-Baked) Story behind the Pork Ban in Federal Prisons," *Washington Post*, 26 Oct 2015, washingtonpost.com/news/federal-eye/wp/2015/10/26/the-sort-of-story -behind-the-ban-on-pork-in-federal-prisons/?utm_term=.e43ae3b7ce8f; and "Obama Administration Bans All Pork Products from Prison Menus," 9 Oct 2015, www. cnsnews .com/news/article/cnsnewscom-staff/federal-government-bans-pork-prison-menus. Other articles as well as blogs appeared but few have appended comments by readers.

3. The term "culinary nationalism" was coined by Priscilla Parkhurst Ferguson, "Culinary Nationalism," *Gastronomica*, vol. 10 (2010), pp. 102–9. On food and national- ism, see also Arjun Appadurai, "How to Make a National Cuisine: Cookbooks in Con- temporary India," *Comparative Studies in Society and History*, vol. 30 (1988), pp. 3–24; Michaela DeSoucey, "Gastronationalism: Food Traditions and Authenticity Politics in the European Union," *American Sociological Review*, vol. 75 (2010), pp. 432–55; Bill Ellis, "Whispers in an Ice Cream Parlor: Culinary Tourism, Contemporary Legends, and the Urban Interzone," *Journal of American Folklore*, vol. 122 (2009), pp. 53–74; Michelle T. King, editor, *Culinary Nationalism in Asia* (Bloomsbury Academic, 2019); Lucy M. Long, "Introduction: Culinary Nationalism," *Western Folklore*, vol. 80 (2021), pp. 5–14; Margaret Magat, *Balut: Fertilized Eggs and the Making of Culinary Capital in the Filipino Diaspora* (Bloomsbury Academic, 2019); Jeffrey Pilcher, *¡Que vivan los tamales! Food and the Making of Mexican Identity* (U of New Mexico P, 1998); Krishnendu Ray, "Nation and Cuisine. The Evidence from American Newspapers ca. 1830–2003," *Food and Foodways*, vol. 16 (2008), pp. 259–97; LuAnne Roth, "Do the [White] Thing: What Oppositional Gaze Narratives Reveal about Culinary Nationalism and Whiteness," *Western Folklore*, vol. 80 (2021), pp. 81–117; Alison K. Smith, "National Cuisines," *The Oxford Handbook of Food History*, edited by Jeffrey M. Pilcher (Oxford UP, 2012), pp. 444–60; and Richard Wilk, *Home Cooking in the Global Village: Caribbean Food from Buccaneers to Ecotourists* (Berg Publishers, 2006).

4. In recent years the population in prisons and jails has grown to nearly 2.4 million; an additional 853,000 adults were on parole in 2013, and more than 3.9 million had proba- tion status. These figures do not include juvenile offenders. The United States spends $167 billion per year on the criminal justice system. See "Nation Spends $167 Billion on Criminal and Civil Justice Services" (press release, Office of Justice Programs, Bureau of Justice Statistics), bjs.gov/content/pub/press/jeeus01pr.cfm.

5. Incarcerated in the US penitentiary system beginning in Sep 1998 at the facility in Leavenworth, Robert Rosso contends that salad bars contained such toppings as croutons and bacon bits while breakfast often included eggs and bacon and weekend brunch of- fered eggs made to order along with bacon, ham, or sausage links. The food was similar at the Lewisburg facility in Pennsylvania, where he was transferred four years later, but by the time he was in the Butner Correctional Complex in North Carolina in 2010, the

federal Bureau of Prisons had instituted the national menu, which excluded fried foods and emphasized more healthful fare. See Robert Rosso, "Bureau of Prison's National Menu," 23 Oct 2015, gorillaconvict.com/2015/10/bureau-of-prisons-national-menu-by-robert-rosso.

6. Rein, "Finally."

7. Rein, "Finally."

8. For pork expenditures, see letter dated 23 Oct 2015 from Newton E. Kendig, Assistant Director of Health Services Division of Bureau of Prisons to Charles E. Grassley, Chairman, Committee on the Judiciary, grassley.senate.gov/sites/default/files/judiciary/upload/Prisons,%2010–23–15,BOP%20response%20on%20pork.pdf. For annual food expenditures, see US Department of Justice, *FY 2014 Performance Budget Congressional Submission: Federal Prison System Salaries and Expenses*, 26, justice.gov/sites/default/files/jmd/legacy/2014/05/08/bop-se-justification.pdf.

9. Rein, "After Firestorm."

10. See bls.gov/regions/mid-atlantic/data/AverageRetailFoodAndEnergyPrices_USandMidwest_Table.htm. Retail prices per pound in Aug 2015 were $8.70 for sirloin steak, $4.40 for boneless pork chops, and $3.41 for boneless chicken breast. Salisbury steak, beef meatloaf, and spaghetti and meatballs appeared on weekly menus in 2012. Although beef's cost often exceeds that of pork, more than a dozen beef entrees were listed on the 2015 survey; while most involve ground beef, which is relatively cheap, one was for roast beef.

11. agweb.com/mobile/article/record-hog-production-puts-plenty-of-pork-on-menu-blmg.

12. One hundred grams (approximately 3.5 ounces) of pork loin consists of 147 calories, 26 grams of protein, and 3.96 grams of fat; a boneless ribeye filet contains 199 calories, nearly 29 grams of protein, and 9.2 grams of fat; and skinless, boneless chicken breast has 157 calories, 32 grams of protein, and 3.24 grams of fat. There are other micronutrients, including minerals and vitamins, but Warner's comment about the healthfulness of pork loin is generally true compared to other meats. See ndb.nal.usda.gov/ndb/search/list. See also http://rhythm-of-food.net and foodb.ca for other lists of micronutrients.

13. Pigs are divided into two major categories: meat types (containing more lean meat and less fat) and lard types (having large deposits of fat that are easier to butcher and render). Document ARS 22–31 titled "The Meat-Type Hog" (Oct 1956), published by the US Agricultural Research Service, notes on the first page that "More and more breeders are producing streamlined meat-type hogs, and better animals are becoming available to farmers as seedstock." Further, "Large 'lardy' hogs served our needs for the first 100 years of the Nation's existence, partly because of domestic preference, partly because of a lively export market for lard." The document attributes the increasing trend toward leaner meat to the reduction of manual labor by greater reliance on machinery and hence less "need for so much fat in the working man's diet," movement of people to cities who are "adopting more sedentary occupations, with a resulting change in diet," and "a spectacular rise in public favor" of vegetable oil. See archive.org/stream/meattypehog31unit/meattypehog31unit_djvu.txt. Because of even greater health consciousness today, the meat-type hogs have much less fat owing to improved genetics, breeding, and feeding. See the US

Department of Agriculture Food Safety and Inspection Service report "Fresh Pork from Farm to Table," fsis.usda.gov/wps/wcm/connect/27f02652-e30e-4772-83af-23aaabba220b/Pork_from_Farm_to_Table.pdf?MOD=AJPERES.

14. Sean Alfano, "How and Where America Eats," CBS News, 20 Nov 2005, cbsnews.com/news/how-and-where-america-eats.

15. See, for example, the Federal Bureau of Prisons' *Food Service Manual*, 13 Sep 2011, acfsa.org/documents/stateRegulations/Fed_Food_Manual_PS_4700-006.pdf,

"Meal Planning: Pork Is Not Served as the Only Entree on Holiday Meals" (18):

"The mainline meal will contain a non-pork entrée" (25); and "Transportation meals: When a box lunch is provided, minimum contents are one non-pork meat sandwich with two ounces of protein, one no-flesh sandwich with two ounces of protein, one portion of fruit, and one beverage" (30–31).

16. On the 2015 survey, the number of and preferences for pork items diminished somewhat, thus giving a degree of support to the bureau's contention that pork might be falling in popularity. Of the approximately thirty-seven thousand respondents in 2015, 51.1 percent liked hot dogs, 42.7 percent roast pork, and 37.7 percent kielbasa sausage. Heading the list of disliked items in 2012 were hummus at 67.4 percent, farina at 51.1 percent, and chicken lo mein at 50.5 percent. Hummus wrap at 70 percent and hummus at 68.5 percent were close behind. Soy taco salad (69.6 percent), soy BBQ (69.3 percent), soy lasagna (66.3 percent), and soy burger (65.3 percent) also found disfavor. Tofu, made from soy milk, did not fare well: 67.5 percent disliked tofu chef salad, 66.3 percent spurned tofu and rice, 64 percent objected to tofu stir fry, and 63.8 percent rejected tofu and fried rice.

17. Kimberly Hartke, "Budget Shortfalls Hit Illinois Prison Diet," Weston A. Price Foundation, 19 Jul 2010, www.westonaprice.org/press/budget-shortfalls-hit-illinois-prison-diet.

18. The Illinois governor justified a diet of soy in order to lower costs, although political payback has been suggested in that the main supplier of soy products to Illinois prisons contributed heavily to the governor's campaign. Six inmates sued, contending that soy-laden food (at four times the recommended daily allowance in meals composed of soy cheese, main dishes of 60–70 percent soy, and baked goods) violates the Eighth Amendment regarding cruel and unusual punishment as well as the Fourteenth concerning due process rights. The National Menu set forth by the federal Bureau of Prisons differs from some state systems in that by 2015 inmates could opt for the regular items that included fried or grilled meat, a "Heart Healthy" selection (e.g., baked chicken or fish and oven-baked potatoes rather than fried), or a nonflesh dish comprising soy, cottage cheese, beans, or peanut butter. See Bob Unruh, "Judge Orders Trial to Decide if Jail Food Really Is 'Torture,'" *WorldNetDaily*, 25 Oct 2011, wnd.com/2011/10/360301.

19. Although franks, kielbasa, chili dogs, and breakfast sausages might have contained beef, chicken, soy, or a mixture rather consisted entirely or largely of pork, this seems unlikely because the Bureau of Prisons offers nonflesh and pork-free dishes that are clearly distinguished from meat and pork items.

20. According to the Federal Bureau of Prisons, the inmate population as of 27 May 2017 was 33.6% Hispanic, 37.7% Black, and 58.7% White. See bop.gov/about/statistics/statistics_inmate_ethnicity.jsp and bop.gov/about/statistics/statistics_inmate_race.jsp.

21. As of 27 May 2017, 6.8% of prisoners were females and 93.2% were males; see gov /about/statistics/statistics_inmate_gender.jsp.

22. Martha C. White and Mike Brunker, "The Big Bucks of Bacon: American Meat Industry by the Numbers," *NBC News*, 26 Oct 2015, nbcnews.com/business/economy /look-u-s-meat-industry-numbers-n451571.

23. Anna Willetts, "'Bacon Sandwiches Got the Better of Me': Meat Eating and Vegetarianism in South East London," *Food, Health, and Identity*, edited by P. Caplan (Routledge, 1997), pp. 111–30.

24. "Religion in Prisons—A 50-State Survey of Prison Chaplains," Pew, 22 Mar 2012, pewforum.org/2012/03/22/prison-chaplains-exec.

25. Susan Eleuterio with Barbara Banks, Phillis Humphries, and Charlene Smith, "Even Presidents Need Comfort Food: Tradition, Food, and Politics at the Valois Cafeteria," *Comfort Food Meanings and Memories*, edited by Michael Owen Jones and Lucy M. Long (UP of Mississippi, 2017), pp. 65–81.

26. Kim LaCapria, "Sausage Pest: A Claim That the San Bernardino Shooting Was Due to Pork Served at a Christmas Party Was Fabricated," Snopes, 4 Dec 2015, snopes.com /san-bernardino-shooting-pork-insult.

27. Benjamin D. Steiner, William J. Bowers, and Austin Sarat, "Folk Knowledge as Legal Action: Death Penalty Judgments and the Tenet of Early Release in a Culture of Mistrust and Punitiveness," *Law & Society Review*, vol. 33 (1999), pp. 461–506.

28. Onno Oerlemans, "Shelley's Ideal Body: Vegetarianism and Nature," *Studies in Romanticism*, vol. 34 (1995), pp. 531–52; and Wayland D. Hand, *Magical Medicine* (U of California P, 1980).

29. Frederick J. Simoons, "Traditional Use and Avoidance of Foods of Animal Origin: A Culture Historical View," *BioScience*, vol. 28 (1978), pp. 178–84.

30. M. Heather Tomlinson, "'Not an Instrument of Punishment': Prison Diet in the Mid-nineteenth Century," *Journal of Consumer Studies and Home Economics*, vol. 2 (1978), pp. 15–26. See also John Pratt, "Norbert Elias and the Civilized Prison," *British Journal of Sociology*, vol. 50 (1999), pp. 271–96; and Edward W. Sieh, "Less Eligibility: The Upper Limits of Penal Policy," *Criminal Justice Policy Review*, vol. 3 (1989), pp. 159–83.

31. Sandy Fitzgerald, "Federal Prison Pork Ban Revoked," *Newsmax*, 16 Oct 2015, news max.com/Newsfront/federal-prison-pork-ban/2015/10/16/id/696612/#ixzz4Lwp7eOf4.

32. Cyrus Naim, "Food & Drug Law," 2005, dash.harvard.edu/handle/1/8848245.

33. Mark Curriden, "Hard Time," *ABA* [American Bar Association] *Journal*, vol. 81 (Jul 1995), pp. 72–75.

34. Gresham M. Sykes, *The Society of Captives: A Study of a Maximum Security Prison* (Princeton UP, 1958).

35. Bill Hanna, "Inmates, Industry Decry Feds Pulling Pork from Menus," *Fort Worth Star-Telegram*, 6 Oct 2015, star-telegram.com/news/local/community/fort-worth/ar ticle37990749.html#storylink=cpy.

36. Setting bacon and sausages aside for the moment, several old canards go whole hog in describing the fate of pig actors. The movie *Babe*, released in 1995, is an Australian-American comedy-drama featuring a cast of real and animatronic animals. The story tells of an orphaned piglet wanting to be a sheepdog. A box office success that also won

critical acclaim, the film inspired activists to stake out theaters with flyers detailing real life abuses to pigs; aroused greater interest in vegetarianism, especially among the young; and prompted the actor James Cromwell (the film's character Farmer Hoggett) to become an ethical vegan (Smith, "A Pig's Best Friend") who in 1996 organized a nonflesh Christmas dinner for the homeless in Los Angeles as a means of reversing the image that "Christmas is carnage." See Scott Smith, "A Pig's Best Friend: James Cromwell on Social Issues, Vegetarianism and the New Babe," *Vegetarian Times* (Nov 1998), p. 20; and "In the News," *Vegetarian Times* (Mar 1997), p. 24. Accounts circulated that at the "wrap party" following completion of the filming, the inconsiderate cast and crew fired up a barbeque grill, then cooked and ate the actor who portrayed Babe. A similar story has circulated about unfeeling film staff roasting and pigging out on Arnold Ziffel, the porker starring in the television series *Green Acres* who is pampered, lives in the house, and understands English. Whether such accounts are presented as factual or told to elicit shock, disgust, or amusement, the theme of insensitivity prevails. Charges of too little sensitivity, or more often too much of it toward a particular group, informs yet other stories and retorts.

37. See comments on the Islamophobic website barenakedislam.com/2015/02/28 /are-you-shopping-at-one-of-targets-islamic-sharia-compliant-stores.

38. Julie Jargon, "Subway Runs Past McDonald's Chain," *Wall Street Journal*, 8 Mar 2011, wsj.com/articles/SB10001424052748703386704576186432177464052.

39. Sean Poulter, "Subway Removes Ham and Bacon from Nearly 200 Stores and Offers Halal Meat Only after 'Strong Demand' from Muslims," *Daily Mail*, 30 Apr 2014; updated 31 Jan 2016, http://www.dailymail.co.uk/news/article-2616576/Subway-removes-ham -pork-nearly-200-stores-strong-demand-Muslims-eat-Halal-meat.html.

40. LaCapria, "Sausage Pest"; Rebecca Perring, "Germany 'Bans' Sausages: Pork Removed from Cafes and Schools," *Sunday Express*, 22 Mar 2016, express.co.uk/news /world/650246/Germany-bans-pork-cafes-schools-offending-Muslim-migrants.

41. Tara Dodrill, "Germany Banning Pork to Avoid Offending Muslims," *Inquisitr* [sic], 7 Mar 2016, inquisitr.com/2864144/germany-banning-pork-to-avoid-offending-muslims.

42. Sara Malm, "German Politicians Campaign to Make Pork Mandatory in Public Canteens after Sausages and Bacon Were Removed 'to Prevent Offending Muslims,'" *Daily Mail*, 7 May 2016, www.dailymail.co.uk/news/article-3480491/Wurst-case-scenario-Call -stop-German-cafes-banning-pork-prevent-offending-Muslims.html.

43. Angelique Chrisafis, "Pork or Nothing: How School Dinners Are Dividing France," *The Guardian*, 13 Oct 2015, theguardian.com/world/2015/oct/13/pork-school-dinners -france-secularism-children-religious-intolerance.

44. Chrisafis, "Pork or Nothing."

45. "City Fires New Salvo in Denmark's 'Meatball War,'" 19 Jan 2016, thelocal.dk/20160119 /city-fires-new-salvo-in-denmarks-meatball-war; and Michael Booth, "Can a Meatball Define a Culture?" 1 Jul 2014, thelocal.dk/20140701/can-a-meatball-define-a-culture.

46. snopes.com/politics/business/targetsharia.asp.

47. pork.org/pork-quick-facts/home/stats/u-s-pork-exports/world-per-capita-pork -consumption-2.

48. S. Jonathan Bass, "How 'bout a Hand for the Hog: The Enduring Nature of the Swine as a Cultural Symbol of the South," *Southern Culture*, vol. 1 (1995), pp. 301–20;

Lauren Collins, "America's Most Political Food," *The New Yorker*, 24 Apr 2017, http://www
.newyorker.com/magazine/2017/04/24/americas-most-political-food; Marcie Cohen
Ferris, *The Edible South: The Power of Food and the Making of an American Region*
(Chapel Hill: U of North Carolina P, 2014); and Sam Hilliard, "Hog Meat and Cornpone:
Food Habits in the Ante-Bellum South," *Proceedings of the American Philosophical Society*,
vol. 113 (1969), pp. 1–13.

49. Hilliard, "Hog Meat and Cornpone," 3.

50. Frederick L. Olmstead, *A Journey in the Back Country* (Mason Brothers, 1863).

51. Hilliard, "Hog Meat and Cornpone," 4.

52. nationalchickencouncil.org/about-the-industry/statistics/per-capita-consumption
-of-poultry-and-livestock-1965-to-estimated-2012-in-pounds.

53. Susan C. Schena, "'Bacon Intern' Needed for Restaurant Pig-Out Gig, and It Pays
Big," 6 Aug 2019, https://patch.com/california/lakeelsinore-wildomar/bacon-intern
-needed-restaurant-pig-out-gig.

54. Alexandra Starr, "Pork. It's What's for Dinner Once More at Federal Prisons,"
National Public Radio, 16 Oct 2015, npr.org/sections/thetwo-way/2015/10/16/449180734
/pork-its-whats-for-dinner-once-more-at-federal-prisons.

55. Benedict Anderson, *Imagined Communities* (2nd ed., Verso, 1983 [2006]).

56. Trevor J. Blank, editor, *Folklore and the Internet Vernacular Expression in a Digital
World* (Utah State University, 2009), p. 9.

57. Gary Alan Fine, "Rumors of Apartheid: The Ecotypification of Contemporary
Legends in the New South Africa," *Journal of Folklore Research*, vol. 29 (1992), pp. 53–71.

58. Regina Marchi, "With Facebook, Blogs, and Fake News, Teens Reject Journalistic
'Objectivity,'" *Journal Communication Inquiry*, vol. 36 (2012), pp. 246–62; and Charlie
Warzel and Lam Thuy Vo, "Here's Where Donald Trump Gets His News," BuzzFeed,
3 Dec 2016, buzzfeed.com/charliewarzel/trumps-information-universe?utm_term
=.tnjmgn6Gj#.bab4mo1wy.

59. William Saletan, "How Trump's 'Unpredictability' Dodge Became the Dumbest
Doctrine in Politics," *Slate*, 3 May 2016, slate.com/articles/news_and_politics/politics/2016
/05/trump_s_moronic_unpredictability_doctrine.html.

60. Peter Coy, "Trump's Uncertainty Principle," *Bloomberg Businessweek*, 26 Jan 2017,
bloomberg.com/news/articles/2017-01-26/trump-s-uncertainty-principle.

61. Tala Ansari, "Anti-Muslim Bills Based on Conspiracy Theories Have Been
Introduced in Two States," *BuzzFeed*, 12 Jan 2017, buzzfeed.com/talalansari/two-new-anti
-sharia-bills?utm_term=.mmZe1zVaN#.xgbrNeE9A.

CHAPTER 7. MARY SHELLEY'S NIGHTMARE AND PERCY SHELLEY'S DREAM

1. Mary W. Shelley, "Introduction," *Frankenstein; or, The Modern Prometheus* (Henry
Colburn and Richard Bentley, 1831), paragraph 11.

2. Rossiter Johnson, *Author's Digest: The World's Great Stories in Brief*. Vol. 7: *Walter
Scott to Laurence Sterne* (Author's Press, 1908; reprinted by Forgotten Books, 2018),
p. 238.

3. Carol J. Adams, *The Sexual Politics of Meat: A Feminist-Vegetarian Critical Theory* (Polity; Continuum, 1990).

4. Frederick A. Pottle, *Shelley and Browning: A Myth and Some Facts* (Archon Books, 1965).

5. Michael Holroyd, *Bernard Shaw* (5 vols., Chatto and Windus, 1988), vol. I, p. 84.

6. Rod Preece, *Sins of the Flesh: A History of Ethical Vegetarian Thought* (U of British Columbia P, 2009), 253.

7. Anita Guerrini, "A Diet for a Sensitive Soul: Vegetarianism in Eighteenth-Century Britain," *Eighteenth-Century Life*, vol. 23 (1999), pp. 34–42.

8. Colin Spencer, *The Heretic's Feast: A History of Vegetarianism* (UP of New England, 1995).

9. Howard Williams, *The Ethics of Diet* (F. Pitman, 1883), p. 206.

10. I am citing Shelley's *A Vindication* that was edited with an introduction by Salt and Axon, 1884, which is available online at https://archive.org/details/vindicationof natooshelrich and http://www.gutenberg.org/cache/epub/38727/pg38727.txt.

11. See, for example, "Queen Mab"; the poem inserted between stanzas 51 and 52 of the 5th canto of "Laon and Cythna," which Henry Stevenson Salt claimed was called "The Lyric of Vegetarianism"; and Shelley's paean to the "brotherhood" of nature in the opening lines of "Alastor."

12. Percy Bysshe Shelley, *Queen Mab: A Philosophical Poem* (P. B. Shelley, 1813 [1831]), p. 51.

13. Shelley, *Vindication of Natural Diet*, 10–11.

14. Shelley, *Vindication of Natural Diet*, 17.

15. Shelley, *Vindication of Natural Diet*, 20.

16. Shelley, *Vindication of Natural Diet*, 18.

17. Shelley, *Vindication of Natural Diet*, 19.

18. Alan Beardsworth and Teresa Keil, "The Vegetarian Option: Varieties, Conversions, Motives, and Careers," *The Sociological Review*, vol. 40 (1992), pp. 253–93; Malcolm Hamilton, "Eating Death: Vegetarians, Meat, and Violence," *Food, Culture, and Society*, vol. 9 (2007), pp. 155–77; and Preece, *Sins of the Flesh*.

19. Shelley, *Vindication of Natural Diet*, 20.

20. Shelley, *Vindication of Natural Diet*, 21.

21. Shelley, *Vindication of Natural Diet*, 25.

22. Omno Oerlemans, "Shelley's Ideal Body: Vegetarianism and Nature," *Studies in Romanticism*, vol. 34 (1995), pp. 531–52.

23. Preece, *Sins of the Flesh*.

24. Peter Singer, *Animal Liberation* (Jonathan Cape, 1977).

25. Oerlemans, "Shelley's Ideal Body."

26. Williams, *Ethics of Diet*, 206.

27. Williams, *Ethics of Diet*, 208.

28. George Cheyne, *The English Malady: or, a Treatise of Nervous Diseases of All Kinds, as Spleen, Vapours, Lowness of Spirits, Hypochondriacal, and Hysterical Distempers, Etc.* (J. Leake, 1733).

29. William Lambe, "Reports on the Effects of a Peculiar Regimen in Scirrhous Tumours and Cancerous Ulcers," *The Annual Medical Review and Register for 1809*, vol. II

(1810), pp. 146–50; and William Lambe, *Water and Vegetable Diet in Consumption, Scrofula, Cancer, Asthma, and Other Chronic Diseases* (Fowlers and Wells, [1815] 1850).

30. William Lambe, "An Investigation of the Properties of Thames Water," *The Medico-chirurgical Review*, vol. 13 (1828), pp. 268–70.

31. Tobias Smollett, *The Expedition of Humphry Clinker* (3 vols., 2nd ed., W. Johnson and B. Collins, 1772), vol. II, p. 6.

32. Rhian Harris, "The Foundling Hospital," 2012, http://www.bbc.co.uk/history/british/victorians/foundling_01.shtml.

33. David Cutler, Angus Deaton, and Adriana Lleras-Muney, "The Determinants of Mortality," *Journal of Economic Perspectives*, vol. 20 (2007), pp. 97–120.

34. Sally Osborn, "Health in the 18th Century," 2010, http://18thcenturyrecipes.wordpress.com/2010/06/17/health-in-the-18th-century.

35. Shelley, *Vindication of Natural Diet*, 25.

36. John Oswald, *The Cry of Nature; or, An Appeal to Mercy and to Justice, on Behalf of the Persecuted Animals* (J. Johnson, 1791), note 4.

37. Shelley, *Vindication of Natural Diet*, 23.

38. Shelley, *Vindication of Natural Diet*, 25–26.

39. Shelley, *Vindication of Natural Diet*, 24.

40. Shelley, *Vindication of Natural Diet*, 26.

41. Shelley, *Vindication of Natural Diet*, 27.

42. Edward Dowden, *The Life of Percy Bysshe Shelley* (2 vols., Kegan Paul; J. B. Lippincott, 1887), vol. I, p. 69.

43. Thomas Medwin, *The Life of Percy Bysshe Shelley* (Oxford UP, [1847] 1913); and Alethea Hayter, "'The Laudanum Bottle Loomed Large': Opium in the English Literary World in the Nineteenth Century," *Ariel: A Review of International English Literature*, vol. 11 (1980), pp. 37–51.

44. Richard Holmes, *Shelley, The Pursuit* (Weidenfeld and Nicolson, 1974).

45. H. F. B. Brett-Smith, *Peacock's Memoirs of Shelley, with Shelley's Letters to Peacock* (Henry Frowde, 1909).

46. Thomas Jefferson Hogg, *Life of Shelley* (2 vols., E. Moxon, 1858), vol. II, pp. 335–37.

47. Edward John Trelawny, *Records of Shelley, Byron, and the Author* (2 vols., Basil, Montagu, Pickering, 1878), vol. II, p. 23.

48. Holmes, *Shelley, The Pursuit*, 91.

49. Brett-Smith, *Peacock's Memoirs of Shelley*, 48.

50. Hayter, "The Laudanum Bottle Loomed Large."

51. William E. A. Axon, *Shelley's Vegetarianism* (The Shelley Society, University College, London, 12 Nov 1891), 1–2.

52. Quoted in Spencer, *Heretic's Feast*, 248.

53. Trelawny, *Records*, 26.

54. Hogg, *Life of Shelley*, II:328.

55. Ian Gilmour, *The Making of the Poets: Byron and Shelley in Their Time*, (Chatto and Windus, 2002).

56. Hogg, *Life of Shelley*, II:328.

57. Thomas Jefferson Hogg, *Shelley at Oxford*, edited with an introduction by R. A. Streatfeild (Methuen and Co., 1904), pp. 10–11.

58. James Bieri, *Percy Bysshe Shelley, A Biography: Youth's Unextinguished Fire, 1792–1817* (U of Delaware P, 2004).

59. Hogg, *Life of Shelley*, II:319–20.

60. Medwin, *The Life of Percy Bysshe Shelley*, 76.

61. Hogg, *Life of Shelley*, II:319–20.

62. Hogg, *Life of Shelley*, II:321.

63. Hogg, *Shelley at Oxford*, 114.

64. John Addington Symonds, *Shelley* (Macmillan, [1909] 1878).

65. Hogg, *Life of Shelley*, II:372–73.

66. Malcolm Elwin Macdonald, editor, *The Autobiography and Journals of Benjamin Robert Haydon* (Macdonald and Co, [1853] 1950).

67. Timothy Morton, "Re-Imagining the Body: Shelley and the Languages of Diet" (PhD Dissertation, Magdalen College, Oxford University, 1992).

68. Dan Wesley, "Food Consumption in America," http://www.creditloan.com/blog /food-consumption-in-america/#ixzz10×3QOn3m.

69. One of the Inspectors of the Prison, "An Account of the State Prison, or Penitentiary-House in New York," *The Belfast Monthly Magazine*, vol. 7 (30 Sep 1811), pp. 167–77.

70. Trelawny, *Records*, 65.

71. Emily W. Sunstein, *Mary Shelley: Romance and Reality* (Little, Brown, 1989), p. 104.

72. Hogg, *Shelley at Oxford*, 114.

73. Hogg, *Life of Shelley*, II:28.

74. Brett-Smith, Peacock's Memoirs of Shelley.

75. Holroyd, *Bernard Shaw*, I:86.

76. Carole A. Bisogni, Margaret Connors, Carol M. Devine, and Jeffery Sobal, "Who We Are and How We Eat: A Qualitative Study of Identities in Food Choice," *Journal of Nutrition Education and Behavior*, vol. 34 (2002), pp. 128–40.

77. Hogg, *Life of Shelley*, II:24, 422–23.

78. Hogg, *Life of Shelley*, II:34–36.

79. Willetts, "Bacon Sandwiches."

80. Hogg, *Life of Shelley*, II:426.

81. Hogg, *Life of Shelley*, II:32–34.

82. Matthew B. Ruby, "Vegetarianism. A Blossoming Field of Study," *Appetite*, vol. 58 (2012), pp. 141–50.

83. Susan I. Barr and Gwen E. Chapman, "Perceptions and Practices of Self-Defined Current Vegetarian, Former Vegetarian, and Nonvegetarian Women," *Journal of the American Dietetic Association*, vol. 102 (2002), pp. 354–60; Katie Haverstock and Deborah Kirby Forgays, "To Eat or Not to Eat. A Comparison of Current and Former Animal Product Limiters," *Appetite*, vol. 58 (2012), pp. 1030–37; and Hal Herzog, "Why Do Most Vegetarians Go Back to Eating Meat?" *Psychology Today*, 2011, http://www.psychologyto day.com/blog/animals-and-us/201106/why-do-most-vegetarians-go-back-eating-meat.

84. Henry Stevenson Salt, *Percy Bysshe Shelley: A Monograph* (Swan Sonnenschein, Lowrey and Co, 1888), p. 242.

85. Brett-Smith, *Peacock's Memoirs of Shelley*, 54–55.

86. Brett-Smith, *Peacock's Memoirs of Shelley*, 38–39.

87. Gilmour, *The Making of the Poets*, 313.

88. Phyllis Grosskurth, *Byron: The Flawed Angel* (Houghton Mifflin, 1997).

89. J. H. Baron, "Illnesses and Creativity: Byron's Appetites, James Joyce's Gut, and Melba's Meals and Mésallilances," *British Medical Journal*, vol. 7123 (20 Dec 1997), http://www.bmj.com/content/315/7123/1697.

90. Mark Bostridge, "On the Trail of the Real Lord Byron," *The Independent*, 4 Nov 2002, http://www.independent.co.uk/arts-entertainment/books/features/on-the-trail-of-the-real-lord-byron-603280.html.

91. Quoted in Baron, "Illnesses and Creativity."

92. Jeffrey D. Hoeper, "The Sodomizing Biographer: Leslie Marchand's Portrait of Byron," 2002, http://web.archive.org/web/20030510053432/http://engphil.astate.edu/gallery/marchand.html.

93. Terry Castle, "'Mad, Bad and Dangerous to Know,'" *New York Times*, 13 Apr 1997.

94. Wilma Paterson, *Lord Byron's Relish: Regency Recipes with Notes Culinary and Byronic* (Dog and Bone, 1990), pp. 133–34.

95. Hogg, *Life of Shelley*, II:318.

96. Trelawny, *Records*, 50.

97. Christine Kenyon Jones, "'Man Is a Carnivorous Production': Byron and the Anthropology of Food," *Prism(s): Essays in Romanticism*, vol. 6, no. 1 (1998), pp. 41.

98. Trelawny, *Records*, 50–51.

99. Thomas Moore, *Life, Letters, and Journals of Lord Byron* (John Murray, 1839), p. 319, note 3.

100. Marguerite Blessington, *A Journal of Conversations with Lord Byron. With a Sketch of the Life of the Author* (3rd ed., G. W. Cottrell, n.d. [1834]).

101. Baron, "Illnesses and Creativity."

102. Arthur Crisp, "Commentary: Ambivalence toward Fatness and Its Origins," *British Medical Journal*, vol. 7123 (20 Dec 1997), http://www.bmj.com/content/315/7123/1703.

103. Castle, "Mad, Bad and Dangerous."

104. Quoted in Fiona MacCarthy, *Byron: Life and Legend* (Farrar, Straus and Giroux, 2002).

105. Bieri, *Percy Bysshe Shelley*, 296.

106. Holmes, *Shelley, The Pursuit*.

107. Richard Garnett, "Hogg, Thomas Jefferson," *Dictionary of National Biography, 1885–1900*, vol. 27, http://en.wikisource.org/wiki/Hogg,_Thomas_Jefferson; and Carol L. Thoma, "Hogg, Thomas Jefferson (1792–1862)," *Oxford Dictionary of National Biography*, online edition, edited by Lawrence Goldman (Oxford UP, 2004), http://www.oxforddnb.com/view/article/13475.

108. Hogg, *Life of Shelley*, II:318–19.

109. Hogg, *Life of Shelley*, II:222.

110. Hogg, *Life of Shelley*, II:422–23.

111. Hogg, *Life of Shelley*, II:316–17.

112. Hogg, *Life of Shelley*, II:419–20.

113. Edward Dowden, *The Life of Percy Bysshe Shelley* (2 vols., Kegan Paul; J. B. Lippincott, 1887).

114. John Davis, "Shelley—'The First Celebrity Vegan,'" 2011, http://www.vegsource .com/john-davis/shelley-the-first-celebrity-vegan.html.

115. Timothy Morton, "Joseph Ritson, Percy Shelley and the Making of Romantic Vegetarianism," *Romanticism*, vol. 12 (2007), pp. 52–61.

116. Ritson, *Essay on Abstinence from Animal Food*; emphasis added.

117. Keith Thomas, *Man and the Natural World: Changing Attitudes in England 1500–1800* (Allen Lane, 1983).

118. Quoted in Reay Tannahill, *Food in History* (Eyre Methuen; Stein and Day, 1973), p. 343.

119. Ritson, *Essay on Abstinence from Animal Food*, 84–85.

120. Spencer, *Heretic's Feast*, 214.

121. Thomas Tryon, *The Way to Health and Long Life* (2nd ed., printed by H. C. for R. Baldwin, 1691), p. 258.

122. Julia Twigg, Julia, "Food for Thought: Purity and Vegetarianism," *Religion* , vol. 9 (1979), pp. 13–35.

123. Oerlemans, "Shelley's Ideal Body"; Wayland D. Hand, *Magical Medicine* (U of California P, 1980).

124. William Smellie, *The Philosophy of Natural History* (2 vols., Charles Elliot, 1790–1799), pp. 60–61.

125. Ritson, *Essay on Abstinence from Animal Food*, 406.

126. Williams, *Ethics of Diet*, 331.

127. Brett-Smith, *Peacock's Memoirs of Shelley*, 25.

128. Salt, *Percy Bysshe Shelley*, 242.

129. Leslie A. Marchand, *Byron: A Biography* (3 vols., Alfred A. Knopf, 1957), vol. III, p. 1066.

130. Hogg, *Life of Shelley*, II:425.

131. Hogg, *Life of Shelley*, II:425.

132. Michael W. Allen, Marc Wilson, Sik Hung Ng, and Michael Dunne, "Values and Beliefs of Vegetarians and Omnivores," *The Journal of Social Psychology* vol. 140 (2000), pp. 405–22; Hamilton, "Eating Death"; Haverstock and Forgays, "To Eat or Not to Eat"; and Ruby, "Vegetarianism."

133. M. Connors, C. A. Bisogni, J. Sobal, and C. M. Devine, "Managing Values in Personal Food Systems," *Appetite*, vol. 36 (2001), pp. 189–200.

134. Quoted in Oerlemans, "Shelley's Ideal Body," 547.

135. See Oerlemans, "Shelley's Ideal Body." Spencer writes that Gandhi went to England in 1888 to study law. He stumbled upon a vegetarian restaurant, where he "had his first big meal since leaving home. At the restaurant he was immediately impressed and influenced by what he read there, both Shelley and Henry Salt's *A Plea for Vegetarianism*, two writers who fused abstinence from animal flesh with much greater social reforms." Gandhi also

read *The Ethics of Diet* by Howard Williams. Salt published a monograph on Shelley, and Williams's book includes chapters about many authors recommending a vegetable diet, including Cheyne, Oswald, Lambe, Newton, and Shelley, whose ideas are discussed in the present work; it also has an "appendix" containing comments by Tryon and Bryon, among others. See Spencer, *Heretic's Feast*, 291.

CHAPTER 8. WHAT THE TWO PRESIDENTIAL FINALISTS ATE IN 2016, AND WHY IT'S IMPORTANT

1. Matthew Jacob, "Politically Correct Eating on the Campaign Trail," CNN, 28 Oct 2010, http://www.cnn.com/2010/OPINION/10/28/jacob.food.politics/index.html.

2. Michael Y. Park, "Paleo, Vegetarian, or Teetotaling? What the Presidential Candidates' Food Habits Say about Them," *Bon Appétit*, 19 Oct 2015, https://www.bonap petit.com/entertaining-style/pop-culture/article/prezcandidates-food.

3. Alexander Bolton, "Gillibrand Becomes Latest Candidate Scrutinized for How She Eats on Campaign Trail." *The Hill*, 10 Feb 2019, https://thehill.com/homenews /campaign/429345-gillibrand-becomes-latest-candidate-scrutinized-for-how-she-eats-on.

4. An exception is the brief essay by Alex Ketchum for the Historical Cooking Project about several Canadian, British, and American politicians in the past. He contends, "The three ways in which eating and drinking play a role in the political campaign are as an enabler of activities, a symbol of identity, and as an aesthetic prop that can either bolster or undermine a candidate's public image." I do not take issue with his hypotheses but rather seek to present a more complete analysis of the uses and abuses of politicians' food habits as they campaign for office, especially that of US president. See Alex Ketchum, "Political Foods: Food and Drink on Campaign," Historical Cooking Project, 13 Oct 2015, http:// www.historicalcookingproject.com/2015/10/political-foods-food-and-drink-on.html.

For another short academic report on the politics of eating in American political campaigns, see Jan Wilson, "The Politics of Food on the Campaign Trail," Oklahoma Center for the Humanities, n.d., https://humanities.utulsa.edu/politics-food-campaign-trail.

Two significant historical events bear mentioning. Not on the campaign trail but in office at the time, Franklin Roosevelt in 1939 treated the king and queen of England to a picnic of hotdogs at his Hyde Park Estate to warm the American public to support the United States intervening to aid Britain in the coming war. See David Levine and Polly Sparling, "Franklin Delano Roosevelt: The Picnic That Won the War, the Royal Visit, the Hot Dog Summit of 1939, and Hyde Park on the Hudson Movie," *Hudson Valley Magazine*, Dec 2012, http://www.hvmag.com/core/pagetools.php?pageid=9913&url=%2fhudson -valley-magazine%2fdecember-2012%2ffranklin-delano-roosevelt-the-picnic-that-won -the-war-the-royal-visit-the-hot-dog-summit-of-1939-and-hyde-park-on-the-hudson -movie%2f&mode=print.

The other food-related event is the presidential election of 1840 pitting William Henry Harrison against incumbent Martin Van Buren, the first election to invoke food as a signifier of class and social differences, "an ongoing cultural symbol to be played upon by politicians and marketers ever since," writes Bruce Kraig in "The Election That Defined What

'Real Americans' Ate and Drank," *Atlas Obscura*, 15 Jan 2018, https://www.atlasobscura
.com/articles/1840-election-food-william-henry-harrison. "When American politicians
hold pancake breakfasts and dutifully eat corn dogs at state fairs, they are following the
tradition established by William Henry Harrison: the man who dominated the vote and
won the presidency on the promise that he ate like real Americans." See also Bruce Kraig,
A Rich and Fertile Land: A History of Food in America (Reaktion Books, 2017).

5. Katie Rogers and Anie Karni, "Home Alone at the White House: A Sour President,
with TV His Constant Companion," *New York Times*, 23 Apr 2020, https://www.nytimes
.com/2020/04/23/us/politics/coronavirus-trump.html.

6. George T. Conway, III, published a long, blistering article in *The Atlantic* on 3 Oct
2019, titled "Unfit for Office: Donald Trump's Narcissism Makes It Impossible for Him to
Carry Out the Duties of the Presidency in the Way the Constitution Requires." Like me,
Conway is not a psychological scientist. He writes, however, "Any intelligent person who
watches Trump closely on television, and pays careful attention to his words on Twitter
and in the press, should be able to tell you as much about his behavior as a mental-health
professional could." He contends, following analysis in a scholarly article, that such
laypersons' interpretations might even be more accurate, particularly in regard to narcissistic personality disorder and antisocial personality disorder, which frequently have been
ascribed to Trump. My explanations of Trump's eating habits tied to his character, values,
and personality are, to be sure, speculative, but they are not unethical or beyond the realm
of possibility, or even likelihood.

7. Ashley Parker, "Donald Trump's Diet: He'll Have Fries with That," *New York Times*,
8 Aug 2016, https://www.nytimes.com/2016/08/09/us/politics/donald-trump-diet.html.

8. Tom Sietsema, "The World Is Trump's Oyster, but He Prefers Filet-O-Fish,"
Washington Post, 24 Mar 2016, https://www.washingtonpost.com/lifestyle/food/trump
-can-afford-to-eat-the-finest-food-instead-he-eats-the-most-generic/2016/03/24/63aedb18
-eafo-11e5-bc08-3e03a5b41910_story.html?utm_term=.8987b3141738.

9. Corey R. Lewandowski and David N. Bossie, *Let Trump Be Trump: The Inside Story
of His Rise to the Presidency* (Center Street, 2017), p. 89.

10. Daniela Galarza, "Donald Trump Celebrates Delegate Victory with McDonald's
Big Mac," *Eater*, 27 May 2016, https://www.eater.com/2016/5/27/11796092
/donald-trump-mcdonalds-private-jet.

11. Michael Wolff, *Fire and Fury: Inside the Trump White House* (Henry Holt, 2018).

12. Brenna Houck, "Everything Donald Trump Ate in 2017," *Eater*, 28 Dec 2017, https://
www.eater.com/2017/12/28/16797530/donald-trump-president-what-he-ate-2017.

13. Trump is also notorious for slathering ketchup on steak that, according to his longtime butler, "would rock on the plate, it was so well done." See Jason Horowitz, "A King in His
Castle: How Donald Trump Lives, from His Longtime Butler," *New York Times*, 15 Mar 2016,
https://www.nytimes.com/2016/03/16/us/politics/donald-trump-butler-mar-a-lago.html.
Trump has been observed partaking of Thousand Island dressing while dinner guests
were served vinaigrette on the salad course, extra sauce with his entrée, and a slice of
chocolate cake or pie with two scoops of ice cream (preferably cherry vanilla) while
others received one scoop (see Houck, "Everything Donald Trump Ate"). At a summit
meeting with North Korean leader Kim Jong Un in Feb 2019, the White House repeatedly

adjusted the menu so that finally it featured shrimp cocktail with Thousand Island dressing, grilled sirloin, and chocolate lava cake rather than the shredded mango salad with scallops, Hanoi spring rolls, and grilled cod that had been proposed by representatives of North Korea. See Greg Morabito, "Menu for Trump's Dinner with Kim Jong-un Gets Last-Minute Rewrite," *Eater*, 27 Feb 2019, https://www.eater.com/2019/2/27/18242897 /trump-dinner-menu-kim-jong-un. In Mar 2019, Trump honored North Dakota State University's Bison football players and coaches at the White House with Big Macs, french fries, and Chick-fil-A chicken sandwiches. He jokingly remarked that he could have served a meal prepared by White House chefs, but "I know you people." See Tom Schad, "President Donald Trump Serves Fast Food to Another Title Team, North Dakota State, the FCS Champions," *USA Today*, 4 Mar 2019, https://www.usatoday.com/story/sports /ncaaf/2019/03/04/donald-trump-north-dakota-state-fast-food-white-house/3056111002. For a study of the Trump-sponsored feast for the Clemson football team in Jan 2919, see Sheila Bock, "Fast Food at the White House: Performing Foodways, Class, and American Identity," *Western Folklore*, vol. 80 (2021), pp. 15–43.

14. David Smith, "Donald Trump: The Making of a Narcissist," *The Guardian*, 29 Feb 2018 (originally published 16 Jul 2016), https://www.theguardian.com/us-news/2016 /jul/16/donald-trump-narcissist-profile.

15. Parker, "Donald Trump's Diet."

16. David Martosko, "Air Force Trump," *Daily Mail*, 24 May 2015, https://www .dailymail.co.uk/news/article-3093304/On-757-Donald-Trump-dishes-Rand-Paul-Mitt -Romney-100-million-wont-help-Jeb-Bush.html#ixzz3tkKh8i2B.

17. Whitney Fillon, "Donald Trump Burger Gets the Axe from Canadian Restaurant," *Eater*, 21 Dec 2015, https://www.eater.com/2015/12/21/10636490/donald-trump-burger -nuburger-winnipeg.

18. Wolff, *Fire and Fury*, 85.

19. Paul H. Elovitz, "A Psychobiographical and Psycho-Political Comparison of Clinton and Trump," *Journal of Psychohistory*, vol. 44 (2016), p. 104; and Dan Mangan, "Donald Trump Says He's a 'Germaphobe' as He Dismisses Salacious Allegations," CNBC, 11 Jan 2017, https://www.cnbc.com/2017/01/11/donald-trump-says-hes-a-germaphobe-as-he -dismisses-salacious-allegations.html.

20. Jess Bolluyt, "The Real Reason Donald Trump Always Eats Fast Food Will Make You Feel Bad for Him," *Cheat Sheet*, 14 Jan 2019, https://www.cheatsheet.com/culture/real -reason-donald-trump-always-eats-fast-food.html.

21. Michael Richardson, "The Disgust of Donald Trump," *Continuum*, vol. 31 (2017), pp. 747–56.

22. Lewandowski and Bossie, *Let Trump Be Trump*.

23. Stormy Daniels, *Full Disclosure* (St. Martin's Press, 2018), 128.

24. Parker, "Donald Trump's Diet."

25. Sietsema, "World Is Trump's Oyster."

26. Leonard L. Glass, "Should Psychiatrists Refrain from Commenting on Trump's Psychology?" *The Dangerous Case of Donald Trump: 27 Psychiatrists and Mental Health Experts Assess a President*, edited by Bandy X. Lee (St. Martin's Press, 2017), p. 157.

27. Richardson, "Disgust of Donald Trump," 751.

28. Richardson, "Disgust of Donald Trump," 748, 752.

29. Houck, "Everything Donald Trump Ate"; and Morabito, "Menu for Trump's Dinner."

30. Khushbu Shah, "Donald Trump Banned from Pizzeria for Being the Worst, *Eater*, 8 Jul 2015, https://www.eater.com/2015/7/8/8913549/donald-trump-banned-from-pizzeria; and Smith, "Donald Trump."

31. Deena Zaru, "Feathers Fly over Donald Trump Eating Fried Chicken with a Fork," CNN, 2 Aug 2016, https://www.cnn.com/2016/08/02/politics/donald-trump-eats-kfc -knife-fork/index.html.

32. Chris Fuhrmeister, "D.C. Diner Celebrates Donald Trump with a Sandwich That's 'Full of Bologna,'" *Eater*, 11 Aug 2015, https://www.eater.com/2015/8/11/9133989/american -city-diner-trump-sandwich-bologna.

33. Galarza, "Donald Trump Celebrates Delegate Victory."

34. Lewandowski and Bossie, *Let Trump Be Trump*, 91.

35. Cari Romm, "Why Comfort Food Comforts," *The Atlantic*, 3 Apr 2015, https://www .theatlantic.com/health/archive/2015/04/why-comfort-food-comforts/389613.

36. Houck, "Everything Donald Trump Ate."

37. Glenn Kessler, "Trump Made 30,573 False or Misleading Claims as President. Nearly Half Came in His Final Year," *Washington Post*, 23 Jan 2021, https://www.washingtonpost .com/politics/how-fact-checker-tracked-trump-claims/2021/01/23/ad04b69a-5c1d-11eb -a976-bad6431e03e2_story.html?utm_campaign=wp_post_most&utm_medium=email &utm_source=newsletter&wpisrc=nl_most&carta-url=https%3A%2F%2Fs2.washington post.com%2Fcar-ln-tr%2F2edd9cf%2F600da33e9d2fdaoefbbef8d4%2F5c709752ae7e8a2db e5401ee%2F8%2F66%2F600da33e9d2fdaoefbbef8d4.

38. Ashley Parker, "The Me President: Trump Uses Pandemic Briefing to Focus on Himself," *Washington Post*, 13 Apr 2020, https://www.washingtonpost.com/politics/trump -pandemic-briefing-focus-himself/2020/04/13/1dc94992-7dd8-11ea-9040-68981f488eed _story.html?utm_campaign=wp_post_most&utm_medium=email&utm_source =newsletter&wpisrc=nl_most.

39. Elovitz, "Psychobiographical and Psycho-Political Comparison," 100; see also 112, notes 53–55.

40. Anton Ashcroft, "Donald Trump: Narcissist, Psychopath or Representative of the People?" *Psychotherapy and Politics International*, vol. 14 (2016), p. 217.

41. Alessandro Nai and Jürgen Maier, "Perceived Personality and Campaign Style of Hillary Clinton and Donald Trump," *Personality and Individual Differences*, vol. 121 (15 Jan 2018), pp. 80–83; and Beth A. Visser, Angela S. Bock, and Anthony A. Volk, "Is Hillary Dishonest and Donald Narcissistic? A HEXACO Analysis of the Presidential Candidates' Public Personas,"*Personality and Individual Differences*, vol. 106 (1 Feb 2017), pp. 281–86.

42. Daniel Berger, "Donald Trump: Profile of a Sociopath," *The Huffington Post*, 3 Aug 2016, http://www.huffingtonpost.com/daniel-berger/trump-profile-of-a-sociopath _b_11318128.html; James A. Herb, "Donald J. Trump, Alleged Incapacitated Person: Mental Incapacity, the Electoral College, and the Twenty-Fifth Amendment," Lee, editor,

Dangerous Case of Donald Trump, 136–47; and Craig Malkin, "Pathological Narcissism and Politics: A Lethal Mix," Lee, editor, *Dangerous Case of Donald Trump*, 57.

43. *Diagnostic and Statistical Manual of Mental Disorders, Fourth Edition* (American Psychiatric Association, 2000).

44. Conway, "Unfit for Office."

45. Justin A. Frank, *Trump on the Couch: Inside the Mind of the President* (Avery, 2018), 107; see also 130.

46. Lewandowski and Bossie, *Let Trump Be Trump*, 90.

47. Allyson Chiu, "President Donald Trump Serves Fast Food to Another Title Team, North Dakota State, the FCS Champions," *Washington Post*, 15 Jan 2019, https://www .washingtonpost.com/nation/2019/01/15/trump-has-turned-white-house-into-white -castle-president-roasted-serving-clemson-fast-food/?noredirect=on&utm_term =.33f34bcfbb92; and Schad, "President Donald Trump Serves Fast Food."

48. Frank, *Trump on the Couch*, 19; and Michael Kruse, "The Mystery of Mary Trump," *Politico*. Nov/Dec 2017, https://www.politico.com/magazine/story/2017/11/03/mary -macleod-trump-donald-trump-mother-biography-mom-immigrant-scotland-215779.

49. Links to two video clips on YouTube are of Martha Stewart preparing meatloaf with the Trumps and another of making a meatloaf sandwich for each of them using thick sourdough bread (and adding dill pickle slices, which Donald Trump in fact eschews; he does not bite into the sandwich that Martha Stewart gives him). See Maxine Shen, "Watch President Trump Make Meatloaf on a Vintage Martha Stewart Episode," *Food and Wine*, 9 Jun 2017, https://www.foodandwine.com/news/watch-president-trump-learning -how-make-meatloaf-scratch.

50. Sietsema, "World Is Trump's Oyster."

51. LuAnne Roth, "Comfort (and Discomfort) Food: Social Surrogacy and Embodied Memory in Real and Reel Time," *Comfort Food Meanings and Memories*, edited by Michael Owen Jones and Lucy M. Long (UP of Mississippi, 2017), p. 188.

52. Marian Burros, "Hillary Clinton's New Home: Broccoli's in, Smoking's Out," *New York Times*, 2 Feb 1993, https://www.nytimes.com/1993/02/02/us/hillary-clinton-s-new -home-broccoli-s-in-smoking-s-out.html.

53. Cortney Drakeford, "What Is Hillary Clinton's Diet? Democratic Presidential Candidate Stays Healthy by Eating Lamb, Hot Peppers and Wine Ice Cream," *International Business Times*, 7 Oct 2016, https://www.ibtimes.com/what-hillary-clintons-diet-demo cratic-presidential-candidate-stays-healthy-eating-2425690.

54. Chris Heasman, "This Is What Hillary Clinton Eats," Mashed, n.d., https://www .mashed.com/118104/hillary-clinton-eats; David S. Martin, "From Omnivore to Vegan: The Dietary Education of Bill Clinton," 2011, http://www.cnn.com/2011/HEALTH/08/18/bill .clinton.diet.vegan/index.html; and Mimi Sheraton, "How Hungry Is Hillary Clinton? An Analysis of the Candidate's Taste Buds," *Slate*, 20 Feb 2008, http://www.slate.com/articles /life/food/2008/02/how_hungry_is_hillary_clinton.html.

55. Shana Lynch, "Here's What Hillary Clinton and Donald Trump Eat on the Campaign Trail," *Delish*, 19 Jul 2016, https://www.delish.com/food-news/a48301/donald -trump-hillary-clinton-eat-campaign-trail.

56. Heasman, "This Is What Hillary Clinton Eats."

57. Hillary Clinton, "Hillary Clinton's Favorite Food & Drink in NY State, according to HRC Herself," *Thrillist*, 18 Apr 2016, https://www.thrillist.com/eat/new-york/hillary-clintons-favorite-food-drink-in-ny-state.

58. Hillary Rodham Clinton, *What Happened* (Simon & Schuster, 2017), p. 91.

59. Clinton, *What Happened*, 91

60. Clinton, *What Happened*, 91

61. Burros, "Hillary Clinton's New Home."

62. Martin, "From Omnivore to Vegan."

63. "While on a jog, a hungry President Bill Clinton (Phil Hartman) stops at a McDonald's, where he talks to customers and eats their food as he answers political questions," Season 18 (1992), https://www.youtube.com/watch?v=eYtokhR_ejo.

64. Burros, "Hillary Clinton's New Home."

65. Martha Sherrill, "Hillary Clinton Takes on the Hill," *Washington Post*, 5 Feb 1993, https://www.washingtonpost.com/politics/hillary-clinton-takes-on-the-hill/2016/07/22/29685e80-5039-11e6-a7d8-13d06b37f256_story.html?utm_term=.2001d890cb89.

66. Clinton, *What Happened*, 118.

67. Clinton, *What Happened*, 118.

68. Clinton, *What Happened*, 119.

69. Kathleen Hall Jamieson, *Beyond the Double Bind: Women and Leadership* (Oxford UP, 1995), 218, note 12; ellipses in the original transcript. See also Karrin Vasby Anderson, "'Rhymes with Rich': 'Bitch' as a Tool of Containment in Contemporary American Politics," *Rhetoric and Public Affairs*, vol. 2 (1999), pp. 599–623; and Karrin Vasby Anderson, "From Spouses to Candidates: Hillary Rodham Clinton, Elizabeth Dole, and the Gendered Office of US President," *Rhetoric and Public Affairs*, vol. 5 (2002), pp. 105–32.

70. Anderson, "Rhymes with Rich"; and Anderson, "From Spouses to Candidates," 111, 113.

71. Visser et al., "Is Hillary Dishonest and Donald Narcissistic?"

72. "Hillary Clinton's Career of Comebacks," Pew Research Center, 21 Dec 2012, https://www.people-press.org/2012/12/21/hillary-clintons-career-of-comebacks.

73. Elovitz, "Psychobiographical and Psycho-Political Comparison," 101.

74. Fedwa Malti-Douglas, *Partisan Sex: Bodies, Politics, and the Law in the Clinton Era* (Peter Lang, 2009), p. 132.

75. Diana B. Carlin and Kelly L. Winfrey, "Have You Come a Long Way, Baby? Hillary Clinton, Sarah Palin, and Sexism in 2008," *Communication Studies*, vol. 60 (2009), p. 332; the authors indicate that this was not simply in jest, for they write, the "Facebook group had tens of thousands of members who ostensibly believed that a woman should be engaged in traditional sex roles." For jokes about Hillary Clinton, see Carlin and Winfrey, "Have You Come a Long Way?"; Jeannie B. Thomas, "Dumb Blondes, Dan Quayle, and Hillary Clinton: Gender, Sexuality, and Stupidity in Jokes," *Journal of American Folklore*, vol. 110 (1997), pp. 277–313; and Walter Shapiro, "Whose Hillary Is She, Anyway?" *Esquire*, Aug1993, https://classic.esquire.com/article/1993/8/1/whose-hillary-is-she-anyway.

76. Burros, "Hillary Clinton's New Home."

77. Shapiro, "Whose Hillary Is She, Anyway?"

78. Tamara Keith, "Cooked Up after A Hillary Clinton Gaffe, The First Spouse Cookie Battle Is Back," WBUR News, 18 Aug 2016, https://www.wbur.org/npr/490478924/cooked -up-after-a-hillary-clinton-gaffe-the-first-spouse-cookie-battle-is-back. The author is quoting Debbie Walsh, a researcher at Rutgers University.

79. Keith, "Cooked Up."

80. Allison Aubrey, "Hillary Clinton's Elixir: Can a Hot Pepper a Day Boost Immunity?" NPR, 21 Jan 2016, https://www.npr.org/sections/thesalt/2016/01/21/463858189 /hillary-clintons-elixir-can-a-hot-pepper-a-day-boost-immunity.

81. Elovitz, "Psychobiographical and Psycho-Political Comparison," 104. See also Kira Hall, Donna M. Goldstein, and Matthew Bruce Ingram, "The Hands of Donald Trump: Entertainment, Gesture, Spectacle," *Hau: Journal of Ethnographic Theory*, vol. 6 (2016), pp. 73, 84.

82. Emily J. H. Contois, "The Spicy Spectacular: Food, Gender, and Celebrity on *Hot Ones*," *Feminist Media Studies* vol. 18 (2018), pp. 769–73; and Paul Rozin and Deborah Schiller, "The Nature and Acquisition of a Preference for Chili Pepper by Humans," *Motivation and Emotion*, vol. 4 (1980), pp. 83, 94.

83. Several studies, however, indicate that personality rather than gender plays a significant role in the liking of spicy foods. See, e.g., Nadia K. Byrnes and John E. Hayes, "Gender Differences in the Influence of Personality Traits on Spicy Food Liking and Intake," *Food Quality and Preference*, vol. 42 (Jun 2015), pp. 12–19; and Contois, "Spicy Spectacular."

84. Lynch, "Here's What."

85. Amy Chozick, "A Homecoming, and a Triumph, for Hillary Clinton in New York," *New York Times*, 19 Apr 2016, https://www.nytimes.com/2016/04/20/us/politics/hillary -clinton-new-york.html.

86. "Stephen Interviews Hillary Clinton at Carnegie Deli," 19 Apr 2016, https://www .youtube.com/watch?v=LmCJIBsQjOY.

87. See FOX 10 Phoenix, 2016, https://www.youtube.com/watch?v=S-Xr1zHUxc4.

88. Visser et al., "Is Hillary Dishonest and Donald Narcissistic?" 282.

89. Mark Leibovich, "In the '60s, a Future Candidate Poured Her Heart Out in Letters," *New York Times*, 29 Jul 2007, https://www.nytimes.com/2007/07/29/us/politics/29letter.html.

90. Meghan Daum, "When Hillary Met Robert," *Los Angeles Times*, 11 Aug 2007, https:// www.latimes.com/la-oe-daum11aug11-column.html.

91. Clinton, *What Happened*, 120.

CHAPTER 9. GAFFES, GIBES, AND GENDER ON THE CAMPAIGN TRAIL

1. "Iowa State Fair," https://www.iowastatefair.org.

2. Syjil Ashraf, "Iowa State Fair Unveils Its Annual 600-Pound Butter Cow," *The Daily Meal*, 10 Aug 2018, https://www.thedailymeal.com/travel/iowa-state-fair-2018-life-sized -butter-cow.

3. Courtney Crowder, "25 Facts about the State Fair's Butter Cow," *Des Moines Register*, 12 Aug 2015, https://www.desmoinesregister.com/story/life/2015/08/12/butter-cow-facts /31569851.

4. "Biographical Note, The Thomas Phillip ('Tip') O'Neill, Jr. Papers, Archives and Manuscripts," John J. Burns Library, Boston College, 15 Aug 2006, https://web.archive.org /web/20100414062330/http://www.bc.edu/bc_org/avp/ulib/oneill_findingaid2.html.

5. Merrill Perlman, "Politics for Sale," *Columbia Journalism Review*, 1 Feb 2016, https:// www.cjr.org/language_corner/politics_for_sale.php.

6. Lynne Vavreck, Constantine J. Spiliotes, and Linda L. Fowler, "The Effects of Retail Politics in the New Hampshire Primary," *American Journal of Political Science*, vol. 46 (2002), pp. 597, 604–5; and Thomas Wood, "What the Heck Are We Doing in Ottumwa, Anyway? Residential Candidate Visits and Their Political Consequence," *The Annals of the American Academy of Political and Social Science*, vol. 667 (2016), pp. 111–12, 118, 123–24.

7. Ed Crews, "Voting in Early America," *CW [Colonial Williamsburg] Journal*, spring 2007, http://www.history.org/foundation/journal/spring07/elections.cfm.

8. Jodi Kantor, "Where the Votes Are, So Are All Those Calories," *New York Times*, 23 Nov 2007, https://www.nytimes.com/2007/11/23/us/politics/23food.htmlPhoto; and Bruce Kraig, "The Election That Defined What 'Real Americans' Ate and Drank," *Atlas Obscura*, 15 Jan 2018, https://www.atlasobscura.com/articles/1840-election-food -william-henry-harrison.

9. Jonathan Deutsch and Megan J. Elias, *Barbecue: A Global History* (Reaktion Books, 2014), p. 37.

10. Elovitz, "Psychobiographical and Psycho-Political Comparison"; Richardson, "Disgust of Donald Trump," 747; and Alan Yuhas, "US Voters Largely Uninfluenced by Meet-and-Greet Campaign Stops, Study Finds," *The Guardian*, 19 Aug 2016, https://www.theguardian .com/us-news/2016/aug/19/us-voters-political-campaign-stops-clinton-romney.

11. Francesca Chambers, "2008 Caucus Winner Huckabee Draws Large Crowd at Iowa State Fair after Tasting a Pork Chop That His Wife Wouldn't Let Him Finish," *Daily Mail*, 14 Aug 2015, https://www.dailymail.co.uk/news/article-3196823/Hawkeye-State-Hearts -Huckabee-2008-caucus-winner-draws-large-crowd-Iowa-State-Fair-tasting-pork-chop -wife-wouldn-t-let-finish.html.

12. Stephen Smith, "Diners Offer Presidential Candidates a Taste of America, *The Guardian,* 27 Nov 2011, https://www.theguardian.com/world/2011/nov/27/diners-pres idential-candidates-america.

13. Darren Garnick, "Eating with the Presidential Candidates," *New Hampshire Magazine*, Feb 2016, https://www.nhmagazine.com/february-2016/eating-with-the -presidential-candidates.

14. Garnick, "Eating with the Presidential Candidates."

15. Garnick, "Eating with the Presidential Candidates."

16. Wood, "What the Heck?" 111.

17. Robynn Tysver, "In Race for the White House, Candidates Must Brave Iowa State Fair Madness—Pork Chop on a Stick and All," *World-Herald*, 19 Aug 2015, https://www .omaha.com/news/politics/in-race-for-the-white-house-candidates-must-brave-iowa /article_00a75b0b-65df-53e1-9d0d-6ac3eaae86a1.html.

18. Paige Sutherland, "Foodstuffs: In Campaign Season, N.H. Diners Offer Comfort Food and Politics," New Hampshire Public Radio, 13 Aug 2015, http://www.nhpr.org/post /foodstuffs-campaign-season-nh-diners-offer-comfort-food-and-politics#stream/0.

19. Garnick, "Eating with the Presidential Candidates."

20. Garnick, "Eating with the Presidential Candidates."

21. Jenna Johnson and Philip Bump, "Hillary Clinton, Donald Trump and the Trumpcopter Descend on the Iowa State Fair," *Washington Post*, 15 Aug 2015, https://www.washingtonpost.com/news/post-politics/wp/2015/08/15/latest-iowa-state-fair-attraction-trump-clinton-sanders-and-a-helicopter/?utm_term=.f80055192dc9.

22. For example, immigrant rights protestors interrupted Chris Christie and animal rights activists jumped on stage, hecklers assailed Jeb Bush regarding the war in Iraq, and critics of Scott Walker's policies on education and labor unions shouted at him; Walker responded, "I will not be intimidated," echoing the title of his 2013 book *Unintimidated*. See Sarah Westwood, "Christie Interrupted by Animal Rights Protest at Iowa State Fair," *Washington Examiner*, 23 Aug 2015, https://www.washingtonexaminer.com/christie-interrupted-by-animal-rights-protest-at-iowa-state-fair; and Trip Gabriel, "At Iowa's State Fair, Candidates Brave Cholesterol and Hecklers," *New York Times*, Aug. 14, 2015, https://www.nytimes.com/2015/08/15/us/politics/candidates-crowd-iowa-fair-in-a-raucous-campaign.html.

23. "The Iowa State Fair Is Famous for Mobile Food on a Stick," https://www.iowastatefair.org/food/food-on-a-stick.

24. Gabriel, "At Iowa's State Fair."

25. Hillary Rodham Clinton, *What Happened* (Simon & Schuster, 2017), 92.

26. See Sarah Gibbens and National Journal, "Photos: 2016 Presidential Candidates at the Iowa State Fair," *The Atlantic*, 17 Aug 2015, https://www.theatlantic.com/politics/archive/2015/08/photos-2016-presidential-candidates-at-the-iowa-state-fair/447888; and Jennifer Jacobs, "20 memorable political moments at Iowa State Fair," *Des Moines Register*, 24 Aug 2015, https://www.desmoinesregister.com/story/news/elections/presidential/caucus/2015/08/24/memorable-political-moments-iowa-state-fair/32201015.

27. Alexis Levinson, "It's the Chuck Grassley Show at the Iowa State Fair," *Congressional Quarterly Roll Call*, 13 Aug 2014, https://www.rollcall.com/news/iowa-state-fair-chuck-grassley.

28. Levinson, "It's the Chuck Grassley Show."

29. Michael Y. Park, "Paleo, Vegetarian, or Teetotaling? What the Presidential Candidates' Food Habits Say about Them," *Bon Appétit*, 19 Oct 2015, https://www.glamour.com/story/paleo-vegetarian-or-teetotalin.

30. Graham Flanagan, "Everything We Know about Trump's Unhealthy Diet," *Business Insider*, 4 Dec 2017, http://www.businessinsider.com/donald-trump-unhealthy-diet-exercise-politics-2016-10.

31. Mimi Sheraton, "How Hungry Is Hillary Clinton? An Analysis of the Candidate's Taste Buds," *Slate*, 20 Feb 2008, http://www.slate.com/articles/life/food/2008/02/how_hungry_is_hillary_clinton.html.

32. Chambers, "2008 Caucus Winner Huckabee Draws Large Crowd at Iowa State Fair after Tasting a Pork."

33. Seema Mehta and Michael J. Mishak, "Candidates Strategize in Final Weeks of Gubernatorial Race," *Los Angeles Times*, 20 Oct 2010, https://www.latimes.com/archives/la-xpm-2010-oct-20-la-me-1020-governor-20101020-story.html.

34. Bob Schieffer, "Dining Tips for Presidential Candidates," CBS News, 29 Mar 2012, https://www.cbsnews.com/news/dining-tips-for-presidential-candidates.

35. Wilson, "Politics of Food."

36. Matthew Jacob, "Politically Correct Eating on the Campaign Trail," CNN, 28 Oct 2010, http://www.cnn.com/2010/OPINION/10/28/jacob.food.politics/index.html.

37. Wilson, "Politics of Food."

38. Craig LaBan, "Photo Oop: Kerry Eats a Cheesesteak Hoagie . . . with Swiss," *The Philadelphia Inquirer*, 2 Jul 2009, https://www.philly.com/philly/food/restaurants /Photo_oop_Kerry_eats_a_cheesesteak_hoagie__with_Swiss.html.

39. Patricia Sullivan and Emma Brown, "Sargent Shriver, Founding Director of Peace Corps, Dies at 95," *Washington Post*, 18 Jan 2011, https://www.washingtonpost.com/local /obituaries/sargent-shriver-founding-director-of-peace-corps-dies-at-95/2011/01/18 /ABqGTSR_story.html?utm_term=.78ce8b85386a.

40. Wyatt Marshall, "How a Plate of Tamales May Have Crushed Gerald Ford's 1976 Presidential Campaign," *Munchies*, 8 Nov 2016, https://munchies.vice.com/en_us/article /ezkvxk/how-a-plate-of-tamales-may-have-crushed-gerald-fords-1976-presidential -campaign.

41. Claude Brodesser-Akner, "Cynthia Nixon's Breakfast of Doom. A Timeline of Funny Food Flubs on the Campaign Trail," NJ Advance Media, 14 Sep 1018, https://www .nj.com/politics/2018/09/cynthia_nixons_depravity_was_revealed_in_a_single .html; and Chris Welsh, "Candidates Descend on Des Moines, Romney Drops Chop," CNN Politics, 1 Aug 2007, http://politicalticker.blogs.cnn.com/2007/08/11/candidates -descend-on-des-moines-romney-drops-chop.

42. Daniela Galarza, "Eating on the Campaign Trail; Why Does Everyone Taste Food Differently?" *Eater*, 14 Jul 2016, https://www.eater.com/2016/7/14/12187594/campaign -eating-tasting-food.

43. Kevin Quealy, "Trump Is on Track to Insult 650 People, Places and Things on Twitter by the End of His First Term," *New York Times*, 26 Jul 2017, https://www.nytimes .com/interactive/2017/07/26/upshot/president-trumps-newest-focus-discrediting-the -news-media-obamacare.html; and Jasmine C. Lee and Kevin Quealy, "The 567 People, Places and Things Donald Trump Has Insulted on Twitter," *New York Times*, 20 Feb 2019, https://outriders.network/database/the-567-people-places-and-things-donald-trump -has-insulted-on-twitter.

44. Hall et al., "Hands of Donald Trump"; David Martosko, "Air Force Trump," *Daily Mail*, 24 May 2015, https://www.dailymail.co.uk/news/article-3093304/On-757 -Donald-Trump-dishes-Rand-Paul-Mitt-Romney-100-million-wont-help-Jeb-Bush. html#ixzz3tkKh8i2B; Richardson, "Disgust of Donald Trump," 747; and Maxwell Tani, "Trump Relentlessly Mocks Kasich: 'I Have Never Seen a Human Being Eat in Such a Disgusting Fashion,'" *Business Insider*, 15 Apr 2015, https://www.businessinsider.com /trump-kasich-eating-2016-4.

45. Allan Smith, "Donald Trump Went on Another Extensive Rant about John Kasich's Eating Habits," *Business Insider*, 28 Apr 2016, https://www.businessinsider.com /donald-trump-john-kasich-eating-2016-4.

46. Hall et al., "Hands of Donald Trump," 89.

47. For more about Trump "for whom disgust is so ever-present and deeply felt," see Richardson, "Disgust of Donald Trump," 747.

48. Tani, "Trump Relentlessly Mocks Kasich."

49. Ruben Vives, "San Francisco Chef Bans MAGA Caps at Restaurant—Then Apologizes for It," *Los Angeles Times*, 1 Feb 2019, https://www.latimes.com/local/lanow/la-me-ln-california-chef-bans-maga-hats-20190201-story.html.

50. Wayne T. Price and Suzy Fleming Leonard, "Restaurants Are Becoming Battleground for Politics and Social Issues," *Florida Today*, 5 Jul 2018, https://www.florida today.com/story/news/2018/06/29/restaurants-becoming-battleground-politics-and -social-issues/742855002.

51. Christopher Klein, "Did William Howard Taft Really Get Stuck in a Bathtub?" *History*, 3 Sep 2018, https://www.history.com/news/did-william-howard-taft-really -get-stuck-in-a-bathtub.

52. Park, "Paleo, Vegetarian, or Teetotaling?"

53. Steve Holland, "On the Hunt for the Presidency, Jeb Bush Adopts a 'Caveman' Diet," Reuters, 22 Apr 2015, https://www.reuters.com/article/us-usa-election-bush-paleo/on -the-hunt-for-the-presidency-jeb-bush-adopts-a-caveman-diet-idUSKBN0ND0CL 20150422.

54. Jessica Roy, "How 6 GOP Presidential Hopefuls Are Slimming Down for the 2016 Election," *New York Magazine*, 19 Feb 2015, http://nymag.com/daily/intelligencer/2015/02 /diets-of-6-gop-presidential-candidates.html.

55. "Food addict" does indeed seem apt for Mike Huckabee; or perhaps "food obsessed" is appropriate. For video examples of his employing food metaphors to refer to phenom- ena such as terrorism in the Middle East, Social Security, the Republic party's slate of candidates for the 2016 presidential election, and surveillance by the National Security Administration, see *The Daily Show with Trevor Noah* on YouTube, 12 Nov 2015, http:// www.cc.com/video-clips/9d7ex9/the-daily-show-with-trevor-noah-mike-huckabee -s-food-based-politics.

56. Meghan Keneally and Gillian Mohney, "Donald Trump Says Campaigning Is 'a Form of Exercise' on 'Dr. Oz,'" ABC News, 14 Sep 2016, https://abcnews.go.com/Politics /donald-trump-talks-weight-dr-oz/story?id=42109718.

57. Sietsema, "World Is Trump's Oyster."

58. House Speaker Nancy Pelosi called Trump "morbidly obese." The president has long insisted that he is six feet three inches, but in photos of him near other people he does not tower above them. Indeed, in one shot of him standing next to Jeb Bush, whose height of six feet three inches is confirmed in several sources, Trump is clearly about three inches shorter. Given Trump's likely height and his reported weight of 243 pounds in mid- February 2019, his body mass index might be as high as 33, i.e., fully in the obese category, which is likely why he claims to be taller and therefore not be categorized as "obese." Darren Samuelsohn, "Trump's Driver's License Casts Doubt on Height Claims," *Politico*, 23 Dec 2016, https://www.politico.com/story/2016/12/trump-drivers-license-height-232948.

59. Kate Bratskeir, "Here's How the Presidential Candidates Eat, Sleep and Work Out," *Huffington Post*, 9 Mar 2016, https://www.huffingtonpost.com/entry/presidential-candi dates-food-exercise-sleep_us_56d865dee4b0000de4038dbd.

60. Jess Bolluyt, "The Weirdest Things You Need to Know about Donald Trump's Exercise Habits, Revealed," *Cheat Sheet*, 2 Oct 2018, https://www.cheatsheet.com/culture /donald-trumps-exercise-habits.html.

61. Bratskeir, "Here's How."

62. Clinton, *What Happened*, 87.

63. For jokes about Hillary Clinton, see Carlin and Winfrey, "Have You Come a Long Way?"; Jeannie B. Thomas, "Dumb Blondes, Dan Quayle, and Hillary Clinton: Gender, Sexuality, and Stupidity in Jokes," *Journal of American Folklore*, vol. 110 (1997), pp. 277–313; and Shapiro, "Whose Hillary Is She, Anyway?"

64. Whitney Filloon, "Iowa Restaurant Honors Donald Trump Visit with 'No-Nonsense' Burger," *Eater*, 26 Jan 2016, https://www.eater.com/2016/1/26/10833758/trump -burger-iowa-northside-cafe.

65. Fuhrmeister, "D.C. Diner Celebrates Donald Trump."

66. Geoff Williams, "Would You Eat a Burger Named after Donald Trump or Hillary Clinton?" *Forbes*, 30 Jul 2016, https://www.forbes.com/sites/geoffwilliams/2016/07/30 /would-you-eat-a-burger-named-after-donald-trump-or-hillary-clinton-some-restaurants -hope-so/#2c89eddc5576.

67. Williams, "Would You Eat a Burger?"

68. Whitney Filloon, "Donald Trump Burger Gets the Axe from Canadian Restaurant," *Eater*, 21 Dec 2015, https://www.eater.com/2015/12/21/10636490/donald-trump-burger -nuburger-winnipeg; and Jessica Scott-Reid, "A Canadian Restaurant Is Dumping Donald Trump's Name from Its Burger," *Vice*, 21 Dec 2015, https://www.vice.com/en_us/article /qkx3dd/a-canadian-restaurant-is-dumping-donald-trumps-name-from-its-burger.

69. Michael Morain, "Hungry for Politics? Try Trumpburger or 'Bernie's Yearning' Ice Cream," *Des Moines Register*, 26 Jan 2016, https://www.desmoinesregister.com/story/news /elections/presidential/caucus/2016/01/25/hungry-politics-try-trumpburger-bernies -yearning-ice-cream/79324550.

70. Lucy Long, "Green Bean Casserole and Midwestern Identity: A Regional Foodways Aesthetic and Ethos," *Midwestern Folklore* 33 (2007), pp. 29–44; reprinted in Long, *The Food and Folklore Reader*, 191–204.

CHAPTER 10. MUST PRISON FOOD SICKEN BODIES AND MINDS?

1. Quoted in John Campanelli, "Jailhouse Slop: If You Don't Behave, It's Nutraloaf for You," *The Plain Dealer*, 16 Nov 2009, http://www.cleveland.com/pdq/index.ssf/2009/11 /post_15.html.

2. Tito David Valdez, Jr., "It's Chow Time! If It's Prison Food, It All Tastes the Same," n.d., http://www.inmate.com/prison-articles/prison-chow-time.htm.

3. For examples of breakfast, lunch, and dinner in a Texas prison over a three-day period, see Bruce Jackson and Diane Christian, *Death Row* (Beacon Press, 1980), pp.125–35. For meals at Men's Central Jail in Los Angeles and at the Oregon State Penitentiary, see respectively, Paul Pringle, "Jail Food Can Be a Hard Sell," *Los Angeles Times*, 8 Jan 2005, https://www.latimes.com/archives/la-xpm-2005-jan-08-me-jailfood8-story.html; and

Joseph Rose, "The Oregon State Penitentiary Surveys Inmates on Its Meals," 2005, http://
www.prisontalk.com/forums/showthread.php?t=113977. For discussions of food quality and gustatory and health issues among prisoners in the Netherlands, Norway, and
Australia, see, respectively, An-Sofie Vanhouche, "Acceptance or Refusal of Convenience
Food in Present-Day Prison," *Appetite*, vol. 94 (Nov 2015), pp. 47–53, http://ac.els-cdn
.com/S0195666315001932/1-s2.0-S0195666315001932-main.pdf?_tid=a663bd10-4a88-11e5
-8d3f-00000aabof6b&acdnat=1440438827_ed817d089029d20e186daa7029fodde5; Thomas
Ugelvik, "The Hidden Food: Mealtime Resistance and Identity Work in a Norwegian
Prison," *Punishment and Society*, vol. 13 (2011), pp. 47–63; and Diane J. Heckenberg and
Danielle Cody, *Food Matters—Issues Surrounding Food in Prison* (Occasional Paper 3.
Technical Report. U of Tasmania, Hobart, Tasmania, 2006), http://www.utas.edu.au
/__data/assets/pdf_file/0005/256064/Occasional_Paper_3_Food_Matters.pdf. Ugelvik
describes how immigrants in an Oslo prison stock up on spices and condiments of their
native countries to transform Norwegian fare into the tastes of their own cultures that are
a crucial part of their identity. The dramatic exception to bland food in prison is the last
meal chosen by inmates before execution, but many are too anxiety ridden to eat what
they have requested.

4. Rose, "Oregon State Penitentiary Surveys Inmates."

5. Quoted in Thomas C. Tobin, "Prison Food Costs Less, but at a Price," *St. Petersburg
Times*, 17 Jun 2002, http://www.sptimes.com/2002/06/17/State/Prison_food_costs_les
.shtml.

6. See also National Audit Office for an audit of British prisons that found high levels
of salt and little dietary fiber in diets owing to the prevalence of processed and convenience foods; National Audit Office, "Serving Time: Prisoner Diet and Exercise." Report
by the Comptroller and Auditor General, 2006, https://www.nao.org.uk/wp-content
/uploads/2006/03/0506939.pdf. Leach and Goodwin's findings regarding South Carolina
facilities were similar: Bethan Leach and Sarah Goodwin, "Preventing Malnutrition in
Prison," *Nursing Standard*, vol. 28 (2014), pp. 50–56.

In addition to repetitious and unhealthful meals, rumors have long circulated about
prisons serving roadkill ("meat so fresh you can still see the tire marks"). On 8 Nov 1989,
the *Lawrence* [Kansas] *Journal-World* carried an AP story titled "'Road Kill du Jour' Tops
Menu of Prison Meals." It reports that prisoners at a minimum security work camp near
Forks, Washington, despaired of eating game from hunters' illegal kills or animals hit by
logging trucks. Nicknamed "Rudy stew" (from Rudolph the Red-Nosed Reindeer), it typically consisted of deer or elk. "These guys who come through that chow line don't have a
choice," said the camp butcher, emphasizing the lack of personal control that imprisonment entails. "That's what it comes down to: Here's the Rudy stew. You eat it. If you don't
like it, right over there is the peanut butter jar."

7. Howard Fischer, "Court Quashes Arpaio's Appeal over Jail Food Order," *East Valley
Tribune*, 13 Oct 2010, http://www.eastvalleytribune.com/local/cop_shop/article_6761d1f8
-d731-11df-bc42-001cc4c002e0.html.

8. Crane-Station, "Food Sunday: Prison Food Privatization and Aramark," 2011, http://
my.firedoglake.com/cranestation/2011/08/14/sunday-food-prison-food-privatization
-and-aramark.

9. Kevin Pang, "Fixed Menu," 24 Mar 2015, http://luckypeach.com/fixed-menu.

10. Jeremy Travis and Bruce Western, editors, *The Growth of Incarceration in the United States: Exploring Causes and Consequences* (National Academies Press, 2014), p. 222.

11. Quoted in Patrick Howe, "Cash-Hungry States Cutting Prison Fare," *Seattle Times*, 14 May 2003, http://community.seattletimes.nwsource.com/archive/?date=20030514 &slug=prison14.

12. However, Robert T. Northup claims that when he was placed in a segregation unit at Washington State Penitentiary in Walla Walla, he was put on a "sack lunch diet" for two weeks, which consisted of "two pieces of dry bread and one piece of hot bologna, contaminated with CO [corrections officer] spit." He was told, "If you want water, drink it from the toilet," which he did in order to wash down the bread. See Robert T. Northup, "Survival of the Fittest," 17 Jan 2002, https://writeaprisoner.com/prison-forum/general -prison-talk/daily-serious-bits-17th-november.

13. Julianne Hing, "Appeals Court Orders Sheriff Arpaio to Be Humane," *Color Lines*, 14 Oct 2010, http://colorlines.com/archives/2010/10/court_orders_sheriff_arpaio_to_com ply_with_court_mandates_for_jail_reforms.html.

14. "Sheriff Runs Female Chain Gang," 29 Oct 2003, http://www.cnn.com/2003/uS /Southwest/10/29/chain.gang.reut.

15. "Sheriff Runs Female Chain Gang."

16. Avi Brisman, "Fair Fare?: Food as Contested Terrain in US Prisons and Jails," *Georgetown Journal on Poverty Law & Policy*, vol. 15 (2008), pp. 49–93; Fischer, "Court Quashes Arpaio's Appeal"; and Kevin Liptak, Daniella Diaz, and Sophie Tatum, "Trump Pardons Former Sheriff Joe Arpaio," CNN, 27 Aug 2017, https://www.cnn.com/2017/08/25 /politics/sheriff-joe-arpaio-donald-trump-pardon/index.html.

17. Dara Kam, 2010, "Prison 'Food Loaf' Not Offensive but Tastes 'Like It's Already Been Eaten Before,'" *Palm Beach Post*, 10 Feb 2010, http://www.postonpolitics.com/2010/02 /prison-food-loaf-not-offensive-but-tastes-like-its-already-been-eaten-before.

18. Campanelli, "Jailhouse Slop." See also Wilson Ring, "Prison Calls It Food, Inmates Disagree," 2008, https://www.highbeam.com/doc/1A1-D8VJ1QB01.html.

19. Tovin Lapan, "When Inmates Act Out, the Loaf Is Served," *Santa Cruz Sentinel*, 17 Dec 2010, http://www.mercurynews.com/breaking-news/ci_16886434?nclick_check=1.

20. Daniel Genis, "Thanksgiving in Prison Is a Beggar's Feast," *Newsweek*, 26 Nov 2014, http://www.newsweek.com/2014/12/05/thanksgiving-prison-beggars-feast-287148.html.

21. Tobin, "Prison Food Costs Less."

22. Lisa Satayut, "State Inmates Sick after Discovering Maggots Inches from Food," mlive.com, 30 Jun 2014, http://www.mlive.com/news/jackson/index.ssf/2014/06/prisoners _sick_after_discoveri.html;

Lisa Satayut, "Maggots Found in Food at Michigan Prison, Second Incident in One Week," mlive.com, 2 Jul 2014, http://www.mlive.com/news/jackson/index.ssf/2014/07 /maggots_found_in_food_at_michi.html; and Matthew Zuras, "Michigan's Prison Food System Is Falling Apart," *Vice*, 7 Jul 2014, http://munchies.vice.com/articles/michigans -prison-food-system-is-falling-apart.

23. Noah Galuten, "Food Safety: Cockroaches Found in Orange County Prison Food (No, the *other* Orange County)," *The Los Angeles Weekly*, 10 Jan 2011, http://www.laweekly

.com/restaurants/cockroaches-found-in-orange-county-prison-food-no-the-other
-orange-county-2378775.

24. Alex Leary, "Inmates Say Prison Food Made Them Sick," *Tampa Bay News*, 13 May
2008, http://www.tampabay.com/news/politics/state/article501936e.

25. Brown, "Prison Food."

26. These instances are reported on the following pages of the Centers for Disease
Control and Prevention website: Wisconsin: http://www.cdc.gov/mmwr/preview
/mmwrhtml/mm5806a2.htm; Colorado: http://www.cdc.gov/mmwr/preview/mmwrhtml
/mm6109a1.htm; Tennessee: http://www.cdc.gov/salmonella/heidelberg-01-14/index.html;
and Arkansas: http://www.cdc.gov/mmwr/preview/mmwrhtml/mm6308a2. htm.

27. Bob Unruh, "Judge Orders Trial to Decide if Jail Food Really Is 'Torture,'"
WorldNetDaily, 25 Oct 2011, http://www.wnd.com/2011/10/360301.

28. Stephen Hudak, "Florida Prisoner's Lawsuit Calls Soy Meals 'Cruel and Unusual'
Punishment," *Orlando Sentinel*, 6 Nov 2011, http://articles.orlandosentinel.com/2011-11-06
/news/os-soy-prison-meals-20111107_1_soy-foods-soy-products-inmate-food.

29. David M. Reuter, Gary Hunter, and Brandon Sample, "Appalling Prison and Jail
Food Leaves Prisoners Hungry for Justice," *Prison Legal News*, 15 Apr 2010, https://www
.prisonlegalnews.org/news/2010/apr/15/appalling-prison-and-jail-food-leaves-prisoners
-hungry-for-justice.

30. Quoted in Patrick Howe, "Cash-Hungry States Cutting Prison Fare."

31. Privatization of food service has brought a host of problems: poorly trained staff,
fewer than the required number of meals, unauthorized substitutions, watered-down or
missing items in menus, food stored or served at the wrong temperature, low food
quality, unsanitary conditions, cooking delays that throw off the prison's schedule, and
not providing enough food—several of which Tobin describes among the "hundreds"
of "food episodes" that Florida corrections officers recorded in "their daily logs from
February to May, which the *St. Petersburg Times* reviewed this month." Tobin,
"Prison Food Costs Less." See also Auditor of Public Accounts, "Audit of Corrections'
$12 Million Contract with Aramark Finds Areas of Noncompliance," kentucky.gov,
7 Oct 2010, http://migration.kentucky.gov/newsroom/auditor/2010+aramark+report
.htm; Paul Egan, "Aramark Pushed to End Prison Meal Shortages or Risk Losing $145M
Contract," *Detroit Free Press*, 24 Jun 2014, http://www.corrections.com/articles/36600;
and Zuras, "Michigan's Prison Food System." A meta-analysis of research on cost and
quality in privately managed and publicly managed prisons indicates that cost savings
from privatization are not guaranteed and are minimal; publicly managed facilities have
better skills training and fewer inmate grievances. See Brad W. Lundahl, Chelsea Kunz,
Cyndi Brownell, et al., "Prison Privatization: A Meta-Analysis of Cost and Quality of
Confinement Indicators," *Research on Social Work Practice*, vol. 19 (2009), pp. 383–94. In
sum, privatization is not necessarily the solution to reducing prison budgets, it comes
with hidden costs, and the state must closely manage the contract; see Leary, "Inmates Say
Prison Food Made." In regard to phasing out private prisons, see Anon., "US Govt.
to Phase Out Use of Private Prisons over Cost, Prisoner Health & Safety Concerns,"
31 Aug 2016, https://www.business-humanrights.org/en/latest-news/us-govt-to-phase-out
-use-of-private-prisons-over-cost-prisoner-health-safety-concerns.

32. Tobin, "Prison Food Costs Less."

33. Egan, "Aramark Pushed to End"; and Zuras, "Michigan's Prison Food System."

34. Reuter et al., "Appalling Prison and Jail Food." Many of the newspaper articles cited in this essay quote legislators and spokespersons for jails and prisons who claim the meals are nutritious even when the food is high in sugar, carbohydrates, fat, and sodium, or when it is served in small portions or less than thrice daily.

For works that describe the food and the assertions about its nutritional benefits in the past in the United States and England, even when the food consisted of burned rye beverage, offal soup, gruel, and mush, see Henry Mayhew and John Binny, *The Criminal Prisons of London, and Scenes of Prison Life.* Vol. 3: *The Great Metropolis* (Griffin, Bohn, and Company, 1862); One of the Inspectors of the Prison, "An Account of the State Prison, Or Penitentiary-House in New York," *The Belfast Monthly Magazine*, vol. 7 (1811), pp. 167–77; and Heather M. Tomlinson, "'Not an Instrument of Punishment': Prison Diet in the Mid-nineteenth Century," *Journal of Consumer Studies and Home Economic*, vol. 2 (1978), pp. 15–26.

35. Catrin Smith, "Punishment and Pleasure: Women, Food and the Imprisoned Body," *The Sociological Review*, vol. 50 (2002), p. 202.

36. Brisman, "Fair Fare?"

37. Smith, "Punishment and Pleasure."

38. Rhonda-Jane Milligan, Glenn Waller, and Bernice Andrews, "Eating Disturbances in Female Prisoners: The Role of Anger," *Eating Behaviors*, vol. 3 (2002), pp. 123–32.

39. Quoted in Smith, "Punishment and Pleasure," 208.

40. Quoted in Smith, "Punishment and Pleasure," 204.

41. Lee Bernstein, "Correctional Dining: Prison Food in the Hudson Valley," 2010, http://ediblehudsonvalley.com/editorial/summer-2010/on-the-line; Mary Bosworth and Jim Thomas, "Food," *Encyclopedia of Prisons and Correctional Facilities*, edited by Mary Bosworth (SAGE, 2005), pp. 330–33; and Aviva Shen, "FBI Agent: Deadly Riot in Corporate-Run Prison Due to Complaints of Inadequate Food and Health Care, 14 Aug 2012, http://thinkprogress.org/justice/2012/08/14/686361/fbi-agent-deadly-riot-in-corporate-run-prison-due-to-complaints-of-inadequate-food-and-health-care/?mobile=nc.

42. Drew Harwell, "Honey Buns Sweeten Life for Florida Prisoners," *Tampa Bay Times*, 2 Jan 2011, http://www.tampabay.com/features/humaninterest/honey-buns-sweeten-life -for-florida-prisoners/1142687.

43. Heckenberg and Cody, *Food Matters.*

44. Erin George, *A Woman Doing Life: Notes from a Prison for Women*, edited by Robert Johnson (Oxford UP, 2010), 86.

45. Bruce Jackson, "Prison Folklore," *Journal of American Folklore*, vol. 78 (1965), pp. 317–29.

46. Jeff Horner, "Dope Fiend Sandwich Recipe? Try Prison Chefs' Cookbook," *USA Today*, 11 Nov 2014, http://www.usatoday.com/news/offbeat/2004-11-11-prison -cookbook_x.htm; Erin George, *A Woman Doing Life: Notes from a Prison for Women*, edited by Robert Johnson (Oxford UP, 2010); Michael Graczyk, "Prison Cookbook: Female Texas Inmates Release 'From the Big House to Your House,'" *Huffington Post*, 1 Feb 2012, http://www.huffingtonpost.ca/2012/02/01/texas-women-inmates-cook_n_1247691.html;

Pringle, "Jail Food Can Be a Hard Sell"; and Amy B. Smoyer, "Making Fatty Girl Cakes: Food and Resistance in a Woman's Prison," *Prison Journal*, vol. 96 (2015), pp. 1–19.

47. Graczyk, "Prison Cookbook"; and N. Mate, "What Is Prison Food Really Like? A Review of the New, Post-National Menu Prison Fare," 1 Aug 2008, https://www.inmateaid .com/pages/details/what-is-prison-food-really-like-a-review-of-the-new-post-national -menu-prison-fare-yahoo.

48. Ceyma Bina, Tina Cornelius, Barbara Holder, et al., *From the Big House to Your House: Cooking in Prison* (Justice Denied, 2010); and Sandra Cate, "'Breaking Bread with a Spread' in a San Francisco County Jail," *Gastronomica: The Journal of Food and Culture*, vol. 8, no. 3 (summer 2008), pp. 17–24.

49. Mate, "What Is Prison Food Really Like?"

50. Torrey Baker, Marco Bland, Donald Dunn, et al., *The Convict Cookbook: A Charity Project by Convicts at the Washington State Penitentiary, Walla Walla, WA*, 2nd ed. (J. G. Narum, 2004).

51. George, *A Woman Doing Life*.

52. Baker et al., *The Convict Cookbook*.

53. Chunksmediocrites, "Dictionary of Prison Slang," 20 Apr 2010, https://www.free thought-forum.com/forum/showthread.php?t=22858&garpg=3.

54. Rick Webb, "Why Do We Cook in Our Cells? Or 'Bad Guys, Good Taste?'" Baker et al., editors, *The Convict Cookbook*, p. 10.

55. Ceyma Bina, Tina Cornelius, Barbara Holder, et al., *From the Big House to Your House: Cooking in Prison* (Justice Denied, 2010).

56. Cate, "Breaking Bread."

57. Cate, "Breaking Bread"; Linda Kjaer Minke, "Cooking in Prison—from Crook to Cook," *International Journal of Prisoner Health*, vol. 10 (2014), pp. 228–38; and Webb, "Why Do We Cook?"

58. John Mandala, "Prison Cuisine: A Creative Challenge," http://www.friendsbeyon dthewall.com/cbc/cellblock_enter.

59. Rose, "Oregon State Penitentiary Surveys Inmates."

60. Mike Ives, "Cruel and Inedible? Sizing Up Vermont's Meanest 'Loaf,'" *Seven Days*, 9 Apr 2008, http://www.7dvt.com/2008/cruel-and-inedible.

61. Dee Riggs, "Jail's Food Service Chief Says Menu Is Restaurant-Level, Thanks to Donated Supplies," *The Wenatchee World*, 14 Jul 2010, http://www.wenatcheeworld.com /news/2010/jul/14/Jails-food-service-chief-says-menu-is-restaurant/?print.

62. Wendy Sawyer, "Food for Thought: Prison Food Is a Public Health Problem," 3 Mar 2017, https://www.prisonpolicy.org/blog/2017/03/03/prison-food.

63. John Bohannon, "The Theory? Diet Causes Violence. The Lab? Prison," *Science*, vol. 325 (25 Sep 2009), pp. 1614–16; and Steven Mihn, "Does Eating Salmon Lower the Murder Rate?" *New York Times*, 16 Apr 2006, http://www.nytimes.com/2006/04/16 /magazine/16wwln_idealab.html.

64. Shayda A. Collins and Sharon H. Thompson, "What Are We Feeding Our Inmates?" *Journal of Correctional Health Care*, vol. 18 (2012), p. 210. See also John S. A. Edwards, Heather J. Hartwell, and Joachim Schafheitle, "Prison Foodservice in England," *Journal of Foodservice*, vol. 20, no. 4 (Aug 2009), pp. 157–66.

65. Rob Perez, "Inmates Lose Weight, Call Prison Food Inadequate," *Star Advertiser*, 22 May 2011, http://www.staradvertiser.com/news/20110522_Inmates_lose_weight_call _prison_food_inadequate.html?id=122409184.

66. National Audit Office, "Serving Time."

67. Rebecca Godderis, "Dining In: The Symbolic Power of Food in Prison," *The Howard Journal*, vol. 45 (Jul 2006), p. 263.

68. Rod Earle and Coretta Phillips, "Digesting Men? Ethnicity, Gender and Food: Perspectives from a 'Prison Ethnography,'" *Theoretical Criminology*, vol. 16 (2012), p. 146. See also Smoyer, "Making Fatty Girl Cakes."

69. Earle and Phillips, "Digesting Men?" 145.

70. Donald L. Beschle, "What's Guilt (or Deterrence) Got to Do with It?: The Death Penalty, Ritual, and Mimetic Violence," *William and Mary Law Review*, vol. 38 (Jan 1996–1997), pp. 487–538.

71. Ives, "Cruel and Inedible?"

72. Quoted in Michael Levenson, "Convicts Shaping Up Before Release/Health Class Offers Them Tips on Diet and Fitness to Improve Future," *Houston Chronicle*, 23 May 2008, p. A24.

73. Kam, "Prison 'Food Loaf.'"

74. Mark Curriden, "Hard Time," *ABA* [American Bar Association] *Journal*, vol. 81 (Jul 1995), p. 73.

75. Emily Gilbert, "Change Agent: Five Urban Garden Programs That Train Inmates and Help Communities," *Christian Science Monitor*, 2 Mar 2012, http://www.csmonitor .com/World/Making-a-difference/Change-Agent/2012/0302/Five-urban-garden -programs-that-train-inmates-and-help-communities.

76. Ken Garcia, "Sentences Reduced to Thyme Served: Unique Gardening Program for Inmates," *SFGate*, 17 Apr 1999, http://www.sfgate.com/homeandgarden/article/Jail -Sentences-reduced-to-Thyme -Served-unique-2935984.php; and Lisa Van Cleef, "Gardening Conquers All/How to Cut Your Jail Recidivism Rates by Half," *San Francisco Gate*, 18 Dec 2002, http://www.sfgate.com/homeandgarden/article/Gardening-Conquers -All-How-to-cut-your-jail-3303782.php#photo-2452879. A caveat is that "recidivism can be defined in different ways. Some states define recidivism as a new arrest of an ex-prisoner, some as a new conviction, and some as a return to prison or jail." The recidivism rates cited in regard to the various programs described here are given by representatives of the institutions and seem to suggest return to a correctional facility, although this is not clearly stated. See Joan Petersilia, "California's Correctional Paradox of Excess and Deprivation," *Crime and Justice*, vol. 37 (2008), pp. 207–78.

77. Jessica Bird, "Prison Garden Programs: Improving Health, Increasing Sustainability and Contributing to Community," 16 Mar 2012, http://www.sustainablecitiesnet.com /models/prison-garden-programs-improving-health-increasing-sustainability-and -contributing-to-community. For several of these along with other projects, see also Eliza Barclay, "Prison Gardens Help Inmates Grow Their Own Food—and Skills," 14 Jan 2014, http://ww2.kqed.org/bayareabites/2014/01/14/prison-gardens-help-inmates-grow -their-own-food-and-skills; Morgan Bulger, "Six U.S. Correctional Facilities With 'Farm to Prison' Local Food Sourcing Programs," 4 Jan 2015, http://seedstock.com/2015/01/04

/six-u-s-correctional-facilities-with-farm-to-prison-local-food-sourcing-programs; James Jiler, "Digging Out from Prison: A Pathway to Rehabilitation," *The Solutions Journal,* 24 Jun 2013, http://www.thesolutionsjournal.com/node/23371; Linda Ly, "Inside a California State Prison," KCET, 24 Feb 2014, http://www.kcet.org/living/homegarden/gardens-of -note/a-look-at-the-first-vegetable-garden-inside-a-california-state-prison.html; Hillary Lyons, "Food, Farming, and Freedom: Promoting a Sustainable Model of Food Justice in America's Prisons," Senior Capstone Project, Vassar College, 2012, http://digitalwindow .vassar.edu/cgi/viewcontent.cgi?article=1073&context=senior_capstone;

Lydia O'Connor, "How a Farm-to-Table Program Could Revitalize Prisons," *Huffington Post,* 29 May 2014, http://www.huffingtonpost.com/2014/05/27/california -inmate-farm-program_n_5400670.html; and Julie Siple, "Garden Program Grows at State Prisons," 31 Jul 2012, http://www.mprnews.org/story/2012/07/31/human-interest/red -wing-prison-garden.

78. Cindy Chang, "Jail Cracks Down on Inmates' Pungent Assaults on Deputies," *Los Angeles Times,* 11 Jul 2014, pp. AA1, AA4.

79. "Key Ingredients: America by Food," sites.si.edu/education/ki%20teacher%27s%20 Guide.pdf.

80. "Michigan Eats," museum.msu.edu/exhibitions/current/michigan_eats.html.

81. Rachelle H. Saltzman, "Taste of Place: Place-Based foods in Iowa," Leopold Center Completed Grant Reports, Paper 288, 2007, http://lib.dr.iastate.edu/leopold_grantreports /288IowaPlace-Based Foods.

82. "Foodways: A 4-h Folkpatterns Project," 4h.msue.msu.edu/uploads/files/4h1329Food waysActivitySheets.pdf.

83. Phillip Curd, Kathleen Ohlmann, and Heather Bush, "Effectiveness of a Voluntary Nutrition Education Workshop in a State Prison," *Journal of Correctional Health Care,* vol. 19 (2013), pp. 144–50; and Philip R. Curd, Sandra J. Winter, and Alison Connell, "Participative Planning to Enhance Inmate Wellness: Preliminary Report of a Correctional Wellness Program," *Journal of Correctional Health Care,* vol. 13 (2007), pp. 296–308.

84. "Eastern State Penitentiary Hosts 'Prison Food Weekend,' Gives Visitors a Taste of Prison Life," 17 May 2013, http://www.easternstate.org/contact/press-room/press-releases /eastern-state-penitentiary-hosts-prison-food-weekend-gives-visit. See also Jesse Smith, "A Plateful of Penitence," The Smart Set (Drexel University), 21 Jun 2013, http:// thesmartset.com/article06211301.

85. Norman Johnston, *Chow: Food and Drink in Eastern State Penitentiary* (Eastern State Penitentiary Historic Site, 2006).

CHAPTER 11. WHAT DIABETES COUNSELING OVERLOOKS

1. Pseudonyms for interviewees are used throughout this essay.

2. E. M. Campbell, S. Redman, P. S. Moffitt, et al., "The Relative Effectiveness of Educational and Behavioral Instruction Programs for Patients with NIDDM: A Randomized Trial," *Diabetes Educator,* vol. 22 (1996), pp. 379–86; Leandris C. Liburd,

"Food, Identity, and African-American Women with Type 2 Diabetes: An Anthropological Perspective," *Diabetes Spectrum*, vol. 16 (2003), pp. 160–66; and R. R. Rubin, M. Peyrot, and C. D. Saudek, "Differential Effect of Diabetes Education on Self-Regulation and Life-Style Behaviors," *Diabetes Care*, vol. 14 (1991), pp. 335–38.

3. Bob Ashley, Joanne Hollows, Steve Jones, et al., *Food and Cultural Studies* (Routledge, 2004), p. 61; and Carole M. Counihan, *The Anthropology of Food and Body: Gender, Meaning, and Power* (Routledge, 1999), p. 123.

4. James, "Factors Influencing Food Choices," 359. An estimated 71 percent of American dietitians are non-Hispanic White; consequently, dietary recommendations often ignore ethnic and non-Western foods. See Priya Krishna, "Is American Dietetics a White-Bread World? These Dietitians Think So," *New York Times*, 7 Dec 2020, https://www.nytimes.com /2020/12/07/dining/dietitian-diversity.html?campaign_id=9&emc=edit_nn_20201211 &instance_id=24930&nl=the-morning&regi_id=90899909&segment_id=46643&te =1&user_id=aa42fdc1969b907497a08056b522916a.

5. Ina Vandebroek, Victoria Reyes-García, Ulysses P. de Albuquerque, et al., "Local Knowledge: Who Cares?" *Journal of Ethnobiology and Ethnomedicine*, vol. 7 (2011), pp. 1–7.

6. Michael Owen Jones, "In Search of Meaning: Using Qualitative Methods in Research and Application," *Inside Organizations: Understanding the Human Dimension*, edited by M. Jones, M. Moore, and R. Snyder (SAGE, 1988), pp. 27–47.

7. R. S. Surwit and M. S. Schneider, "Role of Stress in the Etiology and Treatment of Diabetes Mellitus," *Advances in Psychosomatic Medicine*, vol. 55 (1993), pp. 380–93.

8. R. S. Surwit and P. G. Williams, "Animal Models Provide Insight into Psychosomatic Factors in Diabetes," *Advances in Psychosomatic Medicine*, vol. 58 (1996), pp. 582–89.

9. N. E. Schoenberg, E. M. Drew, E. P. Stoller, et al., "Situating Diabetes: Lessons from Lay Discourses on Diabetes," *Medical Anthropology Quarterly*, vol. 19 (2005), pp. 171–93.

10. For a critique of the compliance model, see Robert M. Anderson and Martha M. Funnell, "Compliance and Adherence Are Dysfunctional Concepts in Diabetes Care," *The Diabetes Educator*, vol. 26 (2000), pp. 597–604.

11. Carmen Rivera Adams, "Lessons Learned from Urban Latinas with Type 2 Diabetes Mellitus," *Journal of Transcultural Nursing*, vol. 14 (2003), pp. 255–68; and Schoenberg et al., "Situating Diabetes."

12. Reported percentages vary widely. See Sharon Brown, Alexandra A. Garcia, Kamiar Kouzekanani, et al., "Culturally Competent Diabetes Self-Management Education for Mexican Americans: The Starr County Border Health Initiative," *Diabetes Care*, vol. 25 (2002), pp. 259–68; Linda M. Hunt, N. H. Arar, and L.L. Akana, "Herbs, Prayer, and Insulin: Use of Medical and Alternative Treatments by a Group of Mexican American Diabetes Patients," *Journal of Family Practic*, vol. 49 (2000), pp. 216–23; Lane Johnson, Hal Strich, Ann Taylor, et al., "Use of Herbal Remedies by Diabetic Hispanic Women in the Southwestern United States," *Phytotherapy Research*, vol. 20 (2006), pp. 250–55; Nasser Mikhail, Soma Wali, and Irwin Ziment, "Use of Alternative Medicine among Hispanics," *The Journal of Alternative and Complementary Medicine*, vol. 10 (2004), pp. 851–59; Vance Pegado, Debbie Kwan, and Lina Medeiros, "'Do You Use Any Herbal Remedies?'—The Impact of Herbal Remedy Use on Diabetes Self-Management in Different Ethnic Groups,"

University of Toronto Medical Journal, vol. 80 (2003), pp. 262–64; Jane E. Poss, Mary Ann Jezewski, and Armando Gonzalez Stuart, "Home Remedies for Type 2 Diabetes Used by Mexican Americans in El Paso, Texas," *Clinical Nursing Research*, vol. 12 (2003), pp. 304–23; Gloria Y. Yeh, David M. Eisenberg, Ted J. Kaptchuk, et al., "Systematic Review of Herbs and Dietary Supplies for Glycemic Control in Diabetes," *Diabetes Care*, vol. 26 (2003), pp. 1277–94; and A. Zaldivar and J. Smolowitz, "Perceptions of the Importance Placed on Religion and Folk Medicine by Non-Mexican-American Hispanic Adults with Diabetes," *The Diabetes Educator*, vol. 20 (1994), pp. 3–6.

13. Hunt et al., "Herbs, Prayer, and Insulin."

14. See especially Jane E. Poss and Mary Ann Jezewski, "The Role and Meaning of Susto in Mexican Americans' Explanatory Model of Type 2 Diabetes," *Medical Anthropology Quarterly*, vol. 16 (2002), pp. 360–77; and G. D. Coronado, B. Thompson. S. Tejeda, et al., "Attitudes and Beliefs among Mexican Americans about Type 2 Diabetes," *Journal of Health Care for the Poor and Underserved*, vol. 15 (2004), pp. 576–88. See also Michael Owen Jones, "Herbs and Saints in the City of Angels: Researching *Botánicas*, Healing, and Power in Southern California," *Journal of American Folklore*, vol. 133 (2020), pp. 53–80.

15. City Terrace is an unincorporated community in eastern Los Angeles with a predominantly Latina/o population. Echo Park is in the central region of Los Angeles just west and slightly north of downtown; 53 percent of residents are foreign born, of which most came from Mexico and El Salvador. Venice is on the west side of Los Angeles abutting the Pacific Ocean; about 22 percent of the population is foreign born, of which 38 percent is from Mexico. Culver City, containing a mixed population of which about one-fourth is of Mexican descent, lies east and south of Venice.

16. Gary Paul Nabhan, "Food, Health, and Native-American Farming and Gathering," *Eating Culture*, edited by Ron Scapp and Brian Seitz (State U of New York P, 1998), p. 175.

17. Yeh et al., "Systematic Review of Herbs."

18. Jose Luis Lopez, Jr. "Use of Opuntia Cactus as a Hypoglycemic Agent in Managing Type 2 Diabetes Mellitus among Mexican American Patients," *Nutrition Bytes*, vol. 12 (2007), n.p.

19. National Institute of Health, "Diuretics Effective for People with Diabetes and High Blood Pressure," 2005, http://nih.gov/news/pr/jun2005/nhlbi-27.htm.

20. L. R. Helton, "Folk Medicine and Health Beliefs: An Appalachian Perspective," *Journal of Cultural Diversity*, vol. 3 (1996), pp. 123–28; and W. B. Jonas, D. Eisenberg, D. Hufford, et al., *Forschende Komplementärmedizin*, vol. 20 (2013), pp. 65–72.

21. R. Davidhizar, G. Bechtel, and J. N. Giger, "When Your Client in the Surgical Suite Is Mexican American," *Today's Surgical Nurse*, vol. 6 (1998), pp. 29–35.

22. Yeh et al., "Systematic Review of Herbs," 1290.

23. Josephine A. Beoku-Betts, "We Got Our Way of Cooking Things: Women, Food, and Preservation of Cultural Identity among the Gullah," *Gender and Society*, vol. 9 (1995), pp. 535–55; Deborah Dale Heisley, "Gender Symbolism in Food" (PhD Dissertation, Marketing, Northwestern University, 1990); and Jeffrey Sobal, "Men, Meat, and Marriage: Models of Masculinity," *Food & Foodways*, vol. 13 (2005), pp. 135–58.

24. Mary O. Douglas, "Deciphering a Meal," *Daedalus*, vol. 101 (winter, 1972), pp. 54–72; and M. Kerr and N. Charles, "Servers and Providers: The Distribution of Food within the Family," *The Sociological Review*, vol. 34 (1986), pp. 115–57.

25. David G. Schlundt, Margaret K. Hargreaves, and Maciej S. Buchowski, "The Eating Behavior Patterns Questionnaire Predicts Dietary Fat Intake in African American Women," *Journal of the American Dietetic Association*, vol. 103 (2003), pp. 338–45.

26. James, "Factors Influencing Food Choices."

27. Teri A. Hall, "Designing Culturally Relevant Education Materials for Mexican American Clients," *The Diabetes Educator*, vol. 13 (1987), p. 283.

28. For example, the kinds of interview guides suggested by Coronado et al., "Attitudes and Beliefs among Mexican Americans"; and James, "Factors Influencing Food Choices."

29. Toni Tripp-Reimer, Eunice Choi, Lisa Skemp Kelley, et al., "Cultural Barriers to Care: Inverting the Problem," *Diabetes Spectrum*, vol. 14 (2001), pp. 13–22.

30. As a team of researchers asserts: "Learning about the identities that clients bring to and derive from eating can help practitioners to think about food through the eyes of their clients and forces practitioners to see beyond their own personal or professional meanings for food and eating." See Carole A. Bisogni, Margaret Connors, Carol M. Devine, et al., "Who We Are and How We Eat: A Qualitative Study of Identities in Food Choice," *Journal of Nutrition Education and Behavior*, vol. 34 (2002), p. 137.

31. Jessica Greene and Michael J. Yedidia, "Provider Behaviors Contributing to Self-Management of Chronic Illness among Underserved Populations," *Journal of Health Care for the Poor and Underserved*, vol. 16 (2005), pp. 808–24.

32. Robin Whittemore, "Culturally Competent Interventions for Hispanic Adults with Type 2 Diabetes: A Systematic Review," *Journal of Transcultural Nursing*, vol. 18 (2008), pp. 157–66.

SELECTED BIBLIOGRAPHY

Adams, Carol J. *The Sexual Politics of Meat: A Feminist-Vegetarian Critical Theory.* Polity; Continuum, 1990.

Adler, Thomas A. "Making Pancakes on Sunday: The Male Cook in Family Tradition." *Western Folklore*, vol. 40, no. 1, 1981, pp. 45–54.

Albala, Ken. "History on the Plate: The Current State of Food History." *Historically Speaking*, vol. 10, no. 5, 2009, pp. 6–8.

Allen, Michael W., Marc Wilson, Sik Hung Ng, and Michael Dunne. "Values and Beliefs of Vegetarians and Omnivores." *Journal of Social Psychology*, vol. 140, no. 4, 2000, pp. 405–22.

Appadurai, Arjun. "How to Make a National Cuisine: Cookbooks in Contemporary India." *Comparative Studies in Society and History*, vol. 30, no. 1, 1988, pp. 3–24.

Auerbach, Susan. "The Brokering of Ethnic Folklore: Selection and Presentation Issues at a Multicultural Festival." *Creative Ethnicity: Symbols and Strategies of Contemporary Ethnic Life*, edited by Stephen Stern and John Allan Cicala, Utah State UP, 1991, pp. 225–38.

Babcock, Charlotte. "Food and Its Emotional Significance." *Journal of the American Dietetic Association*, vol. 24, no. 5, 1948, pp. 390–93.

Banks, Caroline G. "The Imaginative Use of Religious Symbols in Subjective Experiences of Anorexia Nervosa." *Psychoanalytical Review*, vol. 84, no. 2, 1997, pp. 227–36.

Barthel, D. "Modernism and Marketing: The Chocolate Box Revisited." *Theory of Culture and Society*, vol. 6, no. 3, 1989, pp. 429–38.

Bass, S. Jonathan. "How 'bout a Hand for the Hog: The Enduring Nature of the Swine as a Cultural Symbol of the South." *Southern Culture*, vol. 1, no. 3, 1995, pp. 301–20.

Beardsworth, Alan, and Teresa Keil. "The Vegetarian Option: Varieties, Conversions, Motives and Careers." *The Sociological Review*, vol. 40, no. 2, 1992, pp. 253–93.

Belasco, Warren. "Food Matters: Perspectives on an Emerging Field." *Food Nations: Selling Taste in Consumer Societies*, edited by W. Belasco and P. Scranton, Routledge, 2002, pp. 2–23.

Belasco, Warren. *Food: The Key Concepts.* The Berg, 2008.

Belasco, Warren. "Why Food Matters." *Culture & Agriculture*, vol. 21, no. 1, 1999, pp. 27–32.

Bell, David, and Gill Valentine. *Consuming Geographies: We Are Where We Eat.* Routledge, 1997.

Bendix, Regina F., and Michaela Penske. "Eating Politically: Food and Eating in Politics." *Politische Mahlzeiten (Political Meals)*, edited by Regina F. Bendix and Michaela Fenske, Lit Verlag, 2014, pp. 17–29.

Benford, Rebecca, and Brendan Gough. "Defining and Defending 'Unhealthy' Practices: A Discourse Analysis of Chocolate 'Addicts'' Accounts." *Journal of Health Psychology*, vol. 11, no. 3, 2006, pp. 427–40.

Beoku-Betts, Josephine A. "'We Got Our Way of Cooking Things': Women, Food, and Preservation of Cultural Identity among the Gullah." *Gender and Society*, vol. 9, no. 5, 1995, pp. 535–55.

Bisogni, Carole A., Margaret Connors, Carol M. Devine, and Jeffery Sobal. "Who We Are and How We Eat: A Qualitative Study of Identities in Food Choice." *Journal of Nutrition Education and Behavior*, vol. 34, no. 3, 2002, pp. 128–40.

Bock, Sheila. "Fast Food at the White House: Performing Foodways, Class, and American Identity." *Western Folklore*, vol. 80, no. 1, 2021, pp. 15–43.

Brettler, Marc Zvi, and Michael Poliakoff. "Rabbi Simeon ben Lakish at the Gladiator's Banquet: Rabbinic Observations on the Roman Arena." *Harvard Theological Review*, vol. 83, no. 1, 1990, pp. 93–98.

Brisman, Avi. "Fair Fare?: Food as Contested Terrain in U.S. Prisons and Jails." *Georgetown Journal on Poverty Law & Policy*, vol. 15, no. 1, 2008, pp. 49–93.

Bronner, Simon J. "The Paradox of Pride and Loathing, and Other Problems." *Western Folklore*, vol. 40, no 1, 1981, pp. 115–24.

Brown, Linda Keller, and Kay Mussel, editors. *Ethnic and Regional Foodways in the United States: The Performance of Group Identity*. U Tennessee P, 1984.

Brown, Mary Helen de la Peña. "*Una Tamalada*: The Special Event." *Western Folklore*, vol. 40, no. 1, 1981, pp. 64–71.

Brulotte, Ronda L., and Michael A. Di Giovine, editors. *Edible Identities: Food as Cultural Heritage*. Ashegate, 2014.

Brumberg, Joan Jacobs. *Fasting Girls: The Emergence of Anorexia Nervosa as a Modern Disease*. Harvard UP, 1988.

Bynum, Caroline Walker. *Holy Feast and Holy Fast: The Religious Significance of Food to Medieval Women*. U of California P, 1987.

Camp, Charles. *American Foodways: What, When, Why and How We Eat in America*. August House, 1989.

Carson, Gerald. *Cornflake Crusade*. Rinehart, 1957.

Cate, Sandra. "'Breaking Bread with a Spread' in a San Francisco County Jail." *Gastronomica: The Journal of Food and Culture*, vol. 8, no. 3, 2008, pp. 17–24.

Chapman, G., and H. Maclean. "'Junk Food' and 'Healthy Food': Meanings of Food in Adolescent Women's Culture." *Journal of Nutrition Education*, vol. 25, no. 3, 1993, pp. 108–13.

Chen, Yu-Jen. "Ethnic Politics in the Framing of National Cuisine." *Food, Culture & Society*, vol. 14, no. 3, 2011, pp. 315–33.

Cicala, John. "Cuscuszu in Detroit, July 18, 1993: Memory, Conflict, and Bella Figura during a Sicilian-American Meal." *Italian Folk: Vernacular Culture in Italian-American Lives*, edited by Joseph Sciorra, Fordham UP, 2011, pp. 31–48.

Cohen, Nevin, and Kristen Cribbs. "The Everyday Food Practices of Community-Dwelling Lesbian, Gay, Bisexual, and Transgender (LGBT) Older Adults." *Journal of Aging Studies*, vol. 41, 2017, pp. 75–83.

Collins, Shayda A., and Sharon H. Thompson. "What Are We Feeding Our Inmates?" *Journal of Correctional Health Care*, vol. 18, no. 3, 2012, pp. 210–18.

Connors, M., C. A. Bisogni, J. Sobal, and C. M. Devine. "Managing Values in Personal Food Systems." *Appetite*, vol. 36, no. 3, 2001, pp. 189–200.

Cooper, Eugene. "Chinese Table Manners: You Are *How* You Eat." *Human Organization*, vol. 45, no. 2, 1986, pp. 179–84.

Counihan, Carole M. *The Anthropology of Food and Body: Gender, Meaning, and Power.* Routledge, 1999.

Counihan, Carole, and Penny Van Esterik, editors. *Food and Culture: A Reader.* Routledge, 1997.

Curd, Philip, Kathleen Ohlmann, and Heather Bush. "Effectiveness of a Voluntary Nutrition Education Workshop in a State Prison." *Journal of Correctional Health Care*, vol. 19, no. 2, 2013, pp. 144–50.

Dawkins, Nicole. "The Hunger for Home: Nostalgic Affect, Embodied Memory and the Sensual Politics of Transnational Foodways." *Undergraduate Journal of Anthropology*, vol. 1, 2009, pp. 33–42.

DeSoucey, Michaela. "Food Traditions and Authenticity Politics in the European Union." *American Sociological Review*, vol. 75, no. 3, 2010, pp. 432–55.

Deutsch, Jonathan. "'Please Pass the Chicken Tits': Rethinking Men and Cooking at the Urban Firehouse." *Food and Foodways*, vol. 13, nos. 1–2, 2005, pp. 91–114.

Devine, Carol M., Jeffery Sobal, Carole A. Bisogni, and Margaret Connors. "Food Choices in Three Ethnic Groups: Interactions of Ideals, Identities, and Roles." *Journal of Nutrition Education*, vol. 31, no. 2, 1999, pp. 86–93.

Dillinger, Teresa L., Patricia Barriga, Sylvia Escarcega, Martha Jimenez, Diana Salazar Lowe, and Louis E. Grivetti. "Food of the Gods: Cure for Humanity? A Cultural History of the Medicinal and Ritual Use of Chocolate." *Journal of Nutrition*, vol. 130, no. 8, 2000, pp. 2057S–72S.

Douglas, Mary O. *Purity and Danger: An Analysis of the Concepts of Pollution and Taboo.* Routledge; Kegan Paul, 1966.

Dubisch, Jill. "You Are What You Eat: Religious Aspects of the Health Food Movement." *Folk Groups and Folklore Genres: A Reader*, edited by Elliott Oring, Utah State UP, 1989, pp. 124–35.

Egri, Carolyn P. "War and Peace on the Land: An Analysis of the Symbolism of Organic Farming." *Studies in Cultures, Organizations and Societies*, vol. 3, no. 1, 1997, pp. 17–40.

Eleuterio, Susan, with Barbara Banks, Phillis Humphries, and Charlene Smith. "Even Presidents Need Comfort Food: Tradition, Food, and Politics at the Valois Cafeteria." *Comfort Food Meanings and Memories*, edited by Michael Owen Jones and Lucy M. Long, UP of Mississippi, 2017, pp. 65–81.

Ellis, Bill. "Whispers in an Ice Cream Parlor: Culinary Tourism, Contemporary Legends, and the Urban Interzone." *Journal of American Folklore*, vol. 122, no. 483, 2009, pp. 53–74.

Everett, Holly. "Vernacular Health Moralities and Culinary Tourism in Newfoundland and Labrador." *Journal of American Folklore*, vol. 122, no. 483, 2009, pp. 28–52.

Ferguson, Priscilla Parkhurst. "Culinary Nationalism." *Gastronomica*, vol. 10, no. 1, 2010, pp. 102–9.

Ferris, Marcie Cohen. *The Edible South: The Power of Food and the Making of an American Region*. U of North Carolina P, 2014.

Fine, Gary Alan. "The Kentucky Fried Rat: Legends and Modern Society." *Journal of the Folklore Institute*, vol. 17, nos. 2–3, 1980, pp. 222–43.

Fine, Gary Alan. *Kitchens: The Culture of Restaurant Work*. U of California P, 1996.

Fischler, Claude. "Food, Self, and Identity." *Social Science Information*, vol. 27, no. 2, 1988, pp. 275–92.

Flynn, Margaret Tailberi. "Dining with Samuel Pepys in Seventeenth Century England." *American Dietetic Association Journal*, vol. 20, 1944, pp. 434–40.

Georges, Robert A. "You Often Eat What Others Think You Are: Food as an Index of Others' Conceptions of Who One Is." *Western Folklore*, vol. 43, no. 4, 1984, pp. 249–56.

Georges, Robert A., and Michael Owen Jones. *Folkloristics: An Introduction*. Indiana UP, 1995.

Gerhardt, Cornelia. "Language and Food—Food and Language." *Culinary Linguistics: The Chef's Special*, edited by Cornelia Gerhardt, Maximiliane Frobenius, and Susanne Ley, John Benjamins, 2013, pp. 5–49.

Godderis, Rebecca. "Dining In: The Symbolic Power of Food in Prison." *The Howard Journal of Criminal Justice*, vol. 45, no. 3, 2006, pp. 255–67.

Godderis, Rebecca. "Food for Thought: An Analysis of Power and Identity in Prison Food Narratives." *Berkeley Journal of Sociology*, vol. 50, 2006, pp. 61–75.

Gould, Jillian. "Hungry for My Past: Kitchen Comfort with Fried Bread and Eggs." *Comfort Food Meanings and Memories*, edited by Michael Owen Jones and Lucy M. Long, UP of Mississippi, 2017, pp. 99–114.

Grieshop, James I. "The *Envios* of San Pablo Huixtepec, Oaxaca: Food, Homes, and Transnationalism." *Human Organization*, vol. 65, no. 4, 2006, pp. 400–406.

Gutierrez, C. Paige. *Cajun Foodways*. UP of Mississippi, 1992.

Hall, Teri A. "Designing Culturally Relevant Education Materials for Mexican American Clients." *The Diabetes Educator*, vol. 13, 1987, pp. 281–85.

Harris, Jessica B. *High on the Hog: A Culinary Journey from Africa to America*. Bloomsbury USA, 2011.

Hauck-Lawson, Annie. "Hearing the Food Voice: An Epiphany for a Researcher." *Digest— An Interdisciplinary Study of Food and Foodways*, vol. 12, nos. 1–2, 1992, pp. 6–7.

Heckenberg, Diane J., and Danielle Cody. *Food Matters—Issues Surrounding Food in Prison*. Occasional Paper 3. Technical Report. University of Tasmania, Hobart, Tasmania, 2006, http://www.utas.edu.au/__data/assets/pdf_file/0005/256064 /Occasional_Paper_3_Food_Matters.pdf.

Heisley, Deborah Dale. "Gender Symbolism in Food." PhD Dissertation, Northwestern UP, 1990.

Hilliard, Sam. "Hog Meat and Cornpone: Food Habits in the Antebellum South." *Proceedings of the American Philosophical Society*, vol. 113, no. 1, 1969, pp. 1–13.

Howell, Sally. "Modernizing Mansaf: The Consuming Contexts of Jordan's National Dish." *Food and Foodways*, vol. 11, no. 4, 2003, pp. 215–43.

Humphrey, Theodore C., and Lin C. Humphrey, editors. *"We Gather Together": Food and Festival in American Life*. UMI Research Press, 1988.

Jackson, Peter, and Angela Meah. "Taking Humor Seriously in Contemporary Food Research." *Food, Culture & Society*, vol. 22, 2019, pp. 262–79.

James, Delores. "Factors Influencing Food Choices, Dietary Intake, and Nutrition-Related Attitudes among African Americans: Application of a Culturally Sensitive Model." *Ethnicity & Health*, vol. 9, no. 4, 2004, pp. 349–67.

Jiménez, Patricia Vega. "Afro-Caribbean Rice and Beans Conquer the Costa Rican National Cuisine." *Food, Culture & Society*, vol. 15, no. 2, 2012, pp. 223–40.

Jones, Michael Owen. "Afterward: Discovering the Symbolism of Food Customs and Events." *"We Gather Together": Food and Festival in American Life*, edited by Theodore C. Humphrey and Lin T. Humphrey, UMI Research Press, 1988, pp. 235–45.

Jones, Michael Owen. *Corn: A Global History*. Reaktion Books, 2017.

Jones, Michael Owen. "Creating and Using Argot at the Jayhawk Café: Communication, Ambience, and Identity." *Exploring Folk Art: Twenty Years of Thought on Craft, Work, and Aesthetics*, by Jones, UMI Research Press, 1987; reprinted Utah State UP, 1993, pp. 109–17.

Jones, Michael Owen. "The Proof Is in the Pudding: The Role of Sensation in Food Choice as Revealed by Sensory Deprivation." *Exploring Folk Art: Twenty Years of Thought on Craft, Work, and Aesthetics*, by Jones, UMI Research Press, 1987; reprinted Utah State UP, 1993, pp. 97–106.

Jones, Michael Owen. "'Tradition' in Identity Discourses and an Individual's Symbolic Construction of Self." *Western Folklore*, vol. 59, no. 2, 2000, pp. 15–141.

Jones, Michael Owen, Bruce Giuliano, and Roberta Krell, editors. *Foodways and Eating Habits: Directions for Research*. California Folklore Society, 1983.

Jones, Michael Owen, and Lucy M. Long, editors. *Comfort Food Meanings and Memories*. UP of Mississippi, 2017.

Jurafsky, Dan. *The Language of Food: A Linguist Reads the Menu*. W. W. Norton, 2014.

Kalčik, Susan. "Ethnic Foodways in America: Symbol and Performance of Identity." *Ethnic and Regional Foodways in the United States: The Performance of Group Identity*, edited by Linda Kelly Brown and Kay Mussell, U of Tennessee P, 1984, pp. 37–65.

King, Michelle T., editor. *Culinary Nationalism in Asia*. Bloomsbury Academic, 2019.

Kirshenblatt-Gimblett, Barbara. "Playing to the Senses: Food as a Performance Medium." *Performance Research*, vol. 4, no. 1, 2014, pp. 1–30.

Kugelmass, Jack. "Green Bagels: An Essay on Food, Nostalgia, and the Carnivalesque." *YIVO Annual*, vol. 19, 1990, pp. 57–80.

LaChance, Daniel. 2007. "Last Words, Last Meals, and Last Stands: Agency and Individuality in the Modern Execution Process." *Law & Social Inquiry*, vol. 32, no. 3, 2007, pp. 701–24.

Lanser, Susan. "Burning Dinners: Feminist Subversions of Domesticity." *Feminist Messages: Coding in Women's Folk Culture*, edited by Joan Newlon Radner, U of Illinois P, 1993, pp. 36–53.

Last Supper. Directed by Mats Bigert and Lars Bergstrom. SVT, Kultur & Samhalle, Stockholm, Sweden, 2005. DVD, 58 min.

Leitch, Alison. "Slow Food and the Politics of Pork Fat: Italian Food and European Identity." *Ethnos*, vol. 68, no. 4, 2003, pp. 437–62.

Leneman, Leah. "The Awakened Instinct: Vegetarianism and the Women's Suffrage Movement in Britain." *Women's History Review*, vol. 6, no. 2, 1997, pp. 271–87.

Lester, Rebecca J. "Embodied Voices: Women's Food Asceticism and the Negotiation of Identity." *Ethos*, vol. 23, no. 2, 1995, pp. 187–222.

Lévi-Strauss, Claude. "The Culinary Triangle." *Food and Culture: A Reader*, edited by Carole Counihan and Penny Van Esterik, translated by Peter Brooks, 2nd ed., Routledge, pp. 28–35.

Lewis, George H. "From Minnesota Fat to Seoul Food: Spam in America and the Pacific Rim." *Journal of Popular Culture*, vol. 34, no. 2, 2000, pp. 83–105.

Lewis, George H. "The Maine Lobster as Regional Icon: Competing Images over Time and Social Class." *Food & Foodways*, vol. 3, no. 4, 1989, pp. 303–16.

Liburd, Leandris C. "Food, Identity, and African-American Women with Type 2 Diabetes: An Anthropological Perspective." *Diabetes Spectrum*, vol. 16, no. 3, 2003, pp. 160–65.

Linsenmeyer, Whitney, Rabia Rahman, and Daniel B. Stewart. "The Evolution of a Transgender Male's Relationship with Food and Exercise: A Narrative Inquiry." 19 Oct 2020, https://www.tandfonline.com/doi/full/10.1080/15401383.2020.1820924.

Lloyd, Timothy Charles. "The Cincinnati Chili Complex." *Western Folklore*, vol. 40, no. 1, 1981, pp. 28–40.

Locher, Julie L. "Comfort Food." *Encyclopedia of Food and Culture*, edited by S. Katz. Charles Scribner's Sons, 2002.

Locher, Julie L., William C. Yoels, Donna Maurer, and Jillian Van Ells. "Comfort Foods: An Exploratory Journey into the Social and Emotional Significance of Food." *Food and Foodways*, vol. 13, no. 4, 2005, pp. 273–97.

Lockwood, Yvonne R., and William G. Lockwood. "Continuity and Adaptation of Arab-American Foodways." *Arab Detroit: From Margin to Mainstream*, edited by Nabeel Abraham and Andrew Shryock, Wayne State UP, 2000, pp. 515–49.

Lockwood, Yvonne R., and William G. Lockwood. "Pasties in Michigan's Upper Peninsula: Foodways, Interethnic Relations, and Regionalism. *Creative Ethnicity: Symbols and Strategies of Contemporary Ethnic Life*, edited by Stephen Stern and John Allan Cicala, Utah State UP, 1991, pp. 3–20.

Long, Lucy M. "Breaking Bread in Northern Ireland: Soda Farls, Implicit Meanings, and Gastropolitics." *Political Meals*, edited by Regina F. Bendix and Michaela Fenske, LIT Verlag, 2014, pp. 287–306.

Long, Lucy M., editor. *Culinary Tourism*. U of Kentucky P, 2004.

Long, Lucy M., editor. *Ethnic American Food: A Cultural Encyclopedia*. 2 vols. Rowman and Littlefield, 2015.

Long, Lucy M., editor. *The Food and Folklore Reader*. Bloomsbury, 2015.

Long, Lucy M. "Green Bean Casserole and Midwestern Identity: A Regional Foodways Aesthetic and Ethos." *Midwestern Folklore*, vol. 33, 2007, pp. 29–44; reprinted in *The Food and Folklore Reader*, edited by Lucy M. Long, Bloomsbury, 2015, pp. 191–204.

Long, Lucy M. "Introduction." *Journal of American Folklore*, special issue: "Food and Identity in the Americas," vol. 122, no. 483, 2009, pp. 3–10.

Long, Lucy M. "Introduction: Culinary Nationalism." *Western Folklore*, vol. 80, no. 1, 2021, pp. 5–14.

Long, Lucy M. "Learning to Listen to the Food Voice: Recipes as Expressions of Identity and Carriers of Memory." *Food, Culture & Society*, vol. 7, no. 1, 2004, pp. 118–22.

Magat, Margaret. *Balut: Fertilized Eggs and the Making of Culinary Capital in the Filipino Diaspora*. Bloomsbury Academic, 2019.

Magliocco, Sabina. "Playing with Food: The Negotiation of Identity in the Ethnic Display Event by Italian Americans in Clinton Indiana." *Studies in Italian American Folklore*, edited by Luisa Del Giudice, Utah State UP, 1993, p. 107–26.

Malone, Dan F. "Dead Men Talking: Content Analysis of Prisoners' Last Words, Innocence Claims and News Coverage from Texas' Death Row." MA Thesis, U of North Texas, 2006.

Mason, Melissa Caswell. "You Said a Mouthful: Food and Food-Related Metaphors in Folkspeech." *Folklore and Mythology Studies*, vol. 6, 1982, pp. 29–33.

Matejowsky, Ty. "SPAM and Fast-food 'Glocalization' in the Philippines." *Food, Culture & Society*, vol. 10, no. 1, 2015, pp. 23–41.

Mechling, Elisabeth Walker, and Jay Mechling. "Sweet Talk: The Moral Rhetoric of Sugar." *Central States Speech Journal*, vol. 34, no. 1, 1988, pp. 19–32.

Miller, William Ian. *The Anatomy of Disgust*. Harvard UP, 1997.

Milligan, Rhonda-Jane, Glenn Waller, and Bernice Andrews. "Eating Disturbances in Female Prisoners: The Role of Anger." *Eating Behaviors*, vol. 3, no. 2, 2002, pp. 123–32.

Minke, Linda Kjaer. "Cooking in Prison—from Crook to Cook." *International Journal of Prisoner Health*, vol. 10, no. 4, 2014, pp. 228–38.

Mintz, Sidney W. "Foreword." *The Handbook of Food Research*, edited by Anne Murcott, Warren Belasco, Peter Jackson, Bloomsbury Academic, 2013, pp. xxvi–xxx.

Mintz, Sidney W. "Sugar and Morality." *Morality and Health*, edited by Allan M. Brandt and Paul Rozin, Routledge, 1997, pp. 173–84.

Mintz, Sidney W. *Sweetness and Power: The Place of Sugar in Modern History*. Elisabeth Sifton Books/Viking, 1985.

Mintz, Sidney W., and Christine M. Du Bois. "The Anthropology of Food and Eating." *Annual Review of Anthropology*, vol. 31, 2002, pp. 99–119.

Montaño, Mario. "Appropriation and Counterhegemony in South Texas: Food Slurs, Offal Meats, and Blood." *Usable Pasts: Traditions and Group Expressions in North America*, edited by Tad Tuleja, Utah State UP, 1997, pp. 50–67.

Mori, D., S. Chaiken, and P. Pliner. "'Eating Lightly' and the Self-Presentation of Femininity." *Journal of Personality and Social Psychology*, vol. 53, no. 4, 1987, pp. 693–702.

Nemeroff, Carol, and Paul Rozin. "'You Are What You Eat': Applying the Demand-Free 'Impression' Technique to an Unacknowledged Belief." *Ethos*, vol. 17, no. 1, 1989, pp. 50–63.

Nestle, Marion, and W. Alex McIntosh. "Writing the Food Studies Movement." *Food, Culture & Society*, vol. 13, no. 2, 2010, pp. 159–79.

Neuman, Nicklas. "On the Engagement with Social Theory in Food Studies: Cultural Symbols and Social Practices." *Food, Culture & Society*, vol. 22, no. 1, 2019, pp. 78–94.

Newton, Sarah E. "The Jell-O Syndrome: Investigating Popular Culture/Foodways." *Western Folklore*, vol. 51, nos. 3–4, 1992, pp. 249–67.

O'Brien, Gerald V. "Indigestible Food, Conquering Hordes, and Waste Materials: Metaphors of Immigrants and the Early Immigration Restriction Debate in the United States." *Metaphor and Symbol*, vol. 18, no. 1, 2003, pp. 33–47.

Ochs, Elinor, Clotilde Pontecorvo, and Alessandra Fasulo. "Socializing Taste." *Ethnos*, vol. 61, nos. 1–2, 1996, pp. 7–46.

Oerlemans, Onno. 1995. "Shelley's Ideal Body: Vegetarianism and Nature." *Studies in Romanticism*, vol. 34, no. 4, 1995, pp. 531–52.

Opie, Frederick Douglass. *Hog and Hominy: Soul Food from Africa to America*. Columbia UP, 2008.

Palmerino, Claire. "Pleasing the Palate: Diet Selection and Aversion Learning." *Western Folklore*, vol. 40, no. 1, 1981, pp. 19–27.

Pilcher, Jeffrey. *Qu'Vivan los Tamales: Food and the Making of Mexican Identity*. U of New Mexico P, 1998.

Pittet, Diana. "Food Voice Annotated Bibliography." *Food, Culture & Society*, vol. 7, no. 1, 2004, pp. 135–45.

Poe, Tracy N. "The Origins of Soul Food in Black Urban Identity: Chicago, 1915–1947." *American Studies International*, vol. 37, no. 1, 1999, pp. 4–33.

Preece, Rod. *Sins of the Flesh: A History of Ethical Vegetarian Thought*. U of British Columbia P, 2009.

Price, Brian. "The Last Supper." *Legal Affairs*, Mar/Apr 2004, http://www.legalaffairs.org /issues/March-April-2004/feature_price_marapr04.msp.

Price, Brian. *Meals to Die For*. Dyna-Paige Corporation, 2004.

Ranta, Ronald. 2015. "Food and Nationalism: From Foie Gras to Hummus." *World Policy Journal*, vol. 32, no. 3, 2015, pp. 33–40.

Ray, Krishnendu. "Nation and Cuisine. The Evidence from American Newspapers ca. 1830–2003." *Food and Foodways*, vol. 16, no. 4, 2008, pp. 259–97.

Rich, George W., and David F. Jacobs. "Saltpeter: A Folkloric Adjustment to Acculturation Stress." *Western Folklore*, vol. 32, no. 3, 1973, pp. 164–79.

Rikoon, J. Sanford. "Ethnic Food Traditions: A Review and Preview of Folklore Scholarship." *Kentucky Folklore Record*, vol. 28, nos. 1–2, 1982, pp. 12–25.

Rodrigues, Heber, Carlos Goméz-Corona, and Dominique Valentin. "Femininities & Masculinities: Sex, Gender, and Stereotypes in Food Studies." *Current Opinion in Food Science*, vol. 33, 2020, pp. 156–64.

Roth, LuAnne. "Beyond *Communitas*: Cinematic Food Events and the Negotiation of Power, Belonging, and Exclusion." *Western Folklore*, vol. 64, nos. 3–4, 2005, pp. 163–87.

Roth, LuAnne. "Comfort (and Discomfort) Food: Social Surrogacy and Embodied Memory in Real and Reel Time." *Comfort Food Meanings and Memories*, edited by Michael Owen Jones and Lucy M. Long, UP of Mississippi, 2017.

Roth, LuAnne. "Do the [White] Thing: What Oppositional Gaze Narratives Reveal about Culinary Nationalism and Whiteness." *Western Folklore*, vol. 80, no. 1, 2021, pp. 81–117.

Rozin, Paul, and April E. Fallon. "The Acquisition of Likes and Dislikes for Food." *Criteria of Food Acceptances*, edited by J. Solms and R. L. Hall, Forster, 1981, pp. 35–48.

Rozin, Paul, and April E. Fallon. "A Perspective on Disgust." *Psychological Review*, vol. 94, no. 1, 1987, pp. 23–41.

Rozin, P., A. E. Fallon, and M. Augustoni-Ziskind. "The Child's Conception of Food: The Development of Contamination Sensitivity to 'Disgusting' Substances." *Developmental Psychology*, vol. 21, no. 6, 1985, pp. 1075–79.

Rozin, P., E. Levine, and C. Stoess. "Chocolate Craving and Liking." *Appetite*, vol. 17, 1991, pp. 199–212.

Salamanders—A Night at the Phi Delt House. Produced and directed by Ken Thigpen. Documentary Educational Resources, 1982. Videocassette, 13 min.

Schlesinger, Arthur M., Sr. "A Dietary Interpretation of American History." *Massachusetts Historical Society Proceedings*, vol. 68, 1944–47, pp. 199–227.

Shen, Wan, Lucy M. Long, Chia-Hao Shin, and Mary-Jon Lindy, "A Humanities-Based Explanation for the Effects of Emotional Eating and Perceived Stress on Food Choice Motives during the COVID-19 Pandemic," *Nutrients*, vol. 12, no. 9, 2020, p. 10, https://www.mdpi.com/2072-6643/12/9/2712/htm.

Simoons, Frederick J. *Eat Not This Flesh: Food Avoidances from Prehistory to the Present.* 2nd rev. ed., U of Wisconsin P, 1994.

Siporin, Steve. 2015. "The Kosher Con Game: Who's Keeping Kosher in Prison?" *Western Folklore*, vol. 74, no. 1, 2015, pp. 58–79.

Smith, Alison K. "National Cuisines." *The Oxford Handbook of Food History*, edited by Jeffrey M. Pilcher, Oxford UP, 2012, pp. 444–60.

Smith, Catrin. "Punishment and Pleasure: Women, Food and the Imprisoned Body." *Sociological Review*, vol. 50, no. 1, 2002, pp. 197–214.

Smoyer, Amy B. "Cafeteria, Commissary and Cooking: Foodways and Negotiations of Power and Identity in a Women's Prison." PhD Dissertation, City University of New York, 2013.

Smoyer, Amy B. "Making Fatty Girl Cakes: Food and Resistance in a Woman's Prison." *Prison Journal*, vol. 96, no. 2, 2015, pp. 1–19.

Sobal, Jeffrey. "Men, Meat, and Marriage: Models of Masculinity." *Food and Foodways*, vol. 13, nos. 1–2, 2005, pp. 135–58.

Spencer, Colin. *The Heretic's Feast: A History of Vegetarianism.* UP of New England, 1995.

Theophano, Janet S. "'I Gave Him a Cake': An Interpretation of Two Italian-American Weddings." *Creative Ethnicity: Symbols and Strategies of Contemporary Ethnic Life*, edited by Stephen Stern and John Allan Cicala, Utah State UP, 1991, pp. 44–54.

Tomlinson, M. Heather. "'Not an Instrument of Punishment': Prison Diet in the Mid-Nineteenth Century." *Journal of Consumer Studies and Home Economics*, vol. 2, no. 1, 1978, pp. 15–26.

Troisi, Jordan D., and Shira Gabriel. "Chicken Soup Really Is Good for the Soul: 'Comfort Food' Fulfills the Need to Belong." *Psychological Science*, vol. 22, no. 6, 2011, pp. 747–53.

Turner, Patricia A. "Church's Fried Chicken and the Klan: A Rhetorical Analysis of Rumor in the Black Community." *Western Folklore*, vol. 46, no. 4, 1987, pp. 294–306.

Twigg, Julia. "Food for Thought: Purity and Vegetarianism." *Religion*, vol. 9, no. 1, 1979, pp. 13–35.

Twigg, Julia. "Vegetarianism and the Meanings of Meat." *The Sociology of Food and Eating*, edited by A. Murcott, Gowe, 1983, pp. 18–30.

Tye, Diane. "Edible Men: Playing with Food at Bachelorette Parties." *Western Folklore,* vol. 77, nos. 3–4, 2018, pp. 221–48.

Ugelvik, Thomas. "The Hidden Food: Mealtime Resistance and Identity Work in a Norwegian Prison." *Punishment and Society,* vol. 13, no. 1, 2011, pp. 47–63.

Unsain, Ramiro Fernandez, Mariana Dimitrov Ulian, Priscila de Morais, Sato, Fernanda Sabatini, Mayara Sanay da Silva Oliveira, and Fernanda Baeza Scagliusi. "'Macho Food': Masculinities, Food Preferences, Eating Practices History and Commensality among Gay Bears in São Paulo, Brazil." *Appetite,* vol. 144, Sep 2019, pp. 1–7.

Valentine, Gill. "Eating in: Home, Consumption and Identity." *The Sociological Review,* vol. 47, no. 3, 1999, pp. 491–524.

Valentine, Gill, and Beth Longstaff. "Doing Porridge: Food and Social Relations in a Male Prison." *Journal of Material Culture,* vol. 3, no. 2, 1998, pp. 131–52.

van Hagen, Eline. "'A Salisbury Steak Is Not a Steak, It's Ground Beef.' The Significance, Messages and Symbolism of Final Meals on Death Row." *Appetite,* vol. 144, 2020, https://www.sciencedirect.com/science/article/abs/pii/S0195666319302703.

Visser, Margaret. *Much Depends on Dinner.* McClelland and Stewart Weidenfeld, 1986.

Visser, Margaret. *The Rituals of Dinner: The Origins, Evolution, Eccentricities, and Meaning of Table Manners.* Grove, 1991.

Warde, Alan. "The Sociology of Consumption: Its Recent Development." *Annual Review of Sociology,* vol. 41, 2015, pp. 117–34.

Wilk, Richard. 2006. *Home Cooking in the Global Village: Caribbean Food from Buccaneers to Ecotourists.* Berg Publishers.

Willetts, Anna. "'Bacon Sandwiches Got the Better of Me': Meat Eating and Vegetarianism in South East London." *Food, Health, and Identity,* edited by P. Caplan, Routledge, 1997, pp. 111–30.

Williams-Forson, Psyche. *Building Houses out of Chicken Legs: Black Women Food, & Power.* U of North Carolina P, 2006.

Wilson, David, and Angus K. Gillespie, editors. *Rooted in America: Foodlore of Popular Fruits and Vegetables.* U of Tennessee P, 1999.

Yoder, Don. "Folk Cookery." *Folklore and Folklife: An Introduction,* edited by Richard M. Dorson, U of Chicago P, 1972, pp. 325–50.

Yoder, Don. "Pennsylvanians Called It Mush." *Pennsylvania Folklife,* vol. 13, no. 2, 1962–63, pp. 27–49.

Yoder, Don. "Sauerkraut in the Pennsylvania German Folk-Culture." *Pennsylvania Folklife,* vol. 12, no. 2, 1961, pp. 56–69.

Yoder, Don. "Schnitz in the Pennsylvania Folk-Culture." *Pennsylvania Folklife,* vol. 12, no. 2, 1961, pp. 44–53.

INDEX

Page numbers in **bold** refer to figures.